# The Making of Labour Precarity in China since 1949

Globally, most workers live precarious lives. In this examination of China's industrial relations since 1949, Xiaojun Feng explores why this should be. China provides an important case to examine this question because it has gone through both socialist revolution and marketized reforms, the major economic and political dynamics that have shaped the world since the twentieth century. Developing a comprehensive analytical framework for the interpretation of archives, interviews, and participant observation, Feng explores the causes of and remedies for labour precarity in China. Bridging the 1949 and 1976 divides, this study unveils continuities and more fundamental discontinuities across these watershed moments, and sheds fresh light on the extent to which popular policy can counter labour precarity and the future dynamics of labour movements.

Xiaojun Feng is Associate Professor of Sociology at China Agricultural University.

# CAMBRIDGE STUDIES IN THE HISTORY OF THE PEOPLE'S REPUBLIC OF CHINA



---

Cambridge Studies in the History of the People's Republic of China is a major series of ambitious works in the social, political, and cultural history of socialist China. Aided by a wealth of new sources, recent research pays close attention to regional differences, to perspectives from the social and geographical margins, and to the unintended consequences of Communist Party rule. Books in the series contribute to this historical re-evaluation by presenting the most stimulating and rigorously researched works in the field to a broad audience. The series invites submissions from a variety of disciplines and approaches, based on written, material or oral sources. Particularly welcome are those works that bridge the 1949 and 1978 divides, and those that seek to understand China in an international or global context.

A full list of titles in the series can be found at:
www.cambridge.org/HPRC

# The Making of Labour Precarity in China since 1949

Xiaojun Feng
*China Agricultural University*

CAMBRIDGE
UNIVERSITY PRESS

CAMBRIDGE
UNIVERSITY PRESS

Shaftesbury Road, Cambridge CB2 8EA, United Kingdom

One Liberty Plaza, 20th Floor, New York, NY 10006, USA

477 Williamstown Road, Port Melbourne, VIC 3207, Australia

314–321, 3rd Floor, Plot 3, Splendor Forum, Jasola District Centre, New Delhi – 110025, India

103 Penang Road, #05-06/07, Visioncrest Commercial, Singapore 238467

Cambridge University Press is part of Cambridge University Press & Assessment, a department of the University of Cambridge.

We share the University's mission to contribute to society through the pursuit of education, learning and research at the highest international levels of excellence.

www.cambridge.org
Information on this title: www.cambridge.org/9781009640534

DOI: 10.1017/9781009640572



When citing this work, please include a reference to the DOI 10.1017/9781009640572

First published 2026

Cover image: Construction workers at site / Grant Fait / The Image Bank Unreleased / Getty Images

*A catalogue record for this publication is available from the British Library*

*Library of Congress Cataloging-in-Publication Data*
Names: Feng, Xiaojun, 1989- author
Title: The making of labour precarity in China since 1949 / Xiaojun Feng.
Description: Cambridge, United Kingdom ; New York, NY : Cambridge University Press, 2026. | Series: Cambridge studies in the People's Republic of China | Includes bibliographical references and index.
Identifiers: LCCN 2025021418 (print) | LCCN 2025021419 (ebook) | ISBN 9781009640534 hardback | ISBN 9781009640565 paperback | ISBN 9781009640572 epub
Subjects: LCSH: Labor policy–China | Labor market–China | Blue collar workers–China–Economic conditions
Classification: LCC HD5830.A6 F469 2026 (print) | LCC HD5830.A6 (ebook)
LC record available at https://lccn.loc.gov/2025021418
LC ebook record available at https://lccn.loc.gov/2025021419

ISBN 978-1-009-64053-4 Hardback

To my father, Yanbin Feng (1962–2021),
a precarious worker in China.

# Contents

# Figures

# Tables

# Acknowledgements

In late 2015, I was struggling to find a research question for my DPhil study. I read extensively and talked with senior graduate students from both Oxford and other universities, hoping to find inspiration. During a discussion with Kenneth Tsz Fung Ng, a fellow student and friend whom I met at Peking University, who had started his PhD study two years earlier than me in Hong Kong, my attention turned to agency workers. 'There are more labour agencies than restaurants in one street in Suzhou!', he said. I immediately realized the potential of this topic. My interest in agency workers grew and eventually led to this book when I found that the origins of agency workers could be traced way back into the past and understanding the past is integral to understanding the present. Thank you, Kenneth!

I would have been unable to close the gap between conception and completion of this book without the support of so many people and institutions. Fieldwork access is often difficult, but was made easier for me because of the incredible kindness of several figures. It was Kenneth again who added me to a WeChat (the Chinese equivalent of WhatsApp) group in 2015, consisting mainly of Chinese labour scholars. In this group, I met Chun Dai, a labour scholar and activist devoting herself to helping workers with pneumoconiosis, the most common work-related disease in China. Although she had never met me in person, she kindly put me in touch with Yong Yang, a well-connected human resource manager working for the Great China subsidiary of a multi-national. Yong impressed me with his insights into the misalignment between mainstream human resource management practices and ever-evolving industrial relations in China. He introduced me to his friend who ran a labour agency in Beijing.

I worked at this agency in July and August 2016 as a researcher and student intern. There I met Xuduo Meng, an enthusiastic researcher from the Ministry of Human Resources and Social Security, the agency's client. Xuduo introduced me to his colleague who was leading a project about the effect of the 2014 labour dispatch regulation in China.

Through collaboration with Meng's colleague, I interviewed many managers of enterprises and labour agencies, and labour officials.

I am hugely thankful to my interviewees – workers, managers, officials, and scholars. While most worker informants had no idea what a thesis was and I had to tell them that I wanted to write a book instead, they received me with openness, trust, and care, which I will remember forever. They shared with me not only their work experience but also their life stories, lessons, and hot dumplings (on winter nights!), all so valuable for a young student. Some eventually became friends. I am always happy to receive their messages updating me on their lives or asking me about, for example, Excel skills.

As I extended my project to the Mao era, I decided to dig into archives. In this regard, I am blessed with two wonderful teachers – Yanwen Liu and Pan Lin – who introduced me to the archival system in China and historical studies of the Mao era. I owe a great debt to the staff of Beijing Municipal Archives, Shanghai Municipal Archives, and the Universities Service Centre for China Studies at the Chinese University of Hong Kong for their help with retrieving archives and other historical materials. Interviewing workers and cadres working in the Mao era is challenging for scholars of my age. I would like to thank Qianqian Zhao, Fangchun Dai, Fred Engst, Zhongjin Li, Feng Yu, Siyu Kang, Muxuan Song, and Ligang Wang for helping me find informants. Many of them were over eighty or even ninety years old, and interviewing them was like touching history, so thought-provoking.

In turning my rich and complicated materials from fieldwork into a rigorous thesis, I am hugely indebted to my DPhil supervisor Rachel Murphy and several other scholars. Despite the pressures of her own intellectual aspirations, family obligations, and administrative duties, Rachel managed to devote so much time and energy not only to making constructive comments on earlier drafts of this book but also to providing unfailing encouragement and support throughout my study at Oxford. To this day, I still have no idea why Oxford admitted me. While the orientation session for new students on imposter syndrome failed to ease my mind, Rachel's constant reassurance that I was doing well did, motivating me to work harder to live up to her expectations. At Oxford, I also benefitted immensely from advice from Hugh Whittaker, Jenny Chan, and Kyle Jaros in my transfer and confirmation exams, ensuring that I was on the right track to complete my thesis. Comments from Hugh Whittaker and Chris Smith in the final viva enabled me to make full use of the last chance for revision before submission and laid the first stone in transforming the thesis into this book. My study at Oxford was generously funded by the Swire

Educational Trust. My thesis also benefited from grants from St Antony's College and the Oriental Institute at Oxford.

My exchange semester at Johns Hopkins University in 2017 shaped the key ideas and layout of this book tremendously. The influence of my four unforgettable months in this stronghold of comparative-historical sociology goes far beyond this book. I am endlessly grateful to Joel Andreas for sponsoring my visit at Hopkins, organizing the China Labour Workshop through which I collected very helpful feedback on an early draft of this book, and carefully reading several chapters of the draft and giving comments that helped me to avoid embarrassing and fundamental mistakes. I also thank Ryan Calder, Yige Dong, and Smriti Upadhyay in the dissertation workshop at Hopkins in 2017 for their detailed advice on the draft, and their warm companionship and encouragement for a lonely visitor like me in the cold winter of Baltimore.

Thanks must also go to Philip Huang. Although he did not comment on the drafts of this book, his classes at Renmin University of China in 2012 taught me how to treat theories from different traditions, helping me to develop my theoretical framework. Partial drafts of this book were presented at several conferences, workshops, and lectures. I would like to acknowledge the comments from participants in these activities, particularly Beverly Silver, Eli Friedman, Sebastian Link Chaparro, Yu Huang, Hao Qi, Yunxue Deng, Lulu Fan, and Tao Liu. Drafts of this book also benefited from conversations with Tim Pringle, Kai Chang, Biao Xiang, and Chaochao Lin.

Since joining China Agricultural University (CAU), I have been immersed in a very relaxing and supportive intellectual community that rejects the notorious 'publish or perish' culture common in Chinese academia. This community has allowed me to spend month after month transforming my thesis into this book, rather than publishing a few quick articles that would have made it impossible to demonstrate the complexities, discontinuities, and continuities of a seven-decade history. For this, I am tremendously indebted to Jingzhong Ye, the architect of the ethos of my college (College of Humanities and Development Studies) at CAU.

After finishing the book manuscript, I began to write the book proposal, which might not have been accepted by Cambridge University Press without comments from Guanghan Wu, Yige Dong, Fuk Ying Tse, and King Chi Chris Chan. At the Press, I am extremely fortunate to have had Lucy Rhymer as my editor. I am eternally grateful to Lucy, Rosa Martin, and other members of Lucy's team for bringing my manuscript to the bookshelf. The two anonymous reviewers whom the Press invited provided very constructive comments on my manuscript. I also want to thank Joanna Penning for her indexing work.

Research tends to be a lonely endeavour, particularly for work on a long history. I am very grateful to the following friends for pulling me out of academic asceticism into the more colourful and vibrant real world from time to time: Xueni Lan, Yinglei Chen, Yangfan Pan, Guanghan Wu, Xike Cheng, Sophie Ping Sun, Jenny Chan, Qing Zhao, Zixiang Yang, Yanwen Liu, Yunyun Zhou, Camille Boullenois, Amanda Zhang, Pu Yan, Guowei Liang, Tiantian Liu, Yige Dong, Sebastian Link Chaparro, Xuan Wei, Lu Pan, Xiaobo Hua, Yiyuan Chen, Geng Li, Chaoqun Liu, and Weiling Jin. They have made my life since 2015 at Oxford, Hopkins, the International Labour Organization, and CAU enjoyable.

My special thanks go to my husband, Xin Li. Although he only appeared at the very late stage of preparing this book, he has overwhelmed me with care, tenderness, and patience. Living like an ascetic monk (my mother's words), I used to think that I was skinny because I was born this way. I gained nearly 20 pounds in the first year I was with him!

My parents only finished high school and spent most of their careers as precarious workers. My mother, Xiumin Song, took care of my brother and me and worked part-time. My father, Yanbin Feng, worked in the construction sector. Starting as a brick layer, he ultimately became a project manager, a job usually held by college graduates. Projects under his supervision included buildings of over ten storeys. Before I left home for college, a common theme of family conversation was how to get their wages back. I thought of my parents all the time as I prepared this book. Decades of drudgery and psychological pressure from precarious work eventually cost my father's life. He passed away at 59 in 2021 due to a brain haemorrhage. I miss my father very much and dedicate this book to him.

# Abbreviations

| | |
|---|---|
| ACFTU | All-China Federation of Trade Unions |
| BMA | Beijing Municipal Archives |
| BMIURR | Basic Medical Insurance for Urban and Rural Residents |
| BMIUW | Basic Medical Insurance for Urban Worker-Employees |
| BRIURR | Basic Retirement Insurance for Urban and Rural Residents |
| BRIUW | Basic Retirement Insurance for Urban Worker-Employees |
| CAC | Central Archives of China |
| CASS | Chinese Academy of Social Sciences |
| CCP | Chinese Communist Party |
| DOC | dispatch-to-outsourcing conversion |
| FESCO | Foreign Enterprise Service Corporation |
| GCCs | global commodity chains |
| GDP | gross domestic product |
| HR | human resource |
| ILO | International Labour Organization |
| LCL | Labour Contract Law |
| MOHRSS | Ministry of Human Resources and Social Security |
| NBS | National Bureau of Statistics |
| OECD | Organization for Economic Co-operation and Development |
| SMA | Shanghai Municipal Archives |
| SOEs | state-owned enterprises |
| SSTH | Shanghai Suburb Sent-down and Temporary Workers' United Revolutionary Rebel General Headquarters |
| STOH | Shanghai Temporary and Outsourced Workers' Revolutionary Rebel General Headquarters |
| TFC | temp-to-formal conversion |

# 1 Introduction

## Persistent Labour Precarity throughout a Century

In recent years, the term *precarity* has gained popularity in discussions of work and employment. There is no consensus on the precise definition of the term *labour precarity*. However, it is generally used to describe the vulnerability and insecurity of workers' employment and lives.[1] In his 1925 article, *Analysis of the Classes in Chinese Society*, Mao Zedong divided China's labouring people into four strata and discussed their conditions of precarity: (1) the petty bourgeoisie, comprising owner-peasants, master handicraftsmen, and lower-level intellectuals; (2) the semi-proletariat, comprising semi-owner peasants, poor peasants, small handicraftsmen, shop assistants, and peddlers; (3) the proletariat; and (4) the lumpenproletariat, comprising landless peasants and jobless handicraftsmen.[2]

These four strata varied in their scale and degree of precarity. The upper layer of the petty bourgeoisie lived a comfortable life, while the lower layer experienced poorer living standards. The semi-proletariat constituted the vast majority of the population at that time. They had limited means of production and had to sell their labour power to make a living. The industrial proletariat totalled roughly 2 million, forming a negligible share of the 400 million population.[3] They were subjected to ruthless treatment by imperialists, warlords, and the bourgeoisie. The agricultural proletariat worked 'the longest hours, for the lowest wages, under the worst conditions, and with the least security of employment'.[4] The lumpenproletariat was fairly large and led the most precarious existence of all.

Mao contended that the industrial proletariat was the most progressive class, and was the leading force of the revolutionary movement in China. Concerned about these people's sheer precarity, as early as 1922, just a year

[1] Betti 2018.
[2] Mao 1971, 11–22. By owner-peasants, Mao meant middle peasants who had land and seldom hired other people for farming, worked for other people, or engaged in non-agricultural self-employment.
[3] Mi and Jiang 1996. [4] Mao 1971, 18.

after its establishment, the Chinese Communist Party (CCP) declared the introduction of labour protection laws as one of its seven goals. These laws aimed to eliminate the contract labour system (a popular arrangement of precarious employment at that time), implement an eight-hour working day, build healthcare facilities for workers, establish labour insurance schemes, and protect female and child labour and the unemployed.[5]

Since its ascendance to power in 1949, the CCP has made considerable progress on labour protection. Figure 1.1 shows the employment structure of urban China between 1952 and 2019.[6] Clearly, between the mid 1950s and the mid 1990s, roughly 60 to 80 per cent of urban employees worked in state-owned units, where the majority of the workforce enjoyed permanent employment and cradle-to-grave welfare benefits (together called the 'iron rice bowl'). Figure 1.2 takes account of rural employment and shows China's overall employment structure between 1952 and 2019. Between 1957 and 1987, 10 to 20 per cent of labouring people worked in state-owned units, while 75 to 85 per cent were peasants with access to land and welfare services provided by communes.

However, even the CCP under Mao's administration failed to eliminate labour precarity. Figure 1.3 shows the proportion of non-permanent workers in state-owned units between 1957 and 1991. Compared with permanent workers, they had precarious jobs and retrenched benefits. They comprised both peasant workers and those with urban household registration status (urban *hukou*).

Since the late 1970s, China has embarked on the Reform and Opening-up, aiming to replace the planned economy with a market economy and open up China to the world. With reference to Mao's criteria, four similar strata of labouring people can be identified in the present workforce: (1) the petty bourgeoisie, comprising professionals and technical employees, the self-employed, and owner-peasants;[7] (2)

[5] CCP 2011, 133–134.

[6] Unless otherwise specified, this book uses 'urban' in a geographical sense. 'Urban residents' include all people living in urban areas, whether or not they have urban household registration status. Unless otherwise specified, statistics for China in this book include only those for mainland China.

[7] Huang (2008) calls professionals and technical employees who have emerged from the economic development of recent decades the 'new petty bourgeoisie', and calls peasants and the self-employed who have persisted in Chinese society the 'old petty bourgeoisie'. Owner-peasants in present-day China live on land owned by the village collectives of which they are members, rather than on land they own themselves. However, as with the owner-peasants in the 1920s, they rarely hire other people for farming, work for other people, or engage in non-agricultural self-employment. For practical purposes, 'rarely' means less than six months per year. Those working in the non-agricultural sector locally or outside their hometowns for at least six months per year are counted as peasant workers in NBS statistics.

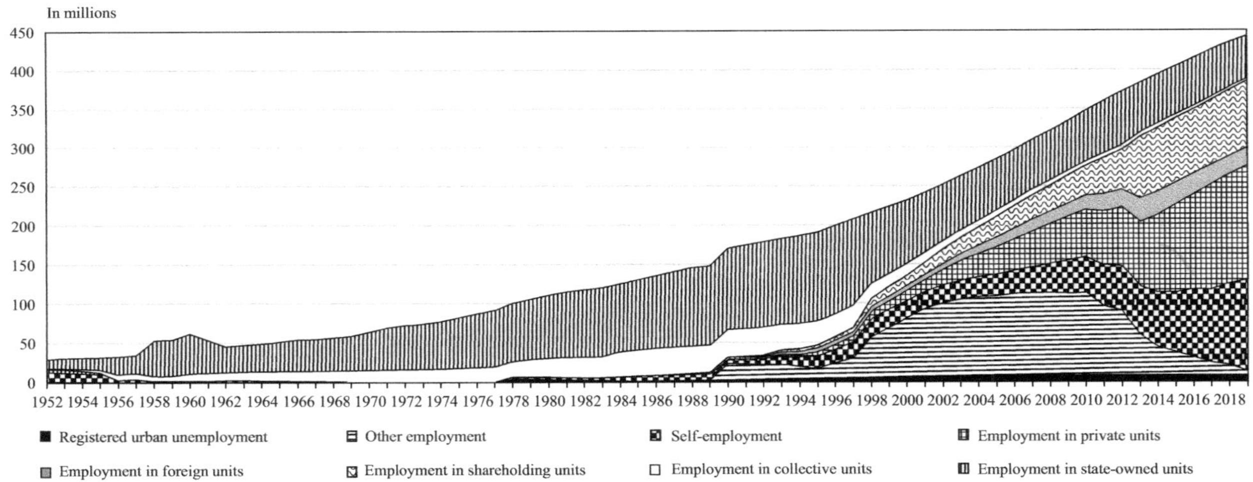


Figure 1.1 Employment structure of urban China, 1952–2019.

*Source*: National Bureau of Statistics (NBS) 1987, 1989, 2000a–2020a; NBS and the Ministry of Labour 1989.

However, in this book, the Western meaning of 'private' is adopted, unless otherwise specified.

The number of peasants was under-estimated in the 1980s. Therefore, this number increased dramatically around 1990 when the fourth national population census was conducted.

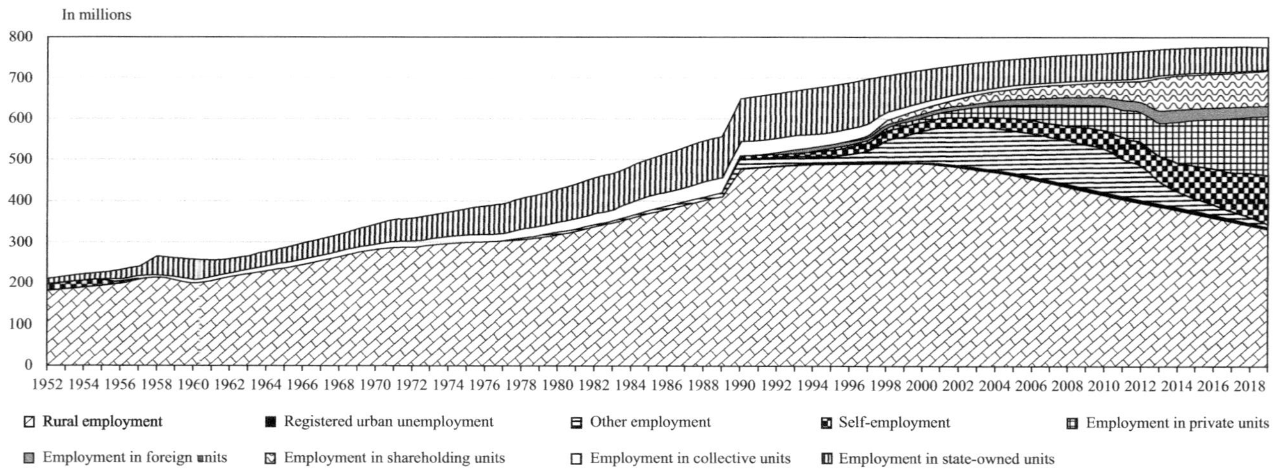


Figure 1.2 Employment structure of China, 1952–2019.

*Source*: NBS 1987, 1989, 2000a–2020a; NBS and the Ministry of Labour 1989.

*Note*: Employment in each type of unit includes both regular and temporary employment at the year-end. Employment in state-owned units between 1952 and 1957 includes employment in public–private joint units. Foreign units refer to those with at least 25 per cent of their investment from outside mainland China. Shareholding units refer to those co-established by multiple shareholders, who may be individuals or organizations, and private or state-owned investors. Those invested solely by state units are a minority in shareholding units. Therefore, figures of employment in state-owned units from the 1980s onwards are smaller than actual numbers. Private units here refer to units owned by natural persons and should not be confused with private units in the Western context. However, in this book, the Western meaning of 'private' is adopted, unless otherwise specified. Other employment refers to the difference between urban employment and the total number of workers in each type of employment specified above. Domestic workers are omitted from this figure. Data on self-employment are unavailable after 2019.

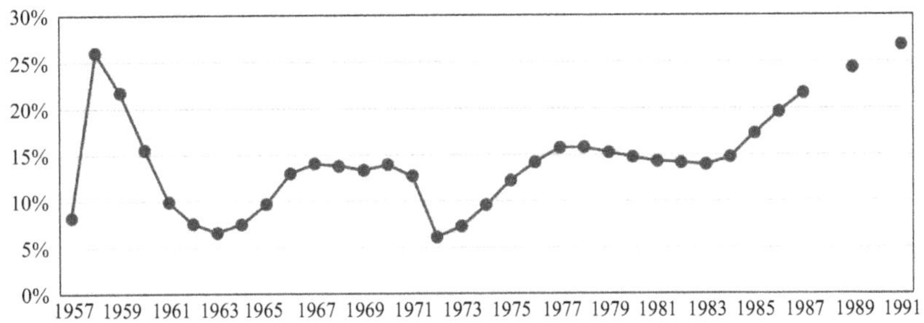


Figure 1.3 Proportion of non-permanent workers in China's state-owned units, 1957–1991.
*Source*: NBS 1987, 1989; NBS and the Ministry of Labour 1990; Ministry of Labour 1991.

the semi-proletariat, consisting of peasant workers with land in wage employment; (3) the proletariat, comprising other rank-and-file wage workers; and (4) the lumpenproletariat, comprising the unemployed.

The distribution of labouring people in the four strata has changed dramatically. Existing data allow only rough estimates of the size of each stratum. In 2019, with regard to the petty bourgeoisie, professionals and technical employees, the self-employed, and workers in the primary sector (mostly owner-peasants) accounted for 7.9, 22.8, and 25.1 per cent of China's employment, respectively;[8] with regard to the semi-proletariat, peasant workers accounted for 37.5 per cent, [9] including those in wage employment and self-account non-agricultural employment, and landless peasant workers. Landless peasants totalled an estimated 40 to 50 million in 2005, and this figure was expected to grow by 2.5 to 3 million every year thereafter.[10] Thus, in 2023, landless peasants may have amounted to around 100 million. With regard to the proletariat, in 2019, those working in urban units accounted for 42 per cent of China's employment, including the employers, professionals and technical employees, and peasant workers with land.[11] With regard to the lumpenproletariat, for most of the 1978–2022 period, registered urban unemployment made up less than 5 per cent of the urban working population.[12] This is an under-estimate of urban unemployment, since it counts only those who had urban *hukou* and were registered.

[8] Huang, Gao, and Peng (2012) estimate that in 2006 hired year-workers totalled only 3 per cent of all labour input in Chinese agriculture. NBS 2020a; NBS and MOHRSS 2020.
[9] NBS 2020a, 2020b. [10] Han 2005. [11] NBS 2020a. [12] NBS 2001a–2023a.

Labour precarity has also become pervasive. Professionals and technical employees tend to work under standard employment arrangements, in the formal economy, and enjoy statutory benefits, including five kinds of social insurance for employees (against work-related injury, illness, retirement, unemployment, and childbirth costs) and the housing fund.[13] However, even their jobs are often unstable; nor are they immune to financial pressure from housing, healthcare, and education expenses. The proletariat may work in the formal or informal economy and are not necessarily covered by statutory social insurance for employees. Peasant workers tend to work under non-standard employment arrangements in the informal economy. Comparing with the proletariat with urban *hukou*, they tend to work longer hours but earn significantly less. When the economy slows down, they are among the first to lose their jobs. After losing their land, their conditions tend to worsen. Being poorly educated and low-skilled, many are unable to secure decent jobs.[14]

Events in China are a manifestation of global trends in industrial relations. In developed economies, labour precarity was alleviated in the three decades after the Second World War. Over the same period in developing economies, labour precarity was the norm, except that some socialist countries countered it with some success. Since the late 1970s, labour precarity has surged worldwide. We now live in a world where most labouring people live in precarity. In response, research on labour precarity has grown rapidly, policy debates have been widespread and intense, and social movements to counter labour precarity have come to the fore.

## Two Paradoxes concerning Persistent Labour Precarity

It is important to recognize that, despite their precarity, the four strata of labouring people now live a materially better life than their 1920s

[13] In China, under standard employment arrangements, employees work full time and are directly employed by de facto employers. Under non-standard employment arrangements, employees work part-time or work for de facto employers through intermediaries. Both types may have short job tenure. State-owned, collective, shareholding, and foreign units together constitute the formal sector, which is closely regulated by the state. The rest form the informal sector, which is largely unregulated. Workers in the formal sector consist of formal workers who are relatively well protected by labour laws, and informal workers who are poorly protected. The formal elements in the formal sector constitute the formal economy. The informal elements in the formal sector and the informal sector together constitute the informal economy. Workers in the informal economy tend to have unstable jobs, receive low wages, and be excluded from the protection of labour laws (see Huang 2009).

[14] Yang, Qiu, and Li 2013.

counterparts, when China was one of the poorest countries globally. In 2010, China passed Japan to become the world's second largest economy.[15] In 2023, China's gross national income per capita reached 13,400 US dollars, exceeding the 13,205 US dollars threshold for classification as a high-income country by the World Bank's 2022–2023 standard.[16] Nevertheless, as shown above, most of today's labouring people by no means enjoy job security. Moreover, the proportion of labouring people who enjoy job security is even smaller than in the Mao era.

These scenarios appear doubly paradoxical. First, according to Marxism, the official ideology of the CCP, socialism is the remedy for labour precarity. Under capitalism, the proletariat suffers from relentless exploitation by the bourgeoisie and becomes precarious, and their only way out is to unite, overthrow capitalism, and embrace socialism.[17] János Kornai argues that socialist economies guarantee full employment by forced growth.[18] Between 1953 and 1956, by collectivizing agriculture and handicrafts and nationalizing capitalist industry and commerce, the CCP transformed China into a socialist country. After over four decades of marketized reforms, the CCP still claims that China is a socialist country, albeit with Chinese characteristics, although this claim is controversial. Mao's China (1949–1976) after 1956 was a quintessential socialist country; yet even then, the proportion of precarious workers was by no means negligible in state-owned units (Figure 1.3). So why do labouring people in a socialist country suffer from precarity?

Second, according to modernization theory, modernization is a remedy for labour precarity. In the two-sector model that lies at the core of this theory, in individual developing economies there are two sectors: a small modern sector that uses capitalist modes of production and provides stable and well-paid jobs, and a large traditional sector that retains traditional modes of production and provides precarious jobs. Modernization is a process whereby the modern sector consumes the traditional sector by absorbing its surplus labour, and thereby reduces labour precarity.[19] China has modernized extraordinarily successfully, particularly in the post-Mao era of marketized reforms. In addition, around just 10 per cent of the population lived in urban areas in the 1950s, whereas 66.2 per cent did so at the end of 2023.[20] So why do labouring people in a country that has so successfully modernized suffer from pervasive precarity?

In light of these two paradoxes, this book asks, what have been the mechanisms that caused and countered labour precarity in China since

[15] Barboza 2010. [16] World Bank 2022, 2024a. [17] Marx and Engels 1988.
[18] Kornai 1992. [19] Lewis 1954. [20] Xing 2024.

1949? China is the largest developing country globally, and has gone through both socialist revolution and marketized reforms, representing the major economic and political dynamics that characterized the world in the twentieth century. Its experience of causing and countering labour precarity may offer lessons for countries worldwide that are struggling with labour precarity.

Examining the conditions of all kinds of precarious labouring people during this period is beyond the scope of this book. Instead, it focuses on precarious labourers in urban enterprises and examines their conditions in relation to that of other labouring people. It traces how the scale, structure, and forms of precarious urban employment have been transformed since 1949, and explores the causes of this transformation, thereby shedding light on the implications of socialist revolution and marketized reforms for labour precarity.

## Two Debates about Labour Precarity

In response to the recent rise in labour precarity around the globe, two key debates have emerged from a rapidly growing body of literature on this issue. This book engages with these using the case of China.

The first debate, which has profound implications for labour movements, is on whether the trend towards greater precarity is a process of deproletarianization or proletarian unification. Guy Standing's *The Precariat: The New Dangerous Class* (2011) has reignited this debate. He argues that the precariat is a new class because its members have neither job security and welfare entitlements nor a wide range of political rights that characterize the working class.[21] Thus, the rise of labour precarity is a movement towards class decomposition and deproletariani zation. This argument builds on a longstanding tradition that emphasizes heterogeneity within the working class.[22] The underlying assumptions are a dichotomous view of working people and equation of the proletariat with workers who have full-time, permanent employment with benefits. Consequently, precarious workers' collective action is interpreted as rallying on the basis of a common experience of precarity, rather than on the basis of a common location within production relations.[23]

In contrast, the counter-argument follows Karl Marx's definition of class, and contends that the precariat is found in locations similar to the proletariat in production relations, and is thus an integral part of the proletariat.[24] Therefore, the rise of labour precarity is a process towards

[21] Standing 2011. [22] Ricketts and Sawhill 1988; Bourdieu 1998, 83.
[23] Standing 2011, 1–4; Lee and Kofman 2012.
[24] Jonna and Foster 2016; Wright 2016; Smith and Pun 2018.

class consolidation and proletarian unification. It may prolong the class formation process, but will not forestall the development of class consciousness and identity.[25] Historically, under capitalism, the image of the proletariat as having secure employment and benefits applied only to white male workers in Western countries in the 1950s and 1960s, and is therefore an exception.[26]

The second key debate is about the extent to which formalization is a remedy for labour precarity. With regard to employment policy, there has been a tendency towards converting informal into formal employment, or in other words to adopt formalization or regularization as a solution. At the international level, in 2015 the International Labour Organization (ILO) issued a recommendation entitled *Transition from the Informal to the Formal Economy.*[27] In developed economies, with nostalgia for the industrial relations of the 1950s and 1960s, some scholars propose re-establishing the social contract between organized labour and organized capital, and therefore shifting from informal to formal employment to reduce labour precarity.[28] In response to the proliferation of non-standard employment following the 1997 financial crisis, in 2007 the South Korean government introduced the Non-standard Employment Protection Act, which requires employers to convert fixed-term and agency workers (*pai-qian gong*) into regular, direct employees after two years of service.[29] Agency workers refer to those who are employed by a labour agency and work for a third party. In China, in requiring enterprises to lower the proportion of agency workers in their workforce to a maximum of 10 per cent, the Interim Provisions on Labour Dispatch were intended to force employers to convert agency workers into formal employees.

However, some scholars note a decay in formal employment.[30] Moreover, labour precarity may be aggravated by the commodification of social reproduction resources, such as housing, education, and healthcare, which usually cannot be offset simply by formalization.[31] In addition, precarity is often embedded in discriminatory social institutions such as gender and citizenship, which are generally beyond the reach of formalization.[32]

Since 1949, the labouring population of China has undergone rounds of making, unmaking, and remaking. Based on the Chinese experience, this book makes a valuable intervention in these two debates. It helps understand the future dynamics of labour movements, and the

[25] Smith and Pun 2018. [26] Mitropoulos 2005. [27] ILO 2015.
[28] Jonna and Foster 2016. [29] Lee 2017b.
[30] Picot and Tassinari 2014; Prosser 2016. [31] Lapavitsas 2009.
[32] Vosko 2000; Anderson 2010.

desirability and limitations of formalization as a popular policy to counter labour precarity.

## Previous Scholarship

Previous scholarship on urban employment in the Mao era focuses on permanent workers, and treats precarious workers largely as the residue of the urban workforce. For example, despite their disagreement on the political implications of permanent job tenure, Andrew Walder and Joel Andreas regard it as a major feature of work units in the Mao era and cover precarious labour in this era only briefly.[33] The dominant discourse on precarious workers in the Mao era concerns status groups. In the Mao era, the state divided citizens into several status groups, granted each group exclusive access to particular jobs, social benefits, and political rights, and largely blocked cross-group mobility.[34] In urban areas, permanent workers enjoyed the iron rice bowl and a wide range of political rights, while temporary workers worked in more difficult, dangerous, and dirty positions but received lower wages and fewer benefits.[35] The latter were also largely excluded from membership of trade unions, party organizations, employee congresses, and Cultural Revolution committees, amongst other bodies, and were ineligible for nomination or election as model workers.[36] Precarious workers were dismissed and sent to the countryside in large numbers following the failure of the Great Leap Forward (1958–1960).[37]

Why did precarious workers exist in Mao's China? The first explanation relates to accumulation: pursuing industrialization in a poor country necessitated labour cost saving, and precarious workers were cheap.[38] In particular, peasant workers, a major source of precarious workers, were cheap because urban units devolved responsibility for their social reproduction to the countryside.[39] The second explanation refers to equality. In urban areas, precarious jobs helped the CCP to fulfil its commitment to full employment.[40] In rural areas, the peasant-worker system was deemed useful for narrowing the rural–urban gap since it reduced rural unemployment and increased the incomes of both rural households and communes.[41] The third explanation concerns flexibility. Precarious workers helped to overcome the rigidity of the system of

[33] Walder 1986; Andreas 2019. [34] Walder 1986, 28–84; Wang 2011.
[35] Walder 1986, 39–55; Naughton 1997; Frazier 2002.
[36] Howard 1991, 100; Harris 2015, 124–125. [37] Luo 2003.
[38] Meisner 1999, 306, 332; Lin 2006; Lee 2019.
[39] Blecher 1983; Sheehan 2002, 85–138; White III 2014, 159–189. [40] Granick 1991.
[41] Blecher 1983; White 1987a.

workforce allocation, making them indispensable for enterprises with seasonal production schedules.[42]

In the Mao era, the state, as the planner and enforcer of the political-economic system, played a key role in both the improvement and deterioration of labour conditions.[43] Labour protests sought to counter precarity. In 1956 and 1957, workers in Shanghai staged various strikes to decry the bureaucratism of cadres in factories, governments, the party, and unions, and to demand welfare benefits. This has been interpreted by Elizabeth Perry as an outpouring of resentment against growing disparities between permanent state employees and other workers, particularly those in newly built joint-ownership enterprises, temporary workers, and apprentices.[44] Between 1966 and 1969, disadvantaged workers rose up and fought against discrimination.[45] In addition to these waves of mass protests, mundane labour protests occurred throughout the Mao era.[46] In line with the discourse of status groups, Ching Kwan Lee argues that struggles against precarity in the Mao era pivoted around recognition, targeting the state: marginalized workers rose up to demand equal recognition, equal compensation, and equal welfare.[47]

The literature on labour precarity in the post-Mao era focuses on replacement of the old labour system characterized by security and dualism, with a new labour system characterized by pervasive precarity. This has involved the unmaking and remaking of workers under the old system (hereafter old workers) and the making of workers under the new system (hereafter new workers). The literature on old workers is dominated by a discourse of anti-exclusion and commodification: the iron rice bowl was smashed because it prevented state-owned enterprises (SOEs) from competing successfully in the market economy; permanent employment in the formal economy was replaced by precarious employment in the informal economy, and even unemployment; the generous cradle-to-grave safety net was replaced by a mean one; and old workers' protests were interpreted as Polanyi-type labour unrest, or in other words resistance to the commodification of labour power.[48]

Generally, new workers are subject to highly coercive discipline, and tend to work without labour contracts or with short-term labour contracts for illegally long hours and in hazardous environments. They

42 Walder 1986, 50–56; Zhang 2014a, 2014b; Zhao 2017.
43 Lee 2019.
44 Perry 1996; Lin 2012.
45 Lee 1980; Perry 1996; Perry and Li 1997; Sheehan 2002, 103–138; White III 2014; Li 2015, 617–662.
46 Sheehan 2002.
47 Lee 2019.
48 Lin, Cai, and Li 1998; Li, Zhang, and Zhao 2000; Chen 2003; Li 2003b; Silver 2003, 20; Tian and Qi 2005; Lee 2007; Xie 2008; Hurst 2009; Wu 2010; Zhao 2012.

receive low wages, are prone to arrears and docking of both wages and social insurance, and are subject to arbitrary dismissals.[49] The vast majority of the extant literature on new workers focuses on peasant workers who have become part and parcel of the urban workforce.

Three discourses can be distinguished in the literature. The exploitation discourse examines the predicament of peasant workers through the lens of labour–capital relations. Accordingly, exploitation is the chief culprit of peasant workers' precarity, facilitated by their second-class citizenship.[50] New workers' struggles are interpreted as Marx-type labour unrest, or struggles of the newly emerging working class against exploitation.[51] In contrast, the exclusion discourse views the plight of peasant workers through the lens of citizen–state relations. Accordingly, being excluded from full citizenship is the chief cause of peasant workers' precarity. They are largely excluded from the protection of labour laws and from essential public services in cities, which are reserved for workers with urban *hukou*. Their insurgent identities tend to be expressed in terms of citizenship rather than class.[52] In the third discourse, scholars note massive dispossession of peasants and rampant commodification of social reproduction resources, particularly housing, healthcare, and education, as well as the financial pressures that such commodification imposes on individuals.[53]

The state, capital, and workers have all played a role in modulating labour precarity in the reform era. The state aims to achieve both economic development and political legitimacy. The drive for growth tends to aggravate labour precarity, while the drive for legitimacy tends to alleviate it. To attract investment, local governments often help investors to circumvent formal rules and regulations on labour use.[54] Labour protection laws are implemented opportunistically, subject to the state's changing economic, political, and social priorities.[55] To reconcile the tension between profitability and legitimacy, enterprises resort to workforce dualism: formal employees enjoy relatively stable jobs and statutory welfare benefits, while informal workers suffer discrimination with regard to income, welfare benefits, and job security.[56]

49 Lee 1998; Pun 2005; Pun, Lu, and Zhang 2012; Swider 2016; Andreas 2019; Chan, Selden, and Pun 2020.
50 Pun and Lu 2010; Pun and Chan 2012; Chan, Pun, and Selden 2013; Feng 2017.
51 Silver 2003, 20.
52 Solinger 1999; Lee 2007, 2016, 2019; Wang 2009; Shen and Guo 2012; Xiong 2012.
53 Meng and Li 2013; Li and Meng 2014; Lee 2019.
54 Lee 2007; Huang 2011; Kuruvilla, Lee, and Gallagher 2011, 1–16; Pun and Chan 2012.
55 Lee 2016.
56 Lüthje, Luo, and Zhang 2013; Zhang 2014a.

Labour activism in China is subject to the state's monopoly over workers' representation and repression.[57] The discourses of exploitation and exclusion are divided on the effectiveness of labour resistance in reducing precarity. According to the exclusion discourse, owing to the fragmentation of workers' interests across localities and work units, new workers' struggles are largely workplace-based and localized. Apart from wage increases, such struggles have failed to make any lasting gains in job security or trade union representation.[58] However, according to the exploitation discourse, different types of employment status, lack of civil rights, and the fragmentation of workers may prolong the class formation process but will not quench their class consciousness and identity. Their collective action has won them both economic and political gains.[59]

The existing literature on labour in the Mao era treats precarious labour as a sideline. It also fails to capture how the dynamics of accumulation, labour policy, and labour movements affected the scale, structure, and forms of precarious labour at different moments in that era. The literature on precarious labour in the post-Mao era appears rich; yet there has been a reductionist tendency to attribute labour precarity to a single mechanism, as the three discourses often appear in separate bodies of literature. Furthermore, most literature on this topic involves cross-sectional case studies at the workplace level, making it difficult to capture longitudinal, national-level transformation throughout the Mao and post-Mao eras and unveil the relationship between workplace dynamics and the larger political economy picture. The literature in the post-Mao era also fails to pay due attention to agency labour, which has become the dominant form of precarious labour (more precarious than formal workers) in urban enterprises since the introduction of the Labour Contract Law (LCL) in 2007.

In light of this, the first half of this book centres on precarious workers in the Mao era. It demonstrates how a hierarchy of precarious labouring people came into being against the background of economic and political dynamics, and how the hierarchy evolved following different paths of industrialization, swings in labour policy, and the rise and fall of labour resistance. The second half of the book first gives a bird's eye view of how various factors in the post-Mao era have recalibrated surplus appropriation and exclusion and activated commodification, and how these three mechanisms have worked together to rapidly proliferate and unevenly distribute precarity among different workers. It then moves to focus on agency workers.

[57] Friedman 2014; Lee 2019; Elfstrom 2021. [58] Lee 2007, 2016.
[59] Leung and Pun 2009; Zhang 2014a; Smith and Pun 2018.

Empirically, by chronicling the history of precarious labour in China since 1949, this book complements existing studies of precarious labour in capitalist countries with a study of it in a socialist country. It also complements existing cross-sectional case studies at the workplace level with a longitudinal study at the country level that combines macro-analysis of the political economy with micro-analysis of working conditions. This facilitates comparison between different periods to unveil continuities and discontinuities in causing and countering labour precarity under socialist revolution and marketized reforms.

## Key Concepts and an Analytical Framework

Labour precarity can arise throughout the life cycle of labour power, from the creation and replenishment of labour power in the sphere of social reproduction to the allocation and consumption of labour power to generate surplus in the sphere of production. This section first introduces the mechanisms that cause labour precarity in each sphere, including their modulators and corresponding counter-mechanisms. It then synthesizes these mechanisms to develop an analytical framework for this book.[60]

### *Surplus Appropriation*

Production is central to the functioning of society. In this sphere, those subject to surplus appropriation are prone to precarity. Surplus is the difference between what is produced and what is required for producers to live.

In class societies, surplus appropriation is called exploitation, involving the 'appropriation of the surplus product of classes of producers by (dominant) classes of non-producers'.[61] In capitalist societies, exploitation takes the form of capitalists' appropriation of workers' surplus value, which is mainly reinvested to generate more surplus value, or in other words for accumulation.[62] Whenever a capitalist mode of production is established, its primary aim is to extract surplus value. Marxism regards labour power as the sole source of value. Thus, labour's desire for decent work is constantly pressured by capital's pursuit of surplus value,

[60] Part of this section was initially published in 'The making of labour precarity: three explanatory approaches and their relationship, Xiaojun Feng, *Labor History*, 2021, Taylor & Francis Ltd', reprinted by permission of the publisher (Taylor & Francis Ltd., http://www.tandfonline.com).
[61] Bernstein 2010, 126. [62] Marx 1996.

which necessarily involves hiring and firing workers according to changing production needs, making them toil hard, and paying them the lowest possible wages.

Such pursuit is enhanced by competition, which is entrenched in capitalism.[63] Those with low profitability risk being forced out of the market. Capital constantly fine-tunes its accumulation strategy, generating fluctuations in labour precarity. In recent decades, capital has increasingly resorted to globalization and financialization to enhance exploitation. The state in capitalist economies tends to stand in alliance with capital. It constantly fine-tunes labour policy to serve capital accumulation. It may introduce anti-labour policy to advance exploitation or pro-labour policy, for example acts of working time limits, to sustain capitalism.[64] The pursuit of surplus value tends to incur labour movements. Marx charges the working class with the mission of overthrowing capitalism, and anchors the hope of eliminating precarity on socialist revolution.[65] Later Marxists focus on non-revolutionary labour resistance, and argue that such resistance may significantly reduce labour precarity.[66]

Capitalism is characterized by a fundamental contradiction between profitability and legitimacy. On the one hand, concessions made by capital and the state to pacify labour movements and reduce labour precarity tend to drive the capitalist system into crises of profitability. On the other hand, efforts to restore profitability by capital and the state entail the intensification of exploitation and the proliferation of labour precarity, thereby producing crises of legitimacy and labour resistance.[67] Thus, a tendency for a double movement exists in capitalist societies between phases characterized by the intensification of labour protection and phases characterized by the intensification of exploitation.

In socialist economies, the means of production are either nationalized or collectivized. However, the imperative of accumulation remains. In reality, socialist revolutions first occurred in the weakest link of the capitalist chain. Thus, when socialist revolutionists took power, they faced economies with massive impoverishment, to which they responded by extracting the surplus of peasants and the proletariat to fuel modernization. In this book, surplus appropriation in socialist economies is referred to as socialist surplus appropriation, which necessarily entails reducing labour costs and thereby generating labour grievances.

Therefore, the contradiction between accumulation and legitimacy also exists in socialist economies, but in a less pronounced way. In contrast to capitalism, which is organized to serve capitalists'

[63] Marx 1973. [64] Marx 1996. [65] Marx and Engels 1988, 203–243.
[66] Wright 2000; Silver 2003. [67] Silver 2003, 20.

accumulation interests, socialism is fundamentally committed to labour welfare, imposing insurmountable constraints on the drive for socialist surplus appropriation. Moreover, among enterprises, competition under capitalism is replaced by co-operation under socialism, further tempering the compulsion for socialist surplus appropriation. Nevertheless, to redress their grievances, workers in socialist economies also resist, in mundane or epic manners.

In socialist economies, the state determines and adjusts accumulation strategies and labour policy, weighing on workers' conditions. Karl Polanyi's analysis of premodern economies and idea of the double movement (discussed later) is enlightening for analysing socialist economies. According to Polanyi, premodern societies ran on three principles: reciprocity, redistribution, and householding (production taking place primarily in individual households).[68] Similar to premodern economies, non-market exchange principles, redistribution in particular, predominate in socialist economies.

Socialist economies are characterized by centralized redistribution by state authorities. However, there is a contradiction between centralization and legitimacy in socialist economies. On the one hand, centralization of redistribution tends to render the grassroots powerless and thereby discourage them from constructing socialism proactively and disable them from holding political elites accountable, thus driving the systems into crises of legitimacy. On the other hand, decentralization of redistribution, which empowers the grassroots, tends to cause disproportions or chaos in the national economy, thus leading to crises of central planning. Therefore, a double movement between centralization and decentralization of redistribution characterizes socialist economies.

### *Exclusion*

Exclusion mainly takes the form of segmentation in job placement and discriminatory distribution of economic, political, and social resources.[69] It guarantees some workers' relative security while leading to others' precarity. Exclusion may be imposed by capital, workers, and the state. These three forms of exclusion are interconnected.

Marxist scholars elaborate on exclusion imposed by capital in capitalist economies. Marxist exclusion is a consequence of capital accumulation. First, according to the general law of capital accumulation, as production expands with advances in productivity, the additional capital employs

[68] Polanyi 2001. [69] Piore 1972; Doeringer and Piore 1985.

fewer labourers than the old capital in proportion to its magnitude, resulting in a relative surplus population or industrial reserve army.[70] Second, to mitigate the contradiction between profitability and legitimacy, capital draws boundaries within the working class at the firm, inter-firm, and international levels.[71] In practice, employers often draw on institutions of Weberian exclusion (discussed later), such as gender, race, religion, and citizenship, to facilitate a divide-and-rule strategy.[72] Given the tension between accumulation and legitimacy in socialist economies, Marxist exclusion also operates there because the state draws boundaries among labouring people. Marxist exclusion is affected by accumulation strategies and can be countered by labour policy and resistance.

Weberian scholars elaborate on exclusion imposed by workers and the state. Weberian exclusion is a consequence of insiders' preservation of self-interests. It means being excluded from resources monopolized by closed social groups. Social relationships may be open or closed. They are likely to be closed if they are achieved through co-operative action or compromise between the interests of different actors, or if such closure consolidates group members' prestige and economic interests.[73] Common social institutions of Weberian exclusion are gender, race, religion, citizenship, ethnicity, and place of origin. Weberian exclusion pursued by workers operates through workers' organizations, such as trade unions, professional associations, and parties, possessing the resources and power necessary to influence conditions of different workers. Weberian exclusion imposed by the state takes the form of citizenship, often drawing on boundaries created by workers.[74] Weberian exclusion operates in both capitalist and socialist economies.

In the transition from traditional to modern societies, Weberian exclusion is recalibrated by market expansion, which breaks down old status groups and gives rise to new ones.[75] Similar scenarios can be observed in economies undergoing the transition from socialism to capitalism. Weberian exclusion can also be adjusted by the state through discrimination-related policies. In particular, the state can counter Weberian exclusion by introducing anti-discrimination laws and by fine-tuning the inclusiveness of citizenship. Mass movements for recognition of equal status across diverse groups can counter Weberian exclusion and reduce the labour precarity of the excluded. For example,

[70] Marx 1996, 607–703.
[71] Friedman 1977, 105–129; Gordon, Edwards, and Reich 1982; Silver and Slater 1999; Silver 2003, 20–21.
[72] Tilly 1999. [73] Weber 1978, 43–46, 339–348.
[74] Marshall 1950; Silver 2003, 21–25. [75] Weber 1978, 638, 936–937.

feminist and gay movements' agendas often include countering gender-based discrimination in the workplace.[76]

### *Commodification*

In the sphere of social reproduction, those suffering from the commodification of labour power are prone to precarity. Commodification operates in market economies. Both Marxism and Polanyianism have contributed to commodification theory.

In Marx's view, generalization of the capitalist mode of production presupposes the existence of large-scale, doubly free labour, meaning workers both free from all means of production, most importantly land, and free to sell their labour power. Marx terms the process of creating doubly free labour 'primitive accumulation', which in essence means the commodification of labour power.[77] Without any means of production, the proletariat is born precarious. Later Marxists find that semi-proletarianized wage labourers, who have meagre means of production, are compatible with and persist under capitalism. Semi-proletarianized wage labourers' means of production often depress their wages.[78]

Moreover, rather than being a one-shot process, as suggested by Marx, primitive accumulation is, in reality, an ongoing process that David Harvey calls 'accumulation by dispossession'.[79] Accumulation by dispossession helps alleviate the over-accumulation crisis of capitalism by releasing assets, including labour power, at very low costs, which can be seized by over-accumulated capital for profitable use. It proceeds not only by displacing peasants but also, for example, by privatizing natural resources (such as land, water, and forests) and public utilities (such as social housing, telecommunications, and transportation), or devaluing existing capital assets and labour power through state-administered austerity programmes.[80] Marxist commodification can be countered by mass movements and collective welfare policy. By eliminating the capitalist mode of production and reconnecting labour with means of production, socialism fundamentally decommodifies labour.

According to Polanyi, traditional societies are based on non-market exchange principles. However, owing to market expansion since the late eighteenth century, natural and human substance has been transformed into commodities, including labour, land, and money, which are not produced for sale. Polanyian commodification contributes to labour precarity in the following ways. First, establishing a labour market means

[76] Raeburn 2004; Cobble 2005. [77] Marx 1996, 704–750. [78] Wallerstein 1983, 27.
[79] Harvey 2003. [80] Harvey 2003, 149–156.

eliminating the protection provided by cultural institutions such as kinship for individuals, and applying the principle of freedom of contract between employees and employers. Consequently, workers 'would die as the victims of acute social dislocation through vice, perversion, crime, and starvation'.[81] Second, workers' lives are affected not only by wage levels but also by other factors such as natural and domestic surroundings and the quality and prices of consumer goods, the commodification of which also aggravates labour precarity.

Polanyi sees the rise of counter-movements against market expansion as inevitable. Counter-movements aim at social protection of humans and nature. He further argues that the history of modern society has been characterized by dynamic, cyclical double movements of market expansion and social protection: at one moment, the harms caused by marketization lead to counter-movements to protect society, while, at the next moment, the problems (including declining profits) caused by waves of social protection lead to counter-movements to restore profit rates.[82] Clearly, the core of both Marxist and Polanyian commodification is to subject workers' lives to the law of the market. Given its purpose, no distinction is made between the two in this book.

### *Towards an Analytical Framework*

As mentioned earlier, surplus appropriation, exclusion, and commodification create labour precarity at different stages of the life cycle of labour power. They are thus complementary. They are also closely intertwined, with combined effects irreducible to the arithmetical sum of each mechanism. Surplus appropriation and exclusion reinforce each other. On the one hand, the contradiction between surplus appropriation and legitimacy in both capitalist and socialist economies leads to boundary-drawing among workers. On the other hand, exclusion facilitates surplus appropriation of not only the excluded but also the included.[83]

Surplus appropriation and commodification are also closely intertwined. On the one hand, the desire for relentless exploitation propels commodification, which dispossesses labour. On the other hand, commodification enables and intensifies exploitation. When labourers are dispossessed, they must sell their labour power to make a living. The greater the pressure to maintain social reproduction is, the greater is the exploitation labourers tend to endure. Exclusion and commodification are also connected. Decommodification arrangements often operate on a

[81] Polanyi 2001, 76. [82] Polanyi 2001. [83] Marx 1996, 631.

discriminatory basis. In addition, the corresponding counter-mechanisms of surplus appropriation, exclusion, and commodification also complement each other in reducing labour precarity.

In light of this, to reach a comprehensive understanding of labour precarity, the three mechanisms that generate it and their corresponding counter-mechanisms must be analysed together. Against this stance, the dichotomous conceptualization of labour precarity that is popular in the existing literature appears problematic. It distinguishes between the haves and the have-nots, and identifies precarious workers with the latter. Employment arrangements (standard versus non-standard) and job quality (good versus bad) are the most common criteria used in the extant literature to distinguish between secure and precarious workers.[84] This conceptualization captures the reality that, in contrast to secure workers, precarious workers tend to work under non-standard employment arrangements and have bad jobs, but fails to explain why. It also downplays how exploitation and commodification contribute to labour precarity.

In contrast, this book defines labour precarity as a situation in which labouring people are subject to three interactive mechanisms that generate labour precarity, namely surplus appropriation, exclusion, and commodification, rendering them vulnerable to economic insecurity. The relevance of these three mechanisms varies with workers, time, and space. This definition implies that, in the real world, most labouring people are likely to be somewhat precarious. Therefore, precarious labour must be treated as a spectrum, rather than as a reified group of people with certain characteristics.

Thus, to understand labour precarity at a national level, one must first gain a panoramic view of the hierarchy of labouring people, rather than focus on a specific layer of precarious workers, and then examine how this hierarchy changes. One must interpret the expansion of a specific layer of precarious labour in the context of a recalibration of the hierarchy. Otherwise, it would be easy, for example, to interpret the dramatic rise of temporary workers in the late 1950s (Figure 1.3) as an increase in labour precarity, which is not entirely true, since this rise was accompanied by the upgrading of collective enterprises into SOEs, and thereby the transformation of workers in collective enterprises into SOE workers, and the enlargement of permanent workers in previous SOEs (for more detail, see Chapter 4).

In this book, the term 'labour tenure regime' is coined to refer to the system that causes and counters labour precarity. The regime determines

[84] Burgess and Campbell 1998, 6–8; Vosko 2000; Standing 2011.

who is rendered precarious, on what scale, and why. Each labour tenure regime consists of a distinct portfolio of interactive mechanisms that generate labour precarity – surplus appropriation, exclusion, and commodification – and their corresponding counter-mechanisms. Changes among mechanisms that generate labour precarity will result in alteration to the labour tenure regime that defines workers' basic conditions. Changes within individual mechanisms will result in variations in the scale, structure, and forms of precarious labour within one labour tenure regime. This book identifies two labour tenure regimes: (1) the regime of marginal labour precarity in the Mao era, which generated small strata of precarious workers and large strata of secure workers; and (2) the regime of general labour precarity in the post-Mao era, which generated large strata of precarious workers.

As an analytical framework, 'labour tenure regime' overcomes the popular reductionist tendency of the extant literature to blame labour precarity on a single mechanism. It accentuates the need to investigate the combined effects of surplus appropriation, exclusion, and commodification and their corresponding counter-mechanisms to generate a comprehensive understanding of labour precarity. By using this framework to explain the ebbs and flows of labour precarity in China since 1949, this book offers a practical example of how to use this framework productively.

Moreover, 'labour tenure regime' provides a powerful tool for comparative dynamic studies of labour precarity in the Mao and post-Mao eras, and between China and other countries, since the relevance of each of its three mechanisms varies with different workers in different places and periods. In addition, it extends the application of the theories of Marx, Weber, and Polanyi, which are traditionally used to analyse capitalist economies, to socialist economies.

## Research Strategy

As mentioned above, the existing literature on precarious labour in the Mao era is scarce, whereas that on the post-Mao era is rich but consists mainly of cross-sectional case studies at the workplace level and downplays agency labour. To complement the extant literature and avoid repetition, a research strategy is required that (1) fills the knowledge gap on precarious labour in the Mao era; (2) captures longitudinal transformation of labour precarity after 1949; and (3) fills the knowledge gap on agency workers in the post-Mao era.

This book pursues a multilayered research strategy that integrates the all-of-China-field-site approach, one-case multi-field-site approach, and one-site-case-study approach. The all-of-China-field-site approach refers to a research design relying on secondary materials, such as news articles, government reports, and research publications, to provide a nationwide picture of an issue. Its strength lies in providing an overview and a sense of the pervasiveness of a particular phenomenon. The one-case multi-field-site approach refers to a research design that involves going to multiple fieldwork sites to study a single phenomenon in depth, rather than studying variations across different sites. This approach is appropriate for uncovering general mechanisms and generating new empirical findings.[85] The combination of these two approaches facilitates cross-checking of information collected from different sources. The one-site-case-study approach, as the name indicates, adds depth and nuance to the one-case multi-field-site approach.

To unveil the labour tenure regime in the Mao era and the longitudinal transformation of the regimes after 1949, this book combines the all-of-China-field-site approach with the one-case multi-field-site approach, which are based on underexploited Chinese-language archives and interviews. Since original archives on precarious labour at the national level are inaccessible to non-official scholars, this study relies primarily on the published multivolume collections of central-government archives co-compiled by the Chinese Academy of Social Sciences (CASS) and the Central Archives of China (CAC). This compilation is ongoing, and as of 2023 covered the period 1949–1965. These archives are supplemented by flagship periodicals of the Ministry of Labour between 1949 and the late 1990s, statistical yearbooks and collections, newspapers, and research publications.[86]

In addition, the author interviewed nineteen people, most of whom once worked as temporary workers or cadres in state-owned units in China between the 1950s and the 1970s. They were reached through personal ties and interviewed via phone in 2023. They were by no means representative of temporary workers or cadres in that period. However, they provided first-hand information about temporary workers' experience and labour management in their units during the Mao era. Detail of these interviewees and their time of being interviewed can be found in the appendix.

To cross-check information at the national level and dig into complexities pertinent to precarious labour at the local level, the study draws

[85] Heimer 2006, 58–77.

[86] Since 1949, the labour ministry of China has changed its name several times. In 2008, the Ministry of Labour and the Ministry of Personnel were amalgamated into the MOHRSS. For the sake of convenience, this book refers to all labour wing predecessors of the MOHRSS after 1949 as the Ministry of Labour.

heavily on original archives on precarious labour in the Beijing Municipal Archives (BMA) and the Shanghai Municipal Archives (SMA). Beijing and Shanghai are not typical of Chinese cities. However, both have been prominent industrial cities since 1949. Their archives are likely to provide the most comprehensive accounts of precarious workers in Mao's China. The BMA and SMA house local archives at the municipal, district, and enterprise levels. In 2017, keywords relating to precarious labour were used to locate relevant archives in the archives' retrieval systems, and the author read the resulting documents.

At the BMA, the retrieval returned 140 volumes of documents, each consisting of multiple files. At the SMA, the retrieval returned nearly 7,000 files. The time frame of these archives spanned from the late 1940s to the early 1980s. Other documentary materials include local annals, memoirs of labour leaders during the Cultural Revolution, newspapers by workers' rebellion organizations, scholarly works, mainly concerning Beijing and Shanghai and, to a lesser extent, other parts of China, and unpublished sources made accessible through personal connections. These materials include those available in mainland China and at the Universities Service Centre for China Studies at the Chinese University of Hong Kong. When reconstructing historical events, the author carefully compared data from different sources and at different administrative levels.

To understand the working conditions of agency workers, the one-case multi-field-site approach was combined with the one-site-case-study approach. To collect data on the general conditions of agency workers and the effects of regulations against the abuse of agency workers, in 2016 a research team consisting of the author, an official from the Ministry of Human Resources and Social Security (MOHRSS), workers from non-governmental labour organizations, and university students visited Shanghai, Guangzhou, Suzhou, Dongguan, Jinan, and several other cities representative of China's top- and second-tier economic powerhouses to conduct semi-structured interviews (Figure 1.4). Individual interviews by the team involved fifty-two agency workers who worked in seven SOEs, nineteen foreign enterprises, and three private enterprises. Group interviews by the team involved provincial labour officials in Guangdong and Shandong, their municipal counterparts in Suzhou and Shanghai, HR managers of eleven SOEs, seven foreign enterprises, and two private enterprises, and managers of nineteen labour dispatch agencies.[87]

[87] Labour dispatch agencies are a subgroup of labour agencies. After the enforcement of the LCL in 2008, labour agencies must obtain a licence for labour dispatch from the local labour bureau, for which they must fulfil certain requirements. In China in the 2010s, labour dispatch was a very popular business of labour agencies.

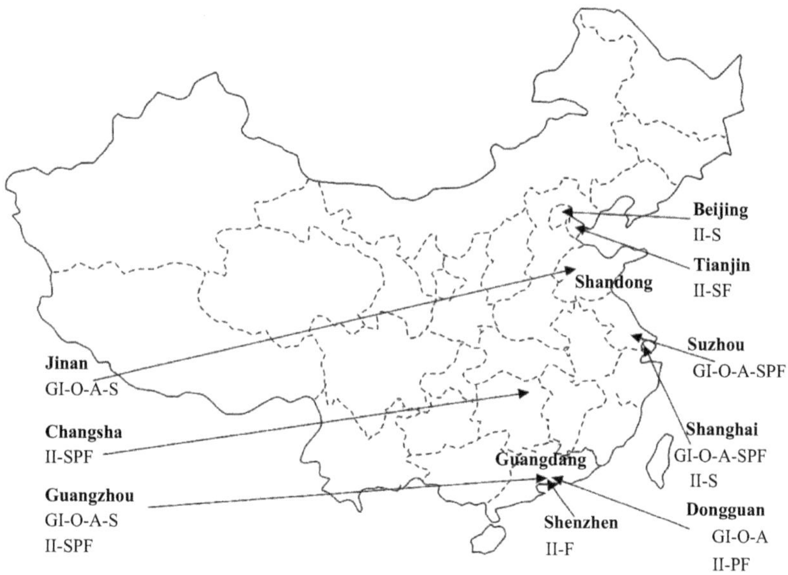


Figure 1.4 Multi-site fieldwork.[88]
*Note*: GI: group interviews with managers or officials; II: individual interviews with workers; O: labour officials; A: managers of labour dispatch agencies; S: interviewees from SOEs; P: interviewees from private enterprises; F: interviewees from foreign enterprises.

To gain a nuanced understanding of the conditions of agency workers at the workplace level, the author conducted participant observation and interviewed thirty current and former agency workers at an SOE called Oriental Express (pseudonym) between July and December 2016. According to a report released by the All-China Federation of Trade Unions (ACFTU) in 2012, among enterprises with different types of ownership, SOEs had the highest proportion of agency workers in their workforce.[89] Thanks to personal connections, in the summer of 2016 the author also worked for a month as an intern at a labour dispatch agency called Talent Pool (pseudonym), which provided agency workers for the Oriental Express, and interviewed thirteen of its staff. In addition, in 2016 and 2017 the author interviewed several scholars and labour officials to gain information about certain labour issues. In 2019, the author

[88] This figure is used with permission of SAGE Publications Ltd. Journals, from 'Regulating labour dispatch in China: a cat-and-mouse game, Xiaojun Feng, *China Information* 33(1), 2019'; permission conveyed through Copyright Clearance Center, Inc.
[89] ACFTU 2012.

revisited several field sites and found that the situation remained fundamentally unchanged. A list of interviewees and their place and time of being interviewed can be found in the appendix.

## Periodization

This book is organized largely in chronological order. To facilitate analysis of precarious labour since 1949, this book divides this period into time blocks, each with a particular labour tenure regime. Although periodization tends to disrupt historical continuity, its absence makes it difficult to distinguish periods with relatively stable characteristics. In light of this, periodization is accompanied by discussion of continuities and discontinuities between different time blocks.

Kornai divides socialism into three stages: revolutionary-transitional socialism, which grows out of capitalism and proceeds towards the completion of basic socialist apparatuses; classical socialism, which follows the trajectory of ready-made socialist apparatuses and proceeds towards sophistication of the socialist system; and reform socialism, which involves dramatic, if not fundamental, reconstruction of classical socialism.[90] Following Kornai's classification, the author divided the post-1949 era in China into three eras: revolutionary-transitional socialism (1949–1956), classical socialism (1957–1976), and reform socialism (1977–present).

The year 1956 marked the completion of the Three Transformations: the transformation of private industrial and commercial enterprises into state-owned units, the transformation of private handicraft workshops into co-operatives, and the transformation of agriculture based on individual peasant households into agriculture based on co-operatives. The year 1978 is often regarded as a pivotal year in post-1949 China because the Third Plenary Session of the 11th Central Committee of the CCP took place in this year. At this meeting, the CCP decided to discard socialist egalitarianism and embrace market-oriented developmentalism. However, a closer look at the policy of Mao's immediate successor, Hua Guofeng, indicates that Hua and Deng Xiaoping were largely in agreement on launching the Reform and Opening-up.[91] Therefore, it seems more apt to regard 1976 as a watershed, marked by Mao's death and the end of classical socialism. Thus, in this book, the post-1949 period is divided into the Mao era (1949–1976) and the post-Mao era (1977–present). They embrace different labour tenure regimes.

[90] Kornai 1992. [91] Teiwes and Sun 2011.

## Outline

The author's aim in this book is to examine the causes of and remedies for labour precarity in China since 1949. The crux of the argument is as follows. The Mao era featured a regime of marginal labour precarity. In this era, relentless socialist surplus appropriation created a tendency to increase labour precarity, which was tempered by the CCP's commitment to labour and labour resistance. To balance legitimacy and accumulation, the state built an exclusion system that privileged some workers over others. The state also decommodified and, to some extent, socialized social reproduction on a discriminatory basis. The boundaries between different groups of labouring people were constantly redrawn, mainly through recurrent shifts of the industrialization path between centralization and decentralization, swings in labour policy between promoting permanent and temporary employment, and ebbs and flows of labour movements. The result was marginal labour precarity and general but differentiated labour security.

The post-Mao era has featured a regime of general labour precarity. In this era, socialist surplus appropriation has been overhauled and marginalized, and has given way to exploitation. The exclusion system has been greatly softened and recalibrated, and social reproduction has been recommodified. The result has been pervasive labour precarity. Agency labour has been the dominant form of precarious labour in urban enterprises since the 2010s. Between the late 1970s and the 2010s, labour dispatch gradually rose to prominence owing primarily to the contradiction between capital's pursuit of profitability and legitimacy. Pro-labour regulations are major tools to counter labour precarity in the post-Mao era. However, they are impotent due to workers' impotence at the local level. In the 2010s, regardless of their employment status, ordinary Chinese workers led precarious lives, because they simultaneously suffered from exploitation, exclusion, and commodification.

Chapter 2 presents a brief overview of how the three mechanisms that generate labour precarity played out for wage labourers before 1949, particularly during the Republican era, and explains the labour institutions that underpinned their functioning, and how they were countered. In doing so, it provides a starting point for explaining the emergence and evolution of labour tenure regimes since 1949. It also serves as a baseline for comparing working conditions between the pre-1949 era and periods thereafter.

Chapters 3, 4, and 5 address labour precarity in the Mao era. Chapter 3 focuses on the 1949–1957 period. It begins by outlining the fundamentals of the regime of marginal labour precarity in the Mao era, which were installed in the early 1950s. It then narrows the focus to the 1949–1957 period, which witnessed the first switch between decentralized and recentralized industrialization in the Mao era, and a reorientation of labour policy, from promoting permanent employment to constraining its expansion, and to promoting the labour contract system. Chapter 4 focuses on the 1958–1965 period, which witnessed the rise and fall of the Great Leap Forward. During this period, China saw the second and most radical switch between decentralized and recentralized industrialization in the Mao era, and a further move of labour policy towards promoting temporary employment. Chapter 5 focuses on the 1966–1976 period, encompassing the rise and fall of the Cultural Revolution. During this period, China experienced a third wave of decentralized industrialization, and the fiercest protests of precarious workers in the Mao era.

Chapters 6, 7, and 8 address labour precarity since 1977. Chapter 6 delineates how the regime of marginal labour precarity was dismantled and replaced by the regime of general labour precarity. Chapter 7 advances Chapter 6 in two respects. First, it explains how the dualism between formal contract workers and agency workers emerged by examining the rise of agency workers. Second, it demonstrates why legal counter-movements in the post-Mao era are incomplete from a Polanyian perspective by examining the effects of two pro-labour regulations. Chapter 8 examines the impacts on workers of cumulative changes since 1949 by presenting a case study of the working conditions of formal and agency workers in an SOE, and accounts of the working conditions of agency workers in export-oriented factories in the 2010s.

Chapter 9 draws conclusions. It summarizes the main findings of this book, and compares the periods before and after 1949, and the Mao and post-Mao eras to unveil their continuities and discontinuities in causing and countering labour precarity. It engages with the paradoxes and debates raised in Chapter 1, and compares China with both socialist and transitional economies and traditional advanced capitalist economies in the transformation of labour precarity. It ends by acknowledging the limitations of this book, speculating on the future dynamics of labour precarity in China, and suggesting directions for future research.

# 2 Precarious Wage Labour before 1949

The pre-1949 era witnessed the rise of wage labour and early efforts to counter labour precarity in China. This chapter gives a brief overview of how the three mechanisms that generate labour precarity played out for wage labourers before 1949, particularly during the Republican era (1912–1949), what labour institutions underpinned their functioning, and how they were countered. As some of these institutions and their variations have remained robust in post-1949 China, this chapter provides a starting point for explaining the emergence and evolution of labour tenure regimes after 1949. By outlining working conditions before 1949, it also serves as a baseline for comparing working conditions between the pre-1949 era and periods thereafter, thus allowing a better understanding of what CCP rule has meant for Chinese workers.

## Wage Labour in the Imperial Era

Worldwide, wage labour is an ancient creation, yet for a long time it was an exceptional, complementary, and transitory form of labour. It only began to prevail when the means of production became concentrated in the hands of capitalists.[1] In China, wage labour existed in the Qin Dynasty (BC 221–207), but its significance was negligible.[2] It began to expand in the Ming Dynasty (AD 1368–1644), owing to a confluence of factors, including the development of trade both at home and abroad, the prevalence of cash crops, concentration of land, and replacement of tax in kind with tax in cash on land ownership in some places.[3] A royal record of the Wanli era (1572–1620) documents the impressive scale and precarious existence of wage workers in the handicrafts industry in the Yangtze River Delta, then the region with the most developed commodity economy in China:

[1] Engels 1987, 257–258. [2] Ma 2012. [3] Hong 1958; Li 1959.

Having large families but little land, Wu[4] people live mainly on weaving. Loom owners provide capital and workers provide labour … These workers lead a precarious life. In the morning, they do not know what will happen in the evening. Employed then live and unemployed then die … When dyeing mills are closed, thousands of dye workers are sacked; when loom owners stop operating, thousands of weavers are displaced.[5]

A civil record of the same era reveals that some of these workers were day workers and could not afford to be unemployed:

We Wu people have little interest in growing crops. The rich live on their looms and the poor live on their hands. Every morning, hundreds of the poor gather at the Xuan Temple, waiting to be called by the rich. If the rich stop operating for a day, they receive nothing; if the poor stop weaving for a day, they go hungry.[6]

In the mining industry in the late Ming Dynasty, publicly run mines using forced labour gradually gave way to privately run ones using both forced labour and free landless peasants. It is recorded that one iron mine in Guangdong employed between 1,800 and 6,000 workers at that time. The booming capitalist mining sector gave rise to a class of metal-workers and towns specializing in metal processing.[7] In agriculture, during the second half of the Ming Dynasty, wage labour also loomed large, particularly in the Yangtze River Delta. These workers' designations indicated a pattern of dualism that has characterized the workforce in many workplaces in China and beyond ever since. Depending on the duration of employment, agricultural wage labour was then divided into two broad categories. Those employed for less than a year were called short-term workers (*duangong*), and included day workers, monthly workers, and seasonal workers. Those employed for at least a year were called long-term workers (*changgong*). Short-term workers were legally free workers even before the Wanli era. In contrast, in the second half of the Ming Dynasty, long-term workers were still subject to feudal bondage and were legally inferior to their employers.[8]

At the same time, the putting-out system (*baomaizhi*), which was popular in Europe prior to the Industrial Revolution,[9] also emerged in China. Under this system, merchants put out materials for processing to

[4] Wu is the ancient name of a region in southeast China.
[5] Royal Archives of Ming, Records of the Shen Emperor Era of the Ming Dynasty (*Ming shen zong shilu*), Ming Dynasty, cited by Editorial Board of Chorography of Jiangsu 1999, 89.
[6] Jiang Yihua, Xitai Notes (*Xitai manji*), Ming Dynasty, cited by Editorial Board of Chorography of Jiangsu 1999, 89.
[7] Li 1959.
[8] Ouyang 1961; Chen 1980; Editorial Board of Chorography of Jiangsu 1999, 88.
[9] Jones 1982.

workers who worked at home using their own means of production. The merchants then purchased these workers' products at piece rates. Some merchants had their own production facilities, and only put out part of the production process. Several historical records describe how the putting-out system worked in the Yangtze River Delta during the Wanli era. One case was the sock industry in Songjiang County:

Since the Wanli era, using Youdun cloth to make soft and light summer socks has been very popular. As a result, merchants operate roughly 100 summer sock stores in the west end of the county. Men and women in the whole county live on making socks and get paid by the stores.[10]

The Youdun cloth from the west end of the county is light, soft, and white. People use it to make socks and sell them to merchants. These socks have developed a household name called Youdun Summer Socks. Women who can't weave sew and get paid for that.[11]

Another case was the cotton textile industry in Jiaxing and Huzhou:

Merchants buy cotton from neighbouring counties and sell it in the market here. People spin and knit the cotton into yarn or cloth. They go to the market and sell the yarn or cloth to buy cotton at dawn. They then spin and knit again, and go to the market for the same trade the next morning.[12]

In the subsequent Qing Dynasty (1644–1912), with the development of the commodity economy, wage labour and labour under the putting-out system became more prevalent in handicrafts, mining, and agriculture. It is documented that, at that time, tens of thousands of workers toiled in handicraft workshops, and the majority were peasants. In Suzhou alone, the number of dye workers during the Yongzheng era (1723–1735) was at least triple that of the Wanli era.[13] In the Qing Dynasty, Suzhou also witnessed waves of strikes by textile- and paper-making craftsmen for pay rises.[14] Strikes and free switching of employers indicate that workers in these industries were free to sell their labour power. However, many workers in the mining sector were still subject to extra-economic coercion, as were many long-term workers in the agricultural sector, although their legal status gradually improved during the Qing Dynasty. These workers were very vulnerable: if dismissed, they

[10] Fan Lian, Yunjian Notes (*Yunjian jumu chao*), Ming Dynasty, cited by Editorial Board of Chorography of Jiangsu 1999, 89.

[11] Chen Menglei (ed.), Collections of Ancient Books (*Gujin tushu jicheng*), Qing Dynasty, cited by Editorial Board of Chorography of Jiangsu 1999, 89.

[12] Zhu Guozhen, Yongzhuang Notes (*Yongzhuang xiaopin*), Ming Dynasty, cited by Chen 1980, 52.

[13] Liu 1962. [14] Editorial Board of Chorography of Jiangsu 1999, 90.

were exposed to hunger and even death. It is recorded that some committed suicide after losing their jobs.[15]

Wage workers appeared in the modern sector in China only after 1840 as a result of the development of modern industries. After the failure of the First Opium War (1840–1842), China entered a century-long era of colonization and humiliation. Between the 1840s and the 1910s, owing to a series of military defeats, the Qing government was forced to open treaty ports, cede territory, and devolve sovereignty to foreign powers, facilitating foreign business operations and giving rise to the first batch of modern enterprises and workers in China. In 1895, the Qing government signed the Treaty of Shimonoseki with Japan, which formally allowed the Japanese to found factories in China. Other colonial powers, citing the principle of equal rights for all foreign powers in China, also exercised this right.

In fact, even before 1895, foreign capital had operated factories in China to facilitate their local trade. For example, in the 1850s in Shanghai, one of the earliest treaty ports and industrial cities in China, there were around ten foreign shipyards, which were the earliest employers of factory workers in that city. In the 1860s, foreign shipping companies loomed large. Moreover, in order to manufacture trading goods, facilitate information circulation, and develop concessions, foreign entrepreneurs established factories, publishing houses, news agencies, and utility companies in the city. By 1894, foreigners had established 45 industrial enterprises in Shanghai, employing around 19,000 workers. The Treaty of Shimonoseki in 1895 further stimulated foreign investment in China, and some foreign factories employed thousands of workers.[16]

In 1861, the Qing government launched the Self-Strengthening Movement (*yangwu yundong*), aiming to modernize Chinese industries by learning from the West. Over the next three decades, the government built various modern military and civil enterprises. The Jiangnan Arsenal (*jiangnan zhizaoju*) in Shanghai was the largest arsenal built during this movement, employing around 2,800 workers in 1870; and in 1889 the Shanghai Mechanical Textile Bureau (*Shanghai jiqi zhibuju*) employed approximately 4,000 workers. Furthermore, since the 1860s, Chinese merchants, landlords, and officials had also begun to invest in modern industries, particularly in silk, flour, tobacco, cotton textiles, and paper-making. Compared with enterprises backed by foreign capital and state authorities, private Chinese enterprises were small in scale. In the late 1890s, most of them employed fewer than 100 workers. Overall, in 1913,

[15] Ouyang 1961; Liu 1962.
[16] Yan et al. 1989, 1570–1574; Yuan 1990, 1–2; Li et al. 1997, 78–81.

factory workers totalled between 140,000 and 150,000 in Shanghai, half of whom worked in factories with a headcount of over 500. Before joining the industrial workforce, most of these workers were poor peasants or handicraftsmen.[17]

In the modern sector, the inside contract system emerged. Under this system, firm owners provided floor space, machinery, and sometimes raw materials and working capital, and arranged sales of finished products. The gap between raw materials and finished products was filled not by the firm owners' paid employees but by contractors, who hired their own employees, supervised the labour process, and received payments from the firm owners. Contractors' income consisted of the difference between their revenues from firm owners and their wage bills to their own employees, as well as the pay they earned as employees of firm owners. Contractors were able to subcontract their share of production, thus forming a multilayered subcontracting chain.[18] Drawing initially on personal bonds in secret societies and the management practices of an army organized to contain the Taiping Rebellion in the 1850s, enterprises built by supporters of the Self-Strengthening Movement developed the inside contract system, and this was then adopted by domestic private enterprises.[19] Meanwhile, foreign capital learned the inside contract system from their home countries and adopted it in their enterprises in China.[20]

The workforce in the modern sector was characterized by dualism. First, there was dualism based on employment arrangements: managers and highly skilled workers tended to be directly employed by business owners and were called 'inside workers' (*ligong*), while low-skilled workers tended to be employed by contractors and were called 'outside workers' (*waigong*).[21] For example, in the foreign shipbuilding industry in the late Qing Dynasty, mechanical workers were generally *ligong*, and carpenters, blacksmiths, riveters, and other workers were *waigong*.[22] Second, there was dualism based on job tenure. Large numbers of temporary workers worked alongside long-term workers. For example, in the late nineteenth century, roughly half of workers at the Hong Kong and Whampoa Dockyard were temporary.[23]

In the modern sector, the standard working day was over ten hours. Although Chinese workers were less productive than their counterparts in developed economies, their wages were even lower. To solicit investment, officials of the Self-Strengthening Movement highlighted Chinese

[17] Yan et al. 1989, 1570–1574; Li et al. 1997, 78–80. [18] Buttrick 1952; Zhu 1999, 309.
[19] Ma 2016. [20] Yuan 1990, 7–8. [21] Liu and Tang 1998, 195–197.
[22] Zhu 1999, 310. [23] Yan et al. 1989, 1572, 1582.

workers' low wages as a guarantee of high returns. A substantial proportion of the wages of those working under the inside contract system went into contractors' pockets. It was reported that, in 1877, contractors for the Shanghai Steam Navigation Company and China Merchants Group extracted 21 per cent of their workers' wages. The management style featured punishment and physical abuse. Against this background, collective labour action in the modern sector emerged almost simultaneously with the arrival of foreign investment into China. In the second half of the nineteenth century, many workers protested against the invasion of foreign powers, exploitation and abuse by business owners, and wage docking by labour contractors.[24] In Shanghai alone, thirteen strikes were recorded between 1868 and 1894, and sixty between 1895 and 1910.[25]

## Wage Labour in the Republican Era

China's last imperial dynasty, the Qing Dynasty, was overthrown in 1912, and the country entered the Republican era. Overall, owing to relentless conflicts between domestic military powers throughout this era, and between China and Japan in 1937–1945, the Chinese economy developed slowly, with short-term booms and long-term stagnation and recession. The national economy was still characterized by dualism, with a small modern sector, and a large traditional sector, which in the 1930s was still using almost the same production technologies and organizations as in the 1840s.[26] During this era, institutions of exploitation and exclusion became more sophisticated, commodification deepened, and attempts at decommodification emerged.

### *Exploitation*

In the workplace of Republican Shanghai, foremen or forewomen imposed despotic control over workers. They controlled virtually every aspect of workers' employment, including access to jobs, remuneration, promotion, and dismissal.[27] In the 1920s, most industrial workers toiled over ten hours per day.[28] The Factory Act of the Republic of China was enacted in 1929, amended in 1932, and re-enforced in 1933. Under this act, which applied to all modern factories with a workforce of over thirty, adult workers' normal working day was eight hours, but this could be extended to twelve hours under certain conditions, and the maximum working day for child labour (under sixteen years old) was eight hours.

[24] Yan et al. 1989, 1581–1596; Li et al. 1997, 258–260. [25] Shen et al. 1998, 470.
[26] Hou 1963. [27] Frazier 2002, 33–34. [28] Li et al. 1997, 118–119.

Table 2.1 *Rates of exploitation by Shanghai companies in the Republican era.*

| Company name | Recorded years | Exploitation rate (%) |
|---|---|---|
| Wing On Cotton Mills | 1923–1936 | 153 |
| Shenxin No. 1 and No. 8 Cotton Mills | 1926–1936 | 208 |
| Shenxin No. 2 Cotton Mill | 1937–1940 | 642 |
| Fuxin No. 1 and No. 3 Flour Mills | 1913–1924 | 1,176 |
| Fuxin No. 7 Flour Mill | 1920–1936 | 830 |
| Nanyang Brothers Tobacco Company | 1933–1936 | 1,158 |
| Shanghai Cement Company | Before 1937 | 480 |
| Department of Electricity and Gas, Shanghai Municipal Council | 1912–1918 | 218 |

*Source*: Li et al. 1997, 153.

Monthly overtime could not exceed forty-six hours, and workers' holiday entitlements included one day off for every six days of work, national holidays (ten days per year), and special holidays according to their years of service in the factory.[29]

In reality, an official survey of 240 (mainly large) factories in forty industries in Shanghai in 1946 found that, on average, workers in eighteen of the industries surveyed worked over ten hours per day.[30] Another official survey of 860 factories (including large, medium, and small ones) in fifty-one major industries in Shanghai in 1946–1948 found that the average working day lasted over ten hours in twenty-one of the industries surveyed, including major ones such as textiles, and that workers worked, on average, twenty-six days per month.[31] Children's working days were as long as adults'. It was common to work between 303 and 308 days per year.[32] Table 2.1 shows the exploitation rates, defined as the ratio of employers' profits (before interest and taxes) to wages, in several major companies in Republican Shanghai. These rates were high in absolute terms.

In the Republican era, inflation was low between 1911 and early 1939, and high between late 1939 and 1949. The real wages of urban workers in Shanghai dropped slightly between 1911 and 1926, plummeted between 1937 and 1945 and between 1947 and 1949, but increased between 1927 and 1936 and in 1946. During the Republican era, on

[29] Li et al. 1997, 295–296. [30] Social Bureau of Shanghai 1947, 22–24.

[31] Industrial Relations Arbitration Committee of Shanghai 1948, 25–26; Zhu, Hu, and Xu 1984.

[32] Li et al. 1997, 104, 120.

average, the wage earnings of a working-class family of two adults and one child provided only around 60 per cent of the minimum they needed to subsist. As a result, many working-class families lived in debt.[33]

Even for those employed on a regular basis, jobs were insecure. Under labour behaviour codes introduced by the municipal government of Shanghai, workers could be dismissed for theft, fighting, drug taking, gambling during work time, absence for a certain number of working days, and disability. Individual enterprises had their own workplace codes, which could be even more stringent.[34] For example, the labour contracts between large commercial companies and their employees in Shanghai often stipulated that, even within the terms of the contract, employers could dismiss workers if they were not needed, were unable to satisfy the employer or comply with workplace codes, picked up bad habits, harmed the reputation and interests of their employer, or were involved in labour mobilization. According to the factory code of the Shanghai Cement Company in 1947, workers could be dismissed if they were not needed or if they participated in strikes or stoppages.[35] In Shanghai in 1927, the Naigai Wata No. 5 Cotton Mill Company fired 120 workers suspected of engaging in labour organizing, the soy sauce industry laid off over 500 workers, and the machinery industry dismissed over 2,000 workers.[36] Between 1933 and 1935, on average, Shenxin No.1 and No. 8 Cotton Mills fired over 30 per cent of their workers every year.[37] In addition, the workplace was hazardous, and work-related injuries and diseases were common.[38]

Workers' grievances often translated into labour disputes. In Shanghai, 11,286 labour disputes, including strikes, were recorded between 1928 and March 1949, and 2,625 strikes between 1918 and March 1949 (see Figure 2.1). Some strikes started in one factory but then quickly extended to involve many others, and even whole industries. In fact, of the 429 strikes recorded in Shanghai between August 1945 and June 1946, 279 involved more than one factory, and 198 of these involved over 100 factories. Dismissals and compensation issues were the major triggers for labour disputes. Of the 1,010 labour disputes recorded between 1933 and 1935, 65 per cent were about dismissals and 21 per cent were about compensation. Dismissals sparked 43 per cent, compensation 35 per cent, and business closures or temporary suspensions 12 per cent of the 3,892 labour disputes recorded between August 1945 and December 1947.

33 Li et al. 1997, 146–155. 34 Shen et al. 1998, 199–200.
35 Zhu, Hu, and Xu 1984; Li et al. 1997, 103, 130. 36 Li et al. 1997, 133.
37 Li et al. 1997, 103. 38 Chen 1929 ; Li et al. 1997, 122–124; Shen et al. 1998, 400.

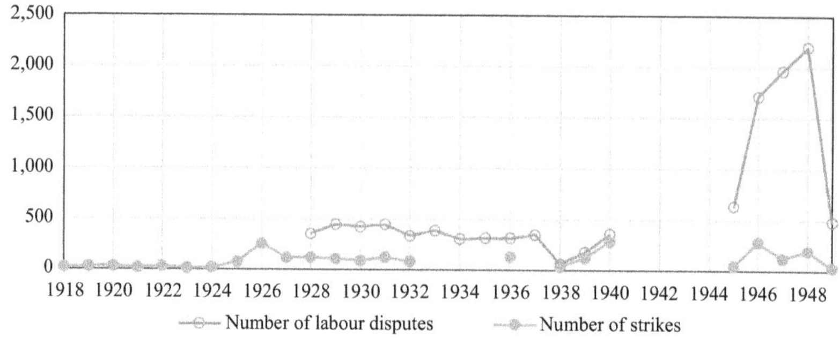


Figure 2.1 Labour disputes and strikes in Shanghai, 1919–1948.
*Source*: Shen et al. 1998, 470–475; Industrial Relations Arbitration Committee of Shanghai 1948, 41.
*Note*: Data for 1945 include only the period from August to December. Data for 1949 include only the period from January to March. Between 1933 and 1936, 383 strikes were recorded in Shanghai.

Many of these strikes were protests against exploitation. Defensive strikes were often launched against arrears, docking of and reductions in wages, dismissals, management abuse, and crackdowns on trade unions. Offensive strikes were often launched for pay rises, working hour reductions, recognition of trade unions, and to support other workers on strike.[39] Since many factories were owned by investors from invader countries, anti-exploitation strikes were often intertwined with anti-imperialism protests. The most famous case of this kind was the May Thirtieth Movement (*wusa yundong*) in 1925, which was triggered by the shooting of a Chinese worker by a Japanese cotton mill manager in Shanghai. It soon escalated into a mass protest against Japanese imperialism throughout China.[40]

The exploitation discourse dominates works on pre-1949 labour history by China's official historians and Marxist scholars. They emphasize the predicament of workers in the workplace, and the class consciousness and solidarity developed during their daily work and collective action.[41]

### *Exclusion*

In China, state-enforced exclusion based on residence prevailed after 1949, whereas prior to 1949 peasants were able to move freely between cities and their home villages, and migrant peasants were, in fact, a major

[39] Deng 1949; Chesneaux 1968; Li et al. 1997, 258–290; Shen et al. 1998, 470–475.
[40] Li et al. 1997, 268–269.
[41] Deng 1949; Chesneaux 1968; Li et al. 1997; Shen et al. 1998.

source of Shanghai's urban workforce.[42] Nevertheless, exclusion pursued by labour and capital was pervasive prior to 1949.

In contrast to the discourse of exploitation, studies conducted by several American historians in the 1980s and 1990s stress exclusion pursued by workers before 1949. Gail Hershatter (*The Workers of Tianjin, 1900–1949*)[43] and Emily Honig (*Sisters and Strangers: Women in the Shanghai Cotton Mills, 1919–1949*)[44] typify this line of argument. Elizabeth Perry (*Shanghai on Strike: The Politics of Chinese Labor*) offers a more balanced version of this discourse, emphasizing both the fragmentation of Chinese workers and cohesion within each fragment. She depicts the history of Chinese workers in pre-1949 Shanghai largely as a history of boundary drawing among workers by the workers themselves. She found that workers with differing skill levels differed in their places of origin, gender composition, educational background, and urbanization, and engaged in different politics.[45]

In parallel, capital often draws on institutions of exclusion to reinforce exploitation. In the Republican era, employment arrangements were important institutions of exclusion. Skilled workers tended to be directly employed by de facto employers and enjoyed the freedom to choose their jobs. In contrast, low-skilled workers tended to work under indirect employment arrangements characterized by extra-economic coercion. Such arrangements not only guaranteed a cheap and stable workforce for de facto employers but also allowed intermediaries to extract commissions.

First, before the late 1940s, the inside contract system continued to prevail in many industries. In Shanghai, in the dock transportation, rickshaw, and construction industries, almost all labour processes were contracted out, as were some processes in the railway transportation and manufacturing industries. In 1935, around a third of the workforces of the Shanghai–Nanjing Railway and the Shanghai–Hangzhou–Ningbo Railway were contract labour. In 1937, in Shanghai's modern shipbuilding industry, in which almost all but mechanical workers were employed by contractors, the proportion of contract workers was roughly 70 per cent.[46] Contract labour was also prevalent in the mining sector: in 1929, workers hired by contractors accounted for 79 per cent of the workforce of Beipiao Coal Mines, 54 per cent of Kailuan Coal Mines, and 66 per cent of Anshan Iron Mines.[47]

Contractors lived on commissions extracted from contract workers' wages. In the 1930s, in Shanghai's dock transportation industry, the commission rate was 70 to 80 per cent (of contract workers' wages); in

[42] Li et al. 1997, 92. [43] Hershatter 1986. [44] Honig 1992. [45] Perry 1993.
[46] Li et al. 1997, 105–106. [47] Yan et al. 1987, 7.

the rickshaw industry, the rate was 30 to 50 per cent; and in the shipbuilding industry, where multilayered contracting prevailed, it was around 40 to 60 per cent. In addition, by controlling access to jobs, contractors were also able to charge recruitment fees and extract bribes from contract workers. Contractors were often members of secret societies, which facilitated the control and abuse of contract workers.[48]

Second, on the shop floor, apprentices and workers-in-cultivation (*yangcheng gong*) worked alongside contract workers. In Shanghai in the 1930s, apprentices made up around 30 per cent of the textiles workforce, 30 to 40 per cent in transportation, furniture, and papermaking, and 50 per cent in metallurgy, metalwork, and machinery. It generally took apprentices three to four years to become formal workers, and during this period their compensation barely covered their subsistence. Workers-in-cultivation were a disguised form of apprentice. A survey conducted in 1936 showed that roughly half of workers in the thirty Japanese-owned cotton mills surveyed were workers-in-cultivation. These were mainly females aged fourteen to eighteen. Some had contracts with the factory; others had contracts with labour contractors and were called enslaved workers (*baoshen gong*). Before 1937, most workers-in-cultivation in Shanghai were enslaved workers. They were sold to labour contractors by their parents for two to three years in return for a payment roughly equal to one month's wage for ordinary workers in cotton mills. During their period of enslavement, these workers received nothing but accommodation and clothes from the contractors who appropriated all of their wages. They were forbidden to go anywhere other than the factory in which they worked and their residence. A survey in the 1930s showed that, for an enslavement period of three years, labour contractors' net profit was around 50 per cent of enslaved workers' wages.[49]

Beyond the shop floor, household workers were organized under the putting-out system to produce for the market. In the Republican era, the putting-out system was particularly common in industries making cotton textiles, silk, lace, hairnets, and braided straw in North China and the Yangtze Delta.[50] In Baodi County, Hebei in 1923, 72 per cent of looms, mainly household-owned, operated under a putting-out system controlled by sixty-seven cloth shops. In Gaoyang County, Hebei in

[48] Li et al. 1997, 106–107; Zhu 1999, 310–312.
[49] Li et al. 1997, 104–116; Shen et al. 1998, 165–170.
[50] Shi, Jianyun. 1992. Guanyu jindai Zhongguo nongcun jiating gongye de jige wenti (Several problems regarding rural family industry in modern China). *Zhongguo shehui kexueyuan jindaishi yanjiusuo jiansuo 40 zhounian xueshu taolunhui lunwenji*, unpublished Yan 1955, 254–297.

1932, 65 per cent of looms were under the control of eighty cloth shops.[51]

By controlling market access, merchants who co-ordinated the putting-out system controlled the prices of household workers' products. Between 1915 and 1920 in Gaoyang County, a bolt of cloth might be sold for 1 to 2 *yuan* on the open market, but for 0.5 *yuan* to merchants who controlled the putting-out system.[52] When demand fell, prices were even lower, and sometimes 80 to 90 per cent lower than normal.[53] Compared with factory owners who invested in fixed capital, merchants who co-ordinated the putting-out system could withdraw from business without significant losses when faced with economic depression, thus rendering household workers more vulnerable to unemployment than their factory counterparts.[54]

On the bottom rung were the unemployed, whose massive presence facilitated the exploitation of those in work. An official survey conducted in Shanghai in September 1928 found that 19.7 per cent of members of the 380 trade unions surveyed were unemployed.[55] In Shanghai, the numbers of unemployed workers were estimated at 300,000 in 1932, 610,000 in 1935, and 300,000 in 1946, amounting to around 40 per cent of the industrial workforce there in 1946.[56]

Moreover, in the Republican era, while skilled workers tended to be employed on a regular basis, low-skilled workers tended to be employed not only under the inside contract system but also on a temporary basis. In Republican Shanghai, temporary workers were widely used in labour-intensive industries such as textiles, tobacco, and flour. In this city in the 1930s, the ratio of dockers employed regularly to those employed temporarily was roughly two to three. Some temporary workers were day workers who waited to be employed by labour contractors each morning. Some were employed for short periods, typically less than three months. For those placed in regular posts, formalization opportunities were rare, and they often became long-term temporary workers. Temporary workers earned less than regular workers because of their shorter working time and lower wage rates. Generally, day dockers were employed for only fifteen to sixteen days per month, and temporary riveters in the shipbuilding industry were employed for only four to five months per year. In the early 1930s, the monthly wage of low-skilled regular workers in the Governing Bureau of the French Concession in Shanghai was

[51] Chao 1977, 204. [52] Wu 1936, 6–17. [53] Shi 1996. [54] Fang 1978, 16.
[55] Li et al. 1997, 133–134. [56] Shen et al. 1998, 69–70.

17 to 30 *yuan*, amounting to 0.65 to 1.15 *yuan* per day,[57] whereas the daily wage rate of their temporary counterparts was 0.55 *yuan*.[58]

Employers also enforced exclusion based on gender and age. Factory surveys in the late 1920s and early 1930s found that female and child labour made up 60 to 70 per cent of the industrial workforce in Shanghai, and comprised mostly low-skilled workers. According to an official survey conducted in 1946–1948, female adult workers made up over 70 per cent of the workforce in knitting, cotton textiles, and tobacco in Shanghai. Child labour was pervasive in the Republican era, often disguised as apprentices. An official survey of 117 textile factories in Shanghai in 1923, with an average headcount of approximately 1,200, found that 15.5 per cent of the workforce was under twelve years old. An official survey of 985 factories in several industries in Shanghai in 1933 found that 6.6 per cent of their workforce was less than sixteen years old. In 860 factories in fifty-one industries officially surveyed in Shanghai in 1946–1948, 5.6 per cent of the workforce was under sixteen.

While the working time of male and female adult workers and child workers was similar within the same factory in Republican Shanghai, female adult workers' wages were roughly 60 per cent of those of male adult workers, and child workers' wages were 50 to 70 per cent of those of female adult workers.[59] In the silk industry of the Yangtze River Delta, male workers tended to enjoy stable employment, while female workers tended to be hired on a seasonal basis.[60]

In addition, there was exclusion based on nationality in companies owned by foreign investors, with foreign employees generally enjoying superior status to Chinese employees.[61] Finally, working conditions also differed by the type of factory ownership. Based on fieldwork in a state-owned arsenal in Yunnan in 1940, Shi Guoheng found that, in the view of local workers, working in state-owned factories could improve one's social status and help evade conscription, and state-owned factories also had more stable jobs and more amiable managers than private ones since they were not primarily concerned about profits.[62]

### *Commodification*

In the Republican era, Chinese life was deeply commodified. The majority of the population consisted of peasants. They increasingly relied on

[57] Employees in the Governing Bureau of the French Concession did not work on Sundays (see Li et al. 1997, 120–121). Therefore, it is assumed here that these employees worked twenty-six days per month.

[58] Li et al. 1997, 100–101, 107; Shen et al. 1998, 173.

[59] Li et al. 1997, 85–87, 103–104. [60] Cliver 2020. [61] Li et al. 1997, 93.

[62] Shi 1946, 120.

the market for daily necessities and agricultural inputs, and needed cash to pay for them and taxes. In the 1930s, over half of peasants did not have enough land to subsist and had to live on wage employment or debts. Subsistence pressure also pushed peasants to grow cash crops, subjecting them to exploitation by merchants.[63] Although the Nationalist Party was in power, the CCP managed to establish many base areas. Anti-commodification efforts in modern industrial sectors differed between regions controlled by the Nationalist Party and those controlled by the CCP.

During most of the Republican era, regions controlled by the Nationalist Party included large cities where workers lived mainly by selling their labour power, as well as large parts of rural areas. The Factory Act of the Republic of China introduced by the Nationalist government was a major piece of national legislation stipulating workers' welfare entitlements. Apart from child labour, maternity leave, working time, and compensation for work-related injury and death, provisions on labour welfare issues in this act were mostly advisory rather than legally binding.[64] Working-class families spent most of their money on food, clothes, and rent, and often failed to make ends meet. A 1926 survey found that, on average, of the living expenses of a two-person household, food accounted for 53.8 per cent, clothes 15.4 per cent, rent 15.4 per cent, fuel 9.5 per cent, and miscellaneous other costs 5.9 per cent. A survey of 305 working-class households conducted in 1930 found that 88.2 per cent of these households were in debt, and 78 per cent had items in pawn.[65]

Some industrial workers were required to eat in factory canteens, while others could choose to eat in factory canteens or private cafes, or bring their own food. An official survey of 860 factories in fifty-one industries in Shanghai conducted in 1946–1948 found that 483 factories had canteens that could serve all workers, and 230 factories had no canteens. Generally, workers had to pay to eat in factory canteens. Most industrial workers in Shanghai lived in cramped rented accommodation, some of which was managed by factories or labour contractors. A survey of 230 households working for cotton mills in Shanghai in 1928 found that, on average, each household had 4.76 people living in 1.42 rooms, amounting to 3.29 people per room.[66]

When workers fell ill, unless from job-related injuries, they were likely to bear all medical costs themselves. When workers retired, except for employees in a few state-owned factories, most had no pensions.[67]

[63] Mao 1982; Huang 1985, 1990; Chen, Xue, and Feng 1987.
[64] Li et al. 1997, 295–296. [65] Li et al. 1997, 154–155. [66] Li et al. 1997, 157.
[67] Li et al. 1997, 125–127; Shen et al. 1998, 352.

Although the Factory Act stipulated that women should have two months' paid maternity leave, in practice pregnant women often ended up being laid off.[68] However, large factories tended to offer more welfare facilities than smaller ones, which included canteens, dormitories, hospitals, and schools for workers and their children. Moreover, in the face of economic difficulties triggered by the Sino-Japanese War and hyperinflation, factories expanded their offerings of welfare services to workers from the late 1930s.[69]

Cost-of-living crises sparked strikes for pay rises. By undermining the real value of wages, inflation fuelled workers' anger and often stirred up mass protests. As workers spent most of their money on food, they were highly sensitive to the price of rice. Strikes for pay rises or rice subsidies at times of rice price increases were common before 1949. For example, in response to the soaring rice price in 1919, workers in Japanese cotton mills in Shanghai protested for pay rises. In Hong Kong in April 1920, metalworkers went on strike against rice price increases and dismissals.[70] In Shanghai between May and July 1920, when the rice price almost tripled while wages stagnated, tens of thousands of workers waged thirty-three strikes, and most succeeded in gaining wage increases or rice subsidies.[71] In Beijing in 1930, postal workers protested for rice subsidies.[72]

During the period of prolonged hyperinflation between late 1939 and 1949, workers in Shanghai rose up to demand that wage rates be linked to the cost-of-living index. Only a few state-owned companies adopted this practice in 1940, but companies in forty-three industries had done so by the end of 1946. In the second half of 1946, war broke out between the Nationalist Party and the CCP. In February 1947, in the context of wartime economic hardships, the Nationalist government froze the nominal wage rate at the January 1947 level. In response, workers in all industries, including civil servants, united in protest, forcing the government to unfreeze the wage rate in May 1947. In 1948, with inflation skyrocketing, workers protested for wages to be calculated on the basis of the current month's rather than the previous month's cost-of-living index, and to be paid in kind, in silver dollars, or in foreign currencies, rather than in the fiat currency issued by the Nationalist government.[73]

For female workers in particular, pregnancy layoffs were a recurring theme of protests. A significant case of this kind was a strike by cotton mill workers in Shanghai in 1946. Under the 1933 Factory Act, female workers were entitled to two months' maternity leave, during which

[68] Shen et al. 1998, 350, 363. [69] Frazier 2002, 60–91; Bian 2005, 127–152.
[70] Deng 1949, 18. [71] Li et al. 1997, 265. [72] Zhou et al. 2005, 362–364.
[73] Li et al. 1997, 145–146, 265, 284–285.

those who had worked for the factory for over six months were entitled to 100 per cent of their usual pay, and those who had worked for less than six months to 50 per cent. In light of poor implementation of these provisions and the cost-of-living crisis, in 1946 approximately 130,000 workers in over forty cotton mills (where female workers were concentrated) in Shanghai participated in protests. They not only defended their legal right to paid maternity leave but also achieved increases to their base pay, the linking of their wages with the cost-of-living index, and reduced working hours.[74]

Following the rupture between the Nationalist Party and the CCP in 1927, the CCP began to establish its own base areas, mainly in remote rural areas where modern industries were minimal. Legislation had long been used as a weapon by the CCP to counter exploitation and commodification. As early as 1922, the Chinese Trade Union Secretariat – the labour wing of the CCP – introduced the Outline of Labour Acts, which stipulated, amongst other things, that workers had a right to organize and strike, that the normal daily working time should be eight hours for workers on day shifts and six hours on night shifts, that women were entitled to paid maternity leave, and that child labour should be abolished. The secretariat then mobilized trade unions across the country to demand the labour rights listed in the *Outline* from authorities and employers.[75]

In its operations in base areas, in the early 1920s the CCP gradually retreated from its one-sided pro-labour stance, and attempted to strike a balance between labour and capital. In the Central Revolutionary Base Area in 1930, it introduced the Provisional Labour Law, which stipulated that employers were responsible for regular workers' medical costs and for two months' paid maternity leave for female workers. These requirements were deemed too high by employers and were not implemented at all. In 1931, the CCP enacted the Labour Law, which required that, in addition to wages, employers should allot money amounting to 10 to 15 per cent of monthly gross wages to a labour welfare fund. This law was amended in 1933 to reduce employers' responsibility for labour welfare. Nevertheless, as the Nationalist Party grabbed back the Central Revolutionary Base Area and the CCP started the Long March in late 1934, this law was hardly enforced either. In addition, individual revolutionary base areas issued their own labour welfare regulations.[76]

In revolutionary base areas, soldiers and staff of the CCP government relied mainly on the free supply system (*gongjizhi*) for their daily necessities, which marked the most pronounced counter-movement against

74 Li et al. 1997, 283; Shen et al. 1998, 350, 363, 474.

75 Yan et al. 1987, 291.

76 Yan et al. 1987, 293–301.

commodification forged by the CCP before it took power. This covered a wide range of necessities, from food, clothes, accommodation, and travel, to assistance for childbirth, disease, ageing, and death, albeit at very low levels. It was egalitarian, and one's rank in the CCP government had little impact on one's access to supplied items.[77] Between 1927 and 1937, most staff in government-run businesses came from armies and bureaus of the CCP government and lived on the free supply system. These businesses also employed skilled workers from society and paid them quite generous wages. In government-run businesses in subsequent years, the co-existence of these two compensation schemes gradually gave way to a mixed compensation scheme combining free supply of some items with wages, and finally to the wage system. There were also some private enterprises in base areas.[78] The extent to which they complied with labour regulations issued by base area governments is unclear.

## Conclusion

China has a long history of wage labour. In the last two dynasties of the imperial era, wage work in the traditional sector expanded significantly, and feudal bondage was gradually abolished. These workers' lives were precarious, and they could not afford to be unemployed. They engaged in collective action to improve their conditions. Workforce dualism based on job tenure and the putting-out system already existed in the Ming Dynasty. From 1840 onwards, wage workers gained prominence in modern industrial sectors, and the inside contract system gained popularity, giving rise to workforce dualism based on employment arrangements.

In the Republican era, wage labour continued to grow. Workers toiled long hours for meagre pay and were constantly exposed to unemployment. During this era, exclusion pursued by the state was insignificant and exclusion by workers was pervasive. Exclusion by capital was salient, relying on institutions such as the inside contract system and the putting-out system, and on workforce fragmentation based on skills, gender, age, and nationality, amongst other factors. In regions controlled by the Nationalist Party, workers in modern sectors lived mainly on their wages, and employers provided limited welfare benefits. In regions controlled by the CCP, the modern industrial sector was very small, and the widely encompassing, low-level free supply system played a key role in decommodification. The Republican era witnessed numerous strikes and other forms of labour disputes. Anti-exploitation and anti-commodification were two major themes of labour protests.

[77] Lü 1997; Lu 1993. [78] Zhai 1990.

# 3 Incipient Socialist Surplus Appropriation, Exclusion, and Decommodification, 1949–1957

The counter-movement against commodification in the 1930s and 1940s reached a milestone on 1 October 1949 when Mao Zedong announced the founding of the People's Republic of China. This was a landmark event in the global wave of social protection beginning around the 1930s to resist laissez-faire principles, together with the abandonment of the gold standard by Great Britain, the initiation of Five-Year Plans in Russia, the launching of the New Deal in the United States, and the ascendance of fascism in Germany and Italy.[1]

This chapter begins by outlining the fundamentals of the regime of marginal labour precarity in the Mao era, which took shape between 1949 and 1956 out of the ashes of the Republican era and remained in effect throughout the Mao era. It then narrows the focus to the period between 1949 and 1957, and examines how these fundamentals were fine-tuned in response to changing circumstances during this period, and how these adjustments affected labouring people.

## Socialist Surplus Appropriation

By 1949, Chinese had successfully toppled the 'three great mountains', namely imperialism, feudalism, and bureaucrat-capitalism. However, torn by a century of foreign invasion, colonization, and civil wars, in 1949 China was a backward and impoverished country. To maintain its hard-won independence, defend socialism, and improve its people's welfare, it had to embark on industrialization. Industrialization in Mao's China fed on surplus appropriated from peasants and industrial workers.

### *Basics of Socialist Surplus Appropriation*

Socialist surplus appropriation in China was greatly facilitated by the Three Transformations, which were completed in 1956. By then, the

[1] Silver and Slater 1999, 197; Polanyi 2001, 24.

basic production units in China had been communes in rural areas and state-owned and collective units in urban areas. In addition to production, communes and urban work units (*danwei*) also performed the functions of controlling and empowering labour, providing welfare, and organizing social life.[2] In replacing private ownership of the means of production with state and collective ownership, the Three Transformations also replaced exploitation with socialist surplus appropriation, which extracted the surplus of agriculture and industry.

Surplus appropriation from agriculture took the forms of agricultural taxes and unequal exchange between agricultural and industrial goods. Between 1952 and 1978, the state extracted an estimated total of 485.2 billion *yuan* from rural areas, including 93.5 billion from agricultural taxes and 391.7 billion from unequal exchange. During the same period, the state invested 173 billion *yuan* in rural areas. The proportion of outflowed value in new value added in agriculture was 24.4 per cent in 1952, 28.4 per cent in 1957, and 27.5 per cent in 1978, respectively.[3] Rural areas also fed industrialization with labourers (discussed later).

Surplus from industry was appropriated by collecting profits from SOEs, and taxes and fees from collective enterprises. In the planned-economy era, SOEs submitted all their profits to the state, and the state then allotted production capital to SOEs from the pool of government revenues. For collective enterprises, the income tax rate rose from 20 per cent in 1955 to 33 per cent in 1958, and to 55 per cent in 1963 for those with annual profits of over 80,000 *yuan*, which were quite common at that time.[4]

Socialist surplus appropriation in China was extraordinarily successful. Figure 3.1 illustrates the accumulation rate (the proportion of gross domestic product (GDP) spent on fixed capital investment rather than consumption) and industry's contribution to GDP in China between 1949 and 1976. In most years between 1952 and 1976, the annual accumulation rate was over 20 per cent, and during the Great Leap Forward and between 1970 and 1976 it was over 30 per cent. Overall, the accumulation level in Mao's China was comparable to that in the Soviet Union between the mid 1950s and the late 1980s,[5] and was much higher than the threshold of 11 per cent required for economic take-off, according to Walt Rostow's celebrated thesis on stages of economic growth.[6] This aggressive accumulation resulted in rapid industrialization in China. As shown in Figure 3.1, industry's contribution to GDP

[2] Walder 1986; Lu 1993; Andreas 2019. [3] Yan et al. 1990, 66. [4] Zhu 1980.
[5] Mazat and Serrano 1995. [6] Rostow 1960.

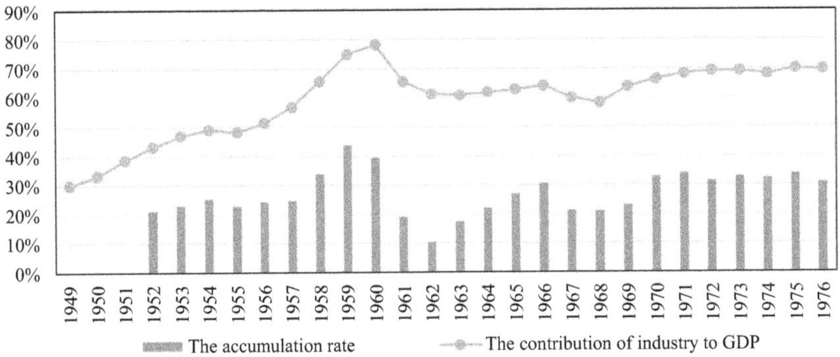


Figure 3.1 Aggressive accumulation and rapid industrialization in China, 1949–1976.
*Source*: Zhuang, Yuan, and Li 1986, 209; NBS 1985, 95.

jumped from roughly 30 per cent in 1949 to 70 per cent in the early 1970s.

Nevertheless, by constraining national consumption, the relentless pursuit of accumulation built into Mao's version of socialism the tendency to pauperize the material lives of Chinese people. Employment of temporary workers, who received lower compensation than permanent employees, conformed with this tendency. Between 1953 and 1978, the average annual growth rate of peasants' real income was 2.2 per cent,[7] and the average annual growth rate of the real wages of workers in state-owned units was 0.5 per cent.[8] Furthermore, public expenditure on workers' welfare benefits as a percentage of gross wages in state-owned units dropped from between 16 and 19 per cent between 1953 and 1956, to around 12 per cent between 1964 and 1976.[9] That said, compared with the Republican era, workers' wages were higher and their working time shorter. The common working time in cities in the planned-economy era was eight hours per day, six days per week.[10]

Despite the great success of industrialization, in the Mao era, China failed to significantly narrow the labour productivity gap with leading economic powers. As shown in Table 3.1, in both farming and manufacturing, the labour productivity gaps were salient between China and three other major economies in 1952 and 1978. The relatively low labour productivity in the Mao era meant that, compared with developed

[7] Wang and Wang 1996, 40. [8] NBS 1984, 166. [9] NBS 1987, 189.
[10] Shen et al. 1998, 424.

Table 3.1 *Comparative labour productivity of China, the Soviet Union, Japan, and the United States, 1952–1978.*

| | Farming | | | | Manufacturing | | | |
|---|---|---|---|---|---|---|---|---|
| | China | Soviet Union | Japan | United States | China | Soviet Union | Japan | United States |
| 1952 | 5.1 | 15.2 | 7.2 | 100 | 5.3 | 29.2 | 18.7 | 100 |
| 1957 | 4.8 | 18.3 | 5.8 | 100 | | | | |
| 1978 | 2.2 | 15.3 | 7.1 | 100 | 5.9 | 35.8 | 80.5 | 100 |

*Source*: Maddison 2007, 77, 82.

economies, China could hardly produce enough to guarantee materially secure lives for all citizens.

### *Double Movement of Socialist Surplus Appropriation*

According to Chapter 1, socialism is characterized by a contradiction between centralization and legitimacy, which leads to a double movement between centralization and decentralization of redistribution. This subsection introduces how the logic of this double movement played out in Mao's China, which is to be elaborated in the following sections and chapters. Industrialization both feeds on and generates surplus, and is therefore an integral part of socialist surplus appropriation. In the Mao era, industrialization swung between centralization (*shou*) and decentralization (*fang*).[11]

Under a centralized industrialization system, management of the national economy is concentrated in the hands of the central government rather than local governments; management of individual enterprises is concentrated in the hands of governments rather than managers of enterprises; and industrialization takes place in large-scale factories rather than wherever feasible. Although it is easier to enforce plans through centralization than decentralization, the former has significant drawbacks. By rendering the grassroots powerless, centralized industrialization tends to discourage the masses from proactively engaging in socialist construction and disable them from monitoring political elites. By rigidifying social exclusion to guarantee smooth implementation of the plans, it allows little room for social mobility. Moreover, centralized industrialization tends to prioritize the development of capital-intensive

[11] Lu 1993; Wang 1997, 31–45.

heavy industry over labour-intensive light industry, contradicting the resource endowment of planned-economy China, with its scarcity of capital and abundance of labour. Between 1949 and 1976, the urban population almost tripled, with an average annual growth rate of 3.93 per cent, whereas rural population growth was slower, at 1.75 per cent.[12] Therefore, centralized industrialization threatened the legitimacy of Mao's socialism both economically and politically, tending to give way to decentralization.

Under a decentralized industrialization system, local states enjoy greater autonomy to manage the local economy; individual enterprises have more autonomy to manage their own business; and industrialization takes place wherever feasible, from large-scale SOEs to workshops affiliated with sub-district governments and rural production teams. By devolving power to the grassroots, decentralization enables mobilization of the masses to devote themselves to industrial development and the supervision of cadres, and also softens the social exclusion system and creates opportunities for social mobility. Moreover, decentralized industrialization can make good use of the resource endowment of the Chinese economy by facilitating the development of labour-intensive industries. However, grassroots spontaneity tends to disrupt the proportionate supply of labour, capital, and raw materials, which is key to the normal function of the socialist economy. In other words, decentralization to restore legitimacy risks undermining central planning. In the Mao era, limits to decentralization were set by grain yields, which determined the reasonable ratio of the non-agricultural to the agricultural population.[13] Therefore, excessive decentralization tends to give way to centralization.

In retrospect, the contradiction between centralization and legitimacy in Mao's China gave rise to three shifts between centralization and decentralization of industrialization. After establishing the central-planning superstructure in the early 1950s, the state embarked on decentralization for the first time in 1956 but began to recentralize the economy in 1957. In 1958, the state decentralized the economy for the second time, only to recentralize it between 1959 and 1963, marking the most radical switch between decentralized and recentralized industrialization in the Mao era. In 1964, the state began to decentralize the economy for the third time, only to be disrupted by the chaotic years of the Cultural Revolution and not reach its zenith until 1971, after which time the state embarked on recentralization again.

[12] Calculated from NBS and the Ministry of Labour 1990, 8.

[13] Chen 2005, 298.

*Countering Socialist Surplus Appropriation*

The drive for socialist surplus appropriation implies a tendency to reduce labour costs and thereby render labourers precarious. In Mao's China, this drive was greatly tempered by the CCP's commitment to labouring people, the core of its legitimacy in the Mao era, and labour resistance.

Mao's China fulfilled its commitment to labouring people in two ways. On the one hand, the CCP greatly reduced class exploitation and oppression and fulfilled the socialist ideal of egalitarianism: it eliminated class differences based on economic capital through the Three Transformations; it substantially reduced class differences based on cultural capital by systematically redistributing access to education and softening the rigid division between mental and manual labour; and it launched ruthless campaigns against bureaucrats to reduce class differences based on political capital, although centralized leadership severely limited the autonomy of the masses to hold bureaucrats accountable.[14] As a result, democratic management in the Mao workplace replaced despotic management in the Republican era.

On the other hand, the CCP regarded unemployment and precarious employment as maladies of capitalism, and promoted full and decent employment of all labouring people. Such promotion was based on aggressive accumulation (see Figure 3.1) to create more jobs, and a pro-labour employment policy. The CCP promoted full and decent employment of urban residents by erecting permanent employment as the dominant employment institution and by socializing essential aspects of social reproduction. In the face of massive urban unemployment after its takeover of China, the CCP even adopted a staffing strategy of 'three people sharing the meals of two people', which meant overstaffing production so that more people had wages.[15] Despite various changes in urban labour policy, the dominance of permanent employment was never challenged during the Mao era (see Figures 1.1 and 1.3). It was guaranteed by labour plans ultimately controlled by the central government. Labour plans, rather than managers of individual enterprises, dictated how many and what type of workers individual enterprises could recruit every year.[16] The CCP promoted full and decent employment of rural residents by guaranteeing their access to land and redistributing educational and health resources to rural areas.

Pro-labour employment policy in urban areas was underpinned by enterprise policy that downplayed profitability. The CCP regarded capitalism as a mode of production for accumulating profits while socialism

[14] Andreas 2009, 2019. [15] Qi 2016, 72–73. [16] Interview M1.

as one for fulfilling needs,[17] leading to the prioritization of production over profitability in enterprises in Mao's China.[18] This priority order was well illustrated by Wang Cheng (pseudonym), the vice director of a state-owned wood processing factory in Beijing between 1969 and 1978:

> As the vice factory director, my basic goal was to complete production plans. There were economic accounting and financial analysis on a monthly basis at that time ... How much did we invest? How much was the profit? How much was to be handed over to the state? ... However, profitability was not emphasized as a big goal. Moreover, if you were overwhelmingly concerned about production affairs, workers would label you as business-oriented (*yewu guashuai*), instead of politics-oriented (*zhengzhi guashuai*). They would also criticize you as only doing small accounting (*zhi suan xiaozhang*), instead of big accounting (*bu suan dazhang*). According to Chairman Mao, the management of enterprises was part of socialist education.[19]

Clearly, at this factory, politics was prioritized over the completion of production plans and then over profitability. This order not only worked at this factory in the Cultural Revolution decade but also worked largely throughout the country and the Mao era after 1956.[20] The meaning of politics in this era varied with time. However, a key part of it was to respect labour rights, including the right of workers to live a decent life and manage the enterprises they were working for. The marginalization of the profit goal was also manifested in the fact that the state covered SOEs' losses.[21]

Meanwhile, the profitability of individual enterprises was disconnected from their existence, since the CCP replaced competition among enterprises under capitalism with co-operation, through centralized distribution of capital, labour, raw materials, and consumers to individual enterprises.[22] In other words, all national activities were co-ordinated like playing chess (*quanguo yipan qi*).[23] An impressive example of socialist co-operation among enterprises was the Beijing Electronic Valve Factory. Following commands from the government, it channelled 2,186 cadres and 1,362 technicians to thirty-one factories, research institutions, and schools that it was required to aid between 1956 and 1984, and transferred around 230 of the over 500 products it developed between 1956 and 1989 to other factories for production.[24]

[17] Lin 2006. [18] Interviews M1, M12, and M18. [19] Interview M1.
[20] Andreas 2019 [21] Yuan 1990.
[22] Interview M4. The production and distribution of industrial input and output were planned, while the distribution of agricultural input such as fertilizer could be out of the plan in the 1970s.
[23] Interview M4. [24] Lu 2016, 24–25.

Therefore, managers in the Mao era had little incentive to reduce labour costs by abusing precarious workers. This differs from the pre-socialist era. For example, in a report submitted by the Shanghai branch of the Chinese Coal and Construction Equipment Company to the local government in 1952 to apply to formalize 919 temporary workers who had worked there for over three months, the company confessed:

> We used to closely follow the capitalistic logic to run the company. We thought using temporary workers could reduce costs and was convenient. We could ask them to come and leave easily. We did not need to be responsible for their daily lives, accommodation, and healthcare, among other issues. Sometimes, we did not even provide hot water for them ... This unveils that we thought about pursuing profits.[25]

The lack of incentive to abuse precarious workers in the Mao era also differs from the post-Mao era. A man who was the director of a fertilizer factory in a county in Shanxi in 1976 recalled:

> The logic of managing enterprises in the Mao era was very different from that in the reform era. In the Mao era, it was impracticable to transform all workers into temporary workers ... They were, after all, human beings. A better way of management was to raise workers' skills and political awareness so that they would work wholeheartedly. In this way, the enterprise could achieve low costs and good financial performance.[26]

In comparison, the first narrative indicates that enterprises before the full establishment of the socialist regime were profit-oriented, which led to the abuse of temporary workers; the second narrative indicates that enterprises in the Mao era were human-oriented and would not pursue cost reductions at the expense of temporary workers. This is where the Mao era diverges fundamentally from the pre- and post-Mao eras in labour protection, which set limits to precarious employment.

Workers' resistance could also temper the drive for socialist surplus appropriation. After the Three Transformations, the antagonistic relationship between capitalists and workers that had prevailed in the Republican era lost its economic basis. Ideologically, the CCP defined itself as the vanguard of the working class and claimed that its policy represented workers' interests. In practice, tension between the party and labour persisted in the Mao era. Aggressive socialist surplus appropriation threatened the living standards of workers. Inequalities between cadres and labour fuelled a view among workers that cadres were more concerned with perpetuating their own privileges than representing workers' interests, against which workers, both core and peripheral,

[25] SMA 1952, B123–2-183-15. [26] Interview M12.

seized every opportunity to voice their grievances.[27] Temporary workers were upset not only by the bureaucratic style of cadres but also by the privilege afforded to formal employees.

The CCP's commitment to labour welfare emboldened workers to fight for their interests by wielding the legitimacy leverage, which is a type of labour power exploiting the CCP's concern with maintaining political legitimacy.[28] While the party attempted to contain labour protests within the political arena, disgruntled workers often made economic demands, only to be condemned as the 'wind of economism' (*jingji zhuyi feng*), that is, an unreasonable longing for material enjoyment, to be cracked down on before long.

The political room for labour resistance varied with swings in state-labour relations. State–labour relations were integral to state–society relations, and were shaped by two countervailing tendencies. In the Mao era, state–society relations swung between strengthening party control over society and countering bureaucratism, meaning opposing the de-radicalization of cadres, their isolation from the masses, and their lack of democratic work style.[29] On the one hand, the CCP wanted the country under its rule, thus tending to minimize the autonomy of society. Independent trade unions were not allowed, and all unions were affiliated with the ACFTU, which was controlled by the CCP. Their main tasks were organizing political studies, socialist emulations, and recreational activities, and providing labour protection and welfare services. Only during the Cultural Revolution were unions involved in monitoring cadres.[30] On the other hand, excessive control over society would lead to bureaucratism, which was regarded as a critical danger to the CCP's political legitimacy. To counter bureaucratism, the CCP would mobilize the masses to check the behaviour of cadres.

These two countervailing impulses were active throughout the Mao era. Workers had less political room for collective action when the pendulum swung towards more party control, and more room when the pendulum swung towards more grassroots freedom. Disgruntled workers often bypassed the union and took to streets directly. This book focuses on labour protests in the 1966–1969 period, when the voices of precarious workers were loudest.

## State-Led Exclusion

In the Mao era, in order to intensify socialist surplus appropriation, the central government, instead of individual enterprises, carried out the

[27] Sheehan 2002, 9–10. [28] Zhang 2014a. [29] Andreas and Dong 2017.
[30] Interview M4.

drive to reduce labour costs, threatening labour welfare, the core of the CCP's legitimacy. To reconcile the tension between accumulation and legitimacy, the CCP established a social exclusion system that privileged some labouring people while discriminating against others, leading to precarious employment of some labourers.

In this era, the state played an overarching role in forging the social exclusion system: exclusion by employers merged with exclusion by the state, and exclusion by workers, which had been prevalent in the Republican era, was weakened. After the Three Transformations, state-owned and collective units monopolized employment opportunities in cities. Following the establishment of a unified labour recruitment and allocation system throughout the country in 1955, all urban units had to recruit through local labour bureaus, which implemented recruitment plans authorized by the State Planning Commission system.[31] In addition, in the 1950s, in the face of pervasive urban unemployment, rapid population growth, and limited industrialization in cities, the government pressurized and assisted the urban unemployed to relocate to the countryside, and also began to constrain the influx of the rural population by establishing the *hukou* system, which remains in effect to this day. During the Mao era, the *hukou* system imposed strict restrictions on rural-to-urban population flows, greatly reducing the salience of native-place politics in urban areas.

Resource allocation priorities were the natural basis on which the state built the social exclusion system. With the help of communes in rural areas and state-owned and collective units in urban areas, the government dominated purchase and allocation of grain and several other agricultural products, recruitment and allocation of labour, and extraction and distribution of capital. Given the scarcity of capital and raw materials for industrialization, the government allocated resources to individual units according to their priority in socialist construction, which was indicated in policy documents produced during the Mao era (see Figure 3.2).

First and foremost, capital was invested overwhelmingly in heavy industry. Second, compared with collective units, state-owned units were prioritized for investment. Under the ideology at that time, state ownership was the optimal socialist form of ownership, while collective ownership was regarded as a transient form of ownership to be transformed into state ownership sometime in the future. The private economy was regarded as capitalistic and to be eliminated. Third, units affiliated with higher-level administrations were more likely to receive investment.

[31] Interviews M12 and M18.

Increasing priority →

Industries: Agriculture → Light industry → Heavy industry

Types of ownership: Private units → Collective units → State-owned units

Administrative levels: Units affiliated with production teams/brigades → Units affiliated with communes → Units affiliated with county governments → Units affiliated with municipal governments → Units affiliated with provincial governments → Units affiliated with the central government

Figure 3.2 Resource allocation priorities in planned-economy China.

To set production in motion, investment priorities had to be matched by priorities in supplies of raw materials and labour power. The national plan system guaranteed provisions of capital, labour, and raw materials to production units proportionate to their designated priority. According to their units' priority, the government distributed subsistence materials and life opportunities to labouring people. In this way, the economic order gave rise to a social order, and a system of state-led social exclusion came into being.

This system ran primarily on the rural–urban divide. This divide was institutionalized by the *hukou* system, which was formally established in 1958 and created perhaps the most crucial foundation of social and spatial stratification and inequality in post-1949 China. In the Mao era, by fixing rural residents largely in agriculture and in the countryside, the *hukou* system contributed to accumulation by facilitating surplus extraction from agriculture and constraining consumption. Under the *hukou* system, Chinese citizens were categorized into two groups, with either rural or urban *hukou*. Those with urban *hukou* relied on the state for employment, housing, food, education, healthcare, transportation, water and electricity, and retirement benefits. In the planned-economy era, these goods and services were subsidized by the state, allowing urban residents to enjoy them at prices below costs. In contrast, those with rural *hukou* depended on self-reliant rural communes for subsistence resources,[32] and even when they became temporary workers in cities they still relied on their home communes for grain.[33]

In urban areas, the exclusion system ran primarily on the basis of the ownership type of work units. It also ran on employment arrangements, *hukou* status, and gender, amongst other factors. One's location in this system largely determined one's wages, entitlement to welfare benefits,

32 Cheng and Selden 1994; Solinger 1999.
33 BMA 1957, 110-00-891, 002-009-00119.

and participation in political life. Mobility between different groups of workers in this system was limited.

The exclusion system was tremendously affected by the double movement between centralization and decentralization of industrialization. Under decentralized industrialization, there were more chances for peasants to become temporary workers, temporary workers to become formal employees, and workers in collective units to become workers in state-owned units (through the transformation of collective units into state-owned units). When the path of industrialization moved towards recentralization, formal workers in state-owned and collective units stopped expanding. In extreme cases, some formal workers were laid off and relocated to rural areas, collective units that had been transformed into state-owned units during decentralization were transformed back to collective units, and temporary workers were more likely to be fired than formalized. In summary, less rigidity in the exclusion system led to more temporary workers in urban areas, and more rigidity led to fewer such workers.

In addition, the exclusion system was affected by labour policy swinging between promoting permanent and temporary employment and labour movements. The next subsections introduce the major categories of labouring people in the exclusion system and their conditions of precarity in employment.

### *Formal Workers in State-Owned Units*

Urban employment consisted of formal workers in state-owned units, formal workers in collective units, and temporary workers in both kinds of units. Formal workers in SOEs, state bureaus, and public institutions (three complementary forms of state-owned units) constituted the most secure layer of the working class at that time. Formal workers in state-owned units made up roughly 60 to 70 per cent of urban employment between 1957 and 1976 (Figure 1.1).

SOEs originated in base areas occupied by the CCP before 1949. Following its takeover of China, the CCP expropriated enterprises owned by foreign and bureaucratic capital, and transformed them into SOEs. These SOEs then gradually absorbed private enterprises by outsourcing production tasks to them, monopolizing their sales, pursuing joint state–private ownership, and redeeming their owners' stakes.[34] SOEs had limited discretion over their own operations: their annual

[34] Central Administrative Bureau of Industry and Commerce 1960.

plans for investment, production, and labour (including annual quotas for new formal and temporary hires, gross wages, average wages, and labour productivity goals) had to be authorized by the central government. Individual SOE's financial performance had little impact on their employees' wages and benefits. They submitted all profits to and had all losses covered by the government. This practice was aptly called 'eating from the big rice pot' (*chi daguofan*).[35]

At the beginning of the Mao era, to ensure a stable handover of power from the Nationalist Party, the CCP implemented the policy of 'taking on all and being responsible for all' (*baoxialai*) for long-term employees of state organs, public institutions, and enterprises owned by foreign and bureaucratic capital.[36] *Baoxialai* meant that the state took responsibility for lifelong employment of these workers, and thus these workers became permanent employees of state-owned units. The *baoxialai* policy was later extended to include graduates of colleges, junior colleges, and technical schools, redundant long-term workers, demobilized servicemen of urban origin, and workers in joint state–private enterprises.[37] Women were under-represented in sought-after state-owned units. In the Mao era, their proportion trended upward both nationally and in Shanghai, but in most years they accounted for less than 35 per cent (Figure 3.3). Women's under-representation in state-owned units and over-representation in collective units and in non-permanent positions (discussed later) demonstrates the limits of the Chinese Revolution in achieving gender equality in the workplace, which dated back to gendered labour politics prior to 1949.[38]

Alongside the rolling-out of the *baoxialai* policy, in the face of pervasive unemployment in urban areas in the early 1950s, the government introduced various regulations to restrict dismissals. For example, in 1952 the State Council required all enterprises to adopt the *baoxialai* policy for workers who were made redundant as a result of upgrading production technologies, and that private enterprises needed permission from authorities to dismiss workers. In 1957, the State Council required enterprises to try their best to reposition redundant apprentices and formal employees, and not to fire them without appropriate repositioning. Failure to comply with this provision resulted in punishment. Gradually, formal workers in state-owned units became permanent or

[35] Yuan 1990; Interview M4. [36] Bo 1991, 15–16.
[37] Deng et al. 2009, 163. These people were major candidates for formal jobs in state-owned units. However, being these people was no guarantee of formal employment in the Mao era.
[38] Cliver 2020.

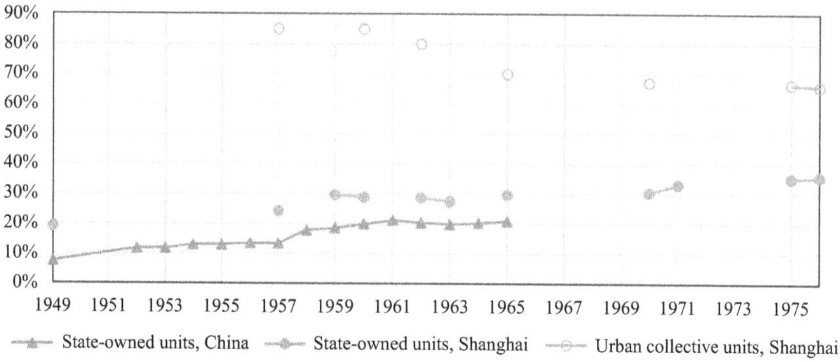


Figure 3.3 Proportions of female employees in state-owned and collective units in China, 1949–1976.
*Source*: Tao and Gao 1991, 241; data for Figure 1.1; Li et al. 1997, 375; Shen et al. 1998, 138–139.

fixed workers (*guding gong*) who tended to stay in the units to which they were assigned until retirement.[39] Their permanent employment was only threatened in extreme circumstances, such as the failure of the Great Leap Forward (more detail in Chapter 4).

Formal workers in state-owned units also enjoyed relatively generous wages and welfare benefits, and generally earned more than their counterparts in collective units. In most years between 1952 and 1976, the average wage of the former was 1.2 to 1.5 times that of the latter.[40] As detailed later, formal workers also enjoyed superior welfare benefits and earned more than temporary workers. In addition, compared with all other workers, formal workers in state-owned units were more likely to become members of the CCP, the Communist Youth League, the ACFTU, and the congress of workers' representatives. Through these organizations, they were able to participate in political activities at the enterprise level and beyond, and climb the ladder of power.[41]

### *Formal Workers in Collective Units*

Formal workers in collective units were less secure than those in state-owned units. In most years between 1957 and 1976, workers in collective units made up 20 to 25 per cent of urban employment,[42] and most were formal employees.

[39] Yuan 1990, 97–99; Lu 1993. [40] NBS 1987, 152.
[41] Howard 1991, 100; Harris 2015, 124–125; Andreas 2019.
[42] Calculated from data for Figure 1.1.

In the Mao era, collective enterprises emerged for many reasons. To eliminate the self-employed economy, the government organized individual handicraftsmen into co-operatives. To reduce unemployment, sub-district administrations (*jiedao banshichu*) and residents' committees (*juweihui*) founded sub-district collective enterprises. To provide enterprise-level welfare benefits, create employment for their employees' family members, and maintain a flexible auxiliary workforce, state-owned units established collectively owned hospitals, nurseries, schools, workshops, factories, and so forth. Some individuals also voluntarily organized collective firms for a livelihood.[43] Unlike state-owned units, collective units' headcount, wages, and finance were controlled by local governments.[44]

In the planned-economy era, collective enterprises were regarded as an inferior form of production organization to SOEs. In order to guarantee the full prioritization of SOEs, the government imposed multifaceted restrictions on collective enterprises to prohibit them from competing with SOEs for capital, raw materials, labour, and product sale.[45] Compared with SOEs, collective enterprises were less likely to employ college graduates and more likely to recruit housewives, and those who were unemployed, disabled, and sick.[46] Women were over-represented in collective units. Between 1957 and 1976, despite a downward trend in the proportion of female employees in collective units in Shanghai, it remained above 70 per cent in most years (Figure 3.3).

Overall, formal workers in collective enterprises were economically and politically inferior to their counterparts in SOEs. Their jobs were less stable as collective enterprises had lower priority in the distribution of production resources. The government also required collective enterprises' wage levels to be lower than SOEs'.[47] In reality, the average annual wage of workers in collective units as a percentage of that in state-owned units dropped from 89.6 per cent in 1957 to 54.2 per cent in 1964, before rising to 76.7 per cent in 1976.[48] As discussed later, the welfare benefits of workers in collective units were also less generous than those of SOE workers. Moreover, given the limited presence of branches of the CCP, the ACFTU, and the Communist Youth League in collective enterprises, many workers there had no institutionalized channels for participation in political activities. As a result, they often felt socially inferior and saw no future in politics.[49]

[43] Ministry of Labour and Personnel 1982, 138–151. [44] BMA 1975, 153-002-00608.
[45] Zhu 1980. [46] Ji et al. 1991, 328–329. [47] Ji et al. 1991, 329–330.
[48] Calculated from NBS 1987, 152.
[49] Research Office for Economic Laws of the Legislative Affairs Commission of the People's Congress 1982.

### *Temporary Workers in State-Owned and Collective Units*

Temporary workers were the least privileged among the urban employed. Their urban employment was precarious. In the Mao era, all those who were not recruited within the quota for formal employees in labour plans were regarded as temporary workers (*linshigong*), whether they worked regularly or for a short period of time. Both state-owned and collective units used temporary workers. The proportion of temporary workers in the workforce of state-owned units peaked at 26 per cent in 1958, and fluctuated between 5 and 15 per cent in the 1957–1976 period (Figure 1.3). While the CCP's commitment to labouring people dictated the dominance of permanent employment in labour policy, it also had incentives to promote temporary employment. Liu Shaoqi, President of China between 1959 and 1968, was a leading promoter of temporary employment in the Mao era.

First, as a backward country with an economy dominated by agriculture and a fast-growing population, Mao's China embraced temporary employment to serve accumulation and to a lesser extent legitimacy. According to the memoir of Qi Benyu, a secretary to Mao Zedong and Jiang Qing (a key figure in the Central Cultural Revolution Group), after being informed of the miseries of temporary workers during the Cultural Revolution, Jiang asked Premier Zhou Enlai why temporary workers could not be treated equally to formal employees, since they were also part of the working class. Zhou listed multiple budget shortfalls faced by the government, and explained that the state could not afford to support all workers as formal employees.[50] Liu Shaoqi pointed out the contradiction between accumulation and labour welfare more clearly in 1958: 'We should care about workers, but not solely about them. We should care about both the lives of workers and the accumulation of the state.'[51]

Under such circumstances, the state's shift in focus between accumulation and legitimacy determined the shift in labour policy and thereby national labour plans between employing more permanent and more temporary workers. Consequently, in the eyes of temporary workers, labour policy in the Mao era had two lines: the politics-oriented line promoting permanent employment, and the profit-oriented line promoting temporary employment.[52] When the state emphasized accumulation and shifted labour policy accordingly, units did not have enough head-count quotas for permanent workers and had to apply for quotas for temporary workers, which were relatively loosely controlled.[53] Moreover,

[50] Qi 2016, 674–675. [51] Liu 1993, 367. [52] SMA 1968, B227-2-54.
[53] Interviews M1 and M12.

under the circumstance of perennial unemployment pressure, the state was more concerned with providing employment for more citizens, rather than permanent employment for a smaller number. Temporary employment was better than unemployment. Thanks to formalization opportunities, temporary workers tended to regard temporary jobs as a stepping stone to formal jobs.[54]

Second, Liu Shaoqi believed that temporary employment, particularly of peasant workers, combined with rural industrialization and educational reform, would help to reduce the Three Great Distinctions (*sanda chabie*): distinctions between workers and peasants, between urban and rural areas, and between intellectual and manual labourers. Liu made this point very clearly in his speeches about reforms to labour and education institutions in the late 1950s and early 1960s. For example,

> Factories shouldn't be too concentrated. Industrial workers should build connections with the countryside ... Industrial workers who are also members of rural communes should contribute to the provident fund of communes. In factories affiliated with county-level administrations and below, peasants can learn non-agricultural skills, and industrial workers can learn farming. Don't distinguish between industrial workers and peasants too much ... This is conducive to the elimination of the distinctions between urban and rural areas, and between industrial workers and peasants.[55]

Although Liu celebrated temporary employment's potential to narrow the Three Great Distinctions, he contended that temporary workers should not be covered by the Labour Insurance Regulation and that urban units should employ peasant workers in their prime, and return them to the countryside when they were ill, disabled, and old.[56] In this case, whether or not temporary employment could help to reduce the Three Great Distinctions was questionable. It is recorded that Mao Zedong agreed with Liu's proposals on reforms to labour and educational institutions on two occasions, in 1958 and 1964, respectively.[57] Promoting temporary employment under the rubric of narrowing the Three Great Distinctions can be reconciled with Mao's imagination of the ideal society in which the rigid social division of labour is broken down, industrial workers also engage in agricultural production, and peasants also engage in industrial production.[58]

Third, Liu argues that putting workers in a dismissible position helps to discipline them. In a speech delivered in 1956, he said: 'Workers who

[54] BMA 1954, 120-001-00142. [55] Liu 1993, 365–366 [56] Liu 1993, 363–364.
[57] Literature Research Centre of the Central Committee of the CCP 1983 258–259; 2013, 361.
[58] Editorial Board of *People's Daily* 1966.

make mistakes should be fired, taken care by the union, and reabsorbed when they are well reformed. In this way, we can strengthen labour discipline and reform laggards.'[59]

Fourth, temporary employment was instrumental in dealing with fluctuations in production and in the permanent workforce, and in softening the rigidity of labour plans.[60] In the early 1950s, private firms often hired temporary workers to hedge against uncertainties during the dramatic handover of power.[61] During the First Five-Year Plan period (1953–1957), industrial production was small-scale and unstable, and was simply unable to accommodate too many permanent workers. When production stoppages were prolonged, even formal employees left to seek alternative livelihoods.[62]

SOEs often employed temporary workers when the headcount quota for formal employees ran out and when there were temporary production needs.[63] They also hoarded temporary workers to ensure completion of the forthcoming production plan, which was prioritized over adherence to the labour plan.[64] Another common motive for hiring temporary workers was to substitute for formal workers who were temporarily absent for reasons such as illness and pregnancy (particularly in textile enterprises where the majority of the workforce was female).[65] In fact, temporary workers directly hired by SOEs, outsourced workers, and workers in collective enterprises together formed a reservoir of flexible workers on which SOEs could draw to buffer fluctuations in production tasks. Finally, hiring the family members of workers who died on duty as temporary workers was a common practice of relief.[66]

At the dawn of the Mao era, temporary work was prevalent. In 1950, the Labour Bureau of Beijing conducted a survey of temporary workers in the city, the findings of which are summarized in Table 3.2. Temporary workers accounted for 34.3 per cent of the workforce in the nationalized enterprises surveyed, and 32.5 per cent in private enterprises. They were particularly common in labour-intensive industries

[59] Liu 1993, 290. [60] Liu 1993, 319–320, 362.
[61] Labour Bureau of Shanghai 1950. [62] BMA 1952, 004-012-00028.
[63] SMA 1957, A54–2-52-21; BMA 1963, 110-001-01467. [64] Mou and Jie 1955.
[65] BMA 1954, 018-009-00043; 1955, 018-009-00065. SMA 1956, C1–1-166-29, B123–3-177-174; 1957, C16–2-191.
[66] SMA 1967, B90–2-144-18, B123–8-15-331, B123–8-107-26, B123–8-107-37, B123–8-107-51, B123–8-107-52, B123–8-107-56, B123–8-107-58, B125–2-552-12; 1968, B98–2-129-36, B98–2-129-38, B98–2-129-40, B98–2-129-42, B98–2-129-65, B103–3-468-45, B103–3-585-6, B103–3-585-8, B103–03-0585-025, B119–4-72-48, B119-4-72-54, B135–4-72-8, B135–4-72-33; 1969, B154–6-80-4, B154–6-80-26, B154–6-80-38, B154–6-80-48, B154–6-344-65, B155–2-432-67; 1971, B125–2-623-11.

Table 3.2 *Proportions of temporary workers in nationalized and private enterprises in Beijing, 1950.*

| Nationalized enterprises (60) | | Private enterprises (2,543) | |
|---|---|---|---|
| Industry | Proportion of temporary workers (%) | Industry | Proportion of temporary workers (%) |
| Construction | 57.8 | Construction | 78.7 |
| Garments | 47.2 | Military uniform | 79.2 |
| Tobacco | 46.9 | Tobacco | 39.7 |
| Wine and beverages | 23.8 | Wine and beverages | 12.0 |
| Flour milling | 16.8 | Flour milling | 8.5 |
| Machinery | 15.9 | Machinery | 21.7 |
| Pulp and paper | 15.2 | Pulp and paper | 29.6 |
| Dyeing | 14.9 | Dyeing | 2.7 |
| Mining | 78.6 | Carpet | 19.4 |
| Printing | 7.8 | Rubber | 7.9 |
| Electricity | 4.9 | Electroplating | 6.5 |
| Telecommunications | 4.4 | Matches | 4.2 |
| Water | 3.5 | Finance | 2.8 |
| | | Leather | 2.1 |

*Source*: BMA 1950, 110-001-00105.
*Note*: This survey does not claim to be representative of all nationalized and private enterprises in Beijing in 1950.

such as construction, mining, garments, tobacco, and wine and beverages. Table 3.3 shows the proportions of temporary workers in state-owned units in different sectors in China between 1957 and 1976. These clearly varied by sector and period. Construction and mining remained leading users of temporary workers,[67] but the proportions in these two sectors were much lower than those in Beijing in 1950 and trended downward between 1957 and 1976, reflecting the CCP's success in countering precarious employment.

Temporary workers did not necessarily work for a pre-fixed term. In fact, many worked in one unit regularly. In enterprises with seasonal production schedules, a creative way of using long-term temporary workers was to reserve them. For example, in Beijing before 1959, construction enterprises would suspend work in winter, dismiss their temporary workers, and sign reservation contracts with them so that they would return to work next spring, but still as temporary workers.[68]

[67] Interviews M4, M8, M9, M14, and M15. [68] BMA 1957–1958, 002-009-00119.

Table 3.3 *Proportions of temporary workers in state-owned units in various sectors in China, 1957–1976 (%).*

| | Overall | Manufacturing | Construction and mining | Agriculture, forestry, water conservancy, and meteorology | Transport and post | Commerce, catering, and other services | Urban utilities | Science, education, and hygiene | Finance and insurance | State organs |
|---|---|---|---|---|---|---|---|---|---|---|
| 1957 | 8.2 | 10.2 | 25.4 | 6.0 | 2.6 | 9.0 | 4.1 | | 0.6 | 0.2 |
| 1958 | 26.0 | 29.5 | 55.0 | 15.4 | 15.5 | 11.6 | 16.8 | 3.4 | 3.0 | 1.3 |
| 1959 | 21.7 | 25.2 | 42.9 | 17.4 | 13.5 | 11.7 | 34.0 | 6.5 | 3.1 | 3.3 |
| 1960 | 15.5 | 17.8 | 27.6 | 16.6 | 10.9 | 9.9 | 26.2 | 5.8 | 1.2 | 2.0 |
| 1961 | 9.9 | 11.2 | 14.5 | 13.7 | 6.8 | 10.1 | 21.4 | 5.0 | 2.3 | 2.7 |
| 1962 | 7.6 | 7.4 | 12.5 | 11.6 | 4.7 | 8.8 | 14.7 | 4.2 | 1.1 | 4.4 |
| 1963 | 6.6 | 5.3 | 10.2 | 12.3 | 2.9 | 8.5 | 12.8 | 4.7 | 1.0 | 3.7 |
| 1964 | 7.5 | 5.8 | 17.3 | 12.3 | 3.0 | 9.3 | 12.8 | 4.3 | 0.6 | 3.1 |
| 1965 | 9.7 | 8.9 | 23.0 | 5.7 | 5.6 | 13.9 | 16.4 | 5.6 | 1.1 | 3.8 |
| 1966 | 13.0 | 13.9 | 32.8 | 6.0 | 6.6 | 15.9 | 16.2 | 6.8 | 2.3 | 3.3 |
| 1967 | 14.0 | 10.3 | 39.4 | 22.7 | 9.8 | 15.7 | 4.7 | 3.6 | 4.4 | 5.8 |
| 1968 | 13.8 | 13.2 | 34.5 | 26.1 | 9.7 | 11.9 | 4.7 | 0.4 | 2.7 | 2.4 |
| 1969 | 13.3 | 8.7 | 35.0 | 25.7 | 9.4 | 12.0 | 5.8 | 5.4 | 3.4 | 10.9 |
| 1970 | 13.9 | 15.1 | 22.7 | 10.8 | 7.4 | 20.7 | 18.4 | 7.4 | 3.0 | 4.0 |
| 1971 | 12.7 | 13.6 | 16.2 | 11.6 | 7.0 | 19.9 | 17.6 | 7.8 | 1.8 | 2.8 |
| 1972 | 6.1 | 5.9 | 6.5 | 9.1 | 2.9 | 9.0 | 6.9 | 3.8 | 2.9 | 3.4 |
| 1973 | 7.3 | 7.4 | 6.4 | 9.7 | 4.8 | 10.4 | 9.9 | 4.4 | 1.4 | 4.7 |
| 1974 | 9.6 | 10.0 | 8.1 | 10.6 | 7.4 | 13.8 | 13.1 | 6.0 | 3.1 | 6.7 |
| 1975 | 12.2 | 13.0 | 9.7 | 12.6 | 9.9 | 17.8 | 16.1 | 7.7 | 4.1 | 8.7 |
| 1976 | 14.2 | 15.2 | 10.7 | 14.1 | 12.2 | 20.9 | 18.6 | 8.7 | 4.5 | 10.2 |

*Source*: Calculated from NBS 1987, 26, 27, 33.

In Beijing's construction and utility sectors between 1953 and 1956, reserved workers made up 24 to 30 per cent of the entire workforce and nearly half of the temporary workforce.[69] In addition to regular and seasonal work, enterprises also employed temporary workers for irregular work such as maintenance and porterage.

Temporary workers were constantly exposed to unemployment. Those who had labour contracts with user enterprises became unemployed when their contracts expired. Temporary workers also tended to be fired when they were not needed, fell ill, became pregnant, or misbehaved, or when there was a campaign against labour squandering.[70] Therefore, some concealed their illness or pregnancy for fear of being dismissed.[71] The narratives below are stories of two temporary workers who worked in a construction company in Shanghai in the 1960s collected by a rebel organization during the Cultural Revolution. These narratives expose the vulnerability of sick and pregnant temporary workers to unemployment, and the challenge posed by temporary employment to the CCP's legitimacy.

> Feng XX … She began to work in 1964 and caught hepatomegaly in 1966. She didn't dare say or hand the sick leave certificate prescribed by a doctor to the manager. Her illness worsened and she asked to be transferred to a less laborious job. She was rejected and the managers wanted to fire her. Instead of paying her promptly, they held back her wage for three days … Feng said: '… I suffered a lot in old society. Now the communist party is running the country, but those in power are still tormenting me! I, a poor person, am still not emancipated.'
>
> … Chen XX … She got pregnant. Owing to fear that she would be fired once the managers knew it, she wrapped her body tightly. In the eighth month of pregnancy, she could hide it no longer. The managers … talked to her and wanted to fire her … Li XX [one manager] said: 'It is against the national policy to keep your job. I fire you on behalf of the party. Are you against the party?' Thus, Chen was fired … Her husband was also a temp. To eke out a living, they sent their clothes to pawnshops. Owing to the tight wrapping during pregnancy, she bled 20 days before her expected delivery date. She had no money to see a doctor, and the child was born dead. Isn't this miserable? Isn't this hateful? We can't help asking: what kind of policy did Li XX implement? Which party did he represent?[72]

Compared with formal employees, temporary workers were more likely to be assigned to laborious and dangerous tasks that formal workers

69 Wang et al. 1999, 56–57.

70 SMA 1956, B76–3-74-40; 1957, B112–4-123-13; Representatives of No. 302 Construction Team 1967.

71 SMA 1960, B127–2-993; Representatives of No. 302 Construction Team 1967.

72 Representatives of No. 302 Construction Team 1967.

were reluctant to do, but were less likely to receive job safety training and personal protective equipment. Labour bureaus often allocated temporary workers to units in need, and turned a blind eye to these units' occupational safety measures pertaining to temporary workers. As a result, temporary workers suffered more work-related injuries than formal employees. For example, in 1955, during railway building in Gansu (a province in northwest China) undertaken by the Railway Construction Group of the Ministry of Railways, 1,058 workers died or were injured, 70 per cent of whom were temporary workers.[73]

Temporary workers tended to work in low-skilled positions, and earned less than formal workers. During most of the Mao era, formal workers were classified into eight grades according to their skill levels, with the eighth grade being the highest, and were paid monthly. In contrast, short-term temporary workers were often paid on piece rates or daily. If they stopped working, they received no pay. While formal workers could expect their wages to climb up the ladder of the eight grades as time went by, long-term temporary workers saw their wages stagnate at the lowest grade. Every time they renewed their working relationship with a unit, even with the same unit, they were treated as new hires.[74] Therefore, many temporary workers lived in poverty. According to a survey of 3,877 temporary workers in Heping district, Shenyang (a major industrial city in northeast China) in 1956, the wages of 30 per cent of those surveyed did not guarantee the minimum subsistence level, and the wages of a further 45 per cent barely met that level.[75]

The compensation gap between formal employees and temporary workers is best illustrated by the fact that some formal workers recruited temporary workers to work for them. It was reported that, at Shanghai Transport Company in 1954, when some formal workers got sick or too old, or wanted to go to school, they called in temporary workers to work for them, and kept the difference in compensation between their own pay as formal employees and what they paid the temporary workers. Some leased their formal jobs out to temporary workers at a good price. Others hired their children or relatives as temporary workers, while they themselves found other jobs.[76] As well as the disparity in wages, the gap in welfare benefits between temporary and formal workers was also significant, as discussed later.

Moreover, temporary workers had no access to certain meetings and political classes. Unlike formal employees, they were largely barred from joining trade unions, the communist party, the congress of workers'

[73] BMA 1956, 002-008-00107. [74] BMA 1954, 004-012-00065.
[75] CASS and CAC 1998a, 145. [76] SMA 1954, B52-2-473-80.

representatives, and similar bodies, and from becoming model workers. While formal employees could complain to their managers, temporary workers were deterred from making complaints for fear of losing their jobs. They were often looked down on by formal workers.[77] Temporary workers were also sometimes forbidden to buy some scarce goods or participate in public activities.[78] Therefore, temporary workers generally felt that they had no future, and their livelihoods were constantly at risk. Many kept a close eye on opportunities for formalization or to join other units as formal employees.[79]

Temporary workers had diverse feelings towards their employment status. On the one hand, some compared their conditions with those of formal workers and felt inferior and vulnerable. Some felt ashamed and tended not to tell others that they were temporary workers. Some even concealed their temporary employment status when on romantic dates for fear of being dumped.[80] A long-term temporary worker who worked at the Bureau of Electricity Services in a Henan county between 1969 and 1971 talked about how temporary employment affected the way he behaved in his unit:

> I didn't dare talk with my formal worker colleagues. I was afraid of offending them. Generally, I didn't talk. I focused on work so that they were less likely to sack me. I didn't complain about my pay. One word from the cadres could sack me. I had no status or job security. So I focused only on work and nothing else … Temporary workers were submissive, unlike some formal workers.[81]

On the other hand, some compared their conditions as temporary workers after 1949 with their even worse conditions before 1949 and felt that they were somewhat better off. For example, a college graduate who became a long-term temporary teacher in a primary school in Henan in 1962 after working there as a formal teacher for one year said:

> In the 1960s, young formal teachers in my school earned roughly thirty *yuan* per month … Long-term temporary teachers earned at most fifteen *yuan* per month … We did the same work as formal teachers … The country was depressed at that time. I felt bad since I didn't have enough food … I didn't complain not because I didn't dare complain, but because I simply shouldn't … At that time, we didn't care about remuneration. Prior to 1949, my family rent land for a living. We had little to eat after handing over the rent … After the CCP built the new China, I was no longer exploited or oppressed. Nobody beat or abused me. How nice this was! Life wasn't easy, but I understood the country's

77 SMA 1950, A39–2-20; 1953, B123–2-183-36; 1957, B54–1-2; Shen 2010.
78 SMA 1960, B127–2-993.
79 SMA 1959, B134–6-285.
80 SMA 1959, B134–6-285; 1960, B127–2-993.
81 Interview M6.

situation. Without enough food, I ate less thick porridge. Without enough wages, I collected and sold firewood on Sundays.[82]

While temporary workers were still discriminated against in the Mao era, this narrative reminds us of the improvement made by the CCP to the life of ordinary labouring people. Temporary workers' origins varied widely. Rural areas were reservoirs for temporary workers in cities. Peasants preferred urban temporary work to farming because the income and working environment of the former were usually better.[83] In urban areas, women, new recruits to the workforce, those without a diploma, and those with suspect political backgrounds were more likely to become temporary workers than men, rehires, those with a diploma, and those with clean political backgrounds. In particular, urban women were over-represented in temporary work because they took the main responsibility for social reproduction in an era when a couple typically had at least three children.[84] The following narrative illustrates how social reproduction responsibility trapped women in temporary work:

My first child was born in 1965, second in 1968, third in 1971, fourth in 1974, and fifth in 1976 ... I could do what the other people did. I was not inferior to others! At that time, many units recruited workers. If I went out to work, I would have been a formal worker. In 1972, my county formalized most temporary workers who had worked for over two months. I wanted to look for jobs, but my husband said no. He said that my wage wouldn't be enough to hire babysitters for my children ... The grain station in my county recruited temporary workers every year ... It paid me daily ... In the 1970s, I also worked as a temp in a construction company.[85]

The politically suspect generally fell into one of three groups: (1) those or their family members who were considered to be members of the exploiter class, including landlords, rich peasants, usurers, and capitalists; (2) those or their family members who had ever worked for the thwarted Nationalist government, including officials, rank-and-file staff, and soldiers; and (3) those who were criticized in political movements. They suffered discrimination in respect of almost all basic human rights, including education, marriage, and employment. The number of people with tainted political backgrounds was by no means small. It was estimated that, before the Cultural Revolution, these people accounted for over 20 per cent of the total population in Wuhan, a major industrial city in central China.[86]

[82] Interview M2. [83] Interviews M9 and M10. [84] Interviews M3, M5, and M7.
[85] Interview M7. [86] Wang 1995.

Temporary workers' diverse origins led to stratification within their ranks. They had urban or rural *hukou*, and the former were prioritized for formalization. With regard to job tenure, temporary workers were either long-term or short-term, and only long-term temporary workers could be formalized. In addition, only those with clean political backgrounds could be formalized. Temporary workers were also distinguished by their relationship with the unit for which they actually worked: ordinary temporary workers were directly employed by the de facto user unit, and outsourced workers (*waibaogong*) worked through intermediaries. The latter were more disadvantaged than ordinary temporary workers: they received lower pay, partly because intermediaries extracted commissions from their wages; they were entirely excluded from labour insurance schemes, to which ordinary temporary workers had limited access; and they were less likely to be formalized.

### *Peasants*

As a result of the *hukou* system, peasants were at the bottom of the exclusion system. Between 1952 and 1976, peasants constituted over three quarters of labouring people in China.[87]

Nevertheless, peasants in Mao's China were by no means precarious. They were entitled to arable land after nationwide land reforms wiped out landlords and landless peasants. They became permanent members of co-operatives and then communes after the collectivization of land ownership. Between 1958 and the early 1980s, they worked in communal businesses, ranging from farming of staple and cash crops to husbandry, industrial production (such as brickmaking), and temporary work in urban units. Their labour input was calculated under the work point system, which assigned a certain number of points to one day of each task and distributed around 80 per cent of the yearly output of individual production units (usually production teams, the basic unit of communes) to households. The other 20 per cent of output was used as the provident fund for future investments and the welfare fund for the care of those who could not live on their own, such as parentless children and the childless elderly.

Output was distributed to households in kind and cash, which were complementary. In-kind distribution involved food grain, cooking oil, and other daily necessities, the amounts of which varied with production team and over time. Food grain was distributed to each household

[87] Calculated from data for Figure 1.1.

according to its headcount and the number of work points it acquired that year. Cash was distributed according solely to the number of work points. If a household had too many mouths to feed and too few hands to earn work points, it would owe its team cash before its young ones could work.[88] Communes also provided rural residents with a range of welfare services, including education and healthcare, as elaborated in the next section.

The ratio of the annual per capita income of rural households to that of urban households was 1 to 3.2 in 1957 and 1 to 2.2 in 1977.[89] Nevertheless, the persistence of the rural–urban divide that characterized the daily life and career prospects of peasants generated a feeling of inferiority among them.[90] Throughout the Mao era, peasants were encouraged by the rural–urban divide to seek non-agricultural jobs in cities, but were discouraged by the *hukou* system from doing so. Between the early 1960s and the early 1980s, rural-to-urban migration was quite limited, and rural residents were largely fixed in their birthplace. In the planned-economy era, rural residents had three official ways to obtain urban *hukou*: joining the army, becoming formal workers in state-owned units, or going to college. During the four decades after 1949, in Gao village, an ordinary village in central China with hundreds of residents, only twelve male villagers became urban citizens.[91] In Shanghai, the proportion of newly recruited formal employees in state-owned units drawn from rural areas was 1.63 per cent between 1964 and 1965, and 5.25 per cent between 1966 and 1976.[92] In Beijing, it was less than 5 per cent in most years between 1960 and 1976.[93]

In the Mao era, apart from sending a few formal employees to cities, rural areas functioned as labour reservoirs, constantly poised to send peasant temporary workers to cities and accept returning peasant temporary workers and urban residents who could not find jobs in cities. Between 1956 and 1979, over 17 million jobless urban youth were mobilized to work in rural areas.[94]

## Decommodification and Discriminatory Socialization of Social Reproduction

Decommodification in Mao's China was more fundamental than in advanced capitalist countries during the same period. These countries decommodified labour by enhancing state welfare provision and labour

[88] Interviews M2, M9, and M10; Jin 2005. [89] NBS 1999, Table A22.
[90] Zhang 2005. [91] Gao 1999, 26–30. [92] Li et al. 1997, 366.
[93] Wang et al. 1999, 17. [94] NBS 1987, 110.

protection regulation without challenging the private ownership of means of production.[95] In contrast, Mao's China collectivized and nationalized means of production throughout the country, including land, reconnecting all labouring people with means of production, albeit in a formalistic manner in urban areas, and determining a production system oriented towards labour welfare in the long term and a distribution system according to one's labour input and needs, instead of one's capital input.

These systems of property ownership, production, and distribution substantiated workers' status as the master of their work units. Instead of selling their labour power for a living as their counterparts in capitalist economies do, they devoted it to the common enterprise that benefitted them and were somewhat controlled by themselves. In the sphere of production, full employment was promoted by the state and was largely achieved, particularly among urban males. Secure job tenure enhanced the power of workers and peasants and allowed them to participate in the management of their work units and went a long way towards holding their managers accountable.[96]

Meanwhile, some aspects of social reproduction were socialized. Schools, hospitals, and other essential social reproduction organizations were state-owned or collective units, oriented towards satisfying public needs, rather than making profits. In urban areas, work units took some responsibility for their members' social reproduction. In the early 1950s, the free supply system that had prevailed in base areas controlled by the CCP prior to 1949 was replaced by the wage system.[97] This was complemented by welfare benefit programmes financed predominantly by individual enterprises, which dated back to the expansion of welfare benefits provided by employers from the late 1930s in response to economic difficulties triggered by the Sino-Japanese War and hyperinflation.[98]

The example of the Anshan Steel Company gives an indication of the range of benefits available in SOEs in the planned-economy era. Since 1949, Anshan Steel has been one of the largest state-owned steel companies in China. At the end of 1949, it had 38 canteens that provided low-priced meals to approximately 30,000 employees. In 1983, the number of company canteens was 181. It ran dozens of dormitories in which workers could live for a meagre rent. It had scores of bathrooms, barber rooms, reading rooms, and recreational rooms scattered across the company. In 1979, it had sixty-six nurseries, and in 1985 it had twenty-four kindergartens, seventeen elementary schools, and fourteen

[95] Esping-Andersen 1990. [96] Zhang 2005, 87–176; Andreas 2019.
[97] Committee of Reforming the System of the National Economy 1983, 192.
[98] Frazier 2002.

secondary schools. In 1985, it also had five large comprehensive hospitals, five specialized hospitals for miners, two sanatoriums, and multiple clinics and healthcare centres.[99]

In addition, in 1951, the government introduced the Labour Insurance Regulation, which, with few exceptions, applied to all factories and mines with a headcount of 100 or more. It required employers to pay all insurance contributions for a range of employee benefits, including relief for illness, injury, death, retirement, pregnancy, and childbirth. This regulation was revised in 1953 to include more workers and more benefits.[100] Between 1957 and 1985, housing (rent), healthcare, and education together accounted for less than 5 per cent of urban households' expenditure.[101]

Workers in different positions in the exclusion system were entitled to different packages of benefits. In the Mao era, formal workers in SOEs enjoyed the most comprehensive and generous welfare benefits. Compared with collective enterprises, SOEs were in a better position to finance their welfare benefit programmes. In 1978, expenditure on labour insurance and benefits accounted for 14.3 per cent of the annual gross wages of state-owned units, and 9 per cent of those of collective units.[102] Table 3.4 lists the major labour insurance programmes enjoyed by formal workers in most SOEs.

In comparison, collective enterprises were often small and beyond the reach of the Labour Insurance Regulation. Individual collective enterprises' coverage of welfare benefits was linked primarily to their financial performance.[103] Compared with SOE workers, workers in collective enterprises often had a shorter maternity leave period and lower wages that barely covered their living costs during this period. Levels of relief for funeral costs and the living expenses of deceased workers' dependents were also significantly lower than in SOEs, nor could their accommodation, canteens, and nurseries compete with those of SOE workers.[104] In 1978, the average annual pension of retired workers in collective units was a mere 58 per cent of that in state-owned units.[105]

Moreover, compared with formal employees, temporary workers enjoyed fewer welfare benefits. Table 3.4 lists the major differences in labour insurance between temporary and formal workers stipulated in the 1953 Labour Insurance Regulation. Temporary workers also faced discrimination with regard to other welfare benefits, ranging from

[99] Li et. al. 1994. Dong (2019) provides detailed accounts of welfare facilities for social reproduction in SOEs in China between 1949 and the early twenty-first century.
[100] CASS and CAC 1994, 5–6, 690–701; CASS and CAC 1998a, 1017–1044.
[101] NBS 1987, 245 [102] NBS 1987, 115, 185, 189. [103] Ji et al. 2000, 237–238.
[104] Ji et al. 1991, 329–330. [105] NBS 1987, 186.

Table 3.4 *Labour insurance for formal and temporary workers stipulated in the 1953 Labour Insurance Regulation.*

| | Formal workers | Temporary workers |
|---|---|---|
| Maternity leave | – 100% wage during maternity leave | – 60% wage during maternity leave |
| Pension | – 50–70% wage until death | – None |
| Illness/non-work-related injury | – 100% of medical costs covered by the employer<br>– 60–100% wage when on sick leave for six months or less<br>– 40–60% wage until recovery or death when on sick leave for over six months<br>– 50% of the medical costs of workers' immediate dependents covered by the employer | – 100% of medical costs covered by the employer for three months<br>– 50% wage when on sick leave for three months or less<br>– Dismissal and a one-off three-month wage for relief when on sick leave for over three months |
| Work-related injury | – 100% of medical costs covered by the employer<br>– 60–75% wage until death when fully disabled<br>– Transferred to a less-demanding job when partially disabled and additional 10–30% wage as disability compensation until death | – 100% of medical costs covered by the employer<br>– Dismissal and a one-off 12-month wage for relief when fully disabled<br>– Transferred to a less-demanding job when partially disabled |
| Non-work-related death | – A one-off two-month wage for funeral costs, and a one-off 6–12-month wage relief for immediate dependents<br>– A one-off 30–50% monthly wage relief for funeral costs when an immediate dependent of the worker died | – A one-off two-month wage for funeral costs, and a one-off three-month wage relief for immediate dependents |
| Work-related death | – A one-off three-month wage for funeral costs, and a monthly 25–50% wage for workers' immediate dependents until they were able to live on their own | – A one-off three-month wage for funeral costs, and a one-off 6–12-month wage relief for immediate dependents |

*Source*: CASS and CAC 1994, 637–646; 1998a, 1017–1044.

substantial ones such as housing to fringe benefits such as holidays for family reunions, weddings, and funerals, thick work uniforms in winter, soap, towels, and cups.[106] When peasant temporary workers lost their

[106] SMA 1956, B154–4-241-8; 1958, B76–1-276-155; 1959, B134–6-285.

jobs in cities, they would have to return to their home villages. Moreover, since peasant temporary workers did not have urban *hukou*, they were excluded from public services in cities and had to raise their children in their home villages. In other words, in the Mao era, the social reproduction of peasant workers who worked in cities was the responsibility of villages. In the post-Mao era, this situation remains largely unchanged for quite some time.

In rural areas, following agricultural collectivization, peasants relied on their communes for welfare benefits, the levels of which were incomparable to those of urban citizens and the content of which varied by commune and over time.[107] While the rural–urban divide persisted throughout the Mao era, the government made earnest efforts to narrow the distinction between peasants and workers by redirecting healthcare and educational resources to rural residents. Most peasants were responsible for their own healthcare until the co-operative medical system began to spread across the country in the 1960s. It covered 93 per cent of rural communes in 1976. This system emphasized preventive public health services and relied on barefoot doctors who came from and lived with peasants, and thus who knew their health conditions and needs well. Under this system, on average half of peasants' medical costs nationwide were covered by communes, while the rest was covered by peasants themselves.[108]

Peasants enjoyed improved access to education in the Mao era as the school system was expanded dramatically and the criteria of higher education admissions were revised to privilege the children of workers and peasants during the Great Leap Forward and the Cultural Revolution. Communes consisted of three administrative levels – the production team, the production brigade, and the commune. Production teams gradually built primary schools, production brigades built junior middle schools, and communes built senior middle schools. Peasant needed only to pay less than 5 *yuan* per year for each child's education within communes, which was a small amount in their annual expenditure, since the communal system was responsible for most educational costs.[109]

Individual peasant households were responsible for building their own houses. However, they only needed to purchase construction materials and the services of skilled workers, while they exchanged their labour for

[107] Gao 1999; Chen 2001. [108] Chen 2001.
[109] Gao 1999; Jin 2005; Zhang 2005, 294–295; Andreas 2009, 44–54; Interviews M3, M9, and M19.

other villagers' labour in low-skilled construction work.[110] Therefore, healthcare, education, and housing – the 'three new great mountains' over Chinese people in the post-Mao era – were not major sources of financial pressure in the Mao era, in both urban and rural areas. Other welfare services provided by the communal system failed to last long or roll out across the country, such as catering, childcare, sewing, haircuts, bathing, recreation, weddings, and funerals.[111]

## Boundary Redrawing between 1949 and 1957

Having presented a full picture of the fundamentals of the regime of marginal labour precarity in the Mao era, it is now possible to examine how these played out in each period of this era. With the help of the Soviet Union, after a short period of economic restoration between 1949 and 1952, the CCP established a planned-economy superstructure and began to implement the First Five-Year Plan (1953–1957) to industrialize the country. During this period, the CCP realized the drawbacks of the highly centralized Soviet mode and embarked on exploring a Chinese mode of industrialization, which was more decentralized. Meanwhile, boundaries among labouring people took shape and were redrawn by swings in the industrialization path from centralization to decentralization, and in labour policy from promoting permanent employment to constraining the expansion of permanent employment and then promoting the labour contract system.

Mao's changing attitudes to the Soviet mode illustrate the above shift. At a conference in 1953, Mao talked about his understanding of the order of priorities in Soviet-style socialist construction. He distinguished between great and small beneficent policies. The former, such as the development of heavy industry and the War to Resist the United States Aggression and Aid Korea (*kangmei yuanchao*), were aimed at the long-term interests of the masses. The latter, including improving peasants' living standards, were aimed at their immediate interests. Although Mao maintained that a balance between the two was necessary, he supported the sacrifice of small beneficent policies for great ones.[112]

However, in April 1956, he delivered the speech *On the Ten Major Relationships*, which reflected on the Soviet mode and served as a manifesto to explore Chinese-style, more decentralized industrialization. In this speech, he proposed more investment in agriculture and light industry to better balance the relationship between heavy industry and

[110] Gao 1999; Interview M3. [111] Hinton 1983; Gao 1999. [112] Mao 1977.

these two, more attention to peasants' income to better balance the relationship between the state and peasants, and more autonomy for grassroots administrations to better balance the relationship between central and local governments.[113] In October 1956, the State Council issued the *Decision on Improving the National Administration Regime*, which granted more autonomy to local governments to establish industrial enterprises, and to individual enterprises to manage their daily operations.[114] Yet before long, the government felt the financial pressure triggered by decentralization, and in 1957 it embarked on recentralization.

At the same time, with rising redundancies from the *baoxialai* policy, in 1955 the government began to constrain the expansion of permanent employment. In January 1956, Liu Shaoqi proposed the introduction of a labour contract system, which had been adopted by the Soviet Union, under which units could dismiss workers, and workers could freely choose their jobs.[115] In the same year, the swing in industrialization towards decentralization resulted in an excessive expansion of permanent workers, which sparked reflection on the promotion of permanent employment. In September 1956, the Ministry of Labour dispatched an investigation group to the Soviet Union to learn about their employment institutions. Its report to Liu Shaoqi in February 1957 proposed introducing the labour contract system in China.[116]

At a national conference in April 1957, Labour Minister Ma Wenrui announced that the institution of permanent employment, which recruited but did not dismiss workers (*zhijin buchu*), must be reformed by introducing the labour contract system, so that enterprises could both recruit and dismiss workers (*youjin youchu*).[117] To facilitate the dismissal of temporary workers, in 1957 the labour contract system was introduced nationwide. However, it was not well implemented. Between 1957 and 1976, only some temporary workers signed labour contracts with the units that they worked for.[118]

### *Two U-Turns in the Expansion of Formal SOE Workers*

Between 1949 and 1957, there were two U-turns in the expansion of formal SOE workers. Owing to the radical rolling out of the *baoxialai* policy, between 1952 and 1954, in SOEs affiliated with the central government in the mechanical, chemical, oil, coal, textile, and

[113] Mao 1986. [114] CASS and CAC 1998b, 83–84. [115] Liu 1993, 289–290.
[116] Yuan 1990, 99. [117] CASS and CAC 2011a, 5.
[118] SMA 1958, B76-1-276-1; Interviews M4, M6, M10–13, and M16.

metallurgical industries, the proportion of non-production workers rose from 11 to 15.8 per cent, and the ratio of managers to workers increased from 0.13 to 1 to 0.17 to 1. Meanwhile, idleness and absenteeism increased rapidly. Under these circumstances, in 1955 SOEs were required by the central government to suspend recruitment from society,[119] prioritize channelling of redundant labour amongst themselves when extra hands were needed, and take measures to reduce redundant labour. In response, SOEs mobilized redundant formal employees who were old, physically weak, ill, or disabled to retire early, and those who had worked in construction enterprises for a short time and had families in home villages to return to their villages.[120]

However, in response to the advocacy of decentralization in 1956, the central government devolved the right to recruit to local labour bureaus.[121] Together with local governments' and individual enterprises' greater autonomy, decentralization led to an economic leap forward. In 1956, China's industrial output value increased by an astonishing 31 per cent. To underpin this dramatic growth, in 1956 state-owned units recruited 2.3 million workers, 1.46 million more than the designated quota.[122] In light of this, in January 1957, the central government took back the right to recruit and prohibited SOEs from recruiting new formal workers from society.[123] Between 1949 and 1956, the transformation of private handicraft workshops into co-operatives was ongoing, and the transformation of collective enterprises into SOEs and the concomitant transformation of workers in collective enterprises into SOE workers were negligible.

### *From Temporary Workers to Formal Employees*

Between 1949 and 1957, two U-turns were also witnessed in temporary workers' formalization opportunities. In the early 1950s, many factories were not running at full productive capacity, or were on the verge of closure.[124] Thus, the government did not rush to formalize temporary workers or lay them off. Rather, it gave travel allowances to temporary workers who were willing to leave their factories and return to their hometowns, and organized those who remained to study or do some auxiliary work, and maintained their employment status as temporary

119 In the Mao era, recruitment from society was different from recruitment from other urban units and of demobilized servicemen.

120 BMA 1955, 002-020-00770; Editorial Board of *People's Daily* 1955; CASS and CAC 1998a, 177–179.

121 BMA 1956, 002-020-00770.

122 Bo 1957.

123 CASS and CAC 1998a, 170.

124 Ministry of Labour 1950.

workers.[125] In 1953, the Ministry of Labour stipulated that the *baoxialai* policy did not apply to temporary workers, that only long-term temporary workers could be formalized, and that construction workers whose employment concluded once the project was completed should not be formalized, even if they had worked with temporary status for years.[126]

In the early 1950s, the CCP's retreat from its 1922 promise to counter precarious labour was particularly clear at the local level. For example, in 1948, when Shanghai was still under the control of the Nationalist government, the Shanghai branch of the ACFTU advocated that factories should limit the proportion of temporary workers in their workforce to a maximum of 10 per cent, should only dismiss temporary workers when their labour contracts expired, and should formalize temporary workers if they were needed regularly or had worked there for three months.[127] Then, in February 1950, the new municipal government of Shanghai issued a document stipulating that private enterprises should seek permission from local labour bureaus to staff over 20 per cent of their positions with temporary workers and that enterprises should formalize these workers once they had worked there for six months. However, before long, the government introduced a notice withdrawing the provision pertaining to formalization after six months.[128] In a labour dispute in 1953, the Labour Bureau of Shanghai vetoed temporary workers' appeal for formalization after six months' work.[129] In a related regulation enacted in 1953, the municipal government required enterprises to use temporary workers only for temporary, substitute, or auxiliary work for six months or less, and to pay temporary workers the same wages as formal employees in comparable positions. It made no mention of any sanctions.[130]

Between 1949 and 1954, enterprises employed temporary workers on a large scale, yet it was easier to formalize temporary workers in this period than in 1955 and 1957. Archives pertaining to temporary workers in Beijing in the 1949–1954 period indicate that the local labour bureau approved almost all requests from enterprises to hire temporary workers.[131] Meanwhile, many temporary workers were formalized after

[125] BMA 1952, 004-012-00028; Li, Yang. 2013. Chujin dagongchang – 1949 nian qianhou zhonggong dui shijingshan gangtiechang de jieguan yu gaizao (The initial entry into giant factories – the takeover and reform of Shijingshan Steel Factory by the CCP around 1949). *Dijiujie Beijing daxue shixue luntan lunwenji*, unpublished.

[126] CASS and CAC 1998a, 137–138.

[127] SMA 1948, Q6-31-445-27.

[128] SMA 1950, B127-1-909.

[129] SMA 1953, B123-2-183-36.

[130] SMA 1953, B127-2-26-20.

[131] BMA 1954, 018-009-00043, 018-009-00053, 018-009-00055; 1954–1955, 018-009-00065; 1956, 019-002-00026; 1957, 019-002-00161.

working for two or three months. In the formalization application forms that enterprises submitted to related bureaus, they simply stated that they wished to formalize specific temporary workers because they were needed regularly.[132]

However, in 1955, when the government changed gear towards downsizing, it required the use of temporary workers to be minimized.[133] In Beijing in 1955, the municipal government tightened its control over formalizing temporary workers.[134] The threshold for formalization was raised dramatically. For example, the Beijing Retailing Company's criteria for formalization in 1955 were that the worker to be formalized must have been unemployed before joining the company, must have a long-term Beijing *hukou* and a clean political background, and must be healthy.[135] Formalization applications in this year were prone to rejection.[136] The municipal government of Shanghai went further and required that no temporary workers should be formalized, no matter how long they had worked as temporary workers.[137]

Then, in 1956, thanks to economic expansion and decentralization of the right to recruit, the number of temporary workers expanded rapidly, with abundant opportunities for formalization. A report prepared by the Labour Bureau of Shanghai indicates that over 60 per cent of temporary workers in Shanghai factories in March 1957 were hired in 1956.[138] In 1956, believing that redundancy in SOEs would be absorbed by the enlarged scale of industrialization enabled by decentralization, the State Council for the first time announced that enterprises could formalize temporary workers who were needed regularly within the authorized quota for formal employees.[139] Of the 47,751 temporary workers in enterprises affiliated with the municipal government of Beijing in mid 1956, 18,103 (37.9 per cent) were formalized, comprising 4,982 (55.3 per cent) of the 9,004 skilled workers and 11,953 (32.4 per cent) of the 36,890 low-skilled workers.[140]

In 1957, the central government began to rein in formalization. In January 1957, in addition to suspending the recruitment of formal employees, the State Council required that all urban units should sign labour contracts with their temporary workers, no contracts should exceed one month, and temporary workers should not be formalized, with the exception that peasants whose land was grabbed automatically

[132] BMA 1952, 018-009-00009, 018-009-00032; 1954, 120-001-00141, 120-001-00142.
[133] CASS and CAC 1998a, 180.
[134] BMA 1955, 110-001-00662.
[135] BMA 1955, 120-001-00177.
[136] BMA 1955, 018-009-00065.
[137] SMA 1955, B112-4-12-36.
[138] SMA 1957, A54-2-52-21.
[139] BMA 1956, 142-001-00352.
[140] BMA 1956, 005-01-807.

qualified for formalization.[141] However, under great pressure from urban units, in February 1957 the State Council suspended its requirement pertaining to temporary workers' job tenure.[142] In practice, in 1957 many temporary workers were dismissed.[143] In Shanghai between February 1957 and January 1958, approximately 7,000 temporary workers lost their jobs.[144]

When they were dismissed or failed to achieve formalization, some temporary workers committed suicide.[145] According to a 1957 document from the municipal government of Beijing:

> One day after being fired on 11 January, an 18-year-old temporary worker from the Textiles Bureau of Tianjin committed suicide on the railway. As far as we know, there have been three cases in Shanghai and another three in Jiangsu in which temporary workers attempted suicide after losing their jobs. Temporary workers at the Jiangdu Food Company in Jiangsu slept at the factory gate, crying that it is better to die than to be fired.[146]

In Shanghai, after a series of suicide protests, in January 1958 the municipal government required enterprises not to fire temporary workers who had begun working there before January 1956, nor those with no other family members in employment.[147] Temporary workers also engaged in collective action, such as strikes and collective petitions, to fight against dismissals and for formalization and the right to join labour unions. While their action against dismissals and for formalization often delivered positive results, their appeals to join unions were rejected outright.[148] Temporary workers were active in the wave of strikes in 1956–1957. In Shanghai's light industry sector, of the roughly 250 collective actions recorded, 4 per cent were waged by incumbent or previous temporary workers for formalization or re-employment.[149]

### *From Peasants to Temporary Workers*

Between 1949 and 1957, similar U-turns were witnessed in flows of peasants into cities. Peasants could improve their living standards by

141 BMA 1957, 071-001-00020; CASS and CAC 1998a, 170.
142 BMA 1957, 002-020-00812; CASS and CAC 1998a, 138.
143 BMA 1957, 026-001-00055; SMA 1957, B1–1-1448-2, B112–4-116, C16–2-191.
144 SMA 1957, B1–1-1448-2.
145 BMA 1957, 026-001-00055, 137-001-00140; SMA 1957, B112–4-116, A54–2-52-21; 1958, B1–1-1448-2.
146 BMA 1957, 137-001-00140.
147 SMA 1958, B1–1-1448-2.
148 BMA 1952, 004-012-00028; 1957, 137-001-00140; SMA 1950, A39–2-20; 1951, B128–2-504-1; 1954, A38–2-19-1; 1957, B54–1-2.
149 SMA 1957, B54–1-5, C16–2-191; Perry 1996.

finding jobs in urban areas. While urban employers were required by the government to prioritize employment of urban residents, they often favoured peasants, who tended to be younger and physically stronger.[150] Between 1949 and 1957, rural-to-urban migration was quite common. Peasants worked as both temporary and formal employees. Between 1952 and 1957, an estimated 8 million peasants migrated to cities for work,[151] and, of the 8.7 million workers recruited to state-owned units, roughly 3.5 million were from rural areas.[152]

From the very beginning of the People's Republic of China, those in urban areas regarded rural areas as a source of workers who could be dismissed at any time. In 1950, in the face of massive unemployment in cities, the government mobilized unemployed workers of rural origin to return to their home villages.[153] However, in 1951, to revitalize the urban economy, the government mobilized approximately 20 million peasants to engage in urban construction, mainly of infrastructure.[154] In 1953, as unemployment in cities persisted and pressure from migrant peasants on cities' supplies of food and accommodation emerged,[155] the government began to prohibit enterprises from recruiting peasants without the permission of local labour bureaus.[156] It was in this context that the government coined the pejorative phrase 'blind flows' (*mangliu*) to condemn peasants who flowed into cities without a pre-arranged recipient unit.[157] In 1955, amid the wave of downsizing, newly hired peasant workers who were not needed were mobilized to return to their home villages.[158] However, in 1956, in response to the expansion of industrialization enabled by decentralization, peasants flooded into cities looking for jobs.[159]

In 1957, against the background of recentralization, the government dramatically intensified its control over migrants. In Beijing, the municipal government required user units to sign tripartite contracts with peasant temporary workers and the agricultural production co-operatives with which they were affiliated. These contracts transformed the relationship between individual temporary workers and their recipient units into a relationship between sending co-operatives and recipient units, which effectively prevented 'blind flows' of peasants into cities. These contracts detailed not only the duration of employment and wages but also the distribution of wages between peasant temporary workers and their affiliated co-operatives. In return, the co-operatives were

[150] BMA 1957, 137-001-00140. [151] Song 1957. [152] CASS and CAC 2011a, 90.
[153] CASS and CAC 1994, 167–174. [154] Wen 2013, 282.
[155] CASS and CAC 1998a, 365. [156] National Bureau of Labour 1980, 321–322.
[157] State Council 1953. [158] BMA 1955, 110-00-662. [159] State Council 1957.

responsible for supplying temporary workers with grain during their employment, and for taking care of them when they returned due to illness or disability.[160]

In December 1957, the State Council enforced this Beijing practice nationwide, and required urban units to prioritize urban residents over peasants when recruiting temporary workers.[161] Earlier that year, the Ministry of Public Security and the Ministry of Grain jointly required that local governments should not transfer the *hukou* of peasant temporary workers to cities, and that the food grain of peasant temporary workers should be supplied by the agricultural co-operatives with which they were affiliated.[162] Moreover, in the same year, the municipal government of Beijing required units to dismiss peasant temporary workers recruited outside the authorized quota,[163] and the municipal government of Shanghai required all local units not to recruit workers from or outsource tasks to people outside Shanghai (mainly peasants).[164]

Last, but not least, between 1949 and 1957, while massive numbers of peasants flowed into cities for jobs, some urban residents were mobilized to work in rural areas to alleviate urban unemployment pressures. In addition to mobilizing the urban unemployed to return to their home villages in the early 1950s, in 1956 the government began to mobilize jobless urban youth to work in rural areas.[165]

## Conclusion

Between 1949 and 1956, the fundamentals of the Mao-era regime of marginal labour precarity took shape, leading to general but differentiated security of labouring people. With regard to the three mechanisms that generate labour precarity, socialist surplus appropriation replaced Republican-era exploitation; it was modulated by swings in the industrialization path between centralization and decentralization, and tempered by the CCP's commitment to labouring people and their resistance. Exclusion led by the state replaced exclusion led by workers and private capital as a result of the contradiction between state-led accumulation and legitimacy. Social reproduction was decommodified and somewhat socialized.

One's location in the exclusion system determined the extent to which one was subjected to socialist surplus appropriation and social reproduction socialization. The Mao-era exclusion system ran mainly on the basis of *hukou* status, the ownership type of one's user unit, and one's

160 BMA 1957, 035-002-00180. 161 State Council 1958.
162 BMA 1957, 002-09-119. 163 BMA 1957, 026-001-00055.
164 SMA 1957, B81-2-115-42. 165 Deng et al. 2009, 13.

employment arrangement. Compared with formal employees in urban units, temporary workers' urban employment was precarious, and they faced discrimination with regard to job tenure, wages, welfare benefits, and political participation. However, despite fluctuations in their numbers, they remained the minority in the urban workforce. The boundaries between different groups of labouring people in the exclusion system were constantly redrawn, mainly by recurrent switches in the industrialization path between centralization and decentralization, swings in labour policy between promoting permanent and temporary employment, and ebbs and flows of labour movements.

Between 1949 and 1957, the state embarked on decentralization for the first time in 1956 but began to recentralize the economy in 1957, and labour policy shifted from promoting permanent employment to constraining the expansion of permanent employment and then promoting the labour contract system. As a result, double U-turns were witnessed in the expansion of formal SOE employees, the formalization of temporary workers, and flows of peasants into cities.

# 4 Radical Inclusion and Radical Exclusion, 1958–1965

The 1958–1965 period witnessed the rise and fall of the Great Leap Forward. During this period, China saw the second and most radical switch between decentralized and recentralized industrialization in the Mao era, and a further swing in labour policy towards promoting temporary employment. This chapter begins by presenting an overview of the economic and political circumstances of this period. It then examines how the rise and fall of the Great Leap Forward, combined with the shift in labour policy, dramatically redrew the exclusion system, thus affecting those in precarious urban employment.

## Chinese Political Economy between 1958 and 1965

The year 1958 saw the beginning of both the Second Five-Year Plan (1958–1962) and the Great Leap Forward. Between 1958 and 1960, the government embarked on dramatic decentralization, in the hope of constructing socialism in a greater, faster, better, and more economical fashion (*duo kuai hao sheng*). Before long, the Great Leap Forward met the hard constraint of grain and began to have disastrous consequences. In response, between 1961 and 1963, the government embarked on economic adjustments characterized by recentralization. Between 1958 and 1965, labour policy shifted further towards encouraging temporary employment. Workers were somewhat quiet during this period, even when tens of millions were dismissed and relocated to the countryside.[1] Reflecting on the masses' reaction to the gigantic scale of relocation in the early 1960s, Mao said: 'Our masses are really nice. Tens of millions of them assemble and disperse at our call.'[2]

### *Industrialization: From Decentralization to Recentralization*

Driven by an eagerness to catch up with Britain and overtake the United States (*ganying chaomei*), at a conference in Chengdu (commonly known

[1] Sheehan 2002, 85–102. [2] Bo 1997, 1094.

as the 'Chengdu Conference') in March 1958, the government set the economic goals for the year. Compared with 1957, gross output from industry was expected to grow by 33 per cent, steel output by 35.5 per cent, and infrastructural investment by 41.5 per cent. These goals were then further raised to impossible levels, both by the blindly optimistic central government and by local governments attempting to over-fulfil the goals as a manifestation of political progressivism.[3]

To achieve these goals, the government intensified accumulation and radicalized decentralization. During the Great Leap Forward, the accumulation rate was raised from around 20 per cent in the early 1950s to 33.9 per cent in 1958, and to 43.8 per cent in 1959 (Figure 3.1). Moreover, in Mao's mind, fulfilling the ambitious goals of the Great Leap Forward necessitated the active participation of local governments and the masses. Thus, the central government once again changed gear towards decentralization and embraced a mass line of industrialization. In fact, although the central government recentralized the right to recruit in January 1957, in November the same year it issued a document outlining plans to hand some enterprises affiliated with the central government to local governments, and to allow the latter to retain 20 per cent of the profits of these enterprises, increase their discretion over resource allocation and labour management, and improve managers' autonomy in running their enterprises.[4]

In April 1958, the central government further decided that all enterprises affiliated with it would be devolved to be affiliated with local governments, with a few exceptions.[5] As a result, of the 1,165 units affiliated with the central government, 885 (76 per cent) were devolved in 1958.[6] In turn, some local governments devolved enterprises affiliated with them to lower levels of government. For example, in Beijing in 1958, a substantial proportion of enterprises affiliated with the municipal government were devolved to district governments.[7] Handing over enterprises to lower levels of government increased the latter's power to manage the local economy, and boosted their revenues to fund local industrialization. As a result, local governments' proportion of total government revenues rose from 19.6 per cent in 1958 to 75.6 per cent in 1959, and remained between 60 and 80 per cent in the following two decades.[8] In addition, in June 1958 the Ministry of Labour devolved the right to recruit to local governments.[9]

[3] Su 2007, 307–322; CASS and CAC 2011b, 3. [4] State Council 1994.
[5] Central Committee of the CCP and State Council 1995, 265.
[6] CASS and CAC 2011b, 3. [7] Yang et al. 1990, 18. [8] Lou et al. 2000, 79.
[9] National Bureau of Labour 1980, 16–24.

In addition to these measures, to encourage local governments to push forward industrialization, in 1958 the central government set the goal that the value of local industry output should match or overtake the value of agricultural output within five to seven years. To achieve this goal, it called on all levels of government to organize industrial production.[10] As a result, in Beijing in 1958, for example, self-made steel-smelting furnaces sprouted up in many factories, schools, residential compounds, and communes. In urban areas, sub-district governments organized housewives to engage in production, and in the suburbs factories mushroomed. In Tong County alone, local communes founded approximately 3,000 factories.[11]

At the national level, in 1958 the number of small-scale factories using traditional technology (*xiaotuqun*) increased by 5.8 times, the number of small-scale factories using modern technology (*xiaoyangqun*) increased by 96 per cent, and *xiaotuqun* and *xiaoyangqun* together employed 33.3 million workers, 180 per cent more than in 1957. In 1959, *xiaotuqun* and *xiaoyangqun* accounted for 99 per cent of industrial enterprises, 69 per cent of the industrial workforce, and around 60 per cent of the overall value of industrial output; and 66.2 per cent of *xiaotuqun* and *xiaoyangqun* were affiliated with rural communes or brigades.[12] Industries developed at the local level tended to be labour-intensive. Between 1957 and 1960, the average annual number of industrial workers increased by 179 per cent, while the value of industrial output increased by 135 per cent.[13]

Before long, this decentralized industrialization met the hard constraint of grain.[14] Between 1958 and 1960, the number of industrial and construction workers increased by 18.2 million, a 1.8-fold increase.[15] In addition, in 1960 China broke up with and began to repay its debt to the Soviet Union, mainly using agricultural products and minerals.[16] To meet these needs, on the one hand, the government raised the amount of grain extracted from rural areas to alarming levels, and lowered grain rations for urban residents. Compared with 1957 levels, in 1961 food grain consumed by rural and urban populations per capita dropped by 25 and 20 per cent, respectively, resulting in famine.[17] On the other hand, grain imported from overseas rose from 0.12 million tons in 1957 to 7.8 million tons in 1961, squeezing imports of other goods.[18]

[10] CASS and CAC 2011b, 6. [11] Yang et al. 1990, 18–19.
[12] CASS and CAC 2011b, 75–76. [13] CASS and CAC 2011b, 716.
[14] Chen 2005, 163. [15] CASS and CAC 2011b, 94.
[16] Wen 2013, 58; Interview M2. [17] CASS and CAC 2011b, 94.
[18] CASS and CAC 2011a, 92.

In addition, as a result of aggressive industrialization, the national fiscal deficit reached 11.5 per cent of government revenues in 1959, and 12.5 per cent in 1960, the peak level during the Mao era.[19] Severe shortages of raw materials, electricity, and machinery often brought production to a halt.[20] Overstaffing also re-emerged, with non-production workers accounting for 17.6 per cent of the industrial workforce in the first half of 1960.[21]

Under these circumstances, the central government recentralized industrialization. In late June and early July 1959, amid an atmosphere of anti-leftist reflection on the Great Leap Forward, Mao proposed to gradually recentralize the four powers (‘*siquan*’) pertaining to labour, finance, commodity circulation, and industrial production, respectively. However, at a conference in Mount Lu (commonly known as the ‘Lushan Conference’) in July 1959, anti-leftist reflections were replaced with anti-rightist criticism, and recentralization attempts were suspended.[22] In late 1959, a new leap forward was launched, and the production goals set for 1960 were even higher than for 1958.[23]

Recentralization did not gain momentum until late 1960. Between late 1960 and 1963, central and provincial governments re-grasped the four powers, retrieved devolved enterprises, retrenched infrastructural investment, shut down poorly performing enterprises, sent redundant urban workers to rural areas, and increased support for agriculture.[24] As a result, between late 1960 and late 1962, the number of SOEs nationwide decreased from 95,000 to 46,000, and the industrial workforce was reduced from 21.4 to 11.8 million.[25] In particular, enterprises founded by communes were shut down in large numbers to enable more people to engage in agricultural production. However, after short-term adjustments, collective enterprises continued to flourish in cities to employ workers dismissed by SOEs.[26]

In 1964, faced by a threat of war owing to the Sino–Soviet split, the United States's intensified aggression towards the socialist bloc, and a renewed threat of strikes on the mainland from the Nationalist party, the CCP began to relocate heavy industries to and develop them in China's interior. This was known as the Third Front Movement *(sanxian jianshe)*.[27]

### *Labour Policy: Towards Greater Flexibilization*

Following the introduction of the labour contract system nationwide in 1957, the government continued to shift labour policy towards greater

19 NBS 1999, Table A09. 20 CASS and CAC 2011b, 104.
21 CASS and CAC 2011a, 131. 22 CASS and CAC 2011a, 237.
23 Su 2007, 345–357. 24 CASS and CAC 2011b, Preface-4, 238–239.
25 CASS and CAC 2011b, 89. 26 Yang et al. 1990, 22–26.
27 CASS and CAC 2011b, 2

flexibilization between 1958 and 1965. Between 1958 and 1964, Liu Shaoqi proposed in a series of speeches that China should have two non-agricultural employment institutions and two education institutions. In addition to the full-time employment institution and the full-time education institution, there should be a temporary employment institution and a part-time education institution. In rural areas, temporary non-agricultural employment could be combined with seasonal farming or schooling. In urban areas, temporary employment could be combined with part-time schooling. By juxtaposing the two employment institutions, Liu raised the status of temporary employment from a residue of the employment system to an essential part of it.

Temporary employment was celebrated as flexible, economical, and conducive to eliminating the Three Great Distinctions by Liu.[28] At the same time, permanent employment was regarded as economically costly and politically reactionary. It not only prevented units from getting rid of redundant workers and those who were old, physically weak, ill, or disabled but also increased the number of urban residents and strained government finances. Moreover, it consolidated the distinctions between workers and peasants, and between urban and rural areas.[29]

Liu's relentless promotion of the two employment institutions translated into regulations that promoted temporary employment. In 1958, in a report seeking permission from higher-level officials, the Ministry of Labour for the first time proposed that units should use fewer formal employees and more temporary workers, and that the majority of new hires should be long-term or short-term temporary workers, except for those with sophisticated skills.[30] As shown later, this proposal was well implemented, at least in 1958. At the end of 1959, the Ministry of Labour required units to tailor their employment arrangements to different circumstances, and allowed them to employ new workers as formal employees, temporary or contract workers,[31] or both-workers-and-peasants (*yigong yinong*). Under the arrangement of both-workers-and-peasants, peasants maintained their status as peasants, but engaged in industrial production on fixed-term contracts. In practice, units tended to employ those with urban *hukou* as normal temporary workers (temporary workers affiliated with their user units) and those with rural *hukou* as both-workers-and-peasants.[32]

[28] Liu 1985, 465–469; Liu 1993, 357–372, 532–544.
[29] CASS and CAC 2011a, 103.
[30] CASS and CAC 2011a, 162.
[31] Following the introduction of the labour contract system nationwide in 1957, contract workers became another name for temporary workers, since formal employees did not sign labour contracts with their units in the Mao era.
[32] CASS and CAC 2011a, 5.

In 1962, the State Council required that all temporary and seasonal work should be performed by temporary workers, and short-term temporary workers should not be formalized. At this time, the state maintained control of the annual quota for temporary workers in individual state-owned units.[33] However, this control was removed in 1965, while the state retained its control of the gross wages of temporary workers in individual state-owned units. In the same policy document, the State Council also made clear that the number and gross wages of outsourced workers were at the discretion of individual units.[34]

## Formal Workers in State-Owned Units: Explosion and Retrenchment

For formal workers in state-owned units, the second and most radical switch between decentralized and recentralized industrialization in the Mao era resulted in another U-turn regarding their scale. Their expansion, triggered by decentralization, was tempered by the promotion of temporary employment. The number of formal workers in state-owned units jumped from 20.8 million in 1957 to 42.6 million in 1960, and then slumped to 30.6 million in 1962, before gradually rising to 33.8 million in 1965.[35]

At the beginning of 1958, following the tendency towards recentralization in 1957, the central government planned to continue downsizing. It not only maintained the ban on new open recruitment, but also mobilized redundant workers in enterprises, demobilized servicemen, and graduates from colleges and middle schools to engage in agricultural production.[36] At the Chengdu Conference in March 1958, the central government emphasized that it would learn the lessons of 1956 and maintain central control of labour planning.[37]

However, in the face of high production goals and radical industrial expansion, in June 1958 the central government believed that the redundant workers recruited in 1956 had been fully absorbed, and that local governments must be granted autonomy to recruit to staff local industrialization. At the end of June 1958, the Ministry of Labour devolved the right to recruit to provincial governments, and these further devolved this right to lower-level authorities.[38]

Devolution of the right to recruit and ambitious production goals led to a massive, rapid expansion of the workforce in state-owned units.

33 BMA 1961–1962, 002-014-00075. 34 CASS and CAC 2011a, 120–122.
35 NBS 1987, 13, 33. 36 CASS and CAC 2011a, 32. 37 CASS and CAC 2011a, 2.
38 National Bureau of Labour 1980, 16–24.

In 1958 alone, 20.82 million new workers were added to state-owned units, amounting to an increase of 84.9 per cent compared with 1957. Of these, 11.04 million were peasants, 5.58 million urban unemployed, 3.27 million handicrafts people and vendors, and 0.93 million students and demobilized servicemen. Owing to the promotion of temporary employment, of the 11.04 million peasants, 8 million (72.5 per cent) became temporary workers, and 3.04 million became apprentices who were guaranteed to become formal employees in future. Of the 5.58 million urban unemployed, 4 million (71.7 per cent) became temporary workers and 1.58 million became apprentices. On average, the wages of new hires in 1958 were 50 per cent lower than those of their predecessors.[39] The net increase in the number of formal employees in state-owned units in 1958 was 11.06 million (an increase of 49.2 per cent from 1957), including newly recruited formal employees and formalized temporary workers and apprentices.[40]

This dramatic expansion of workers in state-owned units put enormous pressure on supplies of grain, finance, and raw materials, amongst other resources. In light of this, in January 1959 the central government required enterprises to suspend their recruitment of new formal employees and formalization of temporary workers, and begin to dismiss redundant workers. At this stage, dismissals affected only temporary workers. Meanwhile, the right to recruit was recentralized into the central government's hands.[41] In May 1959, the government decided that the number of urban employees should be reduced by eight million within a year.[42] Moreover, thanks to anti-leftist reflections on the Great Leap Forward in early 1959, the production goals for that year were lowered substantially. As a result, the number of employees in state-owned units increased by only 0.29 million, reaching 45.6 million in 1959. However, as anti-rightist reflections on the Great Leap Forward boosted the production goals for 1960, the number of employees in state-owned units reached fifty million in that year, the peak level between 1949 and 1970.[43]

In 1961, the grain crisis finally reined in the Great Leap Forward, and formal employees in state-owned units began to feel the chill. The government urged urban workers to leave their units for 'the places where the motherland needed them most' and sugar-coated mass layoffs and relocation to rural areas as more support for agriculture.[44] Between 1961 and 1963, not only was new recruitment suspended but also large numbers of incumbent workers were dismissed. Compared with 1960,

[39] CASS and CAC 2011a, 34, 194. [40] NBS 1987, 33.
[41] Central Committee of the CCP 1996a. [42] Central Committee of the CCP 1996b.
[43] NBS 1987, 26. [44] Interview M2.

the number of formal employees in state-owned units in 1962 was twelve million (28.2 per cent) lower.[45] Many dismissed workers were dispatched to rural areas and had their *hukou* transferred there. Enterprises took this opportunity to get rid of female workers with multiple children, and workers who were old, physically weak, ill, or disabled.[46] Workers in state-owned units were also pushed to retire early, resign, or leave to engage in housework, or were redeployed in collective enterprises.[47] The grain crisis also drove urban workers to leave their units voluntarily for rural areas. 'Being an eighth-grade worker in cities is not as good as being a green onion in hometown villages (*chengli bajigong, buru jiali yike cong*)', according to a popular saying in 1962.[48] In addition to dismissals, some formal workers in state-owned units were transformed into temporary workers.[49]

When the economy recovered and the Third Front Movement was launched, formal employment in state-owned units resumed expansion. In 1964 and 1965, many unemployed urban residents secured formal jobs in state-owned units. In Shanghai, they accounted for 37.3 per cent of formal workers newly recruited to state-owned units in these two years.[50]

## Workers in Collective Units: Upgrading, Downgrading, Inclusion, and Exclusion

For workers in collective units, the Great Leap Forward was a period of upgrading and inclusion. The massive transformation of handicraft cooperatives into quasi-SOEs or SOEs meant that many workers were entitled to better working conditions. With the establishment of new collective units, the under-employed and unemployed, particularly urban housewives, were included in social production on an unprecedented scale. However, the economic adjustment period following the Great Leap Forward was one of downgrading and exclusion, during which many SOEs were transformed back to collective units, development of grassroots industries was discouraged, and their workforces were downsized. As the adjustment period came to an end, the government developed the urban service sector by organizing collective units to reduce urban unemployment.

As already mentioned, state ownership was regarded as the optimal form of ownership in the Mao era. During the Great Leap Forward,

45 NBS 1987, 33.
46 Frazier 2002, 218; Lin 2014.
47 Central Committee of the CCP 1997; Interview M16.
48 Interviews M1 and M4.
49 Interviews M2 and M3.
50 Li et al. 1997, 366.

upgrading handicraft co-operatives into co-operative factories (*hezuo gongchang*) was regarded as a way to accelerate their growth. With this transformation, local governments reclassified collective assets, replaced the profit-sharing scheme prevailing in co-operatives with a fixed-wage system, and determined their production, distribution of output, and financing. Apart from the fact that SOEs submitted their profits to the state whereas co-operative factories paid taxes, the latter were managed in almost the same way as SOEs. After their upgrading, these units were more likely to receive investment and their workers enjoyed better compensation.[51]

Co-operative factories were more often called big collective enterprises (*dajiti*), and were affiliated with governments at district level or beyond. In contrast, small collective enterprises (*xiaojiti*) were affiliated with sub-district governments.[52] Working conditions in *dajiti* were worse than in state-owned units, but better than in *xiaojiti*. Generally, workers in *dajiti* enjoyed stable employment; however, compared with formal employees in state-owned units, for instance in Shanghai, their base wages were approximately 10 per cent lower, their pensions were much lower, and their healthcare insurance did not cover their immediate dependents. However, for workers in *xiaojiti*, their wages were even lower, their employment was precarious, and they were barely covered by labour insurance.[53]

In 1958, of the over 100,000 handicraft co-operatives nationwide, which together had a workforce of over five million (amounting to over 70 per cent of workers in collective units), 37.8 per cent were transformed into state-owned factories affiliated with local governments, 13.6 per cent into co-operative factories affiliated with handicraft confederations, and 35.3 per cent into factories affiliated with communes, while only 13.3 per cent remained intact.[54]

Moreover, in response to the call for local industrialization, many collective units were built in urban areas. They were called sub-district industrial facilities (*jiedao gongye*) as most of them were founded by sub-district governments. They aimed to support large-scale industrial production and serve the daily needs of urban residents, such as necessities, maintenance, catering, nursing, and laundry. In 1959, the value of output from these facilities nationwide increased four-fold over the 1958 level.[55]

Sub-district industrial facilities founded by sub-district governments tended to be small and loosely organized, and their workers tended to be

[51] Ji et al. 1991, 240–245. [52] BMA 1975, 153-002-00608. [53] Li 2015, 5–6.
[54] CASS and CAC 2011b, 616–617. [55] Ji et al. 2000, 133–134.

those with financial difficulties and only assembled to work when they received orders.[56] A minority of such facilities were founded by SOEs, state organs, armed forces, and schools. These tended to be larger in scale and have regular production tasks.[57] The central government required the wages of workers in sub-district industrial facilities to be lower than in SOEs and co-operative factories.[58]

In addition, urban communes sprouted up in 1958 and gained momentum in the first half of 1960, before falling back in the second half of that year. Urban communes were loose organizations incorporating grassroots administrations and production facilities. They took an active role in local industrialization and the provision of welfare services.[59] The Changqiao Commune in Xicheng District, Beijing exemplifies the function of urban communes: between 1958 and mid 1961, this commune founded fourteen factories, three production groups, thirty-four service stations, forty-two nurseries, and thirty-four canteens.[60] In Shanghai between 1958 and 1960, as a result of the development of sub-district industrial facilities and urban communes, over 7,000 production processing groups (*shengchan jiagong zu*) and over 12,000 nurseries, canteens, and service stations for sewing and maintenance were established, which employed a total of 446,600 housewives.[61] At the national level, the proportion of the social production workforce in the working-age population jumped from 72.4 to approximately 90 per cent between 1957 and 1960.[62]

The workforce of these newly established facilities was predominantly females who had been largely excluded from the industrial workforce prior to 1958. In the Mao era, while the government upheld the dictum that 'women hold up half the sky', it never put women in equal positions to men in the social production workforce. In fact, in 1956, when the government declared that unemployment had been essentially eliminated in China, most adult women did unpaid housework at home and were counted as employed.[63] However, in 1958, aggressive industrialization drained the surplus labour and resulted in pervasive labour shortages.[64] Thus, in the government's eyes, women in the domestic sphere suddenly became idle labour to be mobilized into social production.

In urban areas, against the background of rural–urban segregation, the government treated urban males as the primary industrial workforce,

56 Interviews M5 and M16. 57 Ji et al. 2000, 133–134.
58 National Bureau of Labour 1980, 91–97.
59 Gao and Huang 2002; Luo 2003, 85–88. 60 BMA 1961, 110-001-01249.
61 Shen et al. 1998, 79. 62 CASS and CAC 2011a, 69. 63 Yuan 1990, 90
64 Editorial Board of *Labour* 1958a.

urban females as the primary labour reservoir, and peasants as the secondary labour reservoir. Compared with transforming peasants into industrial workers in urban areas, the added cost to the government of transforming urban females into industrial workers was minimal. Moreover, during the downturns of industrialization, mobilizing women to return to the domestic sphere was much easier than mobilizing workers of rural origin to return to their home villages.[65]

Women, particularly housewives, contributed to industrial production in three main ways. First, they were organized into production teams or small factories that complemented large factories' production. Second, they were organized into co-operatives that specialized in housework such as catering, nursing, and laundry, thus freeing other housewives from daily household chores and enabling them to join industrial production. Third, they replaced male workers in service industries to enable the latter to engage in industrial production such as steel smelting. This practice was called 'replacing males with females' (*yi nv dai nan*).[66]

In state-owned units between 1957 and 1960, the total number of employees grew by 106 per cent, while the number of female employees grew by 207 per cent.[67] In autumn 1959, in eleven major industrial cities, including Beijing, Tianjin, Wuhan, Chengdu, and Harbin, female workers accounted for 76 per cent of the workforce in sub-district industrial facilities.[68] The facilities of the previously mentioned Changqiao Commune were run by over 4,400 workers, 90 per cent of whom were women.[69] Between 1958 and 1960, over fifty million domestic workers nationwide were mobilized into social production.[70]

From late 1959 onwards, the central government began to rein in such radical upgrading and inclusion. In August 1959, it required handicraft co-operatives that had been transformed into factories affiliated with communes to be re-managed as handicraft co-operatives and calculate their gains and losses independently, and required handicraft co-operatives that had been transformed into SOEs to undo their transformation if it impeded their operations and caused inconvenience to the people they served. The pressure to downgrade continued in the early 1960s. In addition to downgrading, in September 1960 the central government decided that the development of urban communes and sub-district industrial units should be suspended.[71] Many handicraft factories and co-operatives were thus downsized or even shut down.

65 Jin 2006. 66 Editorial Board of *Labour* 1958b; CASS and CAC 2011a, 161.
67 Calculated from NBS 1987, 26, 32. 68 Ji et al. 1991, 237–239.
69 BMA 1961, 110-001-01249. 70 CASS and CAC 2011a, 69.
71 CASS and CAC 2011b, 614–615, 629–630.

As a result, the number of handicraft workers in SOEs and in factories affiliated with rural and urban communes dropped sharply, while the number in co-operative factories and co-operatives rose. The number of self-employed handicraft workers also increased, from 0.3 million at the end of 1961 to 1 million in 1963.[72] During the wave of downsizing, peasant workers were the first to be laid off, followed by urban women, who were mobilized to return to the domestic sphere to do housework.[73]

In 1963, with economic adjustments coming to an end and unemployment mounting in urban areas, the government mobilized the urban unemployed and the newly grown urban workforce to go to the countryside, and encouraged the development of the urban service sector to create jobs.[74] Thus, sub-district governments once again organized collective units.[75]

Since women made up the majority of the urban unemployed, to encourage units to employ female workers, in 1963 the government decided to grant units that employed female workers on a large scale extra headcount quotas for temporary workers to buffer absences of female workers during pregnancy or for family obligations.[76] In 1964, the Ministry of Labour reiterated that women accounted for two-thirds of the urban unemployed, and that employment of urban females should be prioritized over that of peasants.[77] In practice, the municipal government of Shanghai promoted part-time jobs in the commercial sector, which allowed housewives to balance their employment with family obligations. Many other local governments adopted this practice in their jurisdictions.[78]

## Temporary Workers: Diversification, Stratification, Fluctuation, and Routinization of Formalization

Between 1958 and 1965, on the one hand, the government pushed forward employment of urban workers as normal temporary workers and employment of peasants as both-workers-and-peasants, and the state also allowed the abuse of outsourced workers. The result was stratification of temporary workers. On the other hand, with the rise and fall of the Great Leap Forward, temporary workers' life chances fluctuated greatly. In addition, formalization of temporary workers was routinized,

72 CASS and CAC 2011b, 635. 73 Jin 2006; Deng et al. 2009, 82–83.
74 SMA 1963, B127–1-852.
75 SMA 1965, B127–1-882-57; CASS and CAC 2011a, 73, 127, 131.
76 SMA 1963, B127–1-852; Deng et al. 2009, 83. 77 CASS and CAC 2011a, 149–151.
78 SMA 1965, B98–4-1992-1, B127–2-690; 1966, B123–6-1366.

consolidating the dominance of permanent employment despite the relentless promotion of temporary employment in this period.

### *Diversification*

Labour policy promoting temporary employment was effectively implemented. As previously mentioned, in state-owned units in 1958, 72.5 per cent of newly recruited peasants and 71.7 per cent of the newly recruited urban unemployed were temporary workers. In 1963, of the 1.86 million newly hired peasants and urban unemployed workers in these units, 1.66 million (89.2 per cent) were temporary workers.[79] The equivalent figure for the first half of 1965 was 63.5 per cent (0.4 million of the 0.63 million workers).[80] Compared with the 1949–1957 period, the 1958–1965 period saw greater diversity in temporary employment with regard to both the origins and employment arrangements of temporary workers.

During the Great Leap Forward, urban housewives mobilized to join social production were a major source of temporary workers. In Shanghai, these housewives were called community women workers (*lilong funv*). When they worked as spouses of formal employees in the formal employees' units, they were called spouse workers (*jiashu gong*). These and other previously unemployed workers mobilized by sub-district governments to join existing units or to organize production teams were collectively called community workers (*lilong gong*).[81] In Shanghai at the end of 1958, community workers totalled 112,000, amounting to around 5.5 per cent of the total workforce in state-owned units.[82] In mid 1960, community women workers totalled over 120,000, accounting for over half of temporary workers in urban factories of Shanghai.[83] Urban housewives and the previously unemployed worked not only as normal temporary workers but also as outsourced workers.

Peasants were another major source of temporary workers. In the face of large-scale local industrialization, the central government departed from previous policies curbing the use of peasant workers, and promoted the employment of peasants as both-workers-and-peasants. Compared with the institution of permanent employment, the institution of both-workers-and-peasants was regarded as having several merits. Placing peasants on fixed-term work contracts allowed units to get rid of redundant and underperforming peasants easily, and protected peasants from

[79] CASS and CAC 2011a, 79. [80] CASS and CAC 2011a, 87.
[81] SMA 1959, A54-2-711-11; 1960, A11-2-42-12; 1962, A11-1-69, A62-1-17; 1964, B256-2-68.
[82] Shen et al. 1998, 177. [83] SMA 1960, A11-2-42-12.

occupational diseases by shortening their exposure to hazardous working environments. Since peasants were largely excluded from labour insurance and welfare benefits, labour costs and investment in welfare facilities were lowered. As both-workers-and-peasants had no chance of being formalized or transferring their *hukou* to urban areas, this institution was conducive to controlling urban population growth. Moreover, it increased the incomes of peasant temporary workers and their affiliated communes, and helped them to gain modern and industrial know-how. In the long term, this institution was regarded as having the potential to narrow the rural–urban and worker–peasant distinctions, facilitating the future transformation to communism.[84]

In March 1958, the central government required that, except for some skilled workers and managers, all other workers in county-level units should be temporary workers.[85] In June 1958, the central government celebrated the employment of both-workers-and-peasants in enterprises affiliated with county-level and lower administrations in Sichuan, a province in southwest China. This practice soon gained nationwide popularity. It was largely suspended during the downsizing of 1961–1963, and was re-promoted from 1964 onwards.[86] In 1958, there were nearly seventy million both-workers-and-peasants in China, including fifteen million in enterprises affiliated with rural communes, approximately fifty million engaging in steel smelting in rural areas, and three million in urban factories, mines, and construction sites.[87] In 1965, both-workers-and-peasants nationwide totalled roughly two million.[88] Against this background, temporary workers were concentrated in units affiliated with county-level and lower administrations. Anecdotal evidence from interviews shows that these units commonly had at least one-third of employees being temporary workers in the 1960s and 1970s, well beyond the national average (see Figure 1.3).[89]

The both-worker-and-peasant institution incorporated the tripartite contract institution invented by Beijing's municipal government in 1957, and extended it by routinizing labour exchange between urban units and rural communes. Both-workers-and-peasants took various forms, including regular, temporary, and seasonal workers in both urban and rural enterprises, outsourced workers (where communes, production brigades, or production teams organized peasants to finish tasks contracted out by urban units), and rotation workers (*lunhuan gong*)

[84] CASS and CAC 2011a, 115–116. [85] Central Committee of the CCP 1995.
[86] CASS and CAC 2011a, 12. [87] CASS and CAC 2011a, 100.
[88] CASS and CAC 2011a, 459–460.
[89] Interviews M2, M3, M10, M11, M12, M13, M15, M17, M18, and M19.

who were reassigned every three to five years to limit exposure to workplace hazards. Agricultural product-processing plants and electricity, post, telecoms, and water resource administrations were large users of temporary and seasonal both-workers-and-peasants.[90] Mines and chemical plants were large users of peasant rotation workers.[91]

In addition to normal temporary workers and both-workers-and-peasants, outsourced workers were prevalent between 1958 and 1965. In contrast to normal temporary workers, who were regulated by the government through quotas and recruitment procedures, outsourced workers were entirely beyond the state's control, rendering them particularly popular for user units.[92] In reality, their prevalence was invoked by the constraint on employing normal temporary workers. In Shanghai in the early 1960s, the municipal government rigorously controlled both employment of formal employees and the gross wages of temporary workers, thus forcing SOEs to resort to outsourced workers.[93] Meanwhile, in Beijing, to help units to circumvent the quotas and rigid recruitment procedures for normal temporary workers, sub-district governments organized labour service teams (*laodong fuwu dui*), which provided outsourced workers.[94] As will be discussed in Chapter 7, the 2010s saw the reprise of this practice: when the government began to counter the abuse of agency workers, enterprises embraced 'outsourced' workers, who were barely regulated.

In the early 1960s, textile mills were large users of outsourced workers, owing to the labour-intensive nature of production in the textile industry and rising demand for exports to repay China's debt to the Soviet Union. In 1963, textile mills in Shanghai employed approximately 38,000 workers and used approximately 6,000 full-time equivalent outsourced workers. These mills contracted some processing procedures out to local residents, and equipped them not only with necessary tools but also with supervision by experienced workers. Thus, they maintained a flexible workforce, reduced labour costs, and exploited free space in local communities.[95]

In reality, many outsourced workers worked with formal employees and normal temporary workers in the same workplace. In such cases, they were aptly called outsourced-onsite workers (*waibao neizuo gong*).[96] In Shanghai, outsourced workers organized into labour service teams

[90] SMA 1964, B47–2-6, B102–1-113, B102–1-113-33, B181–1-466-85.
[91] SMA 1964, B127–2-118-20; 1966, B127–2-867; 1967, B84–2-458-17; 1976, B127–4-179, B127–4-179-21; CASS and CAC 2011a, 104, 113, 166–167.
[92] BMA 1963, 110-001-01467. [93] SMA 1967, B227–2-54.
[94] BMA 1963, 110-001-01467. [95] SMA 1964, B202–2-227-50.
[96] SMA 1960, B123–4-688; 1961, A11–1-61.

expanded rapidly between 1964 and 1966. In urban Shanghai in August 1967, these workers totalled 75,000, amounting to roughly 2.7 per cent of the city's workforce, of whom 59,000 (79 per cent) were outsourced-onsite workers.[97] According to data from five major industrial districts in Shanghai, 79 per cent of outsourced-onsite workers worked for contracting-out units regularly, and, among outsourced-offsite workers (*waibao waizuo gong*), 67 per cent worked together in workshops outside contracting-out units and 33 per cent worked at home.[98] In 1964, the Labour Bureau of Shanghai required outsourced-onsite workers to be free from contracting-out units' management and under the management of contractors.[99]

Outsourced-onsite workers managed by contractors resembled those working under the inside contract system, and outsourced workers working offsite in labour service teams were de facto working under the ancient putting-out system. As will be shown in Chapter 7, the practice of using outsourced-onsite workers under the management of the contracting-out unit closely resembled the practice of 'actual labour dispatch, disguised as outsourcing', which prevailed in the 2010s. The practice of distinguishing between outsourced workers and normal temporary workers on the basis of who manages them was activated in the 2010s when the government attempted to draw a line between genuine outsourced workers and those disguised as such.

Various contractors matched demand for outsourced workers with supply. In most cases, labour bureaus and sub-district governments organized the unemployed and under-employed in their jurisdictions into community production teams or labour service teams, which produced goods or services to clients. These formed part of the business of sub-district industrial facilities and urban communes.[100] There were also sectoral contractors. For example, in Beijing, the Transportation Bureau organized labour service teams that provided crane and transport services.[101] In Shanghai, production teams organized by the Bureau of Handicraft were in constant competition with those organized by sub-district governments.[102] Furthermore, according to the Labour Bureau of Shanghai, all collective units automatically qualified as contractors, as long as they were capable of accomplishing certain production tasks.[103] In addition, rural communes and production teams were common

97 Li et al. 1997, 347; Shen et al. 1998, 176.
98 SMA 1968, B227–2-54.
99 SMA 1964, B123–6-181, B200–3-323.
100 SMA 1960, B163–2-1044; BMA 1963, 110-001-01467.
101 BMA 1963, 110-001-01467.
102 SMA 1965, B127–2-690.
103 SMA 1964, B200–3-323.

contractors. Generally, organizers of production and service teams extracted 10 to 25 per cent of outsourced workers' wages as commission.[104]

### *Stratification*

Compared with formal employees, temporary workers suffered discrimination in many ways. In 1959, the average monthly wage of workers was 43.7 *yuan* (1.7 times 25.5 days) in state-owned units and 35.8 *yuan* (1.4 times 25.5 days) in collective units, respectively.[105] In the same year, according to a survey of twenty-four factories in Xuanwu District, Beijing, 48 per cent of temporary workers dispatched by sub-district governments earned less than 25 *yuan* per month, 40 per cent earned 25 to 30 *yuan* per month, and only 11 per cent earned over 30 *yuan* per month.[106] In 1960, Shanghai's municipal government required community women workers who were assigned urgent production tasks to be paid 1 *yuan* per day for those living at home and 1.2 *yuan* per day for those living in the workplace, and jobless youth to be paid 0.8 *yuan* per day for the first six months of work, and thereafter the same rate as community women workers.[107]

The take-home pay of both-workers-and-peasants was even lower. A total of 60 to 70 per cent of their wages were handed over by the units they worked for to the communes with which they were affiliated, in exchange for food grain for their families and themselves and the commune's annual dividend.[108] Outsourced workers were also much cheaper than formal employees. For example, at one construction firm in Shanghai in 1968, for the work of filtering one cubic metre of sand, outsourced-onsite workers received 0.96 *yuan*, while formal employees received 3 *yuan*.[109]

In addition, different kinds of temporary workers had different compensation schemes and different methods for formalization and dismissal. Community and outsourced workers' inferiority was evident in the fact that they were generally not regarded as normal temporary workers. For example, in mid 1960, the No. 1 Steel Mill of Shanghai reported that it had 1,105 temporary workers, 2,229 community women

104 SMA 1959, A20–2-35-68; BMA 1961–1962, 002-014-00075; 1963, 110-001-01467.

105 NBS 1987, 152. In the Mao era, the legal working time was six days per week. In addition, workers had legal holidays totalling seven days a year. Therefore, on average, workers worked 25.5 days per month in this era.

106 BMA 1960, 110-001-01099.

107 SMA 1960, B127–2-993.

108 Editorial Board of *Labour* 1958c; SMA 1964, B184–2-77.

109 SMA 1968, B227–2-54.

workers, and 1,853 outsourced-onsite workers. Its temporary workers were entitled to labour insurance. Community women workers, who were entitled to free healthcare service but not sick pay, complained: 'They call us "comrades" in production meetings and "ladies" when talking about bonuses and welfare benefits. We have worked here for two years but are still treated as "housewives". When can we be treated as "workers"?' This complaint reflects the double consequences of women's participation into social production: on the one hand, they became workers in the public sphere, emboldening them to hope for a lifestyle different from being housewives; on the other hand, they were not regarded by employers as genuine workers, and thus suffered discrimination. Outsourced workers at that company were even worse off because they needed to pay for medical costs.[110]

Being excluded from free healthcare services seemed common among outsourced workers. For example, in Shanghai, two labour service teams, Zhoujiaqiao and Tianshan, together collaborated with fifty-seven units. Only two units provided some healthcare services for outsourced workers. Worse, outsourced workers tended to be poorer than other workers, and many could not afford to see a doctor when they fell ill.[111]

Table 4.1 shows the numbers, profiles, and compensation schemes of five types of temporary workers used by enterprises under the supervision of the City Construction Bureau of Shanghai in 1959. This illustrates how the compensation of contract workers, community workers, spouse workers, both-workers-and-peasants, and outsourced workers were successively worse.

Outsourced workers, as the lowest rung of temporary workers, suffered discrimination in many other respects. A survey conducted by the municipal government of Shanghai in its Changning District in 1968 reported the following:

> Many outsourced workers worked in dirty, laborious, dangerous, and poisonous positions. For example, at one factory, sewing the uppers of shoes was laborious and hazardous to health. Formal employees were reluctant to do this job. So this procedure was done mainly by outsourced-onsite workers. Many factories did not provide protective outfits for outsourced workers … Outsourced-onsite workers at a stone powder plant and a wire drawing factory had to take showers after permanent and normal temporary workers … At another factory, permanent and normal temporary workers did not queue for meals, but outsourced-onsite workers did … In some factories … permanent workers stopped working and specialized in issuing commands and guiding the work of outsourced-onsite workers. Outsourced workers were disgruntled and called them 'labour

[110] SMA 1960, A11-2-42-23. [111] SMA 1968, B227-2-54.

Table 4.1 *An example of stratification among temporary workers in China, 1959.*

| Categories and numbers | Profile | Compensation |
|---|---|---|
| Contract workers 1,462 | – Mainly male<br>– Allocated by labour bureaus<br>– Heavy manual work | – 40.8 (1.6 times 25.5 days) *yuan* or more per month<br>– Paid monthly<br>– Free healthcare service<br>– Paid sick leave (50% of normal wage) for at most three months |
| Community workers 4,936 | – Mainly female<br>– Organized by local labour bureaus<br>– 20% in auxiliary work<br>– 80% in heavy manual work | – 40% of them 30.6 (1.2 times 25.5 days) *yuan* per month, and the rest 1 to 1.2 *yuan* per day<br>– Free healthcare service<br>– Paid sick leave for at most three days |
| Spouse workers 873 | – Mainly female<br>– Recruited mainly to alleviate the financial difficulties of formal employees<br>– 30% in auxiliary work<br>– 70% in heavy manual work | – 25.5 (1 times 25.5 days) or 30.6 (1.2 times 25.5 days) *yuan* per month<br>– Paid monthly<br>– No health insurance unless their direct relatives were formal employees (half reimbursed in this case)<br>– Paid sick leave for at most three days |
| Both-workers-and-peasants 600 | – Supplied by rural communes<br>– Heavy manual work | – Male: 1.4 to 1.6 *yuan* per day<br>– Female: 1 to 1.2 *yuan* per day<br>– No benefits |
| Outsourced workers 2,000 | – Organized by sub-district governments<br>– Heavy manual work | – Piece-rate pay<br>– No benefits |

*Source*: SMA 1959, A54–2-711-11.

contractors'. At one wire drawing factory, one permanent worker managed over fifty outsourced-onsite workers. Influenced by this practice, this worker looked down on outsourced-onsite workers and spoke like a capitalist: 'Getting 100 outsourced workers is easier than getting 100 dogs!'[112]

Clearly, how outsourced workers were treated caused contradictions between permanent and normal temporary workers and these workers, creating tensions with the egalitarian ideology of a socialist country.

[112] SMA 1968, B227–2-54.

Outsourced workers' miserable conditions revealed the downside of constructing socialism economically: while the government sought both legitimacy and accumulation, when the pendulum swung too much towards accumulation, legitimacy was threatened. In light of distinctions within temporary workers, outsourced workers wanted to become normal temporary workers. They were transformed into normal temporary workers when they were needed regularly, or when they suffered from work-related injury or illness.[113]

### *Fluctuation and Routinization of Formalization*

Owing to the shift from decentralization to recentralization of industrialization, the proportion of temporary workers in the workforce of state-owned units fluctuated greatly. It peaked in 1958 (26 per cent), and reached its second lowest level of the Mao era in 1963 (7 per cent, compared with 6 per cent in 1972) (Figure 1.3).

The first nationwide wave of formalization in 1956 was followed by a second wave, albeit with setbacks. In September 1958, Shanghai's municipal government announced that temporary workers who had joined the unit before the end of 1957 could be formalized as long as they worked regularly and had a Shanghai *hukou*, a clean political background, sound health, and certain levels of skills, and that seasonal workers, outsourced workers, and devolved workers who had returned without the permission of previous units should not be formalized, no matter how long they had worked.[114] In fact, from 1958 onwards, *hukou* status, political background, health condition, and skills formed the basic criteria for formalization of temporary workers who were regularly needed both in and beyond Shanghai.[115]

In January 1959, in the face of excessive expansion of the urban workforce the previous year, the central government required enterprises to suspend formalizing temporary workers and dismiss redundant workers. Temporary workers were among the first to be dismissed. In May 1959, the central government decided to reduce urban

113 SMA 1959, B134–6-431-6; 1960, B163–2-1044; 1962, B112–4-659-6, B112–4-659-19, B119–2-866-30.

114 SMA 1958, B76–1-276-155.

115 SMA 1959, B134–6-285, B134–6-285-8; 1960, B127–2-993; 1964, B112–4-1096, B256–2-68; BMA 1960, 125-002-00083; 1963, 002-021-00163, 088-001-00281, 119-001-00732, 119-001-00896, 135-001-01340. Rotation workers in mines were an exception. In April 1961, the Ministry of Labour announced that regular peasant rotation workers in mines could be formalized and acquire urban *hukou* (see BMA 1961, 110-001-01245).

employees by eight million that year, and announced that enterprises could formalize temporary workers after completing their downsizing.[116] It also required that both-workers-and-peasants should be the first to be dismissed, successively followed by apprentices and housewives with family obligations.[117]

As a result, on the one hand, by July 1960 approximately six million industrial workers nationwide had been dismissed, of whom four million were temporary workers, and most were mobilized to return to their home villages.[118] In Shanghai in 1959, of the 112,000 community workers at the end of 1958, approximately 40,000 were dismissed.[119] On the other hand, in 1959 Shanghai's municipal government reiterated its 1958 announcement on formalization, but added that community and spouse workers should not be formalized.[120] In practice, in 1959, of the 10,926 temporary workers recruited by the Construction Engineering Bureau of Shanghai before the end of 1957, 9,855 were formalized (90.2 per cent). Workers with job-related injuries or illnesses automatically qualified for formalization. Apart from counter-revolutionaries, workers who themselves or whose family members were rich peasants or landlords and workers who had served prison sentences could also be considered for formalization, as long as they had demonstrated good performance for at least five consecutive years.[121]

Table 4.2 lists why 1,071 (the difference between 10,926 and 9,855) temporary workers of the Construction Engineering Bureau of Shanghai were not formalized. Clearly, political background and *hukou* status were important. At the No. 17 State-owned Cotton Textile Mill in Shanghai in 1959, of the 431 temporary workers who had joined the factory before the end of 1957, 398 (92.3 per cent) were formalized.[122] Nevertheless, in the same year, community women workers constituted 45.3 per cent of the temporary workforce of the No. 2 Commercial Bureau of Shanghai, none of whom were formalized; and in enterprises affiliated with county-level governments in Shanghai, only those in non-auxiliary positions had a chance of formalization.[123]

In early 1960, during a new round of the Leap Forward, the municipal governments of both Beijing and Shanghai announced that temporary workers who met the criteria for formalization mentioned above and had joined the unit before the end of 1958 should qualify for formalization.

[116] CASS and CAC 2011a, 35.
[117] Central Committee of the CCP 1996a, 1996b; CASS and CAC 2011a, 35.
[118] CASS and CAC 2011a, 172. [119] SMA 1960, A11-2-42-12.
[120] SMA 1959, B127-1-308.
[121] SMA 1959, A54-2-636-1, A54-2-636-5, A54-2-636-7.
[122] SMA 1959, B134-6-285. [123] SMA 1959, A72-2-45-35, B98-4-1069-12.

Table 4.2 *An example of reasons for failure to formalize, 1959.*

| Category | Proportion (%) |
|---|---|
| Counter-revolutionaries and previous criminals *(huai fenzi)* | 27.1 |
| Without a *hukou* in certain areas of Shanghai | 25.5 |
| Underperformance | 14.2 |
| With serious illness | 6.5 |
| Used to be or had relatives who were rich peasants or landlords | 2.8 |
| Political background unverified | 6.5 |
| Other | 17.4 |

*Source*: SMA 1959, A54–2-636-1.

In that year, based on the above criteria and an additional age limit for eligibility (forty for low-skilled workers and forty-five for skilled workers), the Construction Bureau of Beijing formalized 7,100 (69.6 per cent) of the 10,200 temporary workers recruited before the end of 1958.[124]

Moreover, in 1960, Shanghai's municipal government announced that community workers and outsourced-onsite workers who met the above threshold for formalization and had joined the unit before the end of 1958 could also be formalized, and that those who had joined the unit after the end of 1958 could be transformed into normal temporary workers. After formalization, the former's wages remained unchanged, but they were entitled to the welfare benefits exclusive to formal employees.[125] In that year, of the 115,000 community workers in Shanghai's industry, construction, transport, and utility sectors, 75,000 (65.2 per cent) became formal employees.[126]

Between 1961 and 1963, with the recentralization of industrialization, dismissal overtook formalization as the dominant trend, and huge numbers of temporary workers were dismissed.[127] In state-owned units nationwide, the number of temporary workers dropped from 7.8 million in 1960 to 2.2 million in 1963, before subsequently rebounding (Figure 1.3). In construction enterprises in Shaanxi, the proportion of temporary workers in the entire workforce dropped from 43 per cent in 1959 to 18 per cent in 1964.[128] In Shanghai between January and July 1962, approximately 80,000 temporary and spouse workers were dismissed. Some then joined labour service teams and became

124 BMA 1960, 125-002-00083. 125 SMA 1960, A11–2-42-12, A11–2-42-23.
126 Shen et al. 1998, 177.
127 SMA 1961, B163–2-1224, B232–2-15-42; 1962, A11–1-69, G26–2-297; 1963, B134–6-902.
128 CASS and CAC 2011a, 176.

outsourced workers, some ran their own businesses, and some were sent down to rural areas.[129]

Meanwhile, the government seemed to have routinized the formalization of temporary workers who had worked for a unit for two to three years, consolidating the dominance of permanent employment. As previously mentioned, in Shanghai in 1958 and 1959, temporary workers who had joined their units before the end of 1957 were formalized on a large scale. In Beijing and Shanghai in 1960, those who had joined their units before the end of 1958 qualified for formalization. Then, in October 1961, during the wave of downsizing, the State Council withdrew the Ministry of Labour's ban on formalizing temporary workers imposed in February that year, and announced that, of the workers remaining after downsizing, long-term temporary workers who had worked for the unit for two or three years could be formalized.[130] Thus, formalization still took place in 1961 and 1962.[131] In 1963, the State Council announced that long-term temporary workers who had joined the unit before the end of 1960 could be formalized.[132] For temporary workers, the routinization of formalization created an entrenched expectation of formalization in due course, and thus a mindset of using temporary employment as a stepping stone to formal employment.

In 1964 and 1965, as a result of the promotion of temporary employment and the nation's economic recovery, the number of temporary workers again increased (Figure 1.3). Many former formal workers who had been laid off and sent to the countryside between 1961 and 1963 returned to cities to look for jobs, only to be recruited as both-workers-and-peasants. Their *hukou* remained rural, and they had to submit a large portion of their wages to the communes with which they were affiliated.[133]

## Rural Areas: The Labour Reservoir

Between 1958 and 1965, the function of rural areas as labour reservoirs for urban areas was fully exploited. Between 1958 and 1960, large numbers of peasants joined urban industrial production as both-workers-and-peasants. In 1960, the number of agricultural workers dropped by twenty-three million compared with 1957. Of these, nineteen million joined state-owned units, accounting for 76 per cent of the newly

129 SMA 1962, A62–1-17.
130 BMA 1961, 110-00-1245, 163-001-00310; SMA 1961, B123–5-216.
131 SMA 1961, B105–7-1124-1, B273–2-311-26, B273–2-311-28, B273–2-311-49; BMA 1962, 088-001-00281.
132 BMA 1963, 002-015-00183, 110-001-01458.
133 SMA 1964, B127–2-861, B162–2-20-289; 1966, B127–2-867, B134–6-1448.

added workforce to these units and 72 per cent of the newly grown workforce in rural areas during this period.[134] From 1959 onwards, the government began to tighten its control of rural-to-urban migration.[135] In the early 1960s, temporary workers of rural origin in urban areas were among the first to be dismissed . Of the over seventeen million urban workers dismissed in 1961 and 1962, thirteen million were sent down to rural areas.[136] At the same time, in order to reduce urban unemployment, the government continued to mobilize urban youth to work in rural areas. Between 1962 and 1966, approximately 1.3 million urban youth were sent to the countryside.[137]

## Conclusion

The 1958–1965 period revolved around the rise and fall of the Great Leap Forward. This period witnessed the second and most radical switch between decentralized and recentralized industrialization in the Mao era, and a further swing of labour policy towards promoting temporary employment, both of which had enormous impacts on the exclusion system.

The rise of the Great Leap Forward between 1958 and 1960 was characterized by radical decentralization of industrialization and radical inclusion. During this period, the number of workers in state-owned units exploded. With huge numbers of handicraft co-operatives transformed into quasi-SOEs or SOEs, many workers in collective enterprises became entitled to better working conditions. The establishment of sub-district industrial facilities and urban communes allowed the under-employed and unemployed, particularly urban housewives, to join social production on an unprecedented scale. The government pushed forward employment of urban workers as normal temporary workers and employment of peasants as both-workers-and-peasants, and allowed the abuse of outsourced workers. Consequently, the number of temporary workers in the urban workforce peaked during this period in the Mao era. Both the origins and employment arrangements of temporary workers became more diverse, and temporary workers also became more stratified.

The demise of the Great Leap Forward between 1961 and 1963 was characterized by radical recentralization of industrialization and radical exclusion. Tens of millions of formal employees were laid off from state-owned units. Many SOEs were transformed back to collective enterprises, development of grassroots industries was discouraged, and their

[134] CASS and CAC 2011a, 90.
[135] National Bureau of Labour 1980, 321–322; CASS and CAC 2011a, 182–183.
[136] CASS and CAC 2011a, 90. [137] NBS 1987, 110.

workforces were downsized. Huge numbers of temporary workers were dismissed. Together with dismissed urban workers and newly grown urban youth, peasants working in cities were exiled to the countryside in large numbers. Nevertheless, formalization of temporary workers was routinized in the late 1950s and early 1960s, consolidating the dominance of permanent employment. In 1964 and 1965, with economic recovery and the launch of the Third Front Movement, formal and temporary workers in urban areas resumed expansion. Although the working class appeared obedient throughout 1958 to 1965, a violent eruption of labour protests lay around the corner.

# 5 Rebellion, Regularization, and Rebounding, 1966–1976

The period 1966–1976 saw the rise and fall of the Cultural Revolution. During this period, China witnessed the third wave of decentralized industrialization and the fiercest protests of temporary workers in the Mao era. This chapter starts by providing an overview of the political, economic, and international circumstances of this decade. It then looks at how workers in different positions in the urban exclusion system, particularly temporary workers, protested to improve their conditions, and how these protests were quashed by the government. This is followed by an examination of how gains won from temporary workers' protests – most importantly, the largest-scale regularization or formalization in the Mao era – were carried out in 1971 and 1972, and why temporary employment rebounded thereafter.

## Chinese Political Economy between 1966 and 1976

The year 1966 was the opening year of the Third Five-Year Plan (1966–1970). As a result of growing uneasiness about bureaucratism within the party, particularly after the failure of the Socialist Education Movement between 1962 and 1965,[1] Mao and his closest supporters drafted the *Circular of the Central Committee of the CCP*, better known as the *May 16 Circular*, which was passed by the Politburo on 16 May 1966. As the manifesto of the Cultural Revolution, this circular declared that representatives of the bourgeoisie (also called 'capitalist roaders') had infiltrated into the party, the government, the army, and various cultural circles, and must be cleared out or transferred to other positions. This document also announced the establishment of the Central Cultural Revolution Group, which was de facto the most powerful organ in

[1] The Socialist Education Movement is also known as the Four Cleans Movement. Prior to the launch of the Cultural Revolution, it was the broadest, deepest, and most protracted effort to mobilize supervision of cadres from below (see Andreas 2019, 82–98).

China during the Cultural Revolution decade.[2] In this decade, the Cultural Revolution permeated the economic, political, and social lives of the Chinese.

In August 1966, the CCP passed the *Decision of the Central Committee of the CCP Concerning the Great Proletarian Cultural Revolution*, also known as the *Sixteen Points*, which encouraged the masses to join the Cultural Revolution. It declared that the success of the Cultural Revolution hinged on mobilization of the masses, and that cadres must trust the masses, rely on them, and respect their initiative. In addition, it emphasized that the Cultural Revolution aimed to achieve greater, faster, better, and more economical development of social production, and that with fully mobilized masses and appropriate arrangements the Cultural Revolution and production would not hamper each other.[3] The dual emphases on revolution and production placed limits on both: the uprising of the masses disrupted production, and in order to regain social order the government had dissolved most mass organizations by the end of 1969. Temporary workers were able to organize themselves and express their grievances only between mid 1966 and early 1967.

Internationally, following the clash between North Vietnam and the United States in the Gulf of Tonkin in August 1964, the United States's aggression against communist countries escalated dramatically. Moreover, between 1967 and 1969, military conflicts erupted between China and the Soviet Union in Zhenbao Island, dragging the two countries to the brink of war. In response, China speeded up the Third Front Movement. This movement aimed to invest in armaments, machinery, chemicals, petroleum, and railroads, amongst other things, in interior areas (also called the 'Big Third Front'), which were less likely than coastal areas to be bombarded if war broke out. New factories were built there, and many coastal industrial facilities were relocated there.[4]

As a result, during the Third Five-Year Plan period, 70.6 per cent of national investment in infrastructure was diverted to interior areas, around 10 to 15 per cent higher than in any other five-year plan period in the Mao era.[5] In addition to the 'Big Third Front' construction, local governments across the country were mobilized to undertake local industrialization in similar industries (known as the 'Small Third Front' construction).[6] To finance the Third Front Movement, the accumulation rate, which had dropped from 43.8 per cent in 1959 to roughly 20 per cent in the mid 1960s, rebounded to roughly 30 per cent in most years during the Cultural Revolution decade (see Figure 3.1). The tight

[2] Central Committee of the CCP 1966a. [3] Central Committee of the CCP 1966b.
[4] Naughton 1988. [5] NBS 1984, 40. [6] Naughton 1988.

financial conditions during this decade dimmed the prospects of rebellion for economic gains.

In addition, decentralized industrialization staged a comeback. As the economy recovered from the catastrophic consequences of the Great Leap Forward, the central government shifted to decentralization again by granting local governments more discretion in financing and economic management from late 1963 onwards.[7] However, owing to the chaos at the dawn of the Cultural Revolution, the third wave of decentralization did not gain momentum until 1969 when mass movements ebbed away. In 1969 and 1970, the central government devolved the right to manage most civil enterprises affiliated with it to local governments. In 1971, it granted local states even more autonomy in financing and economic planning. In 1973 and 1974, it devolved management of many military enterprises affiliated with it to local governments.[8] As a result of decentralization, local government revenues as a proportion of national government revenues jumped from 68.4 per cent in 1966 to 84 per cent in 1970, and remained at over 85 per cent until 1976.[9]

In 1970, China drafted the Fourth Five-Year Plan (1971–1975), which set high goals for investment and production and aimed to achieve a new round of leap forward, paying particular attention to local industrialization. Under this plan, the central government allocated a special fund of eight billion *yuan* for local governments to develop local industries, including mainly small coal mines, steel plants, fertilizer plants, cement plants, and machinery factories (known as the 'five small industries'), provided tax deductions to county-level enterprises, and mobilized well-established industrial bases to provide technology and equipment to new local industrial enterprises.[10]

The combination of decentralized industrialization and high economic goals generated 'three excesses' in 1971: the number of employees in state-owned units exceeded fifty million, the gross wages of these workers exceeded thirty billion *yuan*, and grain sales exceeded forty billion kilogrammes. All substantially exceeded the planned targets. In light of this, in 1972 the government required workers recruited out of the labour plan to be laid off and control over the labour plans of county-level enterprises to be tightened. In 1973, it decided that recruitment from society should be suspended in that and the following year, and that the workforce of state-owned units should be reduced by two million in these two years. It also revised the Fourth Five-Year Plan to lower the economic goals for this period, and tried to recentralize economic management.

[7] Bai and Zhou 2018. [8] Yu 1998. [9] Lou et al. 2000, 79.
[10] Wang 2001, 309–310.

Nevertheless, owing to chaos throughout the Cultural Revolution era, these policies were not well enforced.[11]

## Wind of Economism and Inclusion in State-Owned and Collective Units

During the Cultural Revolution, formal workers in state-owned units were active rebels. Politically, these workers took power at the local level.[12] Economically, disgruntled by long-term wage stagnation, at the beginning of the Cultural Revolution these workers rose up to improve their material lot. This was allowed by local cadres, who attempted to divert the target of the Cultural Revolution away from themselves by satisfying the rebels' economic claims.[13]

The common practice was as follows. First, workers seized the confidential documents of their units to which they were denied access. They often found that their units were not following instructions issued by higher-level administrations, and raised their wages accordingly. They then organized mass rallies criticizing the cadres of their units, and forced them to pay their back wages.[14] The central government condemned such action as a 'wind of economism' and cracked down on them.[15] In addition, many enterprises suspended recruitment at the beginning of the Cultural Revolution, but gradually resumed it as production was normalized. Between 1966 and 1976, the number of workers in state-owned units jumped from 39.3 to 68.6 million, a third of whom were recruited in 1970 and 1971.[16]

The Cultural Revolution decade witnessed a new round of upgrading of collective units and expansion of workers in collective units. Amid the left-leaning sentiment in this decade, the transformation of collective enterprises into SOEs regained momentum. In January 1967, the Central Committee of the CCP issued the *Circular on Anti-Economism*, which required that collective enterprises should not be transformed into SOEs. Nevertheless, in Beijing in the second half of 1967, collective enterprises that had been transformed into SOEs during the Great Leap Forward but had then been transformed back were once again transformed into SOEs. Several large, collectively owned garment factories and shoe factories also became SOEs.[17] Moreover, nationwide,

[11] He et al. 1990, 137–138; Liu et al. 2006, 307–325. [12] Perry and Li 1997; Li 2015.
[13] Huang, Jinhai. n. d. *Shinian feimeng – Huang Jinhai huiyilu* (*That Decade is not a Dream—A Memoir of Huang Jinhai*), unpublished. Huang Jinhai was one of the leaders of *Gong Zong Si*.
[14] Shen 2010, 296–307. [15] Yang 2016. [16] NBS 1987, 13; He et al. 1990, 137.
[17] Ji et al. 1991, 299–300.

many handicraft co-operatives were transformed into co-operative factories. As a result, in 1965 co-operative factories contributed 20.4 per cent of the workforce in co-operative organizations in the handicraft industry and 28.3 per cent of the output value, but in 1975 this had risen to 47.3 per cent of the workforce and 57.4 per cent of the output value.[18]

This decade witnessed a resurgence of inclusion of the unemployed and under-employed, particularly housewives, into social production, which was known as following the path of the *May Seventh Directive* (*zou wuqi daolu*). In August 1966, the *People's Daily* – the mouthpiece of the CCP – published comments that Mao made on 7 May 1966 on a report from Lin Biao, vice chairman of the CCP and minister of national defence. This letter is better known as the *May Seventh Directive* (*wuqi zhishi*).

In this directive, Mao depicted his ideal society, in which labouring people in different industries would take the main responsibility for production tasks in their industry and engage in study and other tasks. For example, workers should be responsible for industrial production, while studying military and political science and improving their general knowledge, working in agriculture and other jobs, and participating in political activities.[19] On the ground, under the rubric of following the path of the *May Seventh Directive*, cadres were mobilized to the countryside to receive re-education from poor peasants, jobless urban youth were sent to the countryside to farm, and housewives were mobilized into social production.[20]

In 1970, the central government circulated a document entitled the *No. 401 Factory Followed the Path of the May Seventh Directive and Organized Housewives into Collective Production to Serve Military Preparedness*. Coupled with shift of industrialization to decentralization, this document led to a nationwide initiation of May Seventh labour teams (*wuqi laodong lian*), which were collective units founded by sub-district governments, and state-owned or collective units.[21] In those founded by sub-district governments, typical participants were the unemployed or under-employed. They provided goods and services to local residents and larger units by operating commissioned stores, canteens, gas stations, waste recycling stations, and nurseries, amongst other initiatives.[22]

Typical participants in those founded by state-owned or collective units were the spouses of formal employees in these units, mainly

[18] Ji et al. 2000, 173. [19] Editorial Board of *People's Daily* 1966.
[20] Investigation Team from the Institute of Economic Studies, Xiamen University 1976; Zhang 2018.
[21] BMA 1970–1971, 119-002-00251. [22] BMA 1975, 153-002-00608.

housewives, and sometimes retired workers. They formed what were often called May Seventh housewives' teams (*wuqi jiashu lian*). They took advantage of the industrial residues of their founding units, such as materials, water, and gas, to produce supplementary goods and services for these units and beyond, and exploited vacant land in these units to grow vegetables and raise pigs. For example, in 1971, a May Seventh housewives' team was planned by the Beijing Sugar, Cigarette, and Wine Company to package tea and tobacco leaves, repair protective equipment, and dispatch redundant workers to other units. In Beijing in 1970 and 1971, workers of May Seventh housewives' teams were commonly paid according to their days of work, with daily wage rates of 0.8 to 0.9 *yuan* for the first three months and 1.2 *yuan* thereafter.[23] In comparison, in 1970 the average national monthly wages of workers in state-owned and collective units were 50.75 (around 2.0 times 25.5 days) and 33.75 (1.3 times 25.5 days) *yuan*, respectively.[24] In Shanghai, over 35,000 people joined May Seventh labour teams between 1970 and 1972, amounting to around 1.5 per cent of the workforce in Shanghai's state-owned units.[25]

## Rebellion of Temporary Workers

With the legitimatization of mass movements by the *Sixteen Points*, various kinds of temporary workers organized themselves and poured out their grievances. Their most common claim was for non-dismissal. Their organizing efforts benefitted from the circulation of big-character posters criticizing the institution of temporary employment. One entitled *On the Institution of Temporary and Contract Employment* stood out. This poster was written by one of the founders of the National Red Labouring People's Revolt League (*Quan Hong Zong*, a rebel organization), and widely circulated in late 1966. Its gist was as follows:

> Under the institution of temporary and contract employment, temporary workers' right to subsist and work is not protected. Their years of service do not count. They are not entitled to welfare benefits, workplace safety protection, or equal pay for equal work to that of formal employees. They are discriminated against and exploited. If they are fired, the livelihood of their families is immediately under threat … Both temporary and formal employees are members of the working class: why does the disparity in compensation and political opportunities exist?

[23] BMA 1970–1971, 119-002-00251. [24] NBS 1987, 152.
[25] SMA 1972, B104-2-568-29; Li et al. 1997, 351.

… Capitalist roaders within the party divide the working class by deploying the two employment institutions … They attempt to divert the masses' attention away from conflict between the working class and the nascent capitalist class to conflict within the working class … The Proletarian Cultural Revolution sounds the horn to attack capitalist roaders. It is the time for workers, peasants, and all other labouring people to be masters of the country![26]

This incisive poster summarized the discrimination against temporary workers and legitimatized their protests on the basis of the socialist ideology of egalitarianism, a tactic drawing on what Lu Zhang called 'legitimacy leverage'.[27] Moreover, this poster impressively interpreted unequal treatment of formal and temporary workers as being a result of conflict between the working and capitalist classes, rather than within the working class, and associated the institution of temporary employment with the capitalist road. In this way, temporary workers' collective action was anti-capitalist. The *No. 1 Urgent Notice* of the Shanghai Temporary and Outsourced Workers' Revolutionary Rebel United General Headquarters (a rebel organization) reiterated this idea and further interpreted the intention (and the consequences largely) of employing temporary workers, revealing the multiple threats posed by this employment institution to socialism or, in other words, the CCP's legitimacy:

The vicious institution of employing temporary and outsourced workers is the means of capitalist roaders … We know that the fundamental difference between socialist and capitalist societies is that workers are masters of their own country in socialist society and wage labourers that are oppressed and exploited in capitalist society. A small group of people plot to transform should-have-been permanent workers into temporary and outsourced workers … If they succeed, the colour of socialist China will be changed …

The institution of employing temporary and outsourced workers intends to (1) discourage these workers' enthusiasm for socialist construction; (2) erode their revolutionary will by keeping them busy all the time to barely make ends meet; and (3) stratify the working class and widen contradictions within the masses.[28]

However, the initiators of the Revolution associated bureaucratism with the capitalist road, and denounced action that countered temporary employment as the 'wind of economism'. Thus, temporary workers' rebellion contradicted both the designated direction of the Cultural Revolution[29] and the government's relentless pursuit of accumulation, particularly the tight financial condition during the Cultural Revolution era. As a result, the central government quickly cracked down on them.

[26] Fang 2006. [27] Zhang 2014a. [28] SMA 1967, B336-1-43.
[29] Wu (2014) elucidates this point in more detail.

The next subsections delineate the rebellions of normal temporary workers, both-workers-and-peasants, and outsourced workers during the Cultural Revolution. Their brief existence unravels the limit of temporary workers' movements in the Mao era, and consolidates the argument that temporary employment was built into the Chinese version of socialism.

### *Hong Gong Si*

During the Cultural Revolution, the Shanghai Red Workers' Revolutionary Rebel General Headquarters (*Hong Gong Si*)[30] was perhaps the largest rebel organization of temporary workers at the local level. At its peak, it claimed to have 400,000 members, amounting to around 15 per cent of the workforce in urban Shanghai.[31] *Hong Gong Si*'s story shows the typical trajectory of temporary workers' organizations during the Cultural Revolution, the conflict between temporary workers' claims and the Cultural Revolution's designated direction, the divide between permanent and temporary workers during the revolution, and segmentation among temporary worker rebels.

A brief timeline of *Hong Gong Si* from its establishment to liquidation is as follows. Since the release of the *May 16 Circular* in May 1966, the masses had been educated through political meetings organized by grassroots units to exercise 'four great freedoms', namely freedom to speak out, air views, hold debates, and write big-character posters. In Shanghai, at the Jingan Cultural Pavilion, which was the municipal government's reception centre for rebels, temporary workers got to know each other, and organizations were incubated. On 15 November 1966, the Shanghai Temporary and Outsourced Workers' Revolutionary Rebel General Headquarters (STOH, the predecessor to *Hong Gong Si*) held its inaugural meeting. At first, Yu Yongshi, deputy director-general of the Labour Bureau of Shanghai, refused to recognize the STOH as a revolutionary mass organization. In response, the STOH staged a hunger protest, but Yu joined in. To break the impasse, the STOH marched to the Bureau of Eastern China[32] to protest.

30 Unless otherwise specified, all materials on *Hong Gong Si* in this book come from Shen (2010). Shen was one of the leaders of *Hong Gong Si*. The accounts of major events mentioned by Shen (2010) match those by Li (2015) and Huang (Huang, Jinhai. n. d. *Shinian feimeng – Huang Jinhai huiyilu* (*That Decade is not a Dream—A Memoir of Huang Jinhai*), unpublished).

31 Shen et al. 1998, 126.

32 The year 1966 was the last year in which there were regional governments between the central and provincial governments. Between 1949 and 1966, China was divided into six regions, each headed by a regional government, with the Bureau of Eastern China being

On 22 November 1966, the STOH reached an agreement with representatives of the Bureau of Eastern China and Yu. The main contents of this agreement were that (1) the STOH was a legitimate, revolutionary mass organization; (2) the STOH's protests constituted revolutionary action; (3) institutions pertaining to normal temporary and outsourced workers were unreasonable and should be abolished; (4) no one could dismiss normal temporary and outsourced workers under any pretext (apart from those with suspect political backgrounds); (5) the STOH would hold a mass rally of normal temporary and outsourced workers and open fire on the bourgeois reactionary line; and (6) normal temporary and outsourced workers who had been fired after 16 May 1966 should be re-employed within two weeks of the release of this agreement.[33]

Clearly, the STOH's claims were modest. It only demanded non-dismissal of existing temporary workers and re-employment of dismissed ones, rather than formalization. On the day of reaching this agreement, the Labour Bureau of Shanghai issued an official notice that outlawed the dismissal of temporary workers. Meanwhile, the STOH issued the *No. 1 Command*, which asked its members to keep working as usual, and required units not to punish normal temporary and outsourced workers engaged in rebellion, and to re-employ previously dismissed normal temporary and outsourced workers within two weeks. Thereafter, branches of the STOH began to emerge in many districts of Shanghai.

In December 1966, the STOH changed its name to *Hong Gong Si* to downplay its economic intention. On 5 January 1967, *Hong Gong Si* held a mass rally in the People's Square of Shanghai, criticizing the cadres of the municipal government of Shanghai and calling for the establishment of a new employment institution adhering to Mao Zedong's thought. On the same day, *Wen Hui Daily*, a popular newspaper in Shanghai, published *To Shanghainese*. Commissioned by Zhou Enlai, organized by a top cadre in Shanghai, and signed by eleven Shanghai-based rebel organizations, this article called on Shanghai worker rebels to return to their units and resume production. One day later, the railway branch of *Hong Gong Si* organized its temporary workers to operate the No. 14 express train, resuming the paralyzed railway transportation between Beijing and Shanghai, which was praised by Zhou Enlai.

one of them. This bureau was in charge of Shanghai and six provinces: Jiangsu, Zhejiang, Anhui, Fujian, Jiangxi, and Shandong. Its official residence was in Shanghai. Suzhou is a city in Jiangsu.

33 SMA 1966, B6–1-130-245; Shen, 2010, 177.

On 9 January 1967, *Wen Hui Daily* published the *Urgent Circular*. Signed by thirty-two Shanghai-based rebel organizations, this circular reiterated the importance of production and called on rebel organizations to defer their economic claims to a later stage of the Cultural Revolution. The representative of *Hong Gong Si* refused to sign this circular. Two days later, the central government sent greetings to the thirty-two rebel organizations and issued the *Circular on Anti-Economism*. On 17 February 1967, the Central Committee of the CCP and the State Council issued the *Circular on Dealing with Problems regarding Temporary Workers, Contract Workers, Rotation Workers, and Outsourced Workers in the Cultural Revolution*, which outlawed rebel organizations of temporary workers. On 24 February, *Hong Gong Si* was dissolved. Some of its members joined other rebel organizations, and some founded the Criticizing Two Employment Institutions Liaison Station, which was later cracked down on by the municipal government of Shanghai. At the end of 1967, leaders of *Hong Gong Si* were detained and sentenced to years in prison, and some temporary workers involved in *Hong Gong Si* were dismissed.

After *Hong Gong Si* was dissolved, the rebels who took over Shanghai in January 1967 closely followed the instructions from the Central Cultural Revolution Group and swept away temporary workers' gains from protests.[34] Those who had benefitted from the agreement initiated by *Hong Gong Si* and had been re-employed after dismissal were dismissed again.[35] Amid a spirit of anti-economism, formalization of temporary workers was also suspended in Shanghai in 1967.[36]

After this crackdown, temporary workers in Shanghai continued to protest, but in a cellular, wildcat fashion. Some refused to sign fixed-term contracts, and some refused to leave, or even attacked cadres when they were fired.[37] In January 1968, the central government issued the *Circular on Further Countering Anti-Revolutionary Economism and Activities of Speculation and Profiteering*. This circular stipulated that no temporary workers should be formalized until further notice, and that all problems pertaining to wages and benefits should be settled at a later stage of the Cultural Revolution.[38]

From the beginning, *Hong Gong Si* was regarded as an organization fighting for economic interests by the outside and encountered hostility. Before it was founded, temporary workers who wrote big-character

[34] BMA 1967, 047-001-00889; SMA 1967, B76–4-417-11, B109–4-11, B112–5-17, B154–6-20-25.
[35] SMA 1967, B154–6-20, B227–2-66. [36] SMA 1967, B163–4-29.
[37] SMA 1967, B227–2-51. [38] Central Office of Financial Leading Group 1999, 236.

posters criticizing the institution of temporary employment were denounced by red guards[39] as rebelling for private interests (*wei si zaofan*). The inaugural meeting of the STOH was disrupted by red guards with loudspeakers and flyers.

Throughout its brief existence, *Hong Gong Si* oscillated between economic claims and political prudence. On the one hand, it was established to fight for the rights of normal temporary and outsourced workers. This intention was explicitly reflected in its initial name. On the other hand, as a survival strategy, whatever its intention, it was more advantageous to portray itself primarily as a progressive mass organization closely following the designated direction of the Cultural Revolution.

At first, political prudence gained the upper hand. The agreement between the STOH and the government did not include radical economic claims. In the first mass rally, Fei Minzhang, top leader of the STOH and an outsourced worker, did not mention formalization at all. Instead, he quoted Mao – 'It took a rather long time to settle the ideological struggle between socialism and capitalism in our country'[40] – and dismissed the institution of temporary employment as capitalist and profit-oriented, thus portraying the STOH as a revolutionary rebel organization against capitalism. This tactic appeared to demonstrate weak adherence to the designated direction of the Cultural Revolution, when compared with the action of the Shanghai Workers' Revolutionary Rebel General Headquarters (*Gong Zong Si*), which at that moment was fighting against the municipal government of Shanghai. Moreover, the STOH changed its name to *Hong Gong Si*, which was less likely to be linked with the particular interests of temporary workers. However, when Fei's requirement to include provisions distinguishing outsourced workers in the *Urgent Circular* was rejected by other organizations, he refused to sign it. Although *Hong Gong Si* later declared that it was firmly in line with the stance of the *Urgent Circular*, it was too late.

In fact, formal employees, rather than normal temporary and outsourced workers, were the main participants in and beneficiaries of the 'wind of economism' for several reasons. The wages of formal employees in state-owned units were regulated by the government. These workers could take advantage of unpublished official documents in their interests and make claims for back wages, and their wages were paid monthly so that leaving work to participate in rebellions would have little effect on their income. In comparison, the wages of normal temporary and outsourced workers were often informally determined, and these workers

39 Briefly, red guards refer to student rebels in the Cultural Revolution.
40 Mao 1986, 785.

lacked official documents to ground their economic claims. What was worse, their wages were often paid daily, and they received no pay if they stopped working.[41]

As a result, for example, amid the 'wind of economism' between late 1966 and early 1967, the No. 2 Commercial Bureau of Shanghai repaid 637,000 *yuan* to apprentices whose formalization was delayed by a year, and to workers in co-operative factories who requested a pay rise. In comparison, it repaid 79,800 *yuan* to temporary workers who asked to be paid monthly rather than daily, and to outsourced workers who requested payment at hourly rather than piece rates.[42]

The divide between permanent and temporary workers also manifested itself in social movements. Aware of their marginality in both the industrial army and the Cultural Revolution, *Hong Gong Si* actively sought the support of formal employees, only to be both constrained and exploited by them. Founded on 9 November 1966, and endorsed by the Central Cultural Revolution Group four days later, *Gong Zong Si* was one of the most influential rebel organizations in the Cultural Revolution decade. It was composed mainly of formal employees. While *Gong Zong Si* was backed by the Central Cultural Revolution Group, *Hong Gong Si* had no official backing. In light of this, the latter decided to stand and fight together with *Gong Zong Si.*

Leaders of the STOH invited leaders of *Gong Zong Si* to attend their inaugural meeting but were rejected. When members of *Gong Zong Si* were encircled by Red Defenders (*chiweidui*), a conservative workers' organization, at Shanghai's No. 24 Dyeing Mill, *Hong Gong Si* mobilized tens of thousands of members and helped them out. Moreover, *Hong Gong Si* united with *Gong Zong Si* in denying support for an alliance of rebel organizations from the six provinces under the administration of the Bureau of Eastern China.

However, in January 1967 *Gong Zong Si* initiated a petition that resulted in the *Urgent Circular*, which ignored the claims of temporary workers. *Gong Zong Si* also reaped the political gains that should have been shared with *Hong Gong Si* by electing the conductor of the celebrated No. 14 express train, who was a member of *Gong Zong Si*, as the Shanghai representative of the Ninth CCP National Congress. Most of the crew of this train on 6 January 1967, who were members of *Hong Gong Si*, were deliberately omitted.

On top of the divide between permanent and temporary workers, there were divides among temporary workers. Temporary workers' rebel

[41] Shen 2010, 296–307; Li 2015, 617–663. [42] SMA 1967, B248-2-7-28.

organizations were largely isolated from each other. When temporary workers from Suzhou arrived in Shanghai after a long march in late October 1966, they hoped to secure support from their Shanghai counterparts. However, only around ten people joined their parade and meeting with the cadres of the Bureau of Eastern China.

Moreover, although female outsourced workers made up the majority of participants in the inaugural meeting of the STOH and subsequent protests against the municipal government of Shanghai and the Bureau of Eastern China, they were not recognized as members by the STOH. They ultimately founded their own rebel organization called the Red Detachment of Women (*Hongse Niangzijun*). Last, but not least, *Hong Gong Si* and another influential temporary workers' rebel organization, *Quan Hong Zong*, did not collaborate officially. On 8 December 1966, *Hong Gong Si* dispatched a delegation to Beijing. At that time, the leaders of *Quan Hong Zong* were also in Beijing and invited *Hong Gong Si* to affiliate with it as its Shanghai branch. Seeking equal co-operation rather than affiliation, *Hong Gong Si* rejected this invitation.

## *Quan Hong Zong*

During the Cultural Revolution, owing to its engagement with the Central Cultural Revolution Group, *Quan Hong Zong*[43] was the highest-profile rebel organization of temporary workers. Unlike *Hong Gong Si*, which was largely a local organization in Shanghai, *Quan Hong Zong* was established as a national organization. Its first committee included temporary workers from Beijing, Anhui, Guizhou, and Hunan, and it had branches in Beijing, Shanghai, and at least sixteen provinces. *Quan Hong Zong*'s story unravels how the dual contradictions faced by the CCP between accumulation and legitimacy, and between party control and accountability, played out during the Cultural Revolution, defining the prospects of temporary workers' rebellions.

A brief timeline of *Quan Hong Zong* is as follows. It was founded in Beijing on 8 November 1966. On the same day, it launched a sit-in protest at the ACFTU for recognition. This protest lasted ten days, and won oral recognition from the ACFTU as a legitimate rebel organization. On 8 December 1966, with approval from the State Council, the ACFTU officially endorsed *Quan Hong Zong*. On 25 December, after failing to secure an official conversation with the Ministry of Labour and

[43] Unless otherwise specified, materials on *Quan Hong Zong* are drawn from BMA (1966, 002-018-00077) and Bote Li (2003a). Bote Li was one of the founders of *Quan Hong Zong*. His accounts are supported by Fang (2006) and Yang (2016).

the ACFTU, over 50,000 members of *Quan Hong Zong* protested at Tiananmen Square. They then marched to the Ministry of Labour and occupied most of its facilities with the help of its own rebel organizations. One of their slogans was 'It is time to settle all disputes with Boss Liu Shaoqi!', an outpouring of resentment towards Liu's relentless promotion of temporary employment in the late 1950s and 1960s.

On 26 December 1966, representatives of *Quan Hong Zong* were cordially received by the Central Cultural Revolution Group, which instructed it to seize the power of the ACFTU. On 27 December, the ACFTU welcomed *Quan Hong Zong* to occupy its building. The Central Cultural Revolution Group and *Quan Hong Zong* also co-drafted a circular and planned to issue it in the name of the former. According to this circular: (1) temporary workers should have a right to join the Cultural Revolution; (2) they should not be dismissed during the Cultural Revolution; (3) those who had lost their jobs after 1 June 1966 should be allowed to resume their previous work and receive wages from the time of unemployment; and (4) those criticized as counter-revolutionaries after 1 June 1966 should be rehabilitated, apart from those who had engaged in counter-revolutionary activities after 1949. As with the STOH's agreement with the government, this circular only settled temporary workers' most basic concern – unemployment – for a defined period, but omitted other aspects of discrimination.

However, the circular was rejected by the Politburo. In response, *Quan Hong Zong* decided to push forward a regulation in favour of temporary workers through normal administrative procedures, resulting in the *Joint Announcement* with the Ministry of Labour and the ACFTU on 1 January 1967 that reiterated the above provisions. It was under such circumstances that the previously mentioned conversation between Jiang Qing and Zhou Enlai took place, in which Zhou blamed the miseries of temporary workers on government budget shortfalls. In the end, the Central Cultural Revolution Group decided to mothball this announcement and withdraw its support for *Quan Hong Zong*.[44]

Although the central government encouraged the masses to rise up and seize the power of rotten local governments, it by no means tolerated the nationwide solidarity of the masses, which threatened its rule. On 12 February 1967, the central government issued the *Circular on Banning Nationwide Organizations*. On 17 February, the aforementioned circular that outlawed rebel organizations of temporary workers also declared that the *Joint Announcement* was illegal, that all regulations based

[44] Li 2003a.

on it should be invalidated, and that *Quan Hong Zong* and its local branches should be dissolved. *Quan Hong Zong* then decided to relocate to Guangzhou and continued to protest. In March 1967, leaders of *Quan Hong Zong* were detained and sentenced to years in prison.

Unlike *Hong Gong Si*, which had no official backing, *Quan Hong Zong* initially had the support of the Central Cultural Revolution Group. Its gains and losses from such official backing demonstrate the contradiction faced by the CCP between legitimacy and accumulation, and the restraint on temporary workers' rebellions imposed by the drive for accumulation in the Chinese version of socialism. In addition, while *Quan Hong Zong*'s national outreach revealed the prevalence and strength of temporary workers, it also speeded up its liquidation. This fact demonstrates the contradiction faced by the CCP between strengthening party control over society and mobilizing the masses to hold cadres accountable.

### *Rebellion of Both-Workers-and-Peasants*

As mentioned in Chapter 4, as a result of the failure of the Great Leap Forward, many urban workers were mobilized to work in the countryside between 1961 and 1963. They were called 'sent-down workers' (*xiafang gongren*). When the economy recovered, many of them were re-employed as both-workers-and-peasants in urban units. During the Cultural Revolution, together with both-workers-and-peasants of rural origin, they formed rebel organizations and unleashed their grievances. They protested against the particular discrimination against both-workers-and-peasants, in addition to the general discrimination against temporary workers against which *Hong Gong Si* and *Quan Hong Zong* protested.

In Shanghai in 1961 and 1962, approximately 366,000 workers were laid off. Of these, 182,800 were dispatched to rural areas, including 79,800 to villages surrounding this city.[45] Many couples were split up when one was sent down and the other remained in the city. Dramatic decreases in the incomes of sent-down workers often caused financial difficulties, particularly for couples with several children. According to an investigation conducted by the Shanghai Municipal Bureau of Cotton Textile Industry in 1966, which covered 20,542 of its 29,600 sent-down workers, 58.7 per cent of informants reported difficulties in adjusting to rural life. In the mid and late 1960s, sent-down workers became a major source of temporary workers, and earned significantly less than their

[45] Shen et al. 1998, 203.

former colleagues who refused to go to the countryside. For example, at the No. 36 State-owned Cotton Mill of Shanghai in 1966, over half of the workforce were temporary workers, and many were sent-down workers who had been re-employed. On average, these sent-down workers earned 20 *yuan* per month less than their former colleagues in comparable positions. At Chuansha Spinning Mill in Shanghai in 1966, sent-down workers accounted for 62.5 per cent of the workforce.[46]

Sent-down workers were treated as peasants. When they were re-employed, they were treated as both-workers-and-peasants. In Shanghai, both-workers-and-peasants were more often called 'four-six' workers (*si liu gong*) because they kept only 40 per cent of their wages, while the remaining 60 per cent was submitted by the recipient unit to the communes with which they were affiliated, in exchange for the communes' food grain and annual dividend. Both-workers-and-peasants generally felt exploited by this practice. On the one hand, they found it unreasonable that their food grain was supplied by their communes while their urban colleagues' grain was supplied by the state, which was more secure. On the other hand, the communes' annual dividend was often much lower than the wages they submitted. For example, a peasant construction worker in Shanghai in the 1960s would earn 2.5 *yuan* per day, 1.5 *yuan* of which would be handed to the commune. Under the commune's accounting system, 1 *yuan* of cash income translated into five to six work points. Thus, 1.5 *yuan* amounted to at most nine work points. However, in the annual dividend allocation, one work point amounted to 0.05 to 0.15 *yuan*, depending on the performance of the commune. Taking one work point as equal to 0.08 *yuan*, for every 1.5 *yuan* submitted to the commune, the both-worker-and-peasant would ultimately receive at most 0.72 *yuan* (before deductions). Therefore, they sought to overturn the institution of four-six workers.[47]

During the Cultural Revolution, large numbers of sent-down workers and both-workers-and-peasants of rural origin in Shanghai organized under the name of the Shanghai Suburb Sent-down and Temporary Workers' United Revolutionary Rebel General Headquarters (SSTH).[48] On 22 November 1966, the SSTH held a mass rally at the Shanghai Stadium and proclaimed its establishment. At this rally, the SSTH reached an agreement with the director-general of the Labour Bureau of Shanghai, which recognized the SSTH as a legitimate, revolutionary mass organization. Subsequently, branches of the SSTH

[46] SMA 1966, B134–6-1448. [47] SMA 1967, B336–1-17.

[48] Unless otherwise specified, materials on the SSTH are drawn from SMA (1967, B119–4-28-24, B336–1-17).

sprouted up in many districts and counties of Shanghai. Members of the SSTH were reported to total over 100,000, amounting to around 5 per cent of the workforce in Shanghai's state-owned units in 1966.[49] After the inaugural meeting, the SSTH held a series of mass rallies criticizing the institution of both-worker-and-peasant. It also compiled an official newsletter called *Struggle, Criticism, and Transformation* (*Dou Pi Gai*).

The SSTH's claims were mainly economic and reflected the multiple aspects of discrimination against peasant workers as a result of the rural–urban divide in the Mao era. On 30 November 1966, it reached an agreement with the vice mayor of Shanghai granting sent-down temporary workers the same political rights as formal employees. On 29 December, it signed an agreement with the director-general of the Labour Bureau of Shanghai, which allowed sent-down workers to keep 100 per cent of their wages in 1967 (on condition that they gave up their land in rural areas, paid a regular living allowance to the commune and paid for the food grain supplied by the commune), and allowed both-workers-and-peasants of rural origin to keep 90 per cent of their wages. On 7 January 1967, the SSTH and the Labour Bureau of Shanghai reached another agreement, whereby workers who had been sent down before 1957 and had not been re-employed qualified for immediate re-employment, and workers who had been sent down after 1958 would be prioritized in job allocation. Other claims of sent-down workers' rebel organizations included transferring their *hukou* back to cities, extra compensation for their sent-down period,[50] and formalization.[51]

Like *Hong Gong Si*, on 9 January 1967 the SSTH refused to sign the *Urgent Circular*. However, later the same day, aware of increasing pressure on economic claims, it issued a notice declaring that it would change gear to open fire on capitalist roaders from the Bureau of Eastern China and the municipal government of Shanghai. On 16 January, the SSTH stepped back further and announced that it would comply with the *Circular on Anti-Economism*, and that the institution of both-worker-and-peasant should be enforced as it had been before the Cultural Revolution. After the central government outlawed all mass organizations pertaining to temporary workers, on 28 February 1967 the SSTH was dissolved.

### *Rebellion of Outsourced Workers*

Outsourced workers were also keen participants in the Cultural Revolution. In Shanghai, together with normal temporary workers, they

[49] SMA 1967, B336–1-17; Li et al. 1997, 351. [50] Li 2015, 628–630.
[51] SMA 1970, B45–5-48-74.

organized multiple rebel organizations and held mass rallies to make their voices heard. They also successfully reached agreements with the Labour Bureau of Shanghai, the Bureau of Eastern China, and their user units. Their claims reflected the particular discrimination against outsourced workers. In addition to recognizing the legitimacy of their organizations, their main claims in these agreements were as follows:

> Temporary and outsourced workers should be recognized as part of the working class … The affiliation of temporary and outsourced workers should be with the user unit … Temporary and outsourced workers should be entitled to the same political rights as formal employees.[52]

> Our political rights should be the same as employees at our user unit … From this day on, outsourced workers should be directly affiliated with and paid by the user unit, and enjoy the same welfare benefits as normal temporary workers.[53]

> Outsourced-onsite and outsourced-offsite workers should be affiliated with and paid by the factory monthly. Outsourced workers should be directly managed by the factory, and be entitled to the same welfare benefits and join the union as employees of the factory.[54]

These claims were modest. Rather than asking for formalization, outsourced workers only attempted to lift their status from outsourced to normal temporary workers, whose conditions were somewhat better. By transferring their affiliation from de jure employers such as labour service teams to their de facto employers, outsourced workers could become normal temporary workers. In addition, they sought to close not the material gap but the political gap between formal and outsourced workers. These claims were consistent with those of the high-profile rebel organizations of temporary workers mentioned above, and reflected the political prudence of these organizations and the difficulty of fighting for material benefits in the Mao era.

## Regularization of Temporary Workers

Between 1966 and early 1971, although the institution of temporary employment was widely criticized by temporary worker rebels as a plot by capitalist roaders, with no changes in national labour policy, temporary workers' employment continued largely as it had been before 1966. Between 1966 and 1970, the proportion of temporary workers in the workforce of state-owned units remained stable at 13 to 14 per cent

[52] SMA 1966, B6–1-130-252. [53] SMA 1966, B163–4-29-1.
[54] SMA 1966–1967, B336–1-114.

(Figure 1.3). Owing to anti-economism campaigns, formalization of temporary workers was largely suspended between 1967 and 1970.[55]

In November 1971, the State Council issued the *Notice on Reforming the Institution of Temporary and Rotation Workers*, which targeted temporary workers in state-owned units. This notice fulfilled the government's promise to settle issues pertaining to temporary workers at a later stage of the Cultural Revolution, and resumed the routine of formalization. It denounced Liu Shaoqi's proposal of two employment institutions as counter-revolutionary, and retreated from previous labour policy promoting the employment of fewer permanent workers and more temporary workers. It countered the abuse of temporary workers, stipulating that regular positions should be staffed with formal employees, and that temporary and seasonal positions should be staffed with temporary workers.

Moreover, this notice enhanced the protection of temporary workers, stipulating that they should have the same entitlements as formal employees in comparable positions with regard to political rights, food grain rations, work safety equipment, and relief for job-related disabilities or death. In addition, it stipulated that, apart from those working in mines and enterprises affiliated with county-level governments, temporary workers working in regular positions should qualify for formalization, as long as they had a clean political background and proper performance during the Cultural Revolution, and were of sound health and an appropriate age, but that their wages should not generally be changed after formalization.[56] Nevertheless, this notice avoided non-dismissal, the most common claim of temporary workers in 1966 and 1967, and thereby maintained the institution of temporary employment.

Once enforced, this notice brought about the largest-scale formalization of the Mao era. In late 1971 and 1972, of the 9 million temporary workers nationwide, approximately 6.5 million were formalized,[57] resulting in sharp decrease in the proportions of temporary workers in most sectors (see Table 3.3). Unlike previous rounds of formalization, temporary workers with rural *hukou* were also formalized this time.[58] In practice, this notice was applied not only to state-owned units but also to collective units.[59]

In Beijing, conditions that prevented temporary workers from being formalized included working in seasonal or temporary positions, as

[55] Central Office of Financial Leading Group 1999, 236.
[56] BMA 1971, 133-002-00075.
[57] Committee of Reforming the System of the National Economy 1983, 108.
[58] BMA 1971, 133-002-00075; SMA 1971, B103–4-295-3.
[59] BMA 1971, 133-002-00075; 1972, 135-002-00384; SMA 1972, B123–8-621.

outsourced workers, in May Seventh labour teams, or in units affiliated with communes and production brigades or teams.[60] In Shanghai, the bar on formalization similarly applied to those working in seasonal or temporary positions or as outsourced workers.[61]

In Shanghai, long-term temporary workers were categorized into three groups: those qualifying for immediate formalization; those whose formalization was suspended because of immorality, disobedience, long-term sick leave, or suspect political background; and those not qualifying for formalization. Most long-term temporary workers fell into the first category. For example, at the Construction Engineering Bureau of Shanghai in 1971, of the 9,359 long-term temporary workers, 9,025 (96.4 per cent) were formalized, 286 (3.1 per cent) were to be formalized later, and 48 (0.5 per cent) were denied formalization. At the Tractor and Automobile Industrial Company of Shanghai in 1972, of the 2,210 temporary workers, 1,972 (89.2 per cent) were formalized, 207 (9.4 per cent) were to be formalized later, and 31 (1.4 per cent) were denied formalization.[62] In Shanghai in 1974, those whose formalization had been suspended in 1971 were allowed to be formalized on condition that they had made some progress.[63] In addition, in Shanghai in the late 1960s and early 1970s, formalization was commonly used as an incentive to encourage temporary workers to go to interior areas to support the Third Front Movement.[64]

## Rebounding of Temporary Employment

After the great formalization in 1971 and 1972, temporary employment quickly rebounded (Figure 1.3). The majority were recruited outside the labour plan, and were thus aptly called 'out-of-the-plan workers' (*jihua-wai yonggong*).

Between 1966 and 1978, state-owned units were planned to recruit 1.5 to 2 million workers on average every year, including both formal and temporary workers. In fact, they recruited 2.86 million on average every year.[65] The reasons for this rampant extra-quota recruitment were two-fold. On the one hand, the Fourth Five-Year Plan (1971–1975) aimed at a new leap forward in the economy, and a new round of decentralization had gained momentum since 1970. Both boosted demand for workers.

[60] BMA 1971, 133-002-00075; 1972, 153-002-00340. [61] SMA 1972, B123–8-621.
[62] SMA 1971, B89–1-644, B103–4-382-73; 1972, B116–3-671, B119–4-300-59.
[63] SMA 1974, B154–6-294-9.
[64] SMA 1967, B227–2-36; 1969, B173–4-568-44, B173–4-568-177; 1971, B173–4-626-187, B173–4-629, G106–2-99.
[65] Ministry of Labour and the Ministry of Personnel 1991, 111–114.

On the other hand, following temporary workers' uprising, the central government intensified its control over temporary employment. In 1965, the State Council withdrew its control of annual quotas for temporary workers in state-owned units, while maintaining control of the gross wages of these workers. However, in August 1967, to reduce the operating costs of the economy and the ongoing Revolution, the central government required that unless temporary workers' employment was authorized by local governments, the bank should refuse to allocate money to related units to pay their wages.[66] In 1972, following the 'three excesses' in 1971, the central government reiterated that all units should closely follow the labour plan in recruiting temporary workers.[67]

As mentioned in Chapter 4, in the early 1960s, restraint on employing normal temporary workers invoked the prevalence of outsourced workers. Similarly, in the 1970s, intensified control of temporary employment within the labour plan invoked abuse of temporary workers out of the labour plan. While the government openly and repeatedly condemned this practice,[68] it tacitly tolerated it on the ground, as a supplement to the formal labour plan during the Cultural Revolution decade. Generally, the wages of temporary workers recruited within the labour plan were paid from the authorized gross wages of individual units, while the wages of out-of-the-plan workers were paid under the accounting category of miscellaneous expenses.[69] Apart from this subtle difference, these two groups of temporary workers were treated similarly.

Out-of-the-plan workers had long existed in the planned-economy era, but only became a statistical category in 1973. In state-owned units between 1973 and 1978, the number of temporary workers recruited within the labour plan rose slightly, from 2.48 to 2.69 million, while the number of out-of-the-plan workers jumped dramatically from 1.71 to 9.04 million.[70] Of the 9.04 million out-of-the-plan workers, 7.03 million worked in regular positions and approximately 5 million came from rural areas.[71]

Since the number of workers in collective units was relatively loosely controlled, most out-of-the-plan workers who came from urban areas were nominally employed in collective units but actually worked in state-owned units.[72] State-owned units could employ such workers themselves, or receive them from sub-district collective units. During the

66 Central government 1967. 67 He et al. 1990, 137–138.

68 BMA 1957, 026-001-00055, 137-001-00140; 1961–1962, 002-014-00075. SMA 1957, B26-2-503-4, B48-2-1940; 1958, B127-2-732; 1963, B134-6-902.

69 BMA 1972, 153-02-340. 70 NBS 1987, 33, 35; NBS 1989.

71 Ministry of Labour and the Ministry of Personnel 1991, 111–114.

72 Ministry of Labour 1991, 309–312.

Cultural Revolution decade, to encourage sub-district collective units to supply workers to state-owned units, the municipal government of Shanghai allowed them to charge the user unit commission. These workers were called 'support workers' (*zhiyuan gong*).[73] In this sense, these sub-district collective units were doing exactly what labour dispatch agencies are now doing, and the 'support workers' were de facto what we now call agency workers.

In 1977, 56 per cent of out-of-the-plan workers nationwide were employed by enterprises affiliated with county or lower-level governments.[74] As previously mentioned, in the early 1970s, local governments were encouraged to develop the 'five small industries', which needed large numbers of new hires. However, according to the priority order of resource allocation, enterprises affiliated with county or lower-level governments were at the rear of the queue for staff. With tight labour plans, these enterprises simply did not have enough quotas for either formal employees or normal temporary workers, and had to resort to out-of-the-plan workers.[75]

During the Cultural Revolution decade, as had been the case between 1958 and 1965, labour exchanges between rural and urban areas were two-way. On the one hand, around thirteen million peasants flowed into cities,[76] and, on the other hand, as urban unemployment mounted, urban youth were increasingly sent to rural areas for employment. The latter totalled 1.29 million between 1962 and 1966 (0.26 million per year on average) and 15.32 million between 1967 and 1976 (1.53 million per year on average).[77]

## Conclusion

During the Cultural Revolution decade, China witnessed a third wave of decentralized industrialization and the fiercest protests of temporary workers of the Mao era. Formal workers in state-owned units were not only active political actors but also main participants in the 'wind of economism'. Workers in collective units experienced a new round of upgrading, and the inclusion of the unemployed and under-employed, particularly housewives, in social production also made a comeback. Temporary workers of various kinds rose up to organize themselves and make their voices heard. However, the central government quickly

[73] SMA 1981, B127-6-234-59. [74] Ministry of Labour 1991, 309–312.
[75] Ministry of Labour 1991, 309–312; Ministry of Labour and the Ministry of Personnel 1991, 111–114.
[76] Chen et al. 1990, 24–25. [77] NBS 1987, 110.

cracked down on them. The dramatic rise and fall of temporary workers' movements in the Cultural Revolution demonstrates that temporary employment was built into the Chinese version of socialism.

Nevertheless, as a result of temporary workers' rebellions, the government retreated from its previous labour policy of promoting the employment of fewer permanent workers and more temporary workers, and required regular positions to be staffed with formal employees, and only temporary and seasonal positions to be staffed with temporary workers. It also enhanced the protection of temporary workers and formalized over half of them in late 1971 and 1972, which was the largest-scale formalization of the Mao era. However, owing to the expansion and decentralization of industry and intensified control over temporary employment within labour plans in the 1970s, the number of out-of-the-plan temporary workers rose dramatically thereafter.

# 6 Restoring Exploitation, Recalibrating Exclusion, and Recommodification since 1977

On 9 September 1976, Mao passed away. In the following month, the Gang of Four (*sirenbang*, four major supporters of the Cultural Revolution within the central government) were detained. Hua Guofeng became China's top leader, marking the end of the radical socialist experiment and the beginning of marketized reform. Marketized reform in China is part of the global neoliberal turn that began in the 1970s, together with reforms by Margaret Thatcher in Britain and Ronald Reagan in the United States, which featured marketization, privatization, deregulation, austerity, and crackdowns on trade unions.[1] In the face of growing social grievances sparked by marketized reforms, in the early 2000s the Hu Jintao administration (2002–2012) changed gear towards social protection. This chapter outlines the regime of general labour precarity in the post-Mao era.

## Overhauling Socialist Surplus Appropriation and Restoring Exploitation

In the third plenary session of the 11th Central Committee of the CCP in 1978, the leaders pivoting around Deng Xiaoping dismissed the prominence of political movements in the Mao era and decided to adopt economic development as the central task, which replaced the commitment to labouring people as the key basis of the CCP's legitimacy as the ruling party in the new era. While leaders in the Mao era believed that establishing socialist forms of organization was as much a precondition for economic development as its product,[2] leaders in the post-Mao era disconnected economic development with socialist forms of organization, and connected it with marketization. This paved the way for new forms of surplus appropriation.

[1] Harvey 2007. [2] CASS and CAC 1998b, 8; Meisner 1999, 199.

To cultivate political support for the reform, the post-Mao government began by improving the living standards of the masses. Between 1979 and 1981, it spent over 140 billion *yuan* (over 40 per cent of its revenue in these years) mainly on increasing the purchase prices of agricultural products, reducing taxes on peasants, and increasing the wages and welfare benefits of urban employees.[3] The early 1980s were remembered by workers in state-owned units as a period with substantial improvement in wages and benefits, and continued stable employment and power within factories.[4]

However, another line of the reform eroded their job security and political status. In the post-Mao era, rural communes were demolished, state-owned and collective enterprises were reoriented towards profit-seeking entities and most were privatized, and the private economy resumed and expanded. As a result, the institutional infrastructure of the planned economy was dismantled. While the state maintains its ultimate control over the economy and society, it has pushed the market to be the main agent allocating capital, labour, and raw materials. Exploitation has been restored and has marginalized socialist surplus appropriation, which has been carried out similarly to exploitation.

### *Reorientation and Privatization of State-Owned and Collective Enterprises*

In the post-Mao era, SOEs have been reformed to be self-responsible and profit-seeking and have been massively privatized, resulting in a terrible blow to their workers. In the Mao era, SOEs submitted their profits to the state, and the state then allocated funding to them and covered any losses. Thus, the financial performance of individual SOEs had little impact on the wages and benefits of their employees. From 1979 onwards, the state gradually retreated from funding fixed capital investments and daily operations of SOEs, and required them to secure loans from banks for such expenditure and repay these loans themselves. It also stopped appropriating SOEs' profits directly, and instead taxed their revenues.[5] As a result, SOEs became responsible for their gains and losses, and their workers' welfare hinges on their financial performance.

Meanwhile, with the designation of economic development as the government's central task, SOEs' productivity and profitability, which were downplayed in the Mao era, were highlighted in the post-Mao era,

[3] Zhao 1983. [4] Andreas 2019.

[5] Zhang 2008; Gao, Liang. n. d. Guoyou qiye sanshinian gaizhi de zhengce shishi licheng (The implementation of SOE reform policies since 1978), unpublished.

pushing SOEs to reduce labour costs. From 1979 onwards, the government granted SOEs greater autonomy to determine their production and profit distribution. In late 1986, the government began to implement the contract responsibility system in SOEs. Under this system, SOEs signed contracts with governments defining their production goals, and then broke down these goals to their business bureaus, which further broke down the goals to lower-level units. All levels of units in SOEs enjoyed greater discretion over production, with their bonuses linked to their performance.[6]

Wang Cheng, the party secretary of a state-owned wood processing factory in Beijing between 1978 and 1982, put it straightforwardly: 'In my view, factories in the Mao era would inevitably have gone bankrupt [under the new conditions], since they did not care about profitability. As early as in the 1980s, I highlighted profitability in my factory.'[7] In line with Wang, the director of a fertilizer factory affiliated with a county government in Shanxi said: 'After the Reform and Opening-up, enterprises had to make money. If they failed to do so, they would not survive … In the 1970s, every county had a state-owned fertilizer firm. All eleven fertilizer firms in Changzhi and six of the eight such firms in Jincheng went bankrupt, all due to losses.'[8]

In 1993, the central government decided that the direction of SOE reform should be to establish modern enterprise institutions. Under these institutions, the ownership of enterprises is clearly defined, and their rights and obligations are specified, leading to the privatization of SOEs; functions of enterprises are separated from functions of the government, leading to the state's retreat from SOEs in both financing and management, and SOEs' retreat from the sphere of social reproduction; and management follows 'scientific methods', which enhances the power of managers and reduces the role of workers in SOEs' decision-making.[9] As a result, the labour process in SOEs is now similar to that in the private sector. Enterprise managers impose despotic control over workers and have great discretion in determining workers' employment, remuneration, and dismissal.

These reforms, combined with competition from non-state and foreign firms, led to widespread financial difficulties for SOEs, paving the way for their bankruptcy and privatization. Between 1985 and 1998, the

[6] Maschmeyer and Yang 1993. [7] Interview M1. [8] Interview M12.

[9] Research Team of the Institute of the Economic System and Management, the National Development and Reform Commission 2015; Gao, Liang. n. d. Guoyou qiye sanshinian gaizhi de zhengce shishi licheng (The implementation of SOE reform policies since 1978), unpublished.

proportion of loss-making industrial SOEs rose from 9.6 to 47.4 per cent.[10] Rather than taking measures to improve their performance, in 1986 the government introduced the Law of Enterprise Bankruptcy, which legally prepared for the closure of under-performing SOEs.[11] In 1994, the central government launched a scheme called 'optimizing capital portfolio' (*youhua ziben zuhe*), which in practice transferred SOEs' facilities and services for social reproduction to local governments, and bankrupted under-performing SOEs. In 1995, the government introduced the reform principle of restructuring major SOEs and relaxing control of small ones (*zhuada fangxiao*). Over the next few years, most small-scale SOEs were privatized.

In 1997, the government decided to fundamentally change the status quo of SOEs over the next three years by encouraging mergers, formalizing bankruptcy, pushing forward layoffs and repositioning, and launching the Re-employment Project. Between 1997 and the early 2000s, China witnessed large-scale bankruptcy and privatization of SOEs.[12] SOEs that survived these reforms were generally strategically important, large-scale, and capital-intensive. Thereafter, SOE reforms continued in the direction of diluting state ownership, retreating from non-strategic industries, and adopting modern management institutions.[13] Reforms to collective enterprises followed a similar timeline and pattern.[14]

### *Rise of the Private Sector*

The post-Mao era has witnessed the comeback of domestic and international private capital, marginalizing state-owned and collective capital and erecting exploitation as the dominant mode of surplus appropriation.

In the 1950s, domestic private and foreign enterprises were transformed into SOEs, and self-employed handicraftsmen were collectivized. However, in 1980, to counter mounting unemployment, the State Council proposed combining employment allocated by labour bureaus with self-employment of voluntarily organized individuals.[15] In 1984, the government declared that businesses with various types of ownership should be developed.[16] In 1988, a constitutional amendment officially

[10] Lou et al. 2000, 222

[11] Gao, Liang. n. d. Guoyou qiye sanshinian gaizhi de zhengce shishi licheng (The implementation of SOE reform policies since 1978), unpublished.

[12] Research Team of the Institute of the Economic System and Management, the National Development and Reform Commission 2015; Gao, Liang. n. d. Guoyou qiye sanshinian gaizhi de zhengce shishi licheng (The implementation of SOE reform policies since 1978), unpublished.

[13] Zhang 2008. [14] Ji et al. 1991. [15] Deng et al. 2009, 19. [16] Hu et al. 2014.

Table 6.1 *How the fall of SOEs and collective enterprises contributed to the rise of private enterprises, 1992–1996.*

| | 1992 | 1994 | 1996 | 1999 |
|---|---|---|---|---|
| Proportion of private enterprises with SOEs as main material suppliers (%) | 42.8 | 37.9 | 40.3 | |
| Proportion of private enterprises with SOEs as main clients (%) | 34.4 | 26.4 | 28.9 | |
| Proportion of private enterprises' managers from SOEs (%) | 36.4 | | 18.7 | |
| Proportion of private enterprises' managers from collective enterprises (%) | 17.6 | | 20.3 | |
| Proportion of private enterprises' technicians from SOEs (%) | 38.9 | | 17.9 | |
| Proportion of private enterprises' technicians from collective enterprises (%) | 18.0 | | 15.2 | |
| Proportion of urban private business owners from SOEs (%) | 36.4 | 33.3 | 12.2 | 22.9 |
| Proportion of urban private business owners from collective enterprises (%) | 19.3 | 14.2 | 15.3 | 24.5 |
| Proportion of private enterprises that had merged or leased SOEs or collective enterprises (%) | | | 5.5 | 11.3 |
| Proportion of private enterprises that planned to merge or lease SOEs or collective enterprises (%) | | | 17.6 | 15 |

*Source*: All-China Confederation of Industry and Commerce 2007.

recognized the private sector as supplementary to the socialist public sector.[17] In 1997, the 15th National Congress of the CCP escalated the status of the private sector from 'supplementary' to 'an important component of the socialist market economy'.[18] In 2005, the State Council allowed private capital to enter sectors that had conventionally been monopolized or dominated by state capital, such as electricity, telecoms, railways, airlines, infrastructure construction, social services, finance, and national defence, and encouraged private capital to participate in the restructuring of SOEs.[19] Thus, private capital has permeated the whole economy.

On the ground, the fall of SOEs and collective enterprises contributed to the rise of private enterprises. As shown in Table 6.1, in the 1990s, SOEs were both major suppliers of raw materials and major buyers of the products of private enterprises; SOEs and collective enterprises also provided private enterprises with managers and technicians; moreover, some private enterprises expanded by merging and leasing SOEs or collective enterprises. Data from the same investigation series show that, among all private enterprises surveyed, those transformed from SOEs

[17] National People's Congress 1999. [18] Jiang 1997. [19] State Council 2005.

and collective enterprises accounted for 25.7 per cent in 2001 and 20.3 per cent in 2005. Of these transformed in 2001, 60.6 per cent were bought by former top managers of acquired SOEs and collective enterprises, and 23.1 per cent by outside investors.[20]

Meanwhile, against the normalization of the China–United States relationship since the early 1970s, the post-Mao administrations decided to substantially open up China to the world and take advantage of resources both at home and abroad to develop the economy.[21] A milestone moment was 2001, when China joined the World Trade Organization, dramatically lowering the entry barrier of made-in China products to the global market and fuelling the rise of China to be the 'world's factory'. A major contributor in this regard has been foreign-invested companies, the proportion of exports from which in China's exports rose to near 60 per cent in the 2000s and remained at 34.3 per cent in 2021.[22]

The salience of processing trade (importing raw materials, processing, and then exporting finished products) in China's exports reveals its reliance on labour to compete in global commodity chains (GCCs), which subjects Chinese workers to relentless exploitation by global capital. Export value from processing trade as a proportion of China's total export value peaked at 56.9 per cent in 1998 and remained at over 30 per cent in the 2010s.[23] The American company Apple's signature iPhone series was produced mainly in China in the 2010s through processing trade with Foxconn, one of the largest electronics manufacturing service providers globally, with major production facilities in mainland China. In 2010, Apple's profits accounted for 58.5 per cent of the total value of iPhones, while Chinese workers only received 1.8 per cent for their assembly work.[24]

The above processes have fundamentally restructured China's economic landscape. In 1976, state-owned and collective units monopolized national industrial output and urban employment, whereas in 2019 they were marginalized in both respects (Table 6.2). Nevertheless, in 2020 SOEs were estimated to own at least 60 per cent of enterprise assets in China,[25] mainly in strategic fields. In other words, SOEs in present-day China tend to be more capital-intensive than enterprises in the private sector. That said, with the majority of non-agricultural workers employed in the private sector, exploitation, which serves the interests of capitalists, has replaced socialist surplus appropriation, which

[20] All-China Confederation of Industry and Commerce 2007.
[21] Teiwes and Sun 2011. [22] Ministry of Commerce 2022a, 18–19.
[23] NBS 2021, 590. [24] Kraemer, Linden, and Dedrick 2011. [25] Chen 2022.

Table 6.2 *Changing economic landscape of China, 1976 and 2019.*

| | State-owned units | Collective units | Shareholding units | Private units and self-employment | Foreign units |
|---|---|---|---|---|---|
| Share of national industrial output value, 1976 (%) | 78.3 | 21.7 | | | |
| Share of urban employment, 1976 (%) | 78.9 | 20.9 | | 0.2 | |
| Share of revenues of industrial units above the designated size,[26] 2019 (%) | 1.9 | 0.1 | 42.1 | 33.8 | 22 |
| Share of urban employment, 2019 (%) | 12.6 | 0.7 | 19.8 | 60.6 | 5.5 |

*Source*: NBS 2010b, Table 1-34; 2020a, Tables 4-1 and 13-1; data for Figure 1.1.
*Note*: Shareholding units invested solely by state-owned units are counted as shareholding units in the original data. Their share of revenues of industrial units above the designated size, 7.2 per cent in 2019, is not included in that of state-owned units. Private units here refer to units owned by natural persons.

ultimately serves the interests of people across the country, in determining the conditions of Chinese workers.

Moreover, in the post-Mao era, the reorientation of state-owned and collective enterprises towards profitability and the significant development of private enterprises defined the competitive nature of the relationship between enterprises, both at home and abroad. The rise of such competition took place in a context where enterprises in China relied on cheap labour to compete in the global and domestic markets, intensifying surplus appropriation and straining working conditions.

Low-skilled workers in present-day China have poor working conditions typified by Foxconn workers. An investigation in 2014 found that its rank-and-file workers' base wages were barely higher than local minimum wages; in peak seasons, their overtime exceeded sixty hours per month, and overtime pay made up 30 to 40 per cent of their wages; they were subject to coercive management on the shop floor, and were likely

[26] In 2019, in statistical terms, enterprises above the designated size refer to enterprises with an annual revenue of over twenty million *yuan*.

to be dismissed for trivial misbehaviours; they knew very little about the enterprise-level trade union; complaints about management through official channels often invoked retaliation from the managers concerned; and over a dozen Foxconn workers committed suicide in 2010, and suicide protests continued thereafter.[27]

### *Modulating Surplus Appropriation*

In the post-Mao era, with reforms to SOEs and collective enterprises and the rise of the private sector, industrialization is fundamentally decentralized. Surplus appropriation in the post-Mao era is modulated mainly by capital's accumulation strategies, labour policy, and the demographic transition.

Two tendencies in capital's accumulation strategies in present-day China deserve special attention. The first is the shift from globalization to localization. In contrast to the Mao era when China's overseas economic connections were tenuous, the post-Mao era has seen China's ever-closer integration into the global economy. This has created numerous jobs for Chinese workers, but has also subjected them to relentless exploitation by global capital. In 2022, 733.5 million Chinese were in employment, and approximately 180 million of them were in export-related jobs, both directly and indirectly.[28] Therefore, changes in China's relations with the outside world and capital's global strategies tremendously affect Chinese workers.

China's integration into the world economy is at a crossroads. First, owing to rising labour costs and the increasing use of industrial robots, it has been predicted that China will lose many low-skilled jobs as cost-chasing companies disinvest.[29] Between 1995 and 2023, the average monthly nominal wage of peasant workers rose from 456 to 4,780 *yuan*.[30] Second, Brexit in 2016, the election of Donald Trump – an anti-globalization, inward-looking president – in the United States in 2016 and 2024, and the rise of nationalism in many countries in recent years suggest profound doubt about globalization around the world.

China is stuck in a particularly difficult situation. Its economy may be harmed not only by the drive towards deglobalization but also by the United States–China rivalry for global supremacy. The United States, one of China's top trade partners, has attempted to decouple from China to curb its rise. In early 2018, a trade war broke out between the two, which not only pushed export-oriented companies in China to disinvest

[27] Feng 2015. [28] NBS 2023a; Ministry of Commerce 2022b.
[29] De Backer et al. 2016. [30] Lu 2012; NBS 2014b–2024b.

but also created bottlenecks in China's high-tech sector, which relied heavily on suppliers from the United States for key parts and components. The United States–China rivalry is likely to continue in the future. The coronavirus pandemic in the early 2020s further overshadowed the prospects of globalization by accentuating the drawbacks of international interconnectedness.[31]

Under such circumstances, in May 2020 Chinese President Xi Jinping put forward a strategy of dual circulation, which planned to prioritize internal circulation – the domestic cycle of production, distribution, and consumption – for the development of China, while maintaining economic connections with foreign markets and investors, namely external circulation.[32] The transformation of globalization, coupled with the United States–China rivalry and China's emphasis on internal circulation, has profound labour implications that are yet to unfold.

The second is the shift from labour-intensive to capital-intensive industries. The economic mode that has created rapid growth in China depends on investments and exports, and is less driven by domestic consumption and productivity growth.[33] It has created many jobs, but these are often low-skilled and precarious. It has also polluted the country. Moreover, this mode seems to be losing its vigour, as economic growth continues to slow down. The annual GDP growth rate of China dropped from roughly 10 per cent between 2003 and 2011 to around 7 per cent between 2012 and 2018, to 6 per cent in 2019, and further to 5.2 per cent in 2023.[34]

In light of this, as early as 1995 the government placed transformation of the pattern of economic development on its policy agenda. Later, the new mode of economic growth gradually took shape, which features boosting domestic consumption and labour productivity. In 2014, President Xi Jinping emphasized that China needs to adapt to a new normal characterized by slower growth, industrial upgrading, and an innovation-driven economy. In 2015, the government launched the Made in China 2025 Initiative, which set concrete goals and promised multidimensional support to upgrade China's manufacturing for the next decade. In 2016, it launched the National Strategy of Innovation-Driven Development, which aims to build a comprehensive national innovation system to transform China's engine for economic growth.[35] On the ground, between 1996 and 2021, research and development expenditure as a percentage of GDP rose from 0.56 to 2.43 per cent in China, and from 2.45 to 3.46 per cent in the United States.[36]

[31] Feng 2020. [32] Buckley 2020. [33] Naughton 2006. [34] World Bank 2024b.
[35] Feng 2020. [36] World Bank 2024c.

With regard to process upgrading, computer-numerically controlled machine tools, robots, enterprise software, and artificial intelligence, amongst other technologies, are gaining popularity in Chinese enterprises. For example, according to the International Federation of Robotics, robot density (number of robots per 10,000 employees) in China's manufacturing rose from 10 in 2008 to 392 in 2022, albeit still well below those of global leaders.[37]

With regard to product upgrading, while maintaining its dominance as an assembly station in GCCs, China has emerged as a global supplier of parts and components. Between 1992 and 2015, China's share of global exports of assembled products rose from 3.4 to 26.3 per cent, and its share of global exports of parts and components rose from 1.7 to 22.5 per cent.[38] Moreover, Chinese enterprises have established brands in some industries, allowing them to capture a larger share of value from GCCs than pure assemblers. Generally, Chinese brands tend to be at the lower end of the global market, and their profit share significantly underperforms their market share. However, in some niche markets, such as telecoms equipment and electric cars, Chinese companies may have already leapfrogged their foreign competitors in technology, or are about to do so.[39]

The combination of process and product upgrading is on track to shift China's growth path from being labour-intensive to capital-intensive. This will displace some jobs, create new ones, overhaul the employment skills structure, and fine-tune the relative power of labour and capital in China. Similarly, these transformations are at an early stage, and their implications will take some time to unfold.

With the continued tight control of the CCP over society, labour policy remains a key modulator of surplus appropriation. In the post-Mao era, it has swung between flexibilization and protection. On the one hand, in the 1980s and 1990s, to develop the market economy, the government issued various regulations to smash the iron rice bowl and re-establish the labour contract system. On the other hand, in the face of growing labour grievances, the Hu administration introduced a series of pro-labour laws. In 2007, after thirteen years of dormancy since the promulgation of the Labour Law in 1994, the government passed the LCL, the Employment Promotion Law, and the Mediation and Arbitration of Labour Disputes Law. In 2010, it passed the Social Insurance Law. At the end of 2012, it passed an amendment to the LCL to tighten control over labour dispatch.[40]

[37] International Federation of Robotics 2014, 2024. [38] Athukorala 2017.
[39] Feng 2020. [40] Howell and Pringle 2019.

However, the Xi administration (2013–) has been more ambivalent about labour protection. In 2013, to counter the abuse of agency labour, it enacted the Interim Provisions on Labour Dispatch. However, the implementation of this regulation was unsatisfactory. Moreover, in response to economic slowdown, the central government began to promote flexible employment, and local governments lowered employers' social insurance contribution premiums (for more detail, see Chapter 7).

Demographic changes affect surplus appropriation by adjusting the supply of labour power and thereby the scope for labour resistance. In the Mao era, the population grew fast. In the early 1970s, the government began to implement the family planning policy. This evolved into the one-child policy in the early 1980s, which was phased out in 2015 but failed to boost the fertility rate (births per woman) in the long term. China's working population (fifteen to fifty-nine years old) continued to grow until 2012 when it fell by 3.45 million.[41] China's fertility rate was 1.77 in 2016 when Chinese couples were allowed to have up to two children and 1.16 in 2021 when Chinese couples were allowed to have up to three children,[42] both well below the replacement-level fertility rate of 2.1, suggesting that the working population will likely shrink. As a result, since the early 2000s, reports of shortages of low-skilled workers, such as assembly line workers, cleaners, and sales clerks, have been perennial. The ongoing demographic transition helps tighten the labour market, strengthening workers' bargaining power.

### *Countering Surplus Appropriation*

The commitment to labouring people, which fundamentally countered the drive for surplus appropriation in the Mao era, has been largely hollowed out in the post-Mao era through the erection of economic development as the key basis of the CCP's legitimacy and the connection of economic development with marketization. With the reorientation and massive privatization of state-owned and collective enterprises and the rise of private enterprises, class differences based on economic, cultural, and political capital, once narrowed in the Mao era, have widened dramatically in the post-Mao era. In the early 1980s, China was one of the most equal countries globally with an urban Gini coefficient of 0.16. Since then, China has gradually become one of the most unequal countries globally. Its Gini coefficient increased to an alarming 0.491 in

[41] Cary 2013. [42] Silver and Huang 2022.

2008 but dropped to 0.371 in 2020,[43] thanks to social protection measures discussed below.

In the post-Mao era, the counter-movement against surplus appropriation is incomplete from a Polanyian perspective and therefore impotent. Relentless surplus appropriation leads to labour insurgency and the promulgation of pro-labour regulations at the national level. However, the absence of independent trade unions resulting from the CCP's monopoly of political representation of the working class paralyses the enforcement of these regulations at the local level, sustaining poor working conditions and labour insurgency.[44]

The post-Mao government is less concerned about bureaucratism and more concerned about social control, resulting in even smaller room for labour resistance in an era of more relentless surplus appropriation. In 1982, the right to strike was removed from the Constitution and has not yet been reinstated. Independent trade unions are still not allowed, and the major work of trade unions is apolitical. Nevertheless, aggrieved workers are one of the most militant groups in present-day China. According to a study conducted by the CASS, between January 2000 and September 2013, labour disputes accounted for approximately 30 per cent of collective action involving over 100 people, and were the primary cause of collective action involving 100 to 10,000 people.[45] In the late 1990s and early 2000s, the protagonists of collective labour action were SOE workers protesting against the demise of the iron rice bowl. From the 2000s onwards, the protagonists have increasingly been workers in the private sector against relentless exploitation.

As shown in Figure 6.1, the number of strikes increased between 2011 and 2015, and dropped thereafter, partly because of the economic slowdown. Between 2008 and the early 2010s, emboldened by growing labour shortages, new labour laws, and media openness, workers became more assertive in their demands. They increasingly protested to link their wage growth with their employers' productivity growth, on top of protests for back wages and social insurance contributions.[46] As official trade unions have struggled to win workers' recognition, most strikes have been wildcat ones. They have seldom gone across work units or localities. The prospects of such cellular strikes growing into a strengthened and transformational labour movement have been faint.[47]

Growth in labour unrest led the government to be both more repressive by increasing spending on stability maintenance and more

[43] Li 2016; Central Intelligence Agency 2024. [44] Friedman 2014.
[45] Li and Tian 2014. [46] Cai 2010; Elfstrom and Kuruvilla 2014.
[47] Lee 2007, 2017; Hurst 2009; Friedman 2014.

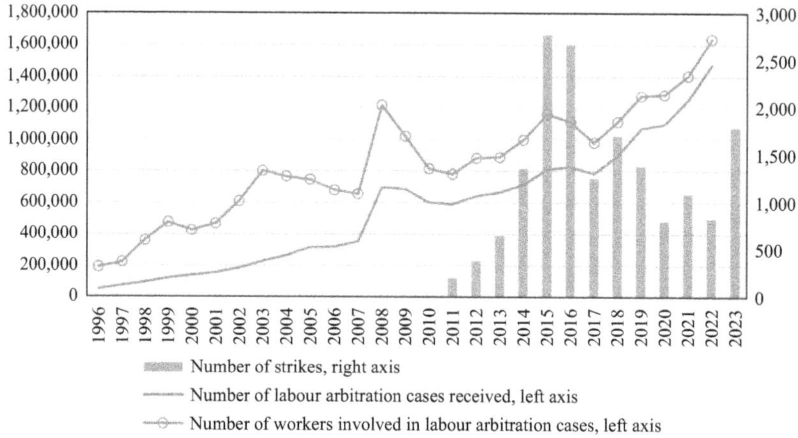


Figure 6.1 Growth in labour disputes in China, 1996–2023.
*Source*: NBS and MOHRSS 2023. China Labour Bulletin 2024 (unpublished source).

responsive by introducing pro-labour regulations.[48] The post-Mao government hopes to resolve labour disputes mainly through labour laws. Between 1996 and 2022, the numbers of both labour arbitration cases[49] received and people involved in such cases trended upward (Figure 6.1). Most labour arbitration cases were about compensation, social insurance, and changes to and termination of labour contracts. During the same time frame, the proportion of cases won solely by workers dropped from 50.9 to 25.2 per cent, the proportion of cases won solely by employers dropped from 20.3 to 10.3 per cent, and those won partly by both parties or with other consequences increased from 28.8 to 64.5 per cent.[50] These trends indicate the great room to manoeuvre in the local implementation of labour laws, resulting from labour's impotence at the local level.[51]

While all post-Mao administrations have been deeply concerned about social control, they have approached it in different ways, thus opening up different opportunities for collective labour action. In the administration led by President Hu, the global economy was sound and the Chinese economy was growing fast. The Hu administration made earnest efforts to address labour grievances, both through reforms within the party

[48] Elfstrom 2021.
[49] Labour arbitration is a compulsory procedure for the settlement of labour disputes before filing a lawsuit in China.
[50] NBS and MOHRSS 2023, Table 8.1. [51] Friedman 2014.

system and by allowing constructive activities of non-party actors. It put forward pro-labour laws and allowed considerable room for civil-society actors such as non-governmental labour organizations and law agencies to influence workers and policies. Moreover, the Hu administration fostered innovation and experimentation relating to collective bargaining, such as grassroots trade union elections, arbitration committees, and elections of worker representatives. However, when President Xi took office in 2013, the global economy was in recession and the Chinese economy was slowing down. The Xi administration renewed restrictions, cracked down on civil-society organizations, and allowed labour protection efforts only from within the party system. The central government has urged the ACFTU to reform itself to be a better mediator between labour and capital, but no significant moves have been made in this regard.[52]

In addition to temporal differences in labour control, there are spatial differences. During both the Hu and early Xi administrations, in the Yangtze River Delta, labour resistance tended to be contained within the workplace, and authorities stuck to state socialist-era programming and focused on welfare provision. In contrast, in the Pearl River Delta, labour resistance tended to be transgressive and boundary-spanning, and authorities experimented with novel forms of worker representation and cracked down harshly on collective labour action.[53]

## Recalibrating Exclusion

Marketized reforms have dramatically softened and recalibrated the social exclusion system, leading to pervasive labour precarity. Compared with the Mao era, the boundaries among labouring people are now less rigid. With the reintroduction of the labour contract system, all workers in enterprises have become de facto contract workers, with or without labour contracts, thus dismantling the dualism between permanent and temporary employment created by the state in the Mao era. Instead, to reconcile the contradiction between profitability and legitimacy, capital has pursued the dualism between formal and informal workers, which has been countered by labour policy and resistance (to be discussed in Chapters 7 and 8). Exclusion based on types of enterprise ownership still exists, but to a lesser extent. Exclusion based on *hukou* status has also softened. Peasants have been included in the urban workforce on a massive scale, but still face various types of discrimination.

[52] Fuchs, Tse, and Feng 2019; Howell and Pringle 2019. [53] Elfstrom 2021.

### *Recalibrating Exclusion Based on Employment Arrangements*

While the CCP under Mao's leadership prioritized creating jobs over increasing labour productivity, reformers have reversed this priority order. In the late 1970s and early 1980s, they blamed the iron rice bowl for lowering labour productivity, and identified the labour contract system as a remedy,[54] eventually leading to the dismantling of permanent employment, the reintroduction of contract employment, and the growth in informal employment. As a result, the dualism between permanent and temporary employment was dissolved, and the dualism between formal and informal employment emerged.

On the one hand, the iron rice bowl was smashed in two steps. First, the government got rid of redundant workers in state-owned units. In 1978, around 15 per cent of the industrial workforce in these units was estimated to be redundant.[55] Subsequently, between 1978 and 1985, the government overhauled many SOEs, and many redundant workers left their jobs. In 1985, the government introduced a scheme to optimize labour combination (*youhua laodong zuhe*) of SOEs. Under this scheme, apart from the enterprise director, all employees had to be selected by a manager in the enterprise to remain in their positions. Those who were not selected became redundant.[56] As a result of this scheme, formal workers who under-performed, or were old, physically weak, ill, or disabled were cleared from SOEs' active workforce, and were at best repositioned to affiliated collective enterprises.[57] At the national level, in 1988, 13.3 per cent of workers in state-owned units were involved in this scheme and around 6 per cent of them became redundant and subject to repositioning.[58]

Second, the government massively laid off workers. In the late 1980s, there were debates about unemployment under socialism. The official magazine of the Ministry of Labour published articles arguing that mild unemployment was conducive to the development of productive forces, and further SOE reforms necessitated the dismissal of redundant workers.[59] Efforts in this direction accelerated after 1992 and gained full momentum in the late 1990s. Between 1997 and 2002, the number of workers in state-owned units dropped by 38.8 million (35.1 per cent), and that in urban collective units dropped by 17.6 million (61.1 per cent; see Figure 1.1).

[54] White 1987b. [55] Deng et al. 2009, 138–140. [56] Zhao 1985; Gong 1989.
[57] Gao, Liang. n. d. Guoyou qiye sanshinian gaizhi de zhengce shishi licheng (The implementation of SOE reform policies since 1978), unpublished.
[58] NBS and the Ministry of Labour 1989, 329; data for Figure 1.1.
[59] He 1989; Song 1989.

To facilitate the re-employment of laid-off workers, the state launched the Re-employment Project, which provided them with employment services such as training and job-matching and a period of living allowances and social insurance.[60] Only formal employees of state-owned units were entitled to such services and benefits, although they might not necessarily have received them because local governments were under financial strain. Temporary workers in state-owned units and workers in collective units were laid off without compensation.[61] There were significant regional variations in the timing and manner of layoffs, the content and implementation of re-employment policies, patterns of workers' protests related to layoffs, and corresponding labour control.[62] In the 2010s, the government's efforts to cut over-capacity in industries such as iron, steel, glass, cement, and aluminium, where SOEs were concentrated, triggered a new round of layoffs, which further reduced the number of formal SOE employees.[63]

On the other hand, the labour contract system is applied to all enterprise workers. In the Mao era, formal workers did not have labour contracts, while in 1957 the government required employers to sign fixed-term labour contracts with temporary workers to facilitate dismissal. In the early 1980s, first Shanghai and then several other regions applied the labour contract system to new hires in regular positions in SOEs.[64] In 1994, the Ministry of Labour mandated the nationwide implementation of the labour contract system by the end of 1996, with only minor exceptions. As a result, between 1983 and 1997, the proportion of contract workers in the workforce of state-owned units rose from 0.6 to 51.6 per cent. Between 1992 and 1997, the proportion in urban collective units rose from 11 to 50.5 per cent, and in other urban units from 29.9 to 60.7 per cent.[65]

In most cases, labour contracts are short. An investigation led by a research team dispatched by the Standing Committee of the National People's Congress found that, in 2005, most labour contracts in China were for one year or less, and many workers did not have labour contracts.[66] As shown in Figure 1.1, 'other employment' expanded rapidly in the 1990s and early 2000s. According to a researcher from the MOHRSS, many workers in this category seemed to be employed

[60] National Committee of Reforming the Economic System 1998; Chinese Labour Academic Association and Beijing Municipal Labour Academic Association 1999.
[61] Yu 2000, 125–139; Wu 2010. [62] Hurst 2009. [63] Wildau and Feng 2017.
[64] SMA 1982, B123-11-130, B127-6-379-26; Chen 2003, 153–154.
[65] NBS 1989; Ministry of Labour 1991, 1993; NBS and the Ministry of Labour 1993,1994, 1996a, 1996b, 1997,1998.
[66] He 2005.

without labour contracts, and this area therefore shrank substantially after the enforcement of the LCL.[67] While labour contracts are no guarantee of the protection of labour laws, working without labour contracts makes it hard for workers to prove their relationship with their employer and safeguard their rights when violations occur.

The expansion of wage workers without labour contracts indicates the rise of informal employment in the post-Mao era. In the Mao era, the government maintained close control over urban employment. From the early 1980s onwards, to reduce unemployment, the government encouraged the development of the informal economy, which was largely beyond the reach of labour regulation. In 1980, the government began to encourage self-employment. In the late 1990s and early 2000s, to create jobs, it encouraged the development of labour-intensive enterprises, small- and medium-sized enterprises, the service sector, the private sector, and flexible employment, including part-time, fixed-term, and seasonal employment, self-employment, and labour dispatch.[68] In Beijing, for example, to create jobs for laid-off workers, the municipal government encouraged the development of catering, retailing, maintenance, childcare, elderly care, gardening, security, and cleaning services, among others. These were poorly regulated. The municipal government also encouraged highly employable laid-off workers to start their own businesses, moderately employable ones to become agency workers, and less employable ones to take part-time jobs.[69]

On the ground, according to a survey involving 4,000 laid-off workers in Shenyang, Qingdao, Changsha, and Chengdu in 1997, over half of the workers surveyed were unemployed, while the rest were self-employed, worked as temporary workers in state-owned or collective units, or worked in private enterprises, all largely outside labour regulation.[70] A study based on data collected in the early 2000s found that self-employment was a main avenue of re-employment for laid-off workers.[71] Compared with the conditions of formal workers, the conditions of informal workers are worse, indicating a dualism between formal and informal employment in the reform era.

### *Recalibrating Exclusion Based on Types of Enterprise Ownership*

In the Mao era, the state took responsibility for providing employment for urban citizens. Most of them worked in state-owned units. Compared

[67] Interview O18.
[68] Central Committee of the CCP and State Council 2003; State Council 2005.
[69] State Council 2002, 3–16. [70] Li, Zhang, and Zhao 2000. [71] Hurst 2009.

with their counterparts in collective units, employees in state-owned units enjoyed superior wages, welfare benefits, and political rights. In the post-Mao era, exclusion based on types of enterprise ownership persists, but to a lesser extent. The state has gradually retreated from the provision of urban employment, which has been increasingly dominated by the private sector. All wage workers have become contract workers. However, in comparison, workers in state-owned and collective units tend to enjoy more stable employment than their counterparts in other units. Wage levels in state-owned units are similar to those in shareholding and foreign units, but significantly higher than in collective and private units (units owned by natural persons). The welfare benefits of formal workers in state-owned units have been significantly curtailed, but remain superior to those in other units. Their political status, as masters of the enterprises, has been largely hollowed out, just as in the private sector.

In 1980, the government began to promote employment in the collective and private sectors, marking the beginning of the state's retreat from the provision of employment. Between 1966 and 1976, the average annual workforce increment was 2.84 million in state-owned units and 0.53 million in collective units. In contrast, between 1977 and 1988, it was 2.6 million in state-owned units and 1.43 million in collective units. In addition, during this period, the number of self-employed workers exploded from 0.15 to 6.59 million. With the reforms of state-owned and collective units and the rise of the private sector, most Chinese workers now work in the private sector (Figure 1.1).

The state's retreat from the provision of employment and the rise of the private sector have led to women's withdrawal from the labour market. According to an investigation conducted by the ACFTU in eleven provinces in 1987, enterprises were reluctant to recruit female workers, and women had to achieve significantly higher scores in recruitment exams than men to be considered. Well-educated women were no exception: units either refused to take in female graduates or were more likely to fire female than male graduates. Female contract workers were mostly recruited at prime age (seventeen to twenty-two years old) and found it difficult to get their contracts renewed after twenty-two, by which time they were regarded as ready to marry and start a family. Women were over-represented amongst redundant workers in SOEs.[72] Amid SOE reforms in the 1990s, women were more likely than men to be forced to retire early, and had greater difficulty getting re-employed.[73]

72 ACFTU 1988.
73 Qingdao branch of the ACFTU and the All-China Federation of Women 1994.

Table 6.3 *Duration of labour contracts in six provinces, 1995, 2002, and 2007.*

| | Category | ≥ Ten years (%) | >One year, < ten years (%) | ≤ One year (%) | No contract (%) |
|---|---|---|---|---|---|
| 1995 | State-owned and collective units | 75.4 | 22.3 | 2.3 | |
| | Other units | 18.5 | 37.5 | 44.0 | |
| 2002 | State-owned and collective units | 62.4 | 24.1 | 9.3 | 4.2 |
| | Other units | 16.8 | 30.7 | 30.2 | 22.3 |
| 2007 | State-owned and collective units | 54.8 | 36.6 | 3.7 | 4.9 |
| | Other units | 17.2 | 53.0 | 12.9 | 16.9 |

*Source*: Chinese Household Income Project Series (1995, 2002) and the Longitudinal Survey on Rural Urban Migration in China (2007), cited by Li and Zhao 2012.
*Note*: The six provinces surveyed were Jiangsu, Anhui, Henan, Hubei, Guangdong, and Sichuan.

With regard to job security, the reintroduction of the labour contract system nationwide eroded permanent job tenure in the Mao era and transformed all wage workers into de jure contract workers, regardless of their employing unit's ownership type. Nevertheless, workers in state-owned and collective units tended to have longer contracts. As shown in Table 6.3, in six provinces in all three years surveyed, the proportion of labour contracts lasting at least ten years in state-owned and collective units was significantly higher than in other units. However, this gap narrowed between 1995 and 2007. Moreover, as shown in Table 6.4, in 2007 the proportion of workers without labour contracts in SOEs and foreign enterprises was lower than in other enterprises.

With regard to income security, in the post-Mao era, wage reforms in SOEs have linked individuals' compensation with the performance of both their employers and themselves. In the Mao era, SOE workers' wages were largely independent of the performance of their employers and themselves, and were aptly called 'iron wages'. In the post-Mao era, 'iron wages' were criticized for being ineffective in motivating workers. In light of this, the state linked the annual gross wages of individual SOEs with their annual performance,[74] and increased the proportion of piece-rate wages and bonuses in SOEs' wages. Between 1978 and 1992, hourly

[74] Ding and Yang 1992.

Table 6.4 *Status of contract workers in enterprises with different types of ownership in China, 2007.*

| | SOEs | Foreign enterprises | Other enterprises |
|---|---|---|---|
| Proportion of contract workers with unexpired labour contracts (%) | 68.5 | 81 | 47.3 |
| Proportion of contract workers with expired labour contracts (%) | 3.0 | 2.7 | 3.7 |
| Proportion of contract workers with labour service contracts (%) | 15.9 | 6.1 | 10.8 |
| Proportion of contract workers without contracts (%) | 12.7 | 10.2 | 38.2 |

*Source*: ACFTU 2010, 231.
*Note*: Contract workers with labour service contracts were predecessors to agency workers before the introduction of the LCL.

rate wages as a proportion of the gross wages of state-owned units dropped from 85 to 45 per cent, and the proportion of piece-rate wages and bonuses increased from 3.1 to 28.9 per cent.[75] Moreover, in the Mao era, wages in state-owned units were significantly higher than in collective units. In the post-Mao era, with regard to wages, state-owned units outperformed shareholding, collective, and private units (units owned by natural persons), but were on a par with foreign units (Figure 6.2).

With regard to welfare benefits, in the 1980s, SOEs significantly increased spending on welfare facilities, enhancing the cradle-to-grave welfare benefits that distinguished formal employees in state-owned units from other labouring people in the Mao era. Since then, however, welfare benefits have been significantly curtailed.[76] In the late 1990s and early 2000s, under the rubric of separating government functions from those of enterprises, SOEs retreated from operating their own labour welfare facilities, including nurseries, schools, and hospitals. These were shut down, handed to local governments, or restructured into profit-seeking entities targeting general customers.[77] SOEs have also retreated from supplying apartments to their employees, and instead provide them with modest subsidies to buy homes in a commodified and even financialized real-estate market.[78]

In addition, SOEs have retreated from fully-funded insurance programmes for healthcare and retirement, and have replaced them with

[75] NBS and the Ministry of Labour 1993, 327. [76] Andreas 2019, 173–175.
[77] Wu 2010, 162–163. [78] Song 2009.

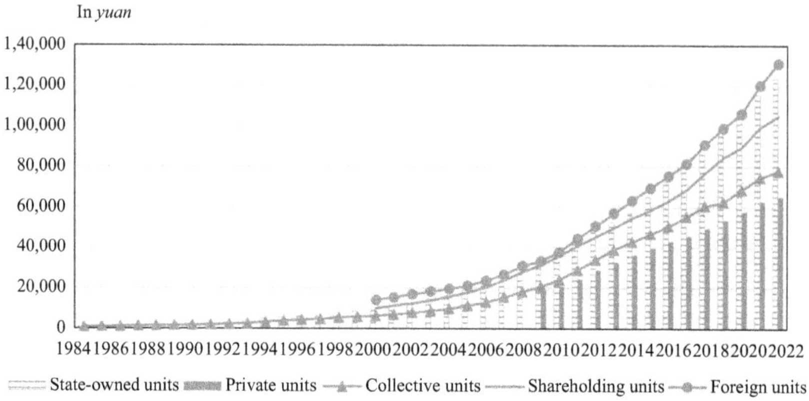


Figure 6.2 Average annual wages of workers in units with different types of ownership in urban China, 1984–2022.
*Source*: NBS 2000a–2023a.

new programmes to which both employees and employers contribute.[79] Nevertheless, workers in SOEs still enjoy better social insurance coverage. As shown in Table 6.5, in 2002 all four types of enterprises failed to provide all workers with statutory social insurance. However, SOEs outperformed shareholding and private enterprises (enterprises owned by natural persons) by wide margins in the provision of all four kinds of insurance. They also outperformed foreign enterprises in the provision of unemployment insurance.

With regard to political rights, the Mao administration significantly enhanced workers' participation in factory management, which helped to maintain their status as masters of the country. In contrast, post-Mao administrations have reduced workers to wage labourers, who are constantly anxious about their future livelihood and care overwhelmingly about short-term pecuniary benefits. In the early 1980s, the government enhanced the functions of the congress of workers' representatives, although these were increasingly concerned about welfare issues. From the mid 1980s, with the implementation of the factory director responsibility system, enterprise-level party organizations and congresses of workers' representatives were sidelined in enterprise management. Moreover, permanent jobs were greatly curtailed through mass layoffs, which uprooted workers' political participation in the

[79] Frazier 2010.

Table 6.5 *Coverage of social insurance in enterprises with different types of ownership in China, 2002.*

| Insurance | Worker's *hukou* status | SOEs | Foreign enterprises with investment from outside China | Foreign enterprises with investment from Hong Kong, Macao, or Taiwan | Shareholding and private enterprises |
|---|---|---|---|---|---|
| Retirement (%) | Rural | 40.4 | 50.4 | 37.4 | 25.6 |
| | Urban | 93 | 86.9 | 67.8 | 47.8 |
| Unemployment (%) | Rural | 21.7 | 15.2 | 13.4 | 5.0 |
| | Urban | 77.9 | 70.4 | 49.4 | 26.1 |
| Healthcare (%) | Rural | 31.5 | 34.4 | 29.6 | 17.6 |
| | Urban | 64.6 | 78 | 59.8 | 33.9 |
| Work-related injury (%) | Rural | 30.8 | 57.2 | 68.6 | 19.9 |
| | Urban | 45.8 | 55.8 | 52.4 | 23.5 |

*Source*: ACFTU 2010, Table 18.

workplace.[80] As a result, the management practices of SOEs in the post-Mao era resemble those in the private sector.[81]

### *Softening Exclusion Based on* Hukou *Status*

In the Mao era, despite the persistence of two-way labour exchanges between rural and urban areas, it was national policy to control rural-to-urban population flows. A few peasants went to urban areas and worked mainly as temporary workers. However, since the early 1980s, although the government still prioritizes the employment of urban citizens, it has opened up the urban labour market to peasants. With the boom of the private sector, hundreds of millions of peasants have joined the urban workforce. Nevertheless, the *hukou* system persists. In other words, marketized reforms have failed to bring full citizenship to peasants.[82] Compared with those with urban *hukou*, peasant workers work longer hours, receive lower wages, and are largely excluded from social insurance and essential public services in cities.

[80] Zhao 2012, 66–67; Andreas 2019, 166–219.
[81] Lau, Qian, and Roland 2000; Gallagher 2011. [82] Solinger 1999.

In the post-Mao era, the government still prioritizes the employment of urban citizens over peasants. Whenever urban unemployment increases, peasant workers bear the brunt. Mao's death in 1976 was followed by a decrease in the number of urban youth sent down to rural areas and an increase in the number returning to their home cities. Between 1978 and 1980, approximately eighteen million people flowed into cities, including both returning urban youth and peasants.[83] Moreover, in the 1980s SOE reforms took off and redundant employees needed to be repositioned.

To reduce urban unemployment, from the late 1970s onwards urban units began to evict peasant workers to take in urban residents. In 1978, the State Council required out-of-the-plan workers of rural origin to be evicted and returned to their home villages.[84] In 1981, the State Council reiterated the necessity to evict out-of-the-plan workers and emphasized that, with few exceptions, urban units should not hire peasants. In 1980, peasants employed by state-owned units as temporary workers totalled 9.31 million.[85] By the end of 1983, over four million out-of-the-plan workers, most of whom were peasants, had been dismissed.[86] When SOE reforms gained momentum in the late 1980s, approximately two million peasant workers were dismissed by their urban employers.[87]

In the 1990s, local governments used several tactics to prioritize the re-employment of laid-off SOE workers over urban employment of peasants. First, they set quotas for the number of peasants that could be recruited by urban units in their jurisdiction. Second, they authorized urban units to recruit peasants only when qualified urban workers were unavailable. Third, they imposed a certificate management system on peasant workers, and required them to acquire various certificates to legally stay and work in cities. These included ID cards, diplomas, and certificates of health, birth control, working in cities, and temporary residence. Acquiring these certificates was costly and time-consuming. Fourth, they restricted jobs open to peasants, and reserved laborious, dirty, and hazardous jobs for them. Fifth, they discouraged urban units from recruiting peasants by charging them fees to manage peasant workers, to expand the urban capacity, to pay for urban non-staple food subsidies, and to contribute to the re-employment fund, among others.

[83] State Council 1981.
[84] Ministry of Labour and the Ministry of Personnel 1991, 111–114.
[85] State Council 1981.
[86] Ministry of Labour and the Ministry of Personnel 1991, 111–114.
[87] Ministry of Labour 1991, 309–312.

Sixth, they prevented peasants from renting private residences, and required urban units to provide accommodation for them.[88]

Nevertheless, in the post-Mao era, peasants have been both pushed and allowed into the urban labour market. In the early 1980s, the government reduced its spending on agriculture and rural areas, and dissolved rural communes. While boosting peasants' enthusiasm for cultivating their land, the dismantling of rural communes and establishment of the household responsibility system atomized peasants and uprooted the provision of collective welfare services, rendering peasants solely responsible for any risks to their families.[89]

Between the early 1980s and mid 2000s, the rural–urban income gap widened. The ratio of annual per capita income in urban areas to that in rural areas dropped from 2.56 to 1 in 1978 to 1.82 to 1 in 1983, and then rose to 3.14 to 1 in 2007, before dropping again.[90] Moreover, peasants have relied increasingly on cash for their daily subsistence. Between 1978 and 2009, the proportion of cash expenditure in the gross expenditure of rural households rose from 44.8 to 89.9 per cent.[91] Finally, owing to urbanization and industrialization, many peasants' land was expropriated by the government or grabbed by investors. Without land, these peasants had to live on selling their labour power. Therefore, although the government abolished all agricultural taxes nationwide in 2006, apart from tax on tobacco leaves, peasants still actively seek wage employment.

In 1983, the State Council granted peasants freedom to migrate to market towns, the lowest level of urban administrative units.[92] With the demolition of rural communes, the sending end's restriction over peasants' flows into cities was lifted. Moreover, the rapid expansion of the private sector since the late 1970s has demonstrated a great appetite for cheap migrant labour. As a result, the number of peasant workers has soared. Between 1985 and 2023, their number grew from 0.67 million to 297.5 million.[93] According to a national survey conducted by the ACFTU, in 2007 peasant workers made up 78.2 per cent of the workforce in construction in China, 71.8 per cent in accommodation and catering, 65.7 per cent in mining, and 61.3 per cent in manufacturing.[94]

Like their predecessors in the Mao era, peasant workers in the post-Mao era remain on the lowest rung of the urban workforce. First, they are more likely to work in the informal sector than urban citizens. As shown in Chapter 7, peasants are a major source of agency workers who are

[88] ACFTU 1999, 263. [89] Wen 2013, 95–97. [90] NBS 2024a.
[91] NBS 2010c, Tables 2-28 and 2-34. [92] State Council 1983.
[93] Lu 2012; NBS 2024b. [94] ACFTU 2010, 36.

poorly regulated by the state. Second, peasant workers tend to work longer hours than workers with urban *hukou.* Since May 1995, the standard working time in China has been eight hours per day, five days per week. According to a national survey conducted by the ACFTU, in 2002 peasant workers worked 53.1 hours per week on average, whereas workers with urban *hukou* worked 44 hours per week.[95] In 2019, the proportion of those working over forty-eight hours per week was 40.3 per cent among peasant workers and 25.8 per cent among workers with urban *hukou.*[96]

Third, the remuneration of peasant workers is generally worse than that of workers with urban *hukou.* In the 1980s, to facilitate the reintroduction of the labour contract system, newly recruited contract workers were entitled to an allowance of 15 per cent of the value of their wages in compensation for welfare benefits reductions compared with veteran permanent workers. In 1992, the Ministry of Labour clarified that contract workers of rural origin were ineligible for this allowance.[97] According to a national investigation by the ACFTU, in 1997 the overall labour costs of a peasant worker were only a sixth to a third of the costs of a veteran permanent worker in the same position.[98] In most enterprises in 2002, coverage of retirement, unemployment, work-related injury, and healthcare insurance was significantly lower among peasant workers than those with urban *hukou* (Table 6.5). Between 2008 and 2013, coverage of the five essential kinds of social insurance among peasant workers remained very low and improved only slightly. In addition, over half of outbound peasant workers[99] worked without labour contracts between 2010 and 2016 (Figure 6.3).

In addition to discrimination in the workplace, peasant workers still find it challenging to settle in cities. In the post-Mao era, the government has gradually lifted restrictions on transfers of rural *hukou* to urban *hukou*, first in small towns and then in larger cities. After being allowed to work in market towns, peasant workers were allowed to settle there in 1984, and in some pilot towns and small cities in 1997, and to transfer their *hukou* there under certain circumstances.[100] By 2023, the government had been lifting restrictions on *hukou* transfers to cities with a population of no more than three million, and loosening such restrictions

[95] ACFTU 2006, 97. [96] NBS and MOHRSS 2020, Table 1-56.
[97] Ministry of Labour 1992. [98] ACFTU 1999, 262.
[99] Outbound peasant workers refer to those who migrate out of local townships to work for over six months in the year surveyed. In contrast, local peasant workers refer to those who work in the non-agricultural sector in local townships for over six months in the year surveyed.
[100] Chan and Zhang 1999.

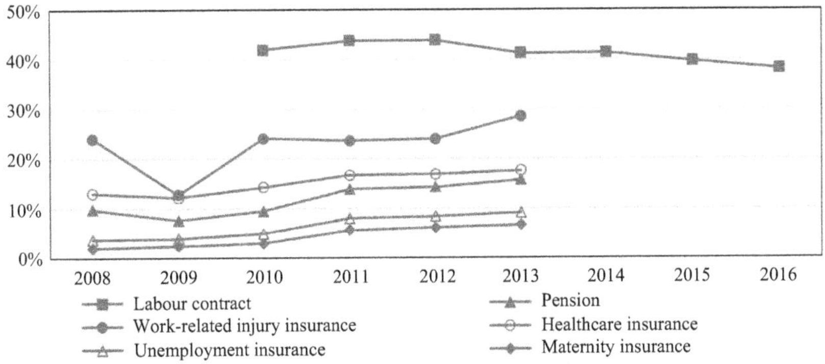


Figure 6.3 Coverage of labour contracts and social insurance for outbound peasant workers in China, 2008–2016.
*Source*: NBS 2014b–2017b.

in cities with a population of three to five million.[101] However, in other cities, restrictions on *hukou* transfers remain. Since peasant workers' jobs in urban areas are often precarious and they must often give up their farmland and homestead to obtain an urban *hukou*, many simply prefer to retain their rural *hukou*.

If they are not allowed or choose not to transfer their *hukou* to their working cities, peasant workers have limited access to public services there, the most important of which is children's education. As a result, in the post-Mao era, rural areas are still responsible for peasant workers' social reproduction. Generally, peasant parents go to work in cities, but leave their children behind in their home villages to be taken care of by the grandparents. In 2010 and 2020, left-behind children (up to seventeen years old) in rural areas were estimated to total 61 million and 41.8 million, accounting for 37.7 and 38.0 per cent of children in rural areas and 21.9 and 14.0 per cent of children nationwide, respectively.[102] In addition to the above general predicament, peasant workers have diverse labour market situations and employment relations, resulting in a diversity of precarious existence.[103]

## Recommodification

In the Mao era, social reproduction was decommodified and somewhat socialized on a discriminatory basis. In the post-Mao era, this sphere has

[101] Li 2023.
[102] All-China Federation of Women 2013; United Nations Children's Fund et al. 2023.
[103] Swider 2016.

been recommodified. The state has significantly retreated from this sphere and encouraged private capital to invest in it. Efforts have been made to counter recommodification, but with limited and uneven effects. This section focuses on the recommodification and decommodification of healthcare, education, and housing – the 'three new great mountains' over Chinese workers in the post-Mao era.

### *Recommodifying Healthcare*

In the Mao era, formal employees in SOEs had all of their medical costs and 50 per cent of those of their immediate dependents covered by their employers. Workers in collective enterprises and some temporary workers enjoyed less generous healthcare services provided by their units. Peasants received low-cost healthcare services provided by communes through the co-operative medical system. However, after a few years into the post-Mao era, the government began to retreat from the healthcare sector.

In the late 1970s and early 1980s, amid debates about the direction of healthcare reform, policymakers reached a consensus that the health sector should pursue not only social benefits but also economic benefits. With the dismantling of rural communes, the co-operative medical system serving peasants was abolished. In the 1980s and early 1990s, the government loosened its control of state-owned hospitals, implemented the contract responsibility system in these hospitals, increased their charges for health services, and encouraged individuals to run private healthcare facilities. In 1998, after several local experiments, the State Council began to replace the Mao-era medical insurance scheme, to which only employers contributed, with the Basic Medical Insurance for Urban Worker-Employees (BMIUW), to which both employees and employers contribute. In the late 1990s and early 2000s, SOEs retreated from operating their own hospitals, which were shut down, handed to local governments, or privatized. Since the early 2000s, reforms to hospital ownership have been on the policy agenda.[104]

As a result, nationwide, the proportion of medical costs covered by the government dropped from 36.2 per cent in 1980 to 15.5 per cent in 2000, before rebounding. In contrast, the proportion borne by individuals rose from 21.3 per cent in 1980 to 60 per cent in 2001, before dropping (Figure 6.4). Between 2005 and 2021, the number of public hospitals decreased, while the number of private hospitals soared; the number of visits to public hospitals increased by 148.8 per cent, but those to private hospitals increased by 821.7 per cent (Figure 6.5).

[104] Chen 2001; Cao 2008.

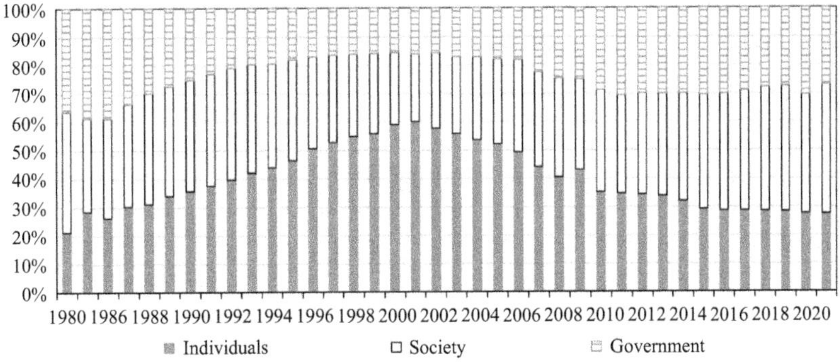


Figure 6.4 Distribution of medical costs between individuals, society, and the government in China, 1980–2021.
*Source*: National Committee of Hygiene and Health 2023, Table 4-1-1.
*Note*: Medical costs covered by society refer mainly to those covered by employers and rural collectives.

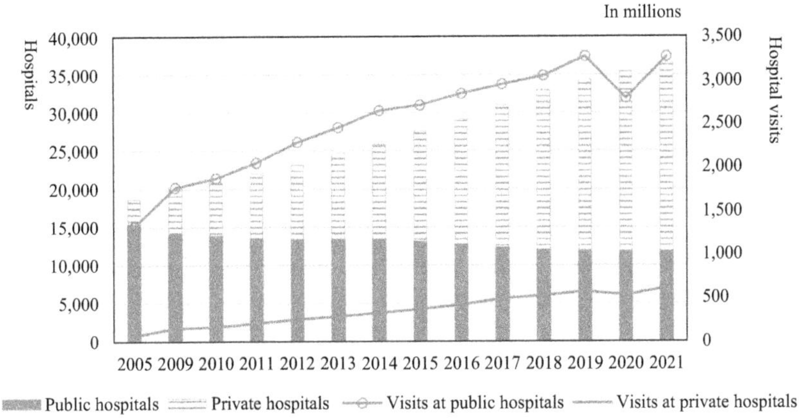


Figure 6.5 Composition of hospitals and hospital visits in China, 2005–2021.
*Source*: National Committee of Hygiene and Birth Control 2014, Tables 1-2-1 and 5-2-2; National Committee of Hygiene and Health 2023, Tables 1-2-1 and 5-2-2.

To counter the drawbacks of marketized reforms, countervailing reforms have pushed the healthcare sector to pursue social benefits, and to extend the coverage of medical insurance. In a national conference on health work in 1996, for the first time in the post-Mao era the government emphasized that the healthcare sector was supposed to serve public welfare. In 2003, it began to experiment with a new co-operative medical system in rural areas. In 2006, it initiated an experiment with a scheme for basic medical insurance, targeting the unemployed and those in the informal economy in urban areas.[105] These two schemes have been unified into the Basic Medical Insurance for Urban and Rural Residents (BMIURR).

Similarly, for those in the formal economy, the government has replaced the pension scheme to which only employers contributed with the Basic Retirement Insurance for Urban Worker-Employees (BRIUW), to which both employees and employers contribute. For those in rural areas, unemployed, or in the informal economy, the government launched the Basic Retirement Insurance for Urban and Rural Residents (BRIURR) scheme. Compared with BMIUW and BRIUW, reimbursements of BMIURR and BRIURR are lower.[106] In 2023, while BMIURR covered 962.9 million people, BMIUW covered 370.9 million;[107] and while BRIURR covered 545.2 million people, BRIUW[108] covered 521.2 million.[109]

### *Recommodifying Education*

Reforms in the education sector have proceeded similarly. In the Mao era, all educational institutions were public. From the outset of the post-Mao era, the government began to encourage social capital to invest in education.[110] During the SOE reforms of the late 1990s and early 2000s, many schools affiliated with SOEs were shut down, handed over to local governments, or privatized. In 2001 alone, the number of kindergartens and elementary schools nationwide dropped by 36.5 per cent and 11.3 per cent, respectively.[111] Between 2003 and 2019, the proportion of students in private regular elementary schools, junior high schools, regular senior high schools, vocational secondary schools, and regular and vocational colleges and universities all showed an upward trend. Most strikingly, the proportion of students in private kindergartens rose from 24 to 56.2 per cent between 2003 and 2019 before dropping to 46 per cent in 2022, reflecting the government's dramatic retreat from the childcare sector (Figure 6.6).

Moreover, as shown in Table 6.6, in 2017 roughly a third of household education expenditure at the pre-university stage was invested in extra-curricular education, mainly provided by private entities and for

105 Cao 2008. 106 Interview O21.
107 National Healthcare Security Administration 2024.
108 Workers in Chinese enterprises view BMIUW and BRIUW as social insurance, but not BMIURR and BRIURR.
109 MOHRSS 2024. 110 Que, Wang, and Wang 2019.
111 Ministry of Education 2012.

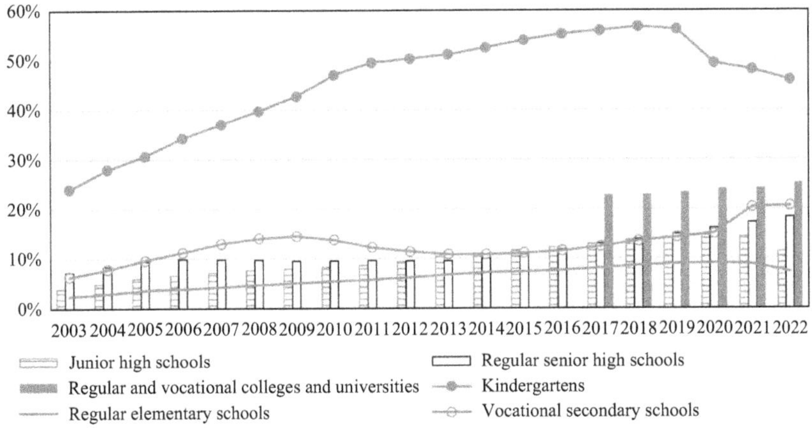


Figure 6.6 Proportions of students in private institutions at different levels of education in China, 2003–2022.
*Source*: Ministry of Education 2024; NBS 2023a, 2024a.

Table 6.6 *Extracurricular education expenditure in China, 2017.*

| | | Elementary schools | Junior high schools | Senior high schools |
|---|---|---|---|---|
| Extracurricular education expenditure as a proportion of household education expenditure (%) | | 38.3 | 32.5 | 26.7 |
| Academic training expenditure as a proportion of household extracurricular education expenditure (%) | | 86.9 | 81.3 | 87.3 |
| Proportion of students enrolled in extracurricular academic training (%) | All | 33.4 | 43.7 | 48.2 |
| | Rural areas | 20.8 | 24.4 | 26.0 |
| | Urban areas | 40.0 | 52.3 | 54.2 |
| Proportion of students enrolled in extracurricular non-academic training (%) | All | 27.9 | 16.2 | 14.6 |
| | Rural areas | 6.8 | 3.1 | 4.1 |
| | Urban areas | 38.8 | 21.9 | 17.4 |

*Source*: China Institute for Education Finance Research 2018.

academic purposes. Depending on the stage of education, 30 to 50 per cent of students participated in extracurricular academic training, and 10 to 30 per cent were involved in extracurricular non-academic training. Urban parents invested significantly more than rural parents.

To counter the commodification of education, the government began to subsidize tuition and miscellaneous fees for students in elementary and junior high schools in 2006, waived these fees for these students in 2008, and banned commercial academic training targeting these students during their weekends and holidays in 2021.

### *Recommodifying Housing*

In the Mao era, urban residents lived mainly in apartments built by their units and the government. Rents were very low. From the outset of the post-Mao era, reformers began to promote the idea of housing as a commodity rather than a public good. In the late 1970s and 1980s, the government experimented with selling public apartments to individuals at subsidized prices, and increased the rents of public apartments to encourage home buying. In the 1990s, the central government encouraged the development of financial services for building and purchasing houses and operating real-estate companies. In 1998, the State Council required local governments and units to stop renting public apartments to individuals, and sell rather than rent newly built public apartments to individuals. It highlighted that the real-estate sector should be reformed to become a new engine for economic growth.[112]

In the first two decades of the new millennium, house prices soared in Chinese cities, driven partly by the country's rapid urbanization, partly by local governments' heavy reliance on revenues from land transfers and taxes from the real-estate sector, and partly by individuals who increasingly regarded urban houses as investments. As a result, while housing costs accounted for a negligible proportion of household expenditure in the Mao era, they have dragged many households into debt in the post-Mao era. According to a national survey conducted by China's central bank, in 2019, 56.5 per cent of urban households surveyed were indebted and 75.9 per cent of their debts were mortgages; among these, indebted households of rank-and-file staff in enterprises spent 22.5 per cent of their monthly income on debt repayments.[113] To buffer house price increases, in the 1990s the government introduced the housing fund, to which employers and employees equally contribute. However, those in the informal economy are excluded from this benefit, and it can only alleviate the financial pressure of housing to a limited extent.

[112] Wang 2018. [113] People's Bank of China 2020.

## Conclusion

China's transition from a planned economy to a market economy is ongoing, as is the transition of its labour tenure regime. However, the fundamentals of the regime of general labour precarity have been laid. The post-Mao government regards economic development as the central task and marketization as the way to achieve this goal. Consequently, with the reorientation of SOEs and collective enterprises towards profit-seeking entities, the massive privatization of these enterprises, and the rise of the private sector, socialist surplus appropriation has been overhauled and given way to exploitation. Both have been enhanced by competition between enterprises. Surplus appropriation in the post-Mao era has been modulated mainly by capitals' accumulation strategies, labour policy swinging between flexibilization and protection, and the demographic transition. It has been countered by labour resistance and pro-labour regulations. However, the impotence of the former has led to the impotence of the latter.

The social exclusion system has been softened and recalibrated by marketization. Exclusion based on employment arrangements has been greatly reduced and taken new forms. With the reintroduction of the labour contract system, all wage workers have become contract workers, thus dismantling the dualism between permanent and temporary employment in the Mao era. Meanwhile, the dualism between formal and informal employment has emerged. Exclusion based on types of enterprise ownership still exists, but to a lesser extent. Exclusion based on *hukou* status has also softened. Social reproduction has been recommodified. Despite efforts of decommodification, the recommodification of healthcare, education, and housing has created the 'three new great mountains' over Chinese workers.

# 7 Rise of Agency Labour and Regulations for Labour Protection

Given the CCP's tight control over labour resistance, in everyday life workers in the post-Mao era rely mainly on pro-labour regulations to protect their rights. This chapter focuses on under-studied agency workers, the dominant form of precarious labour in urban enterprises since the 2010s, and regulations against the abuse of agency workers. It advances the last chapter in two respects. First, it explains how the dualism between formal contract workers and agency workers emerged in the 2010s by examining the origins and expansion of agency workers. Second, it demonstrates why legal counter-movements in the post-Mao era are incomplete from a Polanyian perspective by examining the effects of the LCL and the Interim Provisions on Labour Dispatch, two pro-labour regulations with a focus on agency workers.

## Rise of Agency Labour between the Late 1970s and the 2010s

Labour dispatch already existed in the Mao era. In urban areas, sub-district governments and other organizers of production and service teams dispatched under-employed workers to state-owned units and charged them commissions. In rural areas, communes dispatched their members to urban units and extracted some of their wages. In the post-Mao era, between the late 1970s and the 2010s, employers abused agency workers primarily because they were a cheap and flexible workforce. The state played key roles in this process, as both the initiator of reforms that fostered labour dispatch and as a supplier of agency workers. As a result, dualism between formal contract workers and agency workers replaced the Mao-era dualism between formal permanent workers and temporary workers, defining the employment structure in enterprises of present-day China.

### *Contributors to the Rise of Agency Labour*

In the post-Mao era, labour dispatch was initially used to reduce urban unemployment and buffer the impacts of SOE reforms. In the late 1970s, the central government encouraged local governments to establish labour service companies (*laodong fuwu gongsi*) to lower urban unemployment. These companies were largely a more institutionalized form of Mao-era labour service teams. They pooled together the unemployed, provided them with training, introduced them to jobs, organized workshops and service teams, or dispatched them to other units for temporary work. In the 1980s, many local labour bureaus, local personnel bureaus,[1] sub-district governments, local unions, and SOEs established labour service companies.[2] In 1987, at the national level, a total of 56,051 labour service companies employed 7.3 million workers and managed 1.7 million temporary workers. Of the newly recruited workforce in collective enterprises in 1987, 63 per cent were employed by labour service companies.[3]

The workforce employed or managed by labour service companies included the urban unemployed and redundant SOE workers. When removed from their previous positions, redundant SOE workers were repositioned in labour service companies affiliated with their SOE employers, while maintaining their status as formal SOE workers. When dispatched by labour service companies, they became de facto agency workers. According to the Ministry of Labour, in 1988 approximately 10 per cent of redundant SOE workers were dispatched to other units.[4] An investigation by the ACFTU found that, in 1995, 27 per cent of redundant SOE workers were re-employed, 2.9 per cent of whom became agency workers and 1.4 per cent outsourced workers.[5]

In the late 1990s, the government required SOEs implementing large-scale layoffs to establish re-employment service centres. Apart from distributing living allowances to and paying social insurance contributions for laid-off workers, these centres were charged with responsibilities similar to those of labour service companies in the 1980s. Dispatched workers remained members of sending SOEs, which charged recipient units commissions. Meanwhile, SOEs were encouraged to establish labour dispatch agencies specializing in supplying agency labour to themselves.[6] Labour service companies in the late 1990s were also more involved in labour dispatch than in the 1980s.[7]

In the early 2000s, re-employment service centres were closed. In 2003, the Ministry of Labour permitted labour dispatch agencies to

1 Before the amalgamation of the Ministry of Labour and the Ministry of Personnel into the MOHRSS in 2008, labour bureaus were responsible for blue-collar workers' affairs, while personnel bureaus were responsible for white-collar workers' affairs.
2 Chen et al. 1990. 3 Deng et al. 2009, 59–61, 402–403. 4 Ren 1988.
5 Wu 1995, 69–79. 6 National Committee of Reforming the Economic System 1998.
7 Zhou 2007, 201–216.

dispatch part-time agency workers and sign labour contracts with them. In the same year, President Hu Jintao proposed the proactive development of labour dispatch agencies and other employment service organizations to help laid-off workers to find jobs. At the local level, in Beijing in the early 2000s, the municipal government provided subsidies and tax reductions for labour dispatch agencies employing certain numbers of workers for certain periods, particularly those with laid-off workers in their workforces.[8] In Shanghai in 2002, registered labour agencies totalled approximately 1,800.[9]

Moreover, to lower labour costs and to protect the interests of formal contract workers, SOEs use agency labour on a large scale. To boost SOEs' efficiency, since 1985 the government has linked the annual gross wages of individual SOEs with their annual financial performance, encouraging them to lower labour costs. According to accounting principles for SOEs stipulated by the State-owned Assets Supervision and Administration Commission (hereafter State-owned Assets Commission) and its predecessor, only the wages of formal workers are counted as wages, whereas temporary workers' wages are categorized as operational fees, independent of wage quotas and free from the direct control of the State-owned Assets Commission. In addition, the remuneration of formal workers in many SOEs remains significantly higher than the social average. Under such circumstances, cheap temporary workers have been massively deployed in SOEs as rank-and-file staff.[10]

The LCL, enforced in 2008, and the Social Insurance Law, enforced in 2011, significantly enhanced the legal protection of formal contract workers. These laws required de jure employers to pay five kinds of social insurance and the housing fund (*wuxian yijin*) for their employees. Altogether, employers' compulsory *wuxian yijin* contributions could amount to 30 to 40 per cent of their employees' gross wages.

To comply with these laws without significantly increasing labour costs, enterprises of various types of ownership have abused agency labour. By hiring through a third party, the de jure employer, enterprises, as de facto employers, were able to obfuscate and shirk some responsibilities for workers, including paying *wuxian yijin*. Although labour dispatch agencies, as de jure employers, were legally responsible for employers' *wuxian yijin* contributions, lax regulations enabled them to evade these responsibilities easily. By returning agency workers to labour dispatch agencies when necessary, enterprises could also avoid open-ended contracts and severance fees stipulated in the LCL, which was vital to those managing

[8] Zheng 2010, 22. [9] Tu 2007, 14–22.
[10] Interviews O2, O6, O9, O11, O12, and O15.

fluctuating orders. As discussed below, labour dispatch agencies could eliminate unwanted workers at little cost. Furthermore, many enterprises used agency labour to bypass the maximum probationary term of six months required by the LCL.[11]

The rise of labour-intensive industries also led to the growth in labour agencies, which later engaged in labour dispatch. At the sending end of migrant workers, from the 1980s onwards, with the dismantling of rural communes, rural unemployment surfaced. In response, some county and township governments established labour service companies that served peasants. These companies were both labour dispatch agencies and contractors: they dispatched peasants to urban or local township enterprises, charged these enterprises management fees, and organized peasants into teams to provide services such as building work and baby-sitting.[12] However, most peasant workers migrated to cities without the help of labour service companies.

At the receiving end of migrant workers, for example, in the 1980s, to guarantee the labour supply to labour-intensive processing-trade enterprises, the municipal government of Dongguan (a city near Hong Kong) not only founded labour agencies itself but also encouraged the development of private labour agencies.[13] In Wenzhou, a coastal city in South China, in the 1980s private labour agencies emerged to channel rural surplus labour into booming local private enterprises.[14] These agencies profited by charging jobseekers initially, and then charged employers when labour shortages loomed.[15]

The rise of labour-intensive industries increased relevant enterprises' dependency on labour agencies during labour shortages. In recent years, using agency workers has been employers' common response to labour shortages, the global economic slowdown, and China's diminishing cost advantage in global manufacturing. A former HR manager of a Taiwanese factory in Dongguan put it bluntly in 2016: 'When one founded a factory in the 1990s, one would never run short of either workers or orders. Nowadays, however, it is problematic to secure both enough orders and enough workers to finish these orders.'[16]

On the one hand, decades of demographic transition and economic expansion have led to labour shortages. Perennial labour shortages since the early 2000s have altered power relations between labour agencies and

[11] Interviews O3, O5, O8, and O13.
[12] Labour Bureau of Suzhou 1985; Personnel Bureau of Fenyi, Jiangxi 1985; Wang 1985; Zhu 1985; Solinger 1999.
[13] Ning et al. 2010, 119–121.
[14] Labour Bureau of Wenzhou 1993.
[15] Interview O16.
[16] Interview O16.

factories, and workers' behaviour, contributing to the popularity of labour dispatch. In a context of labour shortages, rather than hiring on their own, factories have relied increasingly on labour agencies for recruitment. Rather than charging one-off recruitment fees, labour dispatch agencies prefer to charge factories monthly commissions for labour supply by maintaining their employment relationships with the workers they recruit. For factories, these workers become agency workers. Factories also rely on labour dispatch agencies to reduce the turnover of agency workers, particularly in peak seasons, because workers are changing jobs more frequently than ever due to labour shortages.[17] In Suzhou, one labour official estimated that in 2015 about 70 per cent of new hires in local factories were obtained through labour dispatch agencies.[18]

On the other hand, the worldwide economic slowdown after the 2008 global financial crisis and China's diminishing cost advantage in global manufacturing have intensified fluctuations of orders for Chinese factories, which have to be matched by a hyper-flexible workforce, such as agency workers. Between 2010 and 2020, China's export growth rate trended downward.[19] Worse, with the increase in wages of Chinese workers, China's conventional role in GCCs as a low-cost manufacturing base is under pressure.[20]

Dongguan was once home to over 160 manufacturers with a workforce of over 10,000. In 2016, fewer than 100 manufacturers there maintained such a large workforce. Many factories had moved to Southeast Asia or closed down. For factories that survived and remained in Dongguan, their orders fluctuated widely. They needed a workforce that could be rapidly summoned in peak seasons and be conveniently got rid of in slack seasons. After the enactment of the LCL, they had to ensure that such dramatic expansion and downsizing of the workforce would not cause legal or financial risks. The solution was agency labour.[21] Owing to their labour-intensive mode of production and fluctuating orders, export-oriented factories in China are huge users of agency labour. In 2015, ASUS, a contract manufacturer for Apple, used over half of the agency labour in the Suzhou New District.[22]

In addition, the constraint on foreign enterprises' recruitment has pushed them to use agency workers. In the late 1970s, newly established representative offices of foreign institutions had limited knowledge of China and were eager to seek local help with HR management. The

[17] Interviews O2, O4–O7, O10–O12, O15, and O16. [18] Interview O14.
[19] Global Economic Database 2024. [20] Sirkin, Zinser, and Rose 2014.
[21] Interview O16. [22] Interview O14.

Table 7.1 *Composition of agency workers in China, 2003, 2008, and 2011.*

| | Peasant workers (%) | Laid-off workers (%) | Other workers (%) |
|---|---|---|---|
| China, 2011 | 52.6 | | |
| Fujian, 2011 | 41.4 | 27.4 | 31.2 |
| Fujian, 2008 | 38.1 | 29.9 | 32.0 |
| Shanghai, 2003 | 50.6 | 21.4 | 28.0 |

*Source*: ACFTU 2012; Zheng 2010, 78; Tu 2007.

government monitored them by prohibiting them from hiring on their own. Instead, it established specialized companies to recruit Chinese staff, dispatch them to these institutions, and charge them commissions.

In 1979, China's first specialized labour dispatch agency, the Foreign Enterprise Service Corporation (FESCO), was established by the financial and commercial division of the municipal government of Beijing. Between 1979 and 1988, the FESCO treated dispatched workers as its formal employees. However, after 1988, workers who were returned and not re-dispatched were provided with living allowances for two years and were then laid off. In 1999, almost half of the 1,300 foreign enterprises in Beijing were clients of the FESCO, including Sony, Microsoft, Nokia, Siemens, and Panasonic.[23]

Although foreign enterprises have been allowed to hire workers directly and have understood China better, some continue to employ workers through labour dispatch agencies. Some foreign enterprises in China use agency workers because their headcount of formal employees is rigidly controlled by their headquarters.[24] Last but not least, small enterprises often find it cheaper to use HR services provided by labour dispatch agencies than to recruit their own HR staff, leading to their use of agency workers.[25]

Owing to the above factors, peasant workers and laid-off workers have been major sources of agency workers (Table 7.1). Many agency workers once worked for the same enterprises as formal contract workers but were later transformed into agency workers. According to an investigation conducted by the Shanghai branch of the ACFTU, of the 4,000 agency workers surveyed in 2003, 1,193 (29.8 per cent) became agency workers after their previous labour contracts with the same employer expired. This practice was particularly common in enterprises transformed from SOEs. A survey of 289 such enterprises in Shanghai in

[23] Chang 1999. [24] Interviews O9 and O12. [25] Interview O1.

2004 by the local ACFTU branch found that, after privatization, the proportion of formal contract workers in these enterprises decreased by 30.2 per cent, while the proportion of agency workers increased by 26.4 per cent.[26]

### *The State as an Agency Labour Supplier*

In the early 1950s and early 1960s, the government ran labour agencies in major cities to facilitate employment of and provide relief to the unemployed.[27] In the 1980s, state organs and SOEs founded labour service companies to take on similar roles. From the late 1980s onwards, with the underperformance and bankruptcy of SOEs with which many labour service companies were affiliated, production activities organized by these companies gradually shrank and they became more like labour agencies. In the 1990s, SOEs founded re-employment service centres and labour dispatch agencies. Most centres were closed down in the early 2000s when mass layoffs receded. Labour dispatch agencies affiliated with SOEs were gradually shut down after the enforcement of the LCL in 2008, which banned employers from establishing labour dispatch agencies to provide agency workers to themselves.[28]

In 1991, of the 13,812 labour agencies nationwide, 70 per cent were owned by local labour bureaus and 30 per cent by local trade unions, local women's federations, local personnel bureaus, and SOEs, among others.[29] In 1992, private registered labour agencies nationwide totalled only 350, mainly for peasant workers.[30] In the 1990s, when the state stopped assigning jobs to college graduates, personnel bureaus expanded their labour agencies to help college students find jobs, including as agency workers.[31] Many local health bureaus and hospitals operated labour dispatch agencies to provide nurses and doctors for themselves. Local propaganda bureaus operated such agencies to provide editors and journalists for themselves.[32]

Furthermore, to satisfy foreign companies' growing labour needs, inspired by the success of the FESCO, many state organs established their own foreign service companies, which later developed into comprehensive HR service suppliers. For example, in 1986 the Ministry of Labour founded what was later known as the China Star International Economic and Technical Corporation; in 1987 the Committee of National Science and Technology (the predecessor to the Ministry of

[26] Tu 2007. [27] Ministry of Labour 1991, 318. [28] Interview O1.
[29] China Labour Data Centre 1993. [30] Zeng et al. 2008, 180. [31] Xu 2013.
[32] Zheng 2010, 27–29.

Science and Technology) founded the China International Intellectech Corporation; and in 1991 the State Administration for Industry and Commerce founded the China International Enterprise Co-operation Corporation. In the mid 1990s, together with the FESCO and the China International Talent Exchange Centre, these companies monopolized labour dispatch to foreign institutions in Beijing.[33] In a 2017 ranking by the Confederation of Chinese Enterprises and the Association of Chinese Entrepreneurs, of the top 500 Chinese enterprises that generated the highest revenue, the China International Intellectech Corporation and the FESCO were the only two HR enterprises shortlisted.[34]

As labour shortages emerged in the early 2000s, private labour dispatch agencies expanded rapidly. After China joined the World Trade Organization in 2001, foreign HR companies such as Manpower and Adecco entered the country by founding joint ventures with Chinese companies.[35] As a result, in China in the 2010s, major players in the labour dispatch industry were (1) state-owned, usually large-scale foreign-service HR companies, which went well beyond providing agency workers to foreign enterprises; (2) labour dispatch agencies run by local labour bureaus and other state organs; (3) private, usually small labour dispatch agencies with limited assets; and (4) joint ventures between foreign and Chinese HR companies.[36] State organs' deep involvement in the labour dispatch business prevented them from genuinely enforcing regulations against abuse of agency workers.[37]

### *New Workforce Dualism*

As a result of the above factors, the number of agency workers grew fast, and the dualism between formal and agency workers defines the employment structure of enterprises in present-day China. According to surveys conducted by the MOHRSS, in Shanghai, the proportion of agency workers in the workforce of enterprises increased from 28.3 per cent in 2003 to 39.7 per cent in 2008.[38] A survey by the ACFTU found that, in 2011, agency workers nationwide totalled forty-two million, including thirty-seven million in enterprises (13.1 per cent of the workforce in enterprises ) and five million in state organs and public institutions.[39]

Enterprises of different ownership types had different proportions of agency workers. According to the ACFTU, in 2011, agency workers accounted for 16.2 per cent of the workforce in SOEs, 14 per cent in

[33] Chang 1999. [34] SOE News 2017. [35] Interview O10.
[36] Zheng 2010, 27–29. [37] ACFTU 2014, 80. [38] Zhang 2012, 62.
[39] ACTFU 2012.

Table 7.2 *Top users of agency workers in China by industry, 2011.*

| China | | Shanghai | | Ningbo | |
|---|---|---|---|---|---|
| Construction | 36.2% | Business services leasing | 68.5% | Mail and telecoms | 72.3% |
| Information communication and computer-related services | 17.9% | Real estate | 63.2% | Petrochemical operations | 56.0% |
| Electricity, gas, and water supply | 15.3% | Wholesaling and retailing | 47.9% | Metallurgy | 54.0% |
| Scientific research and technology services | 12.7% | Hydraulic projects and environment | 40.6% | Ports | 43.0% |
| Finance | 11.1% | Manufacturing | 38.7% | Air transport | 37.5% |
| Manufacturing | 10.1% | Information technologies | 35.1% | Electricity | 32.9% |

*Source*: ACFTU 2012; 2014, 181–189. Shanghai Bureau of Human Resources and Social Security 2011 (unpublished source).

foreign enterprises, and 2.7 per cent in private enterprises.[40] A 2011 investigation by the MOHRSS involving 86 of the 117 central SOEs (*yangqi*) (key SOEs affiliated with the central government) revealed that, of the workforces of the enterprises surveyed, 60.5 per cent were formal contract workers, 12.9 per cent were agency workers, 22.1 per cent were outsourced workers, and 4.5 per cent were recalled retired workers, seconded employees, and other workers; of the agency workers in the enterprises surveyed, 58.5 per cent had worked there for over two years and 21.7 per cent for over five years; half of these enterprises had different compensation schemes for formal and agency workers.[41]

Agency workers were more common in some industries than others. Table 7.2 shows the proportions of agency workers in the workforce of industries using agency labour most extensively in 2011. Clearly, services, construction, and industries dominated by SOEs (for example, telecoms, energy, air transport, finance, and utilities) were large users of agency workers.

Compared with formal contract workers, agency workers face systematic discrimination. They tend to work in low-skilled positions and earn less than formal employees in comparable positions. They tend to have

[40] ACTFU 2012. [41] Zhang 2012, 167–197.

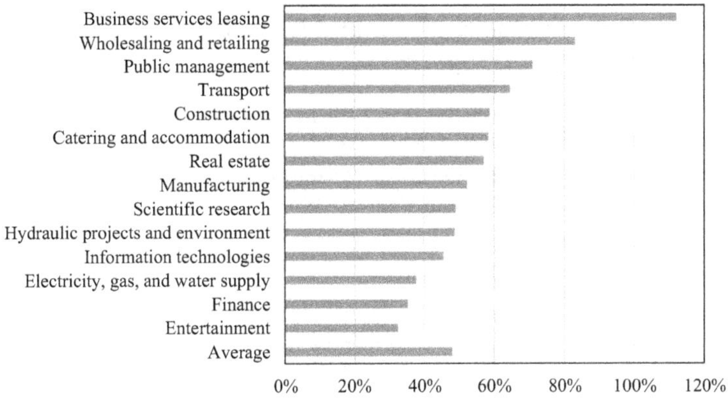


Figure 7.1 Agency workers' wages as a percentage of those of formal employees in Shanghai, 2010.
*Source*: Shanghai Bureau of Human Resources and Social Security 2011 (unpublished source).

limited access to safety education and equipment. However, compensation discrimination forces them to work harder than formal workers to increase their wages, exposing them to greater safety risks. According to a survey conducted by the ACFTU, in China in 2011, the ratio of the average wage of agency workers, peasant workers and urban rank-and-file employees was 0.59:0.77:1, excluding welfare benefits.[42] According to a survey of 363 units using agency workers in Shanghai in 2003, the average monthly wage of agency workers was 80 to 90 per cent of that of formal workers, and agency workers accounted for approximately 80 per cent of all work-related deaths in these units.[43] In Shanghai in 2010, agency workers earned, on average, 48.1 per cent of the wages of formal employees (Figure 7.1). The real compensation gap may have been larger, since discrimination against agency workers with regard to welfare benefits was even worse.[44] In addition, compared with formal employees in comparable positions, agency workers were less likely to join trade unions, receive training, or be promoted.[45]

[42] ACFTU 2014, 94. [43] Tu 2007, 21. [44] ACFTU 2010, 251; 2014, 80.
[45] Shanghai Bureau of Human Resources and Social Security. 2011. Guanyu benshi laowu paiqian yonggong de zongti qingkuang ji guifan laowu paiqian de chubu jianyi (The general conditions of agency labour in Shanghai and preliminary suggestions for labour dispatch regulation), unpublished, collected in fieldwork.

## Introducing the LCL and Its Effects

In the face of growing labour grievances, the Hu administration changed gear towards labour protection and promulgated the LCL in 2007. The divergence between the provisions of the LCL and their implementation illustrates why legal counter-movements in the post-Mao era are incomplete from a Polanyian perspective.[46]

The LCL has been the result of bargaining between various stakeholders in employment relationships, which remains ongoing. The ACFTU, which was the most radical promoter of labour protection among state organs, managed to achieve broad participation of workers at the consultation stage of the LCL. In March 2006, the Standing Committee of the National People's Congress – the legislature of China – publicized a draft of the LCL for public consultation. Within a month, over 190,000 opinions were collected, approximately 70 per cent of which were contributed by workers mobilized by the ACFTU.[47]

Charged with the dual responsibility of employment promotion and labour protection, the MOHRSS was less determined than the ACFTU about labour protection. The MOHRSS and its local branches (labour bureaus) were also deeply involved in the labour dispatch business. Moreover, since SOEs were large users of agency workers, the State-owned Assets Commission, the state organ responsible for the regulation and performance of SOEs, stood firmly against more labour protection.[48] Naturally, employers also pushed hard for less protection.

Disagreements between these parties were cut short by news reports of slave labour in brickyards in Shanxi, which appalled the whole country. In June 2007, the LCL was unanimously passed by members of the Standing Committee of the National People's Congress.[49] The LCL significantly enhances labour protection, reflecting the ACFTU's power at the national level, which has been consolidated by labour insurgency.[50] The LCL aims to formalize and stabilize the employment relationship. It has three key provisions.

First, to counter the pervasive absence of labour contracts, the LCL stipulates that written labour contracts must be drawn up within a month of employment. Otherwise, if the employee has worked for more than a year without a contract, the employer and the employee are deemed to have concluded an open-ended labour contract; and if the employee has worked for over a month but less than a year, the employer must pay the employee double wages for this period. Second, to counter the abuse of

[46] Friedman 2014. [47] Wang 2007. [48] Interviews O18 and O20.
[49] Dong 2011, 3–8. [50] Friedman 2014.

short-term contracts, the LCL stipulates that an open-ended labour contract must be concluded once the employee has worked for the employer for a consecutive period of over ten years, or when fixed-term labour contracts have been concluded on two consecutive occasions. Third, to counter arbitrary dismissals, the LCL stipulates that severance fees should be paid to workers if they are dismissed before their labour contracts expire, and the longer they work for the employer, the higher the fees are. Together with the Social Insurance Law, the LCL also strives to broaden the coverage of social insurance. In addition, the LCL has one chapter countering the abuse of agency workers.

The LCL has delivered some positive results for workers, but has also had unintended consequences, reflecting the impotence of workers at the local level to guarantee the enforcement of the law.[51] Studies indicate that, following the LCL's implementation, the proportion of peasant workers with written contracts increased in 2009,[52] but less progress was made in increasing social insurance coverage.[53] Interview data collected in 2017 revealed that the proportion of workers with contracts lasting for at least three years had also increased.[54] Meanwhile, the effects of the LCL have been found to be larger on SOEs than on private enterprises,[55] and on urban than peasant workers.[56] Ironically, studies report that the LCL itself fuelled precarious employment by invoking layoffs and labour dispatch.[57] According to a survey by the ACFTU, the proportion of agency workers in the enterprise workforce increased by 36.1 per cent in Shanghai between 2007 and 2011, and by 47.1 per cent in Jiangsu between 2008 and 2011.[58]

Employers have constantly attacked the LCL. The six months between its enactment (June 2007) and enforcement (January 2008) witnessed fierce counter-moves from employers. A high-profile case was Huawei, one of the world's largest manufacturers of telecommunications equipment. Between September and December 2007, to evade the LCL's requirement of open-ended contracts, Huawei pushed employees who had worked there for over eight years to resign and then re-sign contracts of one to three years on a competitive basis. Thousands of employees were involved.[59]

[51] Friedman 2014.
[52] Li and Freeman 2015. This article draws on data collected in 2006, 2008, and 2009. Figure 6.3 shows that the proportion of outbound peasant workers with written labour contracts increased between 2010 and 2012 and decreased between 2012 and 2016.
[53] Gallagher et al. 2015. [54] Interview O20. [55] Cui, Ge, and Jing 2013.
[56] Cheng, Smyth, and Guo 2015. [57] Wang et al. 2009; Cairns 2015.
[58] ACFTU 2012. [59] Qiu 2007.

Public debates arose in 2016 on whether the LCL should be revised. Employers and supporting politicians blamed the slowdown in economic growth from 2010 onwards on the LCL. They accused it of rigidifying the labour market, and claimed that it should therefore be revised to lean more towards employers.[60] In contrast, the anti-revision camp comprised mainly scholars and some labour officials. The strongest refutation of the pro-revision camp came from Zhou Guoliang, vice leader of the Labour and Personnel Disputes Arbitration Office of Shanghai. Based on sample data on labour costs of enterprises in Shanghai between 2001 and 2014, he found that the average annual growth rate of per capita labour costs in Shanghai was 10.34 per cent in 2001–2007 and 11.88 per cent in 2008–2014, and the rise in labour costs following enactment of the LCL was accompanied by a rise in profits per unit of labour costs. In addition, social insurance contributions and severance fees as a proportion of gross labour costs hardly increased, reflecting the fact that related provisions were poorly implemented.[61] Moreover, scholars in this camp argued that the increase in labour costs in the 2010s was due primarily to labour shortages.[62] These debates continued thereafter. By mid 2025, the LCL had been amended only once to enhance the protection of agency workers.

## Countering Abuse of Agency Workers and Its Effects

The explosive growth of agency workers threatened the dominance of formal contract workers in enterprises and destabilized employment. The discrimination against agency workers, particularly in wages, was a major trigger for labour unrest, such as the Delphi workers' strike in Beijing in 2013,[63] Nokia workers' strike in Beijing in 2014,[64] and Volkswagen workers' protest in Changchun (a city in northeast China) in 2017.[65] Under such circumstances, to counter the abuse of agency labour, the government introduced the LCL, an amendment to the LCL, and the Interim Provisions on Labour Dispatch (*Interim Provisions* thereafter). This section examines how these agency labour regulations were implemented at the local level, and under what constraints they failed to deliver the expected effects, thus providing another example of the incompleteness of legal counter-movements in the post-Mao era. Such failure made agency labour an expedient backdoor for employers to evade the LCL and sustained abuse of agency labour.[66]

[60] Chen 2015; Jiang and Wang 2016; Wang 2016. [61] Zhou 2016. [62] Xie 2017.
[63] Sina Caijing 2013. [64] RedChinaCn.net 2014. [65] Kohlmann 2017.
[66] Contents of this section are used with permission of SAGE Publications Ltd. Journals, from [Regulating labour dispatch in China: a cat-and-mouse game, Xiaojun Feng, *China*

The 2007 LCL requires that labour dispatch agencies should hold a minimum of 0.5 million *yuan* as registered capital and sign two-year or longer labour contracts with dispatched workers, and that user enterprises should place agency labour 'generally' in temporary, auxiliary, or substitute positions. Moreover, agency workers are entitled to equal pay for equal work to formal employees in the accepting unit. The effects of these provisions, however, had been largely offset by the effects of LCL's provisions pertaining to formal employment, such as open-ended labour contracts, social insurance, and severance fees, leading to the abuse of agency labour.

To counter the growth of agency labour after the enactment of the LCL, an amendment to the LCL was introduced in 2012. It increases the amount of minimum registered capital of labour dispatch agencies to two million *yuan*. It requires labour dispatch agencies to obtain licences before operation. It further details the provision of equal pay for equal work by requiring the unit that uses agency labour to adopt a unified compensation scheme for its own employees and agency workers. The amendment also escalates the wording of 'generally' to 'only' and defines the three kinds of positions open for agency labour: temporary positions lasting less than six months; auxiliary positions providing supplementary services to the primary business; and substitute positions being ad hoc vacancies created by the temporary absence of regular employees.

The Interim Provisions enacted in 2013 has been the most rigorous regulation against the abuse of agency labour. It required that all enterprises lower the proportion of agency workers in their workforce to a maximum of 10 per cent before 1 March 2016. This provision exempted state organs and public institutions, despite their heavy use of agency workers. The question is: how and how well have these regulations been implemented?

The MOHRSS proposed three guiding principles concerning the enforcement of these regulations: these regulations could not result in unemployment, disturb the operation of enterprises, or threaten social stability.[67] After the initial campaign-style enforcement at the local level, the daily enforcement of these regulations adopted a 'no reports from below, no action from above' approach. Aggrieved agency workers could turn to local labour inspectorates and local labour disputes arbitration committees for help, and might then file a lawsuit when necessary.[68]

*Information* 33(1), 2019]; permission conveyed through Copyright Clearance Center, Inc.

67 Interview O3. 68 Interviews O3, O8, O13, O14, and O17.

### *Equal Pay for Equal Work*

Unequal pay for equal work provoked fierce criticisms of labour dispatch. The provision of equal pay for equal work is phrased as: 'Agency workers shall have the right to receive the same pay as that received by employees of the accepting unit for the same work. The accepting unit shall adopt the same compensation policy for agency workers and formal employees in comparable positions according to the principle of equal pay for equal work.' It at best narrowed the gap in wages between formal and agency workers in some enterprises, but failed to narrow the gap in welfare benefits.

Labour officials were sluggish in enforcing equal pay for equal work because employers loathed it. They also found it hard to implement because of the ambiguity of the concept of 'equal work' and 'equal pay'. As a result, formalistic compliance, rather than substantive compliance, was pursued through creative implementation of this provision. When informed of related violations, the local labour inspectorate would ask the enterprise to provide the documentation of its compensation policy to see whether it included agency workers. If it did not, then the enterprise was required to include them. If it did but agency workers were underpaid, the inspectorate would ask the enterprise whether the compensation policy had been approved by the congress of employees' representatives or its equivalents. If it had been approved, the current compensation policy had to be respected even though it discriminated against agency workers. If not, the inspectorate would ask the enterprise to submit the compensation policy to the congress or its equivalents for discussion. However, even labour officials themselves doubted whether the congress of employees' representatives or its equivalents could represent the interests of workers, to say nothing of the fact that they were usually made up only of formal employees.[69]

Litigation could hardly help agency workers either. The Supreme People's Court of China required that judicial documents (with few exceptions) issued by local courts should be available online at wenshu.court.gov.cn from mid 2013. Ninety-two judicial documents issued by courts in Shanghai were available at this website in January 2017, in which plaintiffs, who were all agency workers, asked for equal pay for equal work. No plaintiffs prevailed in court. Judges held that these agency workers lacked evidence of underpayment or job responsibilities comparable to formal employees, or because the employers lawfully differentiated pay based on each worker's diploma, job tenure, work

[69] Interviews O8 and O14.

experience, performance, and the like. This finding is consistent with Philip Huang's findings. Drawing on the adjudication of cases involving labour dispatch disputes between 2012 and 2016 from the database of the Supreme People's Court of China, he found that agency workers had difficulties in claiming equal pay for equal work.[70]

On the ground, to avoid equal work, some employers avoided placing agency workers and formal employees in similar positions. In foreign enterprises of the Xiqing Economic–Technological Development Area in Tianjin in 2016, agency workers were commonly placed in rank-and-file positions while formal employees were mostly in management.[71] Some employers, however, just changed job titles to avoid equal work. For example, agency workers were 'drivers' while formal employees were 'senior drivers', although they might have similar driving skills and work experience.[72]

The remuneration gap between formal and agency workers was the largest in SOEs where the wages of formal workers were beyond market adjustments.[73] According to a manager of a central SOE, equal pay for equal work, once fully realized, could cost twenty-six billion of the thirty billion *yuan* profit in his industry in 2012. Thus, SOEs were strong opponents of this provision, and successfully forced the proponents, including the ACFTU and the MOHRSS, to make a concession: equal pay for equal work should not include social insurance and other welfare benefits.[74]

To avoid legal risks pertaining to equal pay, some employers narrowed the remuneration gap between agency workers and formal employees. For example, Shandong Airways launched several rounds of wage increases for agency workers in the 2010s.[75] Some employers, particularly labour-intensive foreign enterprises, however, obscured equal pay by adopting different compensation schemes between agency workers and formal employees. At Foxconn in Shenzhen in the 2010s, while agency workers were paid solely hourly rates, formal workers were paid structural wages that included base wages, overtime, and bonuses; to earn the same wages, agency workers had to work longer hours than formal employees in comparable positions.[76] After the promulgation of the amendment to the LCL, while some employers adopted a unified payment system for the two groups of workers, they retained the large gap in bonuses between them. For example, in a state-owned steel company in Changsha in the mid 2010s, the normal festive bonuses were

[70] Huang 2017a, 2017b. [71] Interviews W33–W47. [72] Interview O5.
[73] Interview O8. [74] MOHRSS 2014. [75] Interview O5.
[76] Interviews W69–W77.

200 *yuan* for agency workers and 20,000 to 50,000 *yuan* for formal employees when the business was buoyant.[77]

In addition, after the enforcement of the regulations, in SOEs, formal employees enjoyed the five kinds of social insurance, the housing fund, and other benefits; in contrast, agency workers usually enjoyed three kinds of social insurance (for healthcare, occupational disease, and retirement, respectively) and had no access to the housing fund and other benefits, which could amount to a significant percentage of their wages when monetized. In most foreign and private enterprises, social insurance, the housing fund, and overtime pay remained the privilege of formal employees. Labour dispatch agencies would buy agency workers cheap commercial insurance against work-related injury (around 20 *yuan* per month per capita in 2016) instead.[78]

### *Ten Per Cent Cap*

The number of agency workers did decrease after the promulgation of the Interim Provisions. In Shanghai, the number of agency workers dropped from a peak of 1.33 million to 0.88 million at the end of 2015.[79] In Guangdong, the number fell from a peak of 1.63 million to 0.85 million in mid 2016. According to an official of the Labour Bureau of Guangzhou, of the 100 randomly selected enterprises in Guangzhou in 2016, 76 per cent had reduced their number of agency workers by at least 20 per cent after the enactment of the Interim Provisions.[80] The majority of labour dispatch agencies the author investigated in 2016 also reported a significant shrinkage of their business. However, it is too early to conclude that the Interim Provisions successfully curbed the excessive use of agency labour in China.

Employers mainly used two methods to deal with the 10 per cent cap: temp-to-formal conversion (TFC) and dispatch-to-outsourcing conversion (DOC).[81] TFC means that agency workers were transformed into formal employees of the accepting enterprise. It was what the regulation aimed to achieve, since agency workers tended to be better off after a TFC. DOC means that agency workers were transformed into 'outsourced' workers. The standard practice of labour dispatch and outsourcing and the common practice of DOC are specified below.

In standard labour dispatch, the accepting unit signs a labour dispatch contract with the labour dispatch agency; the labour dispatch agency

[77] Interview W54. [78] Interviews O1, O5, and O10. [79] Interview O8.
[80] Interview O3.
[81] This section is based on Interviews O1–O17, unless otherwise specified.

signs labour contracts with agency workers and dispatches them to the accepting unit who manages their labour process; the agency receives a monthly package from the accepting unit, including commissions for itself, wages for dispatched workers, and insurance contributions for local social insurance bureaus; only the commissions are taxed. In standard outsourcing, the issuing party signs an outsourcing contract with the contractor and contracts out certain tasks to it; the contractor signs labour contracts with its employees and manages them to accomplish the task at its premises using its machines, as is the case between Apple and its contract manufacturer Foxconn;[82] the contractor receives a revenue based on the quantity and quality of the task finished; the whole revenue is taxed.

Although there is no legislation clarifying the major difference between labour dispatch and outsourcing in China, in practice, interviewees concurred that the difference lay in who managed the workers (which is reminiscent of the criterion to distinguish outsourced workers from normal temporary workers in Shanghai in the 1960s) and what type of revenue was taxed.

By contrast, the common practice of DOC triggered by the 10 per cent cap was the following: the enterprise re-signed a business outsourcing contract to replace the previous labour dispatch contract, usually with the same labour dispatch agency, or with companies jointly owned by the enterprise and the labour dispatch agency. The latter paid taxes for such a business as contractors, rather than as labour dispatch agencies. Since the regulation does not provide clear definitions of agency workers and outsourced workers, by changing the documentation and the taxation arrangement, user enterprises could disguise agency workers as 'outsourced' workers. 'Outsourced' workers often continued to work at the facilities of the accepting unit and under its management. That is why such practice is called 'actual labour dispatch, disguised as outsourcing'.

Employers might have sought to outsource some business to contractors, as in the case of Apple with Foxconn. However, they simply would not have found enough mature contractors since agency labour was widely and massively deployed in various industries in China, which were at the lower end of GCCs. In addition to labour, production facilities, processing techniques, and management were all crucial for standard contractors, thus creating high-entry barriers for labour dispatch agencies to engage in genuine outsourcing. With formal workers placed in management and the majority of informal workers working in

[82] Chan, Pun, and Selden 2013.

rank-and-file positions, coupled with the need to impose quality control, the issuing enterprise had to be deeply involved in the management of the 'outsourced' work, resulting in 'actual labour dispatch, disguised as outsourcing'. Such practice was so prevalent that labour officials in Shanghai said that the majority of 'business outsourcing' derived from labour dispatch fell into this category.

The lawmakers of the Interim Provisions were aware of the potential prevalence of such creative compliance. In the consultation draft of the Interim Provisions, Article 2 stipulates that 'labour dispatch refers to the employment practice in which the labour dispatch agency dispatches its employees to the accepting unit that manages these workers. Outsourcing business to contractors but retaining the management of workers of contractors is one form of labour dispatch'. According to this provision, the practice of 'actual labour dispatch, disguised as outsourcing' is regarded as one form of labour dispatch, which cannot help enterprises to approach the 10 per cent cap. However, Article 2 in the consultation draft was deleted in the enforced version. Local labour officials concurred that the 10 per cent cap was so stringent that it forced employers to respond creatively. They knew the prevalence of such 'outsourcing' but imposed no penalties on employers involved. They also complained that the 10 per cent cap lacked social support. Employers loathed it while agency workers cared more about income than employment status.

A questionnaire survey of approximately 5,000 enterprises in twenty cities co-conducted by the MOHRSS and the FESCO in mid 2013 indicates that, among enterprises that once had over 10 per cent of the workforce as agency workers, 28.6 per cent hired the majority of agency workers directly, 40.2 per cent transformed the majority of agency workers into 'outsourced' workers, and 2.2 per cent moved labour-intensive businesses out of China.[83] Interviews with local labour officials show that, in Suzhou New District in 2016, 70 to 80 per cent of agency workers worked under the name of 'outsourced' workers;[84] in Guangzhou, after the enactment of the Interim Provisions, around 33 per cent of enterprises surveyed formalized all agency workers, and 54 per cent introduced 'outsourcing'.[85]

At the enterprise level, SOEs were highly responsive to the 10 per cent cap (Table 7.3). While a substantial percentage of agency workers became formal workers, many agency workers and new recruits became 'outsourced' workers (layoffs were rare). Among foreign enterprises,

[83] FESCO 2013. [84] Interview O14. [85] Interview O3.

Table 7.3 *A sample of SOEs' response to the 10 per cent cap.*

| No. | Location | Industry | AW Peak, % | 2016, % |
|---|---|---|---|---|
| 1 | Guangdong | Communication | | OW, 47.6 |
| 2 | Guangdong | Energy | 80 | AW, 6.5; OW, 14.8 |
| 3 | Guangdong | Logistics | 50 | AW, 19; OW, 17.8 |
| 4 | Shanghai | Communication | | AW, 2.6; OW, 39.5 |
| 5 | Shanghai | Logistics | 61 | AW, 36 |
| 6 | Shanghai | Energy | | AW, 1.7; OW, 5.1 |
| 7 | Suzhou | Energy | | OW, 86.8 |
| 8 | Shandong | Communication | 70 | AW, 7 |
| 9 | Shandong | Manufacturing | 37 | AW, 14.9; OW, 8.3 |
| 10 | Shandong | Transport | | AW, 9.9 |
| 11 | Shandong | Logistics | | AW, 24.7; OW, 9.3 |

*Source*: Interviews O2, O6, O9, O11, O12, and O15.
*Note*: AW: agency workers; OW: 'outsourced' workers.

those using agency labour owing to the headcount constraint imposed by their headquarters tended to prioritize compliance with the Chinese law and transform the majority of agency workers into formal employees. Those placing agency workers in labour-intensive businesses such as retailing and manufacturing, however, tended to ignore the cap or transform agency workers into 'outsourced' workers. Labour dispatch remained their best way to cope with fluctuating tasks.[86] In late 2016, agency workers continued to dominate the shop floors of some electronics contract manufacturers in Tianjin, Changsha, and Shenzhen.[87]

The cap had various effects. Both TFC and DOC raised labour costs (Table 7.4). For TFC, employers needed to close the remuneration gap between newly transformed formal workers and previous formal workers in comparable positions in wages, basic social insurance, extra insurance, the housing fund, and bonuses, and pay extra fees associated with formal employees, such as the trade union fee. The enterprise also needed to increase the remuneration of these new formal workers according to length of tenure and pay them pensions after they retired as the enterprise did for previous formal workers. In this way, the increase in labour costs due to TFC was relatively low in the first year of the conversion and would grow annually. DOC was also more expensive than labour dispatch. While only the commission paid by the accepting unit was taxed in labour dispatch, the whole revenue was taxed in outsourcing. Moreover,

[86] Interviews O9 and O12. [87] Interviews W33–W54 and W69–W77.

Table 7.4 *Labour costs increase due to the cap in several enterprises.*

| No. | Location | Ownership | Labour costs increase in the first year |
|---|---|---|---|
| 1 | Guangdong | State-owned | Unknown owing to TFC, at least 8% owing to DOC |
| 2 | Guangdong | State-owned | At least 8% owing to TFC, thirty million *yuan* owing to DOC |
| 3 | Shanghai | Foreign | 12–15% owing to TFC, 17% owing to DOC |
| 4 | Shanghai | State-owned | No TFC, 25% owing to DOC |
| 5 | Shandong | State-owned | At least 12% owing to TFC, unknown owing to DOC |
| 6 | Shandong | State-owned | 10,000–20,000 *yuan* per capita owing to TFC, unknown owing to DOC |

*Source*: Interviews O2, O6, O9, and O11.
*Note*: The base for the percentage increase is previous labour costs of related agency labour.

'contractors' needed money to buy extra business insurance to hedge the risk of more employer responsibility de jure.

For agency workers, their welfare increased when they were formalized, and decreased when they were transformed into 'outsourced' workers. 'Outsourced' workers were more remote from the accepting unit in employment relationships and could not be transformed into formal workers (while agency workers could). Some enterprises even lowered the pay of 'outsourced' workers to offset the cost increase due to DOC. While Chinese labour regulations have specific provisions against the abuse of agency workers, they do not have specific provisions against the abuse of 'outsourced' workers generated by 'actual labour dispatch, disguised as outsourcing'. In response, many 'outsourced' workers invoked by the 10 per cent cap chose to leave the enterprise. For example, the annual turnover rate of agency workers in an SOE in Guangdong used to be about 6 to 7 per cent. However, the company lost around 20 per cent of its 'outsourced' workers between January and September 2016.[88]

### *Other Provisions*

Another major provision to counter the abuse of agency labour was that agency workers were only to be placed in temporary, auxiliary, and substitute positions. Although the amendment to the LCL defines these three kinds of positions, it is still difficult to judge whether the placement

[88] Interview O2.

of agency workers is legitimate in many cases. For example, it is hard to judge whether the positions of HR managers in a toy factory are auxiliary according to the amendment that defines auxiliary staff as those providing supplementary services to the primary business – more legal detail is needed to differentiate 'primary' from 'supplementary'. In practice, as with the implementation of equal pay for equal work, local labour bureaus trusted the congress of employees' representatives or its equivalents in enterprises to delimit the coverage of temporary, auxiliary, and substitute positions. Thus, procedural justice again triumphed over resultant justice.[89] Agency workers were still employed on assembly lines of contract manufacturers, call centres of communication service providers, and other positions alike.[90]

The effort to raise the entry threshold of labour dispatch agencies was also in vain. An increase in the amount of minimum registered capital from 0.5 million to 2 million *yuan* could hardly prevent the proliferation of small, asset-light agencies. In all the cities where the author's research team had interviews with local labour officials, labour dispatch agencies could easily buy from professional asset firms an asset verification report of 2 million *yuan* at a cost of 5,000 to 20,000 *yuan*. Local labour bureaus had no capacity to authenticate these reports. They were exposed to the risk of administrative litigation if they refused to issue licences for labour dispatch to labour agencies with such reports, even if they knew that those agencies were family-run and operated in the owners' home. The entry threshold was so low that, after the enforcement of the regulations, the labour dispatch market remained crowded with tiny, unscrupulous agencies, which made docking of wages and insurance contributions a daily occurrence.[91]

The provision that aims to stabilize the employment of agency workers fails as well. The lawmakers expected to use the requirement of two-year or longer labour contracts with agency workers to force labour dispatch agencies to channel agency workers among enterprises with different peak times. However, none of the agencies interviewed liked this idea because it was risky. Once a worker is returned, the agency is required by the government to pay the local minimum wage before the worker is re-dispatched. This responsibility is too heavy to shoulder, as labour dispatch agencies earn only meagre commissions from enterprises. Even if agency workers were on two-year contracts with agencies but were returned by accepting units halfway, agencies could still circumvent the

[89] Interviews O8, O13, and O14.
[90] Interviews W1–W82.
[91] Interviews O3, O5, and O16.

minimum wage responsibility by, for example, threatening to dispatch them to remote places to force them to resign.[92]

*Constrained Regulation: Old Legacies and 'New Normal'*

The limited success of the regulations reflects the impotence of agency workers at the local level to ensure their enforcement. It also resulted from China's ongoing transformation from a planned economy to a market economy and the 'new normal'.

On the one hand, the legacy of the planned economy is still felt, even if market-orientated reforms have been ongoing for over forty years. One labour official in Shanghai put it bluntly: 'The remuneration gap between agency workers and formal employees is the largest in SOEs, not because agency workers there are too poorly paid but because formal employees there are too well paid.'[93] Equal pay for equal work cannot be achieved in SOEs with the compensation of formal workers protected by the state and the compensation of agency workers determined by the labour market. Moreover, as with the planned-economy era, the wage quota of SOEs in present-day China is still controlled by the government. Although the Interim Provisions requires SOEs to comply with the 10 per cent gap, the State-owned Assets Commission insisted that the wage quota of individual SOEs could only be adjusted according to its financial performance, not according to the number of employees, thus forcing SOEs to transform agency workers into 'outsourced' workers to lower their percentage of agency workers.[94]

The rural–urban dualism institutionalized in the planned-economy era also hampers the enforcement of the regulations by locking migrant agency workers – the majority of agency workers in China – in a state of continuous migration between work cities and their hometown. Interviews with migrant agency workers indicate that working in large cities to make money and settling down in small cities or hometown villages remains the dominant trajectory. Emboldened by the shortage of young blue-collar workers in the 2010s, peasant workers at prime ages interviewed said that they changed jobs frequently and had no worries of unemployment. Under such circumstances, the regulations alone could hardly stabilize their employment.

Meanwhile, although the gap in social insurance between agency workers and formal employees is salient, particularly in foreign and private enterprises, peasant workers are discouraged from contributing

[92] Interviews W69–W82. [93] Interview O8. [94] Interviews O2, O6, O11, and O15.

to or demanding employers to contribute to the social insurance pool of the cities in which they work. Such contributions not only lowered their present income but also might not translate into real benefits owing to their mobility and the obstacles in transferring social insurance entitlements among different regions of China because of the *hukou* system.

On the other hand, the fact that China has been experiencing a 'new normal' has diverted the priority of the government away from labour protection towards economic revitalization and employment promotion. To lower the operating costs of enterprises, particularly labour costs, the government has reduced contributions to social insurance and to the housing fund by employers, and increases to minimum wages. For example, in Guangdong, the provincial government lowered the average premium rate of occupational injury insurance contributed by employers from 0.63 to 0.43 per cent in 2015, lowered the premium rate of unemployment insurance contributed by employers from 1.5 to 0.8 per cent in 2016, and froze minimum wages for three years between May 2015[95] and July 2018, which had been adjusted annually or biennially since 1999. It is worth noting that labour dispatch had already been widely used by employers to avoid contributions to social insurance and the housing fund.

Under such circumstances, the MOHRSS suggested that local labour bureaus should soften the 10 per cent cap and focus more on equal pay for equal work, which excludes social insurance and welfare benefits. Moreover, in 2016 the MOHRSS stopped the initiative of issuing a guideline to distinguish so-called 'outsourcing' from labour dispatch, although considerable preparatory work had been carried out.[96] Thus, labour dispatch and its variations such as 'actual labour dispatch, disguised as outsourcing' were tacitly incorporated into the central government's general plan to cut the operating costs of the real economy. A labour official in Shanghai said incisively: 'It is good news when enterprises are still playing cat-and-mouse games with you. At least, they are still doing business in China. Real troubles come when they stop playing and close down.'[97] Meanwhile, owing to the slowdown of economic growth, in the late 2010s the MOHRSS focused more on employment numbers than before and promoted flexible employment.[98]

## Conclusion

Between the late 1970s and the 2010s, agency workers gradually rose to prominence primarily because they were a cheap and flexible workforce.

[95] Interview O3. [96] Interview O18. [97] Interview O8. [98] Interview O18.

As a result, dualism between formal contract workers and agency workers replaced the Mao-era dualism between formal permanent workers and temporary contract workers, defining the employment structure of enterprises in present-day China. During this process, the state played a double role as both the initiator of reforms that fostered labour dispatch and a supplier of agency workers.

The LCL and the Interim Provisions aim at labour protection with a focus on agency labour. However, these regulations have been poorly implemented, reflecting the impotence of workers at the local level to enforce them and thereby the incompleteness of legal counter-movements in the post-Mao era from a Polanyian perspective. The LCL boosted the coverage of written labour contracts temporarily but not social insurance. Moreover, the LCL led to an explosion of agency workers. Following the enactment of the LCL, the amendment to the LCL, and the Interim Provisions, while some enterprises narrowed the remuneration gap between agency workers and formal employees, others retained large gaps in bonuses and welfare benefits. The regulations reduced the number of agency workers but also invoked the abuse of more precarious 'outsourced' workers. They had little effect in limiting the use of agency labour to temporary, auxiliary, or substitute positions, raising the requirements for engaging in the labour dispatch business, or stabilizing agency workers' employment. In addition to workers' impotence, China's ongoing transformation from a planned to a market economy since the late 1970s, and from high growth to a 'new normal' since the early 2010s, has fundamentally constrained the full implementation of these regulations.

# 8 Formal and Agency Workers in the 2010s

So far, this book has chronicled the evolution of labour tenure regimes since 1949. This provides a basis for examining the impacts of cumulative changes since 1949 on workers. As SOEs and export-oriented factories are large users of agency workers, this chapter presents a case study of both formal and agency workers in a large SOE with relatively stable orders, and accounts of agency workers in export-oriented factories with relatively fluctuating orders. It thus covers the two major types of agency workers in China in the 2010s: one with job tenure of years and managed solely by user enterprises, and another one with job tenure of six months or less and managed by both user enterprises and labour dispatch agencies.

## Formal and Agency Workers in an SOE

Capital Express, the fieldwork site chosen for this study, is the Beijing subsidiary of Oriental Express. Oriental Express is the express mail sector of Oriental Star (pseudonym), a giant SOE with multilayered subsidiary facilities across China. The predecessor to Oriental Star was founded in 1878 and remained in business throughout the Republican era, before being taken over by the CCP. In 2012, 52.65 per cent of workers in Oriental Star were agency workers.[1] Following the promulgation of the Interim Provisions in 2013, Oriental Star adopted the practice of 'actual labour dispatch, disguised as outsourcing'. In 2015, formal workers, agency workers, and 'outsourced' workers accounted for 66.4 per cent, 19.2 per cent, and 13.7 per cent of its workforce, respectively.[2] Oriental Express was founded in 1985. At the end of 2011, it had 82,891 workers engaged in the express mail service, of which 67.9 per cent were agency workers.[3] This section first looks at dualism based on employment

[1] Oriental Star annual report 2012, unpublished.
[2] Oriental Star annual report 2015, unpublished.
[3] Oriental Express initial public offerings prospectus, unpublished.

arrangements in the workforce of Capital Express. It then examines the working conditions of formal and agency workers there.[4]

### *Dualism Based on Employment Arrangements*

Oriental Star has a long history of dualism based on employment arrangements. When the CCP took over Oriental Star's predecessor, it applied the 'taking on all and being responsible for all' policy to its formal employees, and formalized temporary workers who were needed regularly. In the Mao era, Oriental Star established an employment system centring on permanent employment. The proportion of branches operated by contractors dropped from over 80 per cent in 1953 to 51.6 per cent in 1956, and further to 23.8 per cent in 1978. Oriental Star also used both-workers-and-peasants in rural areas. In 1971, it had 605,710 workers, 93.4 per cent of whom were permanent workers. This jumped to 97.9 per cent in 1973 following the great formalization. In the early 1980s, Oriental Star began to roll out the labour contract system and re-encourage outsourcing. At the end of 1985, contract workers accounted for 6.5 per cent of its own workforce, and workers in the 14,278 branches operated by contractors amounted to 30.2 per cent of Oriental Star's own workers.[5]

Data from Capital Star, the Beijing subsidiary of Oriental Star, show that, in the Mao era, over 95 per cent of workers there were permanent workers. In 1983, Capital Star introduced the labour contract system. Contract workers signed fixed-term labour contracts with Capital Star and could not be transformed into permanent workers.[6] In the 1990s, the majority of new workers added to Capital Star's workforce were temporary workers. In 1998, Capital Star established a staffing company, which specialized in providing agency labour to itself. Temporary workers were then transformed into agency workers. In 1990, formal workers (both traditional permanent workers and formal contract workers) made up 98.5 per cent of its workforce, whereas in 2012 agency workers accounted for 48.1 per cent.[7]

In mid 2014, Capital Star transferred its agency workers to several private labour dispatch agencies, one of which was Talent Pool. Owing to the Interim Provisions, Capital Star transformed some agency workers

[4] This section was initially published in [Feng, Xiaojun. Trapped in precariousness: migrant agency workers in China's state-owned enterprises. *The China Quarterly* 238: 396–417. 2019] © Cambridge University Press, reproduced with permission. Unless otherwise specified, all data used in this section come from Interviews W1–W30 and O1.

[5] Editorial Board 1988, 56–67. [6] Hu et al. 2004, 340–341.

[7] Capital Star Yearbook 2000–2014, unpublished.

Table 8.1 *Three career tracks at Capital Star, 2016.*

| Career track | Employment status | Composition | Job security and compensation | Number of employees |
|---|---|---|---|---|
| A | Permanent workers | Veteran managers and frontline workers | Good | Negligible |
| B | Formal contract workers | Majority of managers and minority of frontline workers | Medium | Large |
| C | Agency workers | Minority of managers and majority of frontline workers | Bad | Large |

into 'outsourced' workers,[8] and hired new workers in this way. As shown in Table 8.1, in 2016, three career tracks coexisted at Capital Star. Most rank-and-file workers joined Capital Star on track C and had annual opportunities to enter track B. Workers on tracks B and C made up most of the workforce at Capital Star. Workers on track A were legacies of the old employment system. They were hired as permanent workers, and were later transformed into contract workers with open-ended contracts. Their number was small and decreasing since neither new hires nor those on tracks B or C could enter this track.

In December 2008, Capital Star packaged its express mail business and founded Capital Express, which consisted of several subsidiaries. Each subsidiary consisted of several branch outlets (*yingtoubu*). In 2013, each branch outlet packaged some of its big clients, such as schools and business complexes, into networks. In 2014, Capital Express deployed 8,148 workers in over 100 branch outlets.[9] Each branch outlet was responsible for the collection and delivery of express mail in an area of one or two postcodes. In 2016, depending on the traffic of express mail, the number of workers at each branch outlet ranged from twenty to seventy. Over two-thirds were agency workers on track C, fewer than one-third were on track B, and at most one or two were on track A. Each branch outlet was staffed with one manager, dozens of couriers, and several support workers handling the recording and distribution of inward and outward mail, warehousing, and customer service. They

[8] This section uses the term 'agency workers' to refer to both agency workers and 'outsourced' workers, since 'outsourced' workers at Capital Express were managed by Capital Express itself, and were therefore de facto agency workers.

[9] Capital Star Yearbook 2014, unpublished.

were assisted by drivers affiliated directly with Capital Express who transported mail between sorting centres and branch outlets within Beijing. Managers tended to be on track B while couriers and support staff tended to be on track C.

Generally, couriers at Capital Express were young, low-skilled, male peasant workers capable of lifting parcels of up to 40 kilogrammes. They worked full time. At the end of 2011, 44.2 per cent of Oriental Express workers (including agency workers) were under thirty years old, with another 32.3 per cent aged thirty to thirty-nine; 61.3 per cent had a high school diploma, their equivalents, or lower.[10] After a two-day work trial, shortlisted candidates for rank-and-file positions would be asked to sign labour contracts with labour dispatch agencies, for example, Talent Pool. Every month, Talent Pool calculated the wage bill of its dispatched employees according to attendance records and wage distribution methods updated by Capital Express. After Capital Express authenticated the payroll, Talent Pool would receive a payment that covered wages for its dispatched workers, social insurance contributions to be paid to social insurance bureaus, and commissions for Talent Pool itself – the 2016 rate was 65 *yuan* per person per month.

Couriers' working day at Capital Express began at 7.30 am. Along with the support staff, they made preparations before departing for their first delivery round, which usually commenced at 9 am. Carrying mail on their electric tricycles, they shuttled back and forth across the city, calling clients to arrange delivery and receiving instructions for onsite pickups. They began the second shift at 2.30 pm, the third shift at 4.30 pm, and finished deliveries and collections at approximately 6 pm. The working day ended when couriers completed all type-ins, scanned waybills, and handed over the collected money to the accountant at 7 pm, or sometimes 9 pm. Couriers at Capital Express usually enjoyed one day off each week. However, during peak seasons such as the 'double-eleven' online shopping festival in November, they might work a whole month without a break. Couriers' daily tasks and holidays did not vary much according to their employment status and were managed only by Capital Express.

Why did these couriers willingly endure such exhausting work? One put it bluntly: 'Why are we here? To earn money, to create a better environment for our family.'[11] Couriers' wages were determined mainly by a piece-rate system, which did not vary with their employment status. In 2016, the piece rate for delivering one item of mail ranged from 0.5 to 1.2 *yuan*, and the piece rate for collecting a package ranged between

[10] Oriental Express initial public offerings prospectus, unpublished. [11] Interview W12.

8 and 25 per cent of the shipping fare. These two commissions accounted for over 80 per cent of couriers' wages. Although a courier could earn over 10,000 *yuan* in November, their normal monthly wage was between 3,000 and 6,000 *yuan*. The monthly wage of support workers was set as a certain proportion of the gross wage of the branch outlet, mostly around 2,000 to 4,000 *yuan*.

The income gap between agency workers and formal employees at Capital Express was wide previously but had been gradually reduced in the new millennium. In 2004, the annual wage of agency workers increased by 3,000 *yuan*. In 2005, the monthly wage of agency workers increased by 100 *yuan*, while that of formal employees rose by 110 *yuan*. In 2011, agency workers with urban *hukou* were entitled to the housing fund. In 2012, Capital Express began to prioritize agency workers over formal employees when deciding on awards to facilitate agency workers' temp-to-formal conversions.[12] Moreover, all those working for Capital Express were entitled to the five kinds of social insurance. Nevertheless, formal employees did enjoy some exclusive benefits such as extra retirement insurance, extra medical care, allowances for winter heating, childcare, and the like, which amounted to approximately 500 *yuan* per month in 2016.[13]

The employment status of agency workers worsened their working conditions. Meilan, a young mother of a two-year-old, was from a rural village in Hebei, just one hour by train from Beijing. She became an agency worker at Capital Express in 2012. After two two-year contracts, she signed a three-year contract with Sky Labour (a labour agency) in 2016. Her primary responsibility was to record and distribute incoming mail. In a resentful tone, she recounted:

> Every time I receive a lower wage than I deserve, Capital Express always says, 'We don't dock your money. Sky Labour does' ... Female workers at Capital Express all know that to give birth to a child, we have to quit. Otherwise ... one colleague lost her baby in the eighth month of pregnancy. I know another one. The foetus was strangled to death by the umbilical cord in the seventh month. The mother toiled too much. I know four female workers at Capital Express who suffered miscarriages. I asked for maternity leave when I was pregnant. I was refused. I was only permitted to work for shorter hours later when I found I was bleeding.[14]

Meilan's words cast light on the precarious nature of agency labour at Capital Express, particularly for females. Her experience was not exceptional. During my fieldwork, I was often told that labour agencies made

[12] Capital Star Yearbook 2014, unpublished.
[13] Capital Star Yearbook 2009, unpublished.
[14] Interview W24.

profits by docking wages and extracting social insurance fees. Branch outlets' managers might collude with labour agencies, sharing their gains and helping to hide the deception.

> I have a relative working at Land Staffing (an agency labour supplier to Capital Express). I know how it works. For example, for a monthly wage of 6,000 *yuan*, the agency worker only receives 5,000. For the remaining 1,000, Land Staffing takes 100 while the manager of the branch outlet takes 900. I know one manager who bought an apartment in Shandong after running one branch outlet for two years.[15]

> Once we went to the social insurance bureau ... It showed that we paid about 300 *yuan* each month for insurance. But our wage slips showed that we were charged more than 700 *yuan* for insurance fees monthly. We complained to the manager. He asked us to complain to our labour agency. They kicked us back and forth like this.[16]

The fact that many agency workers had their labour contracts renewed did not necessarily mean that their employment was secure. If they made mistakes, agency workers would be sent back to labour agencies and then usually dismissed, while formal employees might simply receive warnings. In 2014, more than 2,200 agency workers were dismissed when Capital Star transferred agency workers from its own labour agency to other labour agencies.[17] Moreover, agency workers faced dismissal at forty-five years of age (for females) or fifty years of age (for males), despite the mandatory retirement age being fifty for female workers and sixty for male workers in production positions in China in 2016, even if they had made no mistakes. In contrast, formal employees at those ages were transferred to less-demanding positions.

### *Precarious Agency Workers, Protected Formal Workers?*

While formal employees of Capital Express were somewhat better off than agency workers, their employment status did not necessarily guarantee them income security. Rather, the income security of both formal and agency workers was subject to the same following factors, which both types of workers were powerless to fight.

The first factor was market competition. China's express mail is a highly competitive market in which state-owned companies compete with private companies for market share. Between 2007 and 2015, in terms of the number of mail items dealt with, the market share of state-owned express delivery companies, of which Oriental Express was the largest, shrank from 59.3 to 9.9 per cent.[18] Although the express delivery

15 Interview W12. 16 Interview W2. 17 Capital Star Yearbook 2015, unpublished.
18 National Post Bureau and Deloitte 2014; National Post Bureau 2016.

industry in China has expanded massively in recent years, Capital Express's revenue declined by 3.85 per cent in 2014 compared with 2013, and its profits dropped from 140 million *yuan* in 2012 to 60.2 million *yuan* in 2013.[19] In response, in late 2015 Capital Express launched a cost saving and efficiency drive, which almost halved the commission rates for both deliveries and collections. This resulted in wages being nearly halved. Welfare benefits were also significantly reduced. Festive gifts such as mooncakes for the Mid-Autumn Festival and dumplings and meat for the Spring Festival, paid annual leave, and partly funded trips had all but disappeared for the rank-and-file staff. For formal employees, the reimbursement rate of medical care was lowered from 87 to 85 per cent in 2014.[20]

Pervasive penalties accounted for the second factor. Penalties affecting the income of branch outlet staff operated at the outlet, network, and individual levels. At the outlet level, penalties were determined by the overall performance of the outlet, including revenue, rates of successful delivery, rates of complaint, and code compliance. For every failure or offence at the outlet level, one point would be deducted in the performance assessment of the branch outlet, resulting in a deduction of 10,000 *yuan* from the gross wage of the branch outlet that month: this penalty was evenly borne by all outlet staff. At the network level, workers running the network collectively faced a financial penalty amounting to 5 per cent of arrears if they failed to collect monthly shipping payments from clients. They also lost 300 *yuan* for every new major client account that they failed to sign up if they did not hit their targets.

Table 8.2 lists the common individual-level penalties imposed on couriers. Informants reported that some punishable offences were so unavoidable that they expected to incur at least two penalties every month. Most important, a verbal dressing down from the managers of the outlet was grounds enough for a penalty to be issued, a situation which, as explained next, emboldened the arbitrary docking of wages.

The third and most sweeping factor affecting wage security was the docking of wages. Wages were co-determined by multilayered entities. Reports of commissions and bonuses were compiled at the lowest level and were scrutinized and summed up by intermediaries before reaching the headquarters of Capital Express. Wages were decided by the headquarters and then shared among the intermediaries according to their performance before reaching individual workers. Combined with other institutions, this wage determination system allowed room for the

[19] Capital Star Yearbook 2013–2015, unpublished.
[20] Capital Star Yearbook 2015, unpublished.

Table 8.2 *Common individual-level penalties for couriers at Capital Express, 2016.*

| Description | Penalty in *yuan* |
|---|---|
| Failing to notify the receiver before delivery | 50 |
| Failing to deliver the mail in due time | 50 |
| Losing one item of mail | 500 |
| Changing the status of mail as 'delivered' before it is | 500 |
| Invoking one receiver to call the service line to track mail | 50 |
| Failing to reach the monthly required successful delivery rate, usually 95 per cent | (1 – achieved rate) times delivery commission |
| Scanning one waybill later than the designated time | 50 |
| Omitting scanning one waybill | 10 |
| Failing to collect the mail within one hour after being notified | 300 |
| Being complained about for service attitude once | 500–1,000 |
| Being complained about to the State Post Bureau once | 1,000–2,000 |

arbitrary docking of wages. Managers often docked wages for the sake of themselves and those under their patronage, usually relatives or friends. Many informants reported the existence of 'zombie' workers who only showed up for one or two days per week (if they appeared at all) but had their names on the payroll. Underperforming managers received only a living allowance equivalent to the minimum monthly wage in Beijing (1,890 *yuan* in 2016), and so were motivated to boost their income by docking the wages of couriers.

Such behaviour was enabled by the following factors. First, each branch outlet operated in its own distinct environment, making it impossible for Capital Express to set universal commission rates. For instance, couriers serving the central business district might deliver 200 items of mail and collect 100 items per day; those in the suburbs might toil all day and end up with only 40 deliveries and no collections. Therefore, commission rates differed in these two places. Second, to encourage competition and boost revenue, Capital Express endowed its lower levels with great autonomy, including over the distribution of wages. According to one network leader, 'there are multiple ways to allocate the money as long as everyone accepts it'.[21] Generally, for individual couriers, the commission rate for each item of mail delivered or collected depended on whether the mail belonged to a certain network, whether the network hit its monthly performance target, whether the recipient or sender was an enterprise client, and the like.

[21] Interview W7.

Third, it was deemed a privilege, rather than a right, for workers to see their monthly wage slips, which detailed payments and deductions. Therefore, rank-and-file workers only had a vague idea of how much they should earn each month. When they received less than expected and complained to managers, common responses included that the commission rates had been changed, that they had been penalized owing to misdemeanours, or that the labour agency had docked the money. One formal employee once roared to me, 'I earned 5,900 *yuan* last month. This month, I get 100 *yuan* more in bonus, but 1,000 *yuan* less in the total wage. How is this possible?! More bonus, less wage!'[22] Most victims chose to bear it silently since they could not prove that their wages were docked and they did not dare offend managers for fear of losing their jobs.

Although rank-and-file workers at Capital Express were resentful of the excessive penalties and arbitrary wage docking, they were powerless to do anything about them. The trade union at Capital Express, to which formal employees paid monthly union subs, turned a blind eye to these violations of workers' rights. The isolated distribution of individual couriers and branch outlets effectively made mass mobilization and organization across branch outlets nearly impossible. Within the branch outlet, my informants reported that there had been occasional strikes and collective resignations, particularly when Capital Express dramatically cut their commission rates in the cost savings and efficiency drive. Workers involved in the strikes were quickly dismissed. An exception was a strike at Capital Express's sorting centre in Beijing International Airport many years before. The sorters' demands were soon met and sorting work shortly resumed. After all, a strike at this critical transport node would have paralysed the operation of not only Capital Express but also Oriental Express.

Couriers, however, did not have as much strategic power as sorters. Compared with migrant workers in other industries, couriers tended to earn higher wages. The wages of couriers at Capital Express might have been lower than those earned at private courier companies, but the difference was compensated for by social insurance. In addition, the low-skilled nature of their work made them highly replaceable. On the one hand, these factors persuaded the majority of the staff at Capital Express to continue working there under such conditions, albeit with ambivalence or even resentment. On the other hand, they also guaranteed the replacement of workers and supported the continued violations of workers' rights.

[22] Interview W13.

Table 8.3 *Numbers of agency workers converted into formal employees at Capital Star, 2008–2014.*

| | 2008 | 2009 | 2010 | 2011 | 2012 | 2013 | 2014 |
|---|---|---|---|---|---|---|---|
| Capital Star | 160 | 160 | | 389 | 570 | 825 | |
| Of which, Capital Express | | | 12 | | 116 | >600 | 321 |

*Source*: Capital Star, unpublished.[23]

### *Becoming Formal Workers, So What?*

Capital Star began to convert agency workers into formal employees on a large scale from 2008 onwards, and accelerated such formalization when the Interim Provisions were introduced in 2013 (Table 8.3). Workers chosen to be converted were selected through a points-based system, which considered the applicants' educational background, years of service at Capital Express, skills, honours, and awards. Every year, Capital Express would authorize a formalization quota, which was divided among its subsidiaries. Subsidiaries then sequenced the points of all the candidates recommended by branch outlets from the highest to the lowest. Those who fell within the subsidiary quota were entitled to become formal employees.

Becoming a formal employee was an arduous process. Generally, a junior college diploma was the minimum entry requirement; this criterion put it out of reach for most agency workers at Capital Express, who only had middle school or high school diplomas. Worse, their lengthy working hours prevented them from attending junior college courses to obtain a diploma. Of the thirty workers the author interviewed, no one had a junior college diploma recognized by Capital Express. Only one had enrolled on a junior college program because his manager had advised him to do so in preparation for formalization and promotion.

The annual quota issued by Capital Express was so limited that only one or two agency workers in each branch outlet were formalized each year. Although the published rules for the selection of candidates for formalization seemed clear and just, in practice nepotism played an overarching role. Ahead of ordinary workers in the queue to be formalized stood managers, the acquaintances of managers, and workers native to Beijing. Some migrants remained agency workers after working for Capital Express for eight years or so. The demanding formalization

23 Capital Star Yearbook 2009–2015, unpublished.

criteria meant that agency workers tended to regard themselves as being on probation. Formalization was an achievement or reward for competence and seniority, which helped to legitimize their inferior situation as agency workers in their minds.

Furthermore, most rank-and-file staff at Capital Express were young migrant workers, for whom working in one unit for eight years was unimaginable. The average duration of the first job for migrant workers born in and after 1990 in China was estimated to be less than one year.[24] Migrant workers in China tended to move to cities on a temporary basis to make money, rather than to settle down. The following were typical views shared by migrant agency workers at Capital Express:

> It takes seven to even eight years to be formalized. Migrant workers don't care about it. Nobody wants to work as a courier for that long.[25]

> On the one hand, it's hard to be formalized. On the other hand, it's useless to be formalized. Many people may work here for three to five years and quit after they have the money to start a small business. Even if you work here until you are sixty years old, you'll have to return to your hometown (after retirement). Even if you have been formalized, the same, unless you have the money to buy an apartment and transfer your *hukou* here.[26]

These sentiments direct us to the real question: what advantages were there for migrant agency workers to become formal employees of Capital Express? There was a time when Capital Star provided its formal grassroots employees with apartments as part of their welfare entitlements. Those days are long gone. What remains unchanged is Chinese people's attitude towards real estate. Owning a place to live is still considered necessary for settling down and starting a family for young Chinese men.

However, for migrant workers at Capital Express, renting a decent room in Beijing was a luxury. Capital Express did provide some dormitories for its staff, usually with two people to a room. However, dormitories were so scarce that most workers at Capital Express had to rent rooms elsewhere. With limited budgets (generally less than 1,000 *yuan* per month), many lived far from their place of work, usually underground or in undemolished villages within the city, and with other people to share the rent. With the-then ongoing demolition and reconstruction of villages in the city, they had to move from time to time. Jian, an agency worker from North China who had worked for Capital Express for eight years, proudly reported, 'The room I rent is beneath high-voltage power

[24] Department of Sociology, Tsinghua University 2013. [25] Interview W8.
[26] Interview W2.

lines. It won't be demolished for some time.'[27] As house prices soared, so did the rent for low-end rooms. As one agency worker explained in 2016,

> We have no plans to work here for long. What's the point of living in Beijing? We cannot afford to buy an apartment, or rent one either. It's becoming increasingly expensive every day. Initially, the monthly rent of my room was 600 *yuan*; it then jumped to 700, and then 800. So expensive! For a room with bath facilities, the monthly rent was 1,500 to 1,600, and is at least 1,700 now, bills excluded. You may earn at most 5,000 *yuan* per month, 2,000 for rent and 1,000 for eating. Could you end the month with 2,000 in hand? What if you buy some clothes?[28]

Migrant workers are allowed to buy real estate in Beijing but only after they have paid taxes or social insurance fees for five consecutive years. However, with meagre monthly wages ranging from 3,000 to 6,000 *yuan* in the mid 2010s, buying an apartment in Beijing was beyond the wildest expectations of migrant agency workers at Capital Express. In 2015, the average house price in Beijing (including the centre and suburbs) was 22,300 *yuan* per square metre (*yuan*/$m^2$). It would take a couple of average income twenty-three years to buy an apartment of 100$m^2$ in this city without spending on anything else.[29] Moreover, most couriers worked in central Beijing. House prices in central Beijing are at least four or five times more expensive than those in the suburbs.

There was a housing fund at Capital Express to relieve the pressure on house buyers to some extent. However, it did not benefit those with a rural *hukou*, who made up the majority of rank-and-file staff at Capital Express. Jian, who rented a room of sixteen square-metres with his wife under high-voltage power lines, had four spacious houses in his hometown – one in his village and three in a town of his native county. Their combined value did not match the price of a small apartment in Beijing.

Under these circumstances, none of the migrant couriers interviewed planned to buy an apartment in Beijing. Nevertheless, they did not escape soaring house prices. To secure a good match for marriage, or for the sake of their children's future education, young males in China strived to own an apartment not in their home villages but in nearby county towns or even cities where house prices had also been rising. In 2015, Meilan and her husband bought an apartment in urban Zhuozhou, a Hebei county near Beijing, at a price of 8,000 *yuan*/$m^2$. By late October 2016 when the author interviewed her, the price had almost doubled. Qiang, a Henanese courier, spent nearly 300,000 *yuan* buying and furnishing an apartment in a county town near his village

[27] Interview W11. [28] Interview W18. [29] 21st Century Economic Report 2017.

Table 8.4 *Population goals and population realized in Beijing, 2010–2020 (in millions).*

| | Total population | Population with Beijing *hukou* | Immigrant population |
|---|---|---|---|
| 2010 goal, planned in 1993 | 12.5 | 10.0 | 2.5 |
| 2004 realized | 14.9 | 11.6 | 3.3 |
| 2020 goal, planned in 2005 | 18.0 | 13.5 | 4.5 |
| 2015 realized | 21.7 | 13.5 | 8.2 |
| 2020 goal, planned in 2015 | 23.0 | | |

*Source*: Arts Bureau of *Keji wencui* 1994; Municipal government of Beijing 2005, 2016; Statistics Bureau of Beijing 2005; Statistics Bureau of Beijing and the Beijing branch of NBS 2016.

several years ago. His wife was urging him to buy another apartment in Anyang, a city in the north of Henan province, so that their two children could attend quality schools there. In 2016, a decent apartment in Anyang cost approximately 500,000 *yuan*.

Given their meagre wages, migrant couriers at Capital Express could hardly afford to bring up their children in Beijing. The cruel reality was that, even if these workers could afford to do so, their children might not be able to attend schools there, regardless of whether they were agency workers or formal employees of an SOE. At the beginning of the new millennium, the Beijing local government regarded the education of migrant children as its own responsibility and invested over 160 million *yuan* annually in migrant children's education.[30]

However, it changed gears later in the face of excessive migrant inflows (Table 8.4). By limiting migrant children's access to schools, both public and private, the city effectively worked to discourage migrants. Many private nurseries and schools were closed, and public kindergartens and schools significantly raised the entry thresholds for migrant children, actually receiving fewer of them despite the increasing number of incoming migrants.

The municipal government of Beijing dramatically intensified its control over migrant inflows following the release of its Thirteenth Five-Year Plan (2016–2020) in 2015, which sought to cap Beijing's total population at twenty-three million in 2020. In addition to constraining migrant children's access to schools, the municipal government introduced measures to raise the threshold of public service access for migrants, to force

[30] Feng 2002.

them to close their small businesses, and to disrupt their daily life. In August 2016, it introduced the residence permit (*juzhuzheng*) to replace the temporary residence permit (*zanzhuzheng*). The *zanzhuzheng* only granted the holder the legal right to stay in Beijing for a certain period. In contrast, the *juzhuzheng* provided the holder with access to multiple urban public services such as those related to compulsory education, social insurance, participation in exams for professional qualifications, and the like.

To qualify for the *juzhuzheng*, applicants had to prove that they had legal and stable employment and residence in Beijing, or were attending school there. Self-employed migrants, or those who worked for informal firms or who lived in rooms under informal rental agreements were hardly able to provide all the required documentation for this permit. Although they worked for an SOE, some couriers at Capital Express were worried that they might not get residence permits because they lived in villages within the city or in underground rooms.

Meanwhile, the municipal government closed many small businesses run by migrants, claiming that they lacked licences, and evacuated some villages within the city on the pretext of safety concerns. In one village in suburban Beijing, where one of my informants lived and migrants were concentrated, the government frequently cut off water and electricity supplies, destroyed the coal stoves (for winter heating) of many families, and accused local restaurants, grocery stores, barbershops, and the like, of operating illegally. These measures aimed to force the migrant residents to leave. Jiang was an agency worker from South China who had worked for Capital Express for five years. He left Beijing in December 2016 after his wife's grocery store had to relocate from a residential compound to a commercial complex, a location with a prohibitively expensive rent. 'Beijing has successfully driven us away,' he posted on WeChat (a social network app), with a photograph of himself taken at Beijing West Railway Station.

## Agency Workers in Exported-Oriented Factories

The deplorable working conditions of formal employees in export-oriented factories have been well documented. This section examines the working conditions of agency workers there in the 2010s.

### *Creative Labour Dispatch Combining Flexibility with Stability*

In response to previously mentioned domestic and international circumstances, export-oriented factories embraced dualism between formal employees and agency workers on the shop floor. The former were mainly managers, skilled workers, and a certain number of rank-and-file workers, who sustained factories' basic operations during the slack season, and enabled them to secure orders for peak seasons. Generally, formal workers enjoyed social insurance and other welfare benefits. To fill the workforce gap in peak seasons, these factories would resort to agency workers, who consisted mainly of student interns and peasant workers.[31]

Student interns included batches of students organized by their schools or labour dispatch agencies and individual students seeking factory work during holidays for pocket money. In Dongguan, student interns emerged in the late 1990s. At that time, many entered factories when they were thirteen to fifteen years old, and worked for thirteen to fourteen hours per day. Studies have found that, in the 2010s, many students were forced to intern in factories under the government's encouragement of close school–factory co-operation.[32] They often felt constrained, resigned, and powerless, and their classroom studies and work in factories were often misaligned.[33] Factories preferred student interns to peasant workers because they were better disciplined and more productive. According to several managers of labour dispatch agencies in Dongguan in 2016, the productivity of student interns was approximately 80 to 90 per cent of that of formal employees, whereas peasant agency workers' productivity was only half that of formal employees. However, numbers of student interns were often limited, and factories relied mainly on peasant workers to fill the workforce gap.

Dualism in export-oriented factories' workforce was common in the late 2010s. For example, at Xiqing Economic-Technological Development Area of Tianjin (a major industrial city in North China) in 2016, many workers in foreign enterprises and joint ventures reported that agency workers comprised over half of their factory workforce.[34] At Foxconn, Shenzhen, when the author worked at a branch factory in 2012, agency workers were rare. However, interviews with workers there in 2016 revealed that approximately half of the workforce on many shop floors were agency workers.[35] It was reported that in 2018 over 40 per cent of workers at a Foxconn factory in Hengyang, Hunan (a province in interior China) were agency workers.[36] This dualism was also common in export-oriented factories in Suzhou and Dongguan.

[31] Unless otherwise specified, this sub-section is based on Interview O16.
[32] Woronov 2015; Koo 2016. [33] Smith and Chan 2015. [34] Interviews W33–W47.
[35] Interviews W69–W77. [36] Condliffe 2018.

Labour dispatch in export-oriented factories differed markedly from that at Capital Express. SOEs like Capital Express used agency labour mainly to cut labour costs and bypass headcount and wage quotas. These agency workers' labour contracts lasted at least a year. Labour dispatch agencies were not involved in the daily management of these workers. In contrast, export-oriented factories used agency labour mainly to maintain a cheap and flexible workforce. Labour dispatch agencies recruited workers, signed three-to-six-month contracts with them, and dispatched them to these factories. It is worth noting that the LCL stipulates that labour contracts between agency workers and labour dispatch agencies must last at least two years. However, this provision was poorly implemented. The staff of labour dispatch agencies often lived with dispatched workers in export-oriented factories, and tried their best to lower the workers' turnover during the dispatch period.

To avoid legal risks pertaining to returning agency workers to labour dispatch agencies, some factories would also sign three-year labour contracts with agency workers. These workers thus had two labour contracts: one with the labour dispatch agency and the other with the user employer. This was illegal. A three-year labour contract granted employers the right to impose a six-month probationary term. When dismissed within the probationary term, workers could not claim severance fees.

For factories, this practice combined flexibility with stability. In peak seasons, it allowed factories to quickly expand their workforce and maintain its stability. In slack seasons, it allowed them to get rid of redundant workers easily. Labour dispatch agencies were key to maintaining the stability of the workers they dispatched. Factories and labour dispatch agencies would normally agree on acceptable levels of turnover during the dispatch period, such as 15 per cent for student interns and 20 per cent for peasant workers. Unless the factory was to blame for the high turnover (for example, due to a dramatic decrease in overtime), the labour dispatch agency would be fined, for example 200 to 500 *yuan* for each additional early leaver. To avoid any delays in order deliveries due to labour shortages, some factories would require labour dispatch agencies to put down a deposit, which prevented them from transferring workers to factories offering higher wages.

In light of this, labour dispatch agencies would try to lower turnover. On the one hand, they would dispatch their own staff to factories to provide services for dispatched workers. The wages of these staff were paid by both the labour dispatch agency and the user factory, and were linked to the turnover of agency workers under their supervision and to complaints against them from agency workers and factory managers. These onsite labour dispatch agency staff were not involved in managing production at client factories. Instead, their major responsibility was to take care of their agency workers, for example by lending them small amounts of money, caring for their physical and mental health, and mediating relationships between factory managers and agency workers. For student interns organized by their schools, labour dispatch agency staff collaborated with their teachers, and some even kept an eye on whom female student interns were dating for the interns' safety.

On the other hand, to encourage workers to stay until their contracts ended, labour dispatch agencies would link workers' compensation with the length of their working time by lowering the wage rates of early leavers or docking their wages, and by promising a gratuity (*fanfei*) to workers who remained to the end of their contracts. In addition to labour contracts, some agencies would sign additional agreements with agency workers to discourage them from leaving their jobs too early. Below is a translation of such an agreement signed before an agency worker boarded a bus departing for a factory, which the author collected from a labour inspector in Suzhou in 2016. This gives a flavour of his future working conditions and the punishment to which he would be subjected if he left the factory within a month of the start date.

**Confirmation of Voluntary Commitments**

I voluntarily join XXX factory as an operator. The hourly rate is 15.5 *yuan* for the first month, and will rise to 16.5 *yuan* from the second month upon satisfactory performance. The overall wage per month is over 3,000–5,000 *yuan*. A meal bill of 260 *yuan* will be deducted from monthly wages. The working time is twelve hours per day, on day or night shifts. The physical examination fee is fifty *yuan*. The ID card will be returned to me after seven days so that the labour agency has time to sort out issues relating to factory files and bank cards. This agreement will come into effect once I am on the bus departing for XXX factory.

Liabilities for breach of the contract: if I give up this job within a month of the start date, I shall pay 800 *yuan* to the labour agency for its losses regarding recruitment, training, and transport. This agreement is legally binding once I sign my name on it.

I am aware of all the above conditions.

Signature: XXX
Date: XXX

### *Working Conditions of Agency Workers*

On the shop floor, rank-and-file formal employees and agency workers were generally assigned to similar jobs and worked similar hours. However, compared with formal employees, agency workers faced discrimination with regard to compensation, welfare benefits, and job security, among others. Formal employees in export-oriented factories commonly received structured wages, including base wages, overtime pay, and bonuses. Their overtime rates were 1.5 to 3 times the normal rate. In contrast, agency workers were likely to be paid solely on hourly rates, and were therefore called hourly workers (*xiaoshigong*). Their hourly rates sometimes did not discriminate between normal working hours and overtime, which was illegal.[37]

For example, at Foxconn, Shenzhen, in 2016, the monthly wage of a new formal assembly line worker included a base pay of 2,450 *yuan*, overtime pay linked to the level of base pay, and bonuses. In contrast, in December 2016, agency workers there received fifteen or sixteen *yuan* (if they had no unexpected leave) for each hour they worked. Different batches of agency workers had different overtime wage rates: some were paid the same overtime rate as for their normal working hours, while others had a higher rate, albeit not as high as that of formal employees. Agency workers reported that their monthly take-home pay was approximately 400 to 500 *yuan* lower than that of formal employees in comparable positions.

Formal Foxconn workers were entitled to the five kinds of social insurance and the housing fund, while agency workers had, at best, cheap commercial insurance against work-related injuries. Agency workers also had no access to dormitories run by Foxconn. Instead, they lived in dormitories provided by labour dispatch agencies, which were more cramped. In Foxconn's own dormitories, six to eight people shared one room, whereas, in those provided by labour dispatch agencies, ten to twelve people shared a room of similar size. Some were not even provided with work uniforms. Some agency workers at Foxconn waged strikes and threatened to jump off high-rise buildings to protest against discrimination, only to be dismissed.[38]

Avoiding social insurance contributions was a major incentive for factories to use agency workers. In Dongguan, prior to the enforcement of the LCL, to cope with random inspections by local social insurance

[37] Unless otherwise specified, this sub-section is based on Interview O16 and interviews with agency workers in various foreign enterprises and joint ventures in several cities, as specified in the Appendix.

[38] Interviews W69–W77.

bureaus, factories paid social insurance and the housing fund for only a small number of formal employees. After 2008, they generally paid the five kinds of social insurance and the housing fund for formal employees based on the local minimum wage, rather than actual wages as required by the Social Insurance Law enforced in 2011, and paid for commercial insurance against work-related injuries for agency workers. In electronics companies in Tianjin in 2016, formal employees often had the five kinds of social insurance and the housing fund, while agency workers had at best three kinds of social insurance (against work-related injuries, illness, and retirement), and were excluded from most bonuses to which formal employees were entitled.[39]

Moreover, while formal employees' labour contracts lasted at least a year and were often renewed as a matter of course, agency workers' labour contracts in export-oriented factories generally lasted for six months or less, and their renewability hinged on the user factory's needs. In reality, factories with stable orders might use agency workers throughout the year, leaving their employment status unchanged, and might formalize some capable agency workers to retain them. In contrast, factories with fluctuating orders would not hesitate to return unneeded agency workers to labour dispatch agencies, which might re-dispatch them or find ways to get rid of them. In export-oriented enterprises, the latter scenario was more common. In addition, in enterprises with trade unions, agency workers were generally excluded from membership. Finally, informants reported experiences of being looked down on by formal employees.[40]

In addition to discrimination in the workplace, there was predation from labour agencies, which further worsened agency workers' conditions. In the 2010s, unregistered labour agencies (*hei zhongjie*) making profits by cheating workers were common in major manufacturing cities. In Dongguan in 2012, a twenty-one-year-old man stabbed a worker from a labour agency to death when the agency failed to provide the job it had promised and refused to return the 300 *yuan* it had charged.[41] In the same city in 2016, a staff member of a local association of labour agencies estimated that roughly half of labour agencies there were unregistered.

Registered labour agencies might also violate the law. In the 2010s, young people increasingly looked for jobs online. However, internet fraud relating to recruitment was rampant. Many job websites charged those who posted jobs, but did not authenticate their postings. As a result, it was common practice for labour agencies to fabricate job

[39] Interviews W33–W47. [40] Interview W39. [41] Sohu Net 2012.

descriptions to lure jobseekers. Many found they had been cheated only when they started work. Given the broad reach of these websites and the absence of central government regulation, local labour bureaus found it hard to counter online recruitment fraud.[42]

The most abominable crime of labour dispatch agencies was to abscond after receiving payments from user factories. This was committed mainly by small, unregistered labour dispatch agencies with no fixed offices. They lived on repeating this tactic with different batches of workers. For the workers affected, the possibility of getting their wages back hinged on whether they could stage high-profile collective action to capture the government's attention. Labour dispatch agencies commonly concocted various pretexts for docking agency workers' wages. The proportion of wages docked was usually limited to 20 to 30 per cent, a percentage that the agency workers affected were likely to give up in trading off the effort required to get back their wages against the chances of success.

A common pretext for wage docking was that agency workers had failed to work for a certain period. According to the Confirmation of Voluntary Commitments illustrated above, if the worker failed to work for over a month, he would have to pay 800 *yuan* to the labour agency that had dispatched him to the factory. At Foxconn, Shenzhen, in 2016, agency workers dispatched by Golden Light (a labour agency, pseudonym) would be docked 400 *yuan* if they failed to work for over a month.[43] Labour dispatch agencies might also build traps in which agency workers simply could not fulfil the minimum hours required by their contracts and had to accept the loss of wages. In addition, labour dispatch agencies might dock social insurance contributions handed over by user factories that were supposed to be paid to social insurance bureaus.[44]

Labour dispatch agencies were not the only beneficiaries of wage docking. They were often joined by factories that docked wages via labour dispatch agencies to lower labour costs. To transfer recruitment costs to labour dispatch agencies, some factories would persuade the agencies to accept low commissions for the prospect of long-term collaboration. Subsequently, they often successfully coaxed the agencies into wage docking conspiracies for the benefit of both.[45] Wage docking sometimes triggered fierce resistance. In Shenzhen in 2016, two agency workers from Yunnan stabbed to death two labour agency workers who had docked their wages.

[42] Interviews O13 and O14. [43] Interview W77. [44] Interviews O13 and O14.
[45] Interviews O13 and O14.

Dispatched student interns also suffered from wage docking by their own schools. According to the managers of labour dispatch agencies in Dongguan interviewed in 2016, they would take about 10 per cent of what user factories paid them, occupational schools would take 20 to 30 per cent, and the rest was given to student interns. For example, the user factory might pay sixteen *yuan* to the collaborating labour agency for each hour a student intern worked. The agency would take 1.5 *yuan* and give the rest to the collaborating occupational school, which would take 3.5 to 4.5 *yuan*. Ultimately, student interns received ten to eleven *yuan* for each working hour. The municipal government of Suzhou required the hourly rate of student interns to be higher than the local minimum hourly rate for part-time work (15.5 *yuan* per hour in 2016). However, in a case investigated by a local labour inspectorate, the students involved received only 11 *yuan* per hour. In another case, the wage slip provided by the factory indicated that it paid one student intern 4,351 *yuan* that month, while the intern only received 2,000 *yuan*.[46]

As with agency workers at Capital Express, agency workers in export-oriented factories also had opportunities for formalization, which hinged on their performance and seniority, and the willingness of labour dispatch agencies and factories. Generally, those who worked in factories where the compensation gap between formal employees and agency workers was large, who had better awareness of the legal benefits of formal employees, and who planned to work in the factory for a long time were keen to be formalized. In contrast, those who worked in enterprises with narrow wage gaps and who valued freedom more than compensation tended to remain as agency workers. The narratives below illustrate typical reasons why agency workers might or might not wish to be formalized.

I really want to be formalized, because I'll get higher wages and overtime pay after formalization.[47]

I want to be formalized, because only formal workers get severance fees when dismissed. I had a friend who worked at Samsung for eight years. Samsung offered 80,000 *yuan* to dismiss him.[48]

I want to be formalized. I'll feel more secure when formalized. I'll be a genuine member of the company then.[49]

At present I don't want to be formalized. Formal employees have to wait for one month before being permitted to resign. But, as an agency worker, I only need to wait for one week to get my wages and leave. If there are promotion

[46] Interviews O13 and O14. [47] Interview W44. [48] Interview W36.
[49] Interview W42.

opportunities, I might consider being formalized ... It's easy to find a job. Many agency workers enjoy their freedom as agency workers. They don't like the constraints associated with being formal employees.[50]

This raises the same question as at Capital Express about what formalization meant to these workers. The working conditions of formal employees in export-oriented factories were deplorable. Moreover, migrant agency workers in export-oriented factories faced the same barriers to settling down in cities as with their counterparts at Capital Express. Those in Shenzhen, Tianjin, and Guangzhou complained that house prices were so high that with their annual savings they could scarcely afford one square metre. They also faced barriers to transferring their *hukou* to the cities in which they worked. In light of this, formalization also had a limited effect in reducing the precarity of agency workers in export-oriented factories.

## Conclusion

This chapter depicts the conditions of Chinese workers with a focus on agency workers in the 2010s, shedding light on the combined effects of the socialist revolution and marketized reforms on workers. In the 2010s, both Capital Express and export-oriented factories embraced the dualism between formal contract workers and agency workers. At Capital Express, agency workers worked regularly, usually for years, and were managed solely by this enterprise. In contrast, in export-oriented factories, agency workers often worked for six months or less, and were managed by both user enterprises and labour agencies, which combined flexibility with stability.

In both workplaces, agency workers faced discrimination with regard to compensation, social insurance, and job security. That said, at Capital Express, the conditions of both formal and agency workers were concerning owing to the enterprise's shrinking market share in a competitive market, pervasive penalties, arbitrary wage docking, and commodification of social reproduction. In export-oriented factories, formal frontline workers' conditions were also deplorable. In addition, most agency workers in both workplaces were migrant workers who faced barriers to settling down in cities, such as their *hukou* status and high house prices.

[50] Interview W79.

# 9 Labour Precarity in Historical and Comparative Perspective

In Republican China, workers typically worked over ten hours per day, six days per week. Most were constantly at risk of unemployment, and had no labour insurance to hedge against illness, unemployment, or retirement. In 1949, the CCP took over China and has ruled the country ever since. The CCP has long claimed to be the vanguard of the working class, and has also claimed that China is a country ruled by the working class. After over seventy years of CCP rule, a substantial number of wage workers in China still work over ten hours per day, six days per week, and rarely have job security or social insurance. Such striking similarities in labour precarity in two periods over seventy years apart necessitate careful reflection on continuities and changes in working conditions before and after 1949. Based on a combination of archives, interviews, participant observation, and documentary materials, this book has examined the mechanisms that have caused and countered labour precarity in China since 1949.

## Main Findings

This book develops the framework of the 'labour tenure regime' to guide analysis. Drawing on theories by Marx, Weber, and Polanyi, this framework incorporates three interactive mechanisms that generate labour precarity, namely surplus appropriation, exclusion, and commodification, and their corresponding counter-mechanisms, thus overcoming the popular reductionist tendency of the extant literature to blame labour precarity on a single mechanism. It also provides a powerful tool for comparative dynamic studies of labour precarity in the Mao and post-Mao eras and between China and other countries, since the relevance of each of its three mechanisms varies with different workers in different places and periods. Applying this framework to the analysis of labour precarity in the Mao and post-Mao eras extends the application of the theories of Marx, Weber, and Polanyi to socialist economies, and helps to reveal the continuities and discontinuities in causing and countering labour precarity in these two eras. This book has the following findings.

The first half of this book advances the existing literature by studying the causes of and remedies for labour precarity in the Mao era. It does so by examining the formation and evolution of the hierarchy of labouring people with a focus on temporary workers in urban areas. In the early 1950s, the fundamentals of the Mao-era regime of marginal labour precarity took shape, leading to marginal precarity and general but differentiated security of labouring people. With regard to the three mechanisms that generate labour precarity, socialist surplus appropriation replaced Republican-era exploitation. It was modulated by swings in the industrialization path between centralization and decentralization, and tempered by socialism's commitment to labouring people and their resistance.

Exclusion led by the state replaced exclusion pursued by workers and private capital in the Republican era. It was a result of the contradiction between state-led accumulation and legitimacy. The state guaranteed people in different segments of the exclusion system mostly secure but differentiated access to subsistence materials and life opportunities. The exclusion system was based mainly on *hukou* status, the ownership type of one's user unit, and one's employment arrangements. In particular, temporary workers' urban employment was precarious. The boundaries between different groups of labouring people in the exclusion system were constantly redrawn, mainly by recurrent switches in the industrialization path between centralization and decentralization, swings in labour policy between promoting permanent and temporary employment, and ebbs and flows of labour movements. Social reproduction was decommodified and somewhat socialized on a discriminatory basis.

Between 1949 and 1957, these boundaries were revised by swings in the industrialization path between centralization and decentralization, and in labour policy from promoting permanent employment to constraining its expansion, and then to promoting the labour contract system. In the early 1950s, the government established the dominance of permanent employment. Between 1949 and 1954, the number of formal SOE workers expanded steadily, temporary workers were employed on a large scale and had abundant opportunities for formalization, and large numbers of peasants flooded into cities to work. However, in 1955, in light of rising redundancies, the government reined in the expansion of formal SOE workers, formalization of temporary workers, and inflows of peasants. In 1956, in response to the decentralization of industrialization, restrictions on urban workforce expansion were lifted, only to be resumed in 1957 as decentralization gave way to recentralization. In 1957, the labour contract system was introduced nationwide to facilitate the dismissal of temporary workers.

The period 1958–1965 witnessed the second and most radical switch between decentralized and recentralized industrialization of the Mao era, and a further swing in labour policy towards promoting temporary employment. The rise of the Great Leap Forward between 1958 and 1960 was characterized by radical decentralization of industrialization and radical inclusion. During this period, the number of workers in state-owned units exploded. Many workers in collective units enjoyed better compensation because their units were upgraded into quasi-SOEs or SOEs. Many urban housewives were included in social production. Temporary workers surged and became more stratified. Peasants joined the industrial workforce on a large scale. The demise of the Great Leap Forward between 1961 and 1963 was characterized by radical recentralization of industrialization and radical exclusion. Tens of millions of formal workers in state-owned units were laid off. Many SOEs were transformed back to collective units, the development of grassroots industries was discouraged and their workforces downsized, and huge numbers of temporary workers were dismissed. Peasants working in cities were exiled to the countryside in large numbers.

During the Cultural Revolution decade of 1966–1976, China witnessed the third wave of decentralized industrialization and the fiercest protests by temporary workers of the Mao era. Formal workers in state-owned units were not only active political actors but also main participants in the 'wind of economism'. Workers in collective units experienced a new round of upgrading and inclusion. Temporary workers of various kinds organized themselves and made their voices heard, only to be quickly cracked down on by the government. Nevertheless, as a result of temporary workers' rebellions, the government retreated from promoting temporary employment, enhanced protection for temporary workers, and formalized over half of them in late 1971 and 1972. Thereafter, owing to the expansion and decentralization of industrialization and intensified control over temporary employment within labour plans, the number of out-of-the-plan temporary workers increased dramatically.

The second half of this book advances the existing literature by providing a comprehensive analysis of mechanisms that have caused and countered labour precarity in the post-Mao era and examining the rise of agency labour and regulations countering it. China's transition from a planned economy to a market economy is ongoing. However, the fundamentals of the regime of general labour precarity were largely established before 2000. Socialist surplus appropriation has been overhauled and given way to exploitation. Both are enhanced by competition between enterprises. Surplus appropriation in the post-Mao era has been modulated mainly by capital's accumulation strategies, labour policy swinging between flexibilization and protection, and the demographic transition. It has been countered by labour resistance and pro-labour regulations, both of which have been impotent.

The social exclusion system has been softened and recalibrated by marketization. Exclusion based on employment arrangements has been significantly reduced. Dualism between formal contract workers and agency workers has replaced the dualism between formal permanent workers and temporary contract workers in the Mao era, defining the employment structure in enterprises. Exclusion based on types of enterprise ownership still exists, but to a lesser extent. Exclusion based on *hukou* status has also softened. Social reproduction has been recommodified. The recommodification of healthcare, education, and housing has created the 'three new great mountains' over Chinese workers.

Agency labour has been the dominant form of precarious labour in urban enterprises since the 2010s. Between the late 1970s and the 2010s, agency workers gradually rose to prominence primarily because they were a cheap and flexible workforce. During this process, the state played a double role as both the initiator of reforms that fostered labour dispatch and a supplier of agency workers. Pro-labour regulations have been major tools to counter labour precarity in the post-Mao era. Both the LCL and the Interim Provisions aim at labour protection with a focus on agency labour. However, these regulations have been poorly implemented, reflecting the impotence of workers at the local level to enforce them and thereby the incompleteness of legal counter-movements in the post-Mao era from a Polanyian perspective.

In the 2010s, both SOEs and export-oriented factories embraced the dualism between formal contract workers and agency workers. At Capital Express, a subsidiary of a central SOE, agency workers were used on a regular basis, usually for years, and were managed solely by this enterprise. In contrast, in export-oriented factories, agency workers were often used for six months or less, and were managed by both user enterprises and labour agencies, which combined flexibility with stability. In both workplaces, agency workers faced discrimination with regard to compensation, social insurance, and job security. That said, at Capital Express, the conditions of both formal and agency workers were concerning owing to the enterprise's shrinking market share in a competitive market, pervasive penalties, arbitrary wage docking, and commodification of social reproduction. In export-oriented factories, formal frontline workers' conditions were also deplorable. In addition, most agency workers in both workplaces were migrant workers who faced barriers to settling down in cities, such as their *hukou* status and high house prices.

## Continuities and Discontinuities

This book also complements cross-sectional case studies of precarious labour at the workplace level that dominate the existing literature, with a longitudinal study at the country level that combines macro-analysis of the political economy with micro-analysis of working conditions. This facilitates comparison between different periods to unveil their continuities and discontinuities in the transformation of labour precarity in China, which has multiple implications.

In addition to similarities in the conditions of ordinary workers before 1949 and in the 2010s, significant continuities in the mechanisms and institutions that generate labour precarity can be found in the periods before and after 1949, thus unveiling the entrenched nature of labour precarity and advancing the literature on continuities in the Chinese workplace before and after 1949.[1] In the late imperial era, wage labour expanded, and anti-exploitation labour action emerged; production began to be organized through the inside contract and putting-out systems, and workforce dualism based on job tenure and employment arrangements already existed, which persisted throughout the Republican and post-1949 eras. Both eras witness salient surplus appropriation and exclusion. In particular, in the Republican and reform eras, surplus appropriation mainly took the form of exploitation, exclusion was led mainly by capital, and commodification was rampant.

Nevertheless, the discontinuities in labour precarity before and after 1949 are clear-cut, reflecting the CCP's achievement in countering labour precarity. In the Mao era, by nationalizing and collectivizing the means of production, the state replaced the market in distributing life opportunities, leading to general but differentiated security of labouring people. Unlike exploitation prior to 1949, socialist surplus appropriation was for the common good of the masses and was tempered by the CCP's commitment to labouring people. Social reproduction was decommodified and somewhat socialized. In the post-Mao era, although exploitation and commodification have resumed, workers, though precarious, live materially better lives than those before 1949. Prior to 1949, the majority of labouring people were subsistence peasants, whereas, in the 2010s, the majority were wage workers in manufacturing and services.

Similarly, there are profound continuities in labour precarity between the Mao and post-Mao eras, reflecting the shared flaws of socialist revolution and marketized reforms in countering this issue. First, in both

[1] Frazier 2002; Cliver 2020.

eras, there has been an unfailing drive towards surplus appropriation and contradiction between accumulation and legitimacy, which have led to exclusion and framed the basic conditions of labouring people. Second, in both eras, independent trade unions and labour movements have been anathema to the state. The state's monopoly of workers' representation has largely deprived workers of their most important weapon against labour precarity, that is, collective action.

Third, in both eras, peasant workers have constituted a large proportion of the precarious workforce. The state has denied them access to essential public services in urban areas through the *hukou* system. Their employers have drawn on their inferior citizen status to discriminate against them. Urban units have always regarded them as workers who could be dismissed at any time: they have exploited them in their prime age, but have devolved responsibility for their social reproduction to rural areas. Fourth, in both eras, women have been over-represented in the precarious workforce. In the Mao era, they were mobilized into social production by the government during labour shortages, and dismissed when there was downsizing. In the post-Mao era, with the private sector replacing the state as the main provider of urban employment, discrimination against female workers has become more rampant.

Nevertheless, the discontinuities in labour precarity between the Mao and post-Mao eras are more fundamental. The fact that labour precarity was reduced by socialist revolution but resumed by marketized reform entails lessons for countering labour precarity in the future. The CCP has ruled China in both eras. In the Mao era, it was preoccupied with labour welfare improvement and regarded economic development as a means to this end. In contrast, in the post-Mao era the CCP has been preoccupied with economic development and has regarded labour welfare improvement as its natural result. Moreover, in the Mao era the CCP believed that establishing socialist forms of organization was as much a precondition for economic development as its product. In contrast, in the post-Mao era, the CCP believes that marketization is the precondition for economic development.

As a result, in the Mao era means of production were nationalized or collectivized, and the CCP was committed to labouring people, leading to decommodification, state-led distribution of life opportunities, and thereby general labour security. In contrast, in the post-Mao era means of production have been substantially privatized, and the CCP has prioritized economic development over labour welfare, leading to recommodification, market-led distribution of life opportunities, and thereby general labour precarity. Within this general picture, in both eras the contradiction between accumulation and legitimacy has given rise to exclusion. In the Mao era, however, state-led exclusion formalized the segmentation of labouring people, causing general but rigidly differentiated security among them. In the post-Mao era, state-led exclusion has softened and been marginalized by capital-led exclusion, and workers are impotent in ensuring the implementation of pro-labour regulations, giving capital leeway to drive down working conditions for all.

Several lessons can be drawn from the Chinese experience of countering labour precarity: (1) socialist revolution can counter labour precarity more effectively than marketized reform; therefore, the drive to reduce labour precarity can benefit from adopting elements of socialist revolution, such as labour-centred development, nationalization and collectivization of means of production, and decommodification; (2) exclusion, while privileging some workers, leads to the precarity of other workers; therefore, the drive to reduce labour precarity of the excluded can benefit from fighting exclusion, including exclusion led by capital, the state, and workers; and (3) collective labour action can counter precarity effectively, regardless of political-economic systems; therefore, the drive to reduce labour precarity can benefit from labour organizing.

## Engaging with the Paradoxes and Debates

The above findings enable this book to engage with the two paradoxes and two debates introduced in Chapter 1, which have implications for labour movements and policy.

According to classical Marxism, socialism is the remedy for labour precarity. Thus, workers in China, a country that experienced a socialist revolution and still claims to be socialist, should enjoy security. The reality is different, although this is not to say that socialism is entirely ineffective in reducing labour precarity. The Mao administration did lift the majority of labouring people out of precarity and into lifelong security; yet a minority of the working population still had precarious urban employment. In the post-Mao era, labour precarity has become pervasive. In this sense, the Chinese experience challenges classic Marxism and unveils socialism's limitations in reducing labour precarity.

Owing to marketized reforms in the post-Mao era, Mao's China was better positioned to expose such limitations. First, Mao's China was poor and incapable of guaranteeing materially secure lives for all labouring people. Although the socialist revolution dramatically changed the ownership structure of the means of production in society, it did not have equally dramatic effects in boosting productivity to a level that materially improved the lives of the masses. Second, as a poor country, Mao's China had to resort to surplus appropriation to industrialize the country, which squeezed consumption and fundamentally constrained labour security for all. Third, to reconcile the contradiction between accumulation and legitimacy, rather than distributing scarce resources to the masses equally, Mao's China built an exclusion system that privileged some workers and discriminated against others. The lesson is that nationalization and collectivization of the means of production – the achievement of the socialist revolution – does not automatically lead to equal distribution of resources among members of society.

Moreover, the Chinese version of socialism demonstrates that different ways of constructing socialism have different labour implications. Centralized industrialization tends to rigidify the exclusion system and reduce precarious urban employment. In contrast, decentralized industrialization tends to soften the exclusion system and create opportunities for social mobility, including the transformation of peasants and urban housewives into temporary workers. Workers face greater security and exclusion when the government promotes permanent employment, and less of both when it promotes temporary employment. In addition, they are likely to be better off with greater political space for collective action. Overall, with regard to reducing labour precarity, socialism can help, but its success in a constrained time frame depends on the circumstances under which the socialist revolution takes place, and on the path of socialist construction.

Modernization theory sees modernization as a remedy for labour precarity. Accordingly, workers in China, a country that has been so successfully modernized, particularly in the post-Mao era, should generally enjoy security. However, the reality is otherwise, although modernization has enlarged the material base underpinning labour security. As a result of economic development in both the Mao and post-Mao eras, most Chinese now earn their living from non-agricultural work, and live materially better lives than in the pre-1949 period. However, their working hours are still inhumanely long, their jobs are still unstable, and they remain vulnerable to illness, unemployment, and unsupported retirement. In this sense, the Chinese experience also challenges modernization theory and exposes the limitations of modernization in reducing labour precarity.

Socialist revolution as a means of modernization has limitations in reducing labour precarity, yet so do marketized reforms. Despite creating economic success, the reforms have resumed both exploitation and commodification. Furthermore, having dismantled the Mao-era exclusion system, they have given rise to a new one. Different ways of carrying out marketized modernization have different labour implications. China's integration into the global economy and labour-intensive growth mode have been double-edged swords for workers. China is now recalibrating its economic connections with the outside world and pursuing technological upgrading, the labour implications of which are yet to unfold. Working conditions tend to improve when the government loosens social control and promotes labour protection, and deteriorate when the government tightens social control and promotes labour flexibility. Overall, with regard to reducing labour precarity, marketized modernization may help, but it also has an in-built tendency to increase it. Different ways of carrying out marketized modernization also have different labour implications. That said, the Chinese experience shows that marketized modernization is less effective in reducing labour precarity than socialist modernization.

As to the debate about whether the current trend towards greater labour precarity is a process of de-proletarianization or proletarian unification, the Chinese experience supports the latter. In the Mao era, over half of urban workers enjoyed the iron rice bowl. However, they were only part of the proletariat, and their security was based on excluding the rest of the proletariat and peasants from such security. In the post-Mao era, the iron rice bowl has been smashed, and those who once enjoyed it have ended up living like their previously disadvantaged workmates. In other words, the two parts of the proletariat have been unified, given the convergence of their working conditions. In the case of Capital Express, compared with the gap in working conditions between permanent and temporary workers in the Mao era, the gap between formal contract workers and agency workers was insignificant in the 2010s, which supports the argument for proletarian unification in China.

Unification of the previously bifurcated working class has profound implications for labour movements. On the one hand, it suggests expanding ground for working-class solidarity, as workers can more easily relate their conditions to those of their fellow workers, in the spheres of both production and social reproduction. On the other hand, it suggests expanding ground for working-class segmentation pursued by workers, who face increasing competition from fellow workers for decent employment. The worldwide rise of nationalism hints at this trend.

Regarding the debate about the extent to which formalization is a remedy for labour precarity, the Chinese experience recognizes its desirability and exposes its limitations. In the Mao era, formalization granted individual workers in SOEs genuine security by entitling them to the iron rice bowl. However, as temporary employment was built into the economic system, formalization could not apply to all temporary workers. Similarly, in the post-Mao era, temporary employment is built into capital's pursuit of profits. Therefore, formalization can apply only to individual temporary workers, rather than these workers as a whole. Moreover, deteriorating formal employment, the *hukou* system, and commodification all compromise formalization's effectiveness in alleviating labour precarity.

Both the Capital Express case study and the accounts of working conditions in export-oriented factories demonstrate that formalization does little to reduce the precarity of agency workers in China, particularly migrant agency workers. Thus, to reduce labour precarity, it is worth promoting formalization, but further measures are necessary to curb relentless exploitation, soften exclusion, and rein in commodification of social reproduction.

## The Chinese Experience in Comparative Perspective

This section compares labour precarity in China with that in socialist and transitional economies and in traditional advanced capitalist economies after the Second World War. Clearly, the Chinese experience is set within global trends. In the first three decades after the Second World War, both countries embracing socialism and those embracing capitalism made earnest efforts to resist laissez-faire principles and counter labour precarity. Since the late 1970s, the capitalist world has witnessed a neoliberal turn, which has resumed market expansion and rolled back workers' gains in the previous three decades. Marketized reforms in China and in former socialist countries around the same time are part of this global turn.

### *Labour Precarity in Socialist and Transitional Economies*

By the early 1930s, the Soviet Union had nationalized the urban economy, collectivized the rural economy, and built a highly centralized planning system.[2] Like Chinese workers, Soviet workers suffered from socialist surplus appropriation and benefited from decommodification and socialization of social reproduction. Unlike Mao's China, which faced a perennial labour surplus and implemented a social exclusion system, the Soviet Union faced chronic labour shortages during most of its existence, and social exclusion was less of a concern amongst rank-and-file Soviet workers. Moreover, unlike China, the capitalist transition of many Soviet and Eastern European countries was dramatic. However,

[2] Lu 2007.

as in China, marketized reforms have intensified labour precarity by resuming exploitation and commodification.

To fuel industrialization, the Soviet government extracted the surplus of peasants and the industrial proletariat.[3] The accumulation rate rose from 14 per cent in 1950 to a peak of 33 per cent in 1982, before dropping to 16 per cent in 1990.[4] As a result, the real wages of non-agricultural workers in the Soviet Union declined between 1928 and the late 1940s, before slightly rebounding in the early 1950s.[5] Although real wages did increase thereafter, their growth rate lagged far behind that of productivity[6] until the accession of Mikhail Gorbachev. He launched the 1985–1991 *Perestroika* (Russian for 'reconstruction'), which allowed Soviet enterprises to use a significantly larger share of profits for wages.[7] Soviet trade unions contributed to the decline and slow growth of workers' real wages by prioritizing economic development over workers' interests.[8]

In addition to wages, once in employment, Soviet workers were covered by the state-led social insurance system. They were entitled to compensation for wage losses due to illness, accidents, pregnancy, and childbirth, pensions for permanent disability and retirement, funeral benefits, allowances for dependent survivors of deceased workers, and, until 1930, the unemployment allowance.[9] Moreover, in Soviet Russia, all citizens were entitled to employment, free healthcare, free education, and free vocational training. Housing and many mass consumption goods were heavily subsidized. The state also provided very cheap recreation and childcare services.[10]

The Soviet Union was long haunted by labour shortages, which uprooted the basis for social exclusion among rank-and-file workers. In 1930, the Soviet government declared the liquidation of unemployment. Thereafter, a chronic labour shortage haunted most Soviet Union states.[11] While there was no sign of mass unemployment in the Soviet Union, partial, concealed, and frictional unemployment did exist. Surplus labour, whether disguised or not, was found in factories due to overmanning,[12] in peripheral areas due to over-concentration of industry in large towns, and in cities due to technological progress and factory closures,[13] as well as in agriculture,[14] particularly among former capitalists, landowners and other rich people,[15] and women.[16] Nevertheless,

[3] Gregory and Stuart 1974. [4] Mazat and Serrano 1995. [5] Chapman 1963, 144.
[6] Adam 1987, 131. [7] Mazat and Serrano 1995. [8] Clarke 2007, 40–41.
[9] Chapman 1963, 122–123. [10] Mikhalev 1996.
[11] Conquest 1967, 22; Adam 1987. [12] Porket 1989, 114. [13] Conquest 1967, 35.
[14] Schwarz 1960. [15] Kornai 1992, 204–205. [16] Porket 1989, 101.

unemployment was rarely a problem in most Soviet economies. The Soviet Union's actual unemployment rate in the 1970s was estimated to be 1 to 2 per cent.[17]

However, the Soviet working class was still stratified. Despite the ideology of egalitarianism, in 1931, to boost productivity, Joseph Stalin launched a movement encouraging incentives based on the functions that individuals performed in production and management. As a result, within the working class, those with the highest skills were well paid, those with medium skill levels earned the average wage, and the low-skilled earned the minimum wage.[18]

In a context of chronic labour shortages, fixed-term labour contracts had limited impact on workers' job security. The Soviet Labour Code, enacted in 1922, required employers to sign labour contracts with their workers. Labour contracts could be open-ended, fixed-term, or last until the completion of specific tasks. For most of the time before 1971, while Soviet workers had a right to quit their jobs before their contracts expired, employers could fire workers only on grounds stipulated by law and with the agreement of local trade unions.[19]

Emboldened by pervasive labour shortages, Soviet workers changed jobs frequently. Between the late 1950s and the mid 1970s, the average annual labour turnover was 19 to 22 per cent in industry, and 24 to 41 per cent in construction.[20] To lower labour turnover, the new Soviet Labour Code introduced in 1971 prohibited workers from freely exiting from fixed-term contracts, which allowed employers, particularly those in inhospitable and remote regions, to retain workers using fixed-term contracts.[21] In contrast, in both the Mao and post-Mao eras, China has resorted to fixed-term labour contracts to get rid of redundant workers. Moreover, in a context of labour shortages, Soviet industrialization relied heavily on workers from rural areas. As a result, the Soviet Union's share of agricultural employment dropped from 48 per cent in 1950 to 20 per cent in 1980.[22] In contrast, China's share of agricultural employment dropped from 91.5 per cent in 1949 to 77.6 per cent in 1976.[23]

In the late 1980s and early 1990s, communist parties lost their monopoly of power in many Eastern European countries. In 1991, the Soviet Union collapsed. In the early 1990s, many countries in the socialist bloc embraced shock therapy, including Albania, Bulgaria, Czechoslovakia (split into the Czech Republic and Slovakia in 1993), Estonia, Latvia, Poland, and Russia. Shock therapy aimed to get prices right by abruptly

17 Gregory and Collier 1988. 18 Inkeles 1950. 19 Conquest 1967, 15–21.
20 Porket 1989, 93. 21 Muravyev 2014. 22 Mazat and Serrano 1995.
23 NBS 1987, 5.

privatizing SOEs, withdrawing price and currency controls and subsidies, and liberalizing trade.[24] SOEs had once almost monopolized Russia's industrial sector. Following mass privatization in the 1990s, in 1999 SOEs made up 5.2 per cent of industrial enterprises and 15.8 per cent of the workforce. In contrast, private enterprises made up 88.4 per cent of industrial enterprises and 39.9 per cent of the workforce. Joint ventures co-funded by the state and private capital (both domestic and foreign) made up 5.9 per cent of enterprises and 43.6 per cent of the workforce.[25]

Shock therapy laid the basis for revived exploitation, exclusion, and commodification of social reproduction. It pushed Russia into recession in the 1990s, and drove up the unemployment rate. Between 1991 and 1999, Russia's GDP dropped by 62.2 per cent.[26] According to data from the World Bank, the unemployment rate jumped from nearly zero in most of the Soviet period to 13.3 per cent in 1998.[27] Meanwhile, Russia witnessed a plunge in real wages and proliferation of non-standard employment such as part-time work, agency work, and independent contracting.[28] In addition, the social security system has been drastically restructured, with four identifiable trends: privatization of provision, individualization of risks, monetization of access, and decentralization of management.[29]

### *Labour Precarity in Traditional Advanced Capitalist Economies*

In traditional advanced capitalist economies, the three decades after the end of the Second World War were a golden age for workers. During this period, Fordism was the dominant mode of growth in these economies, apart from Japan. Fordism is based on mass production and mass consumption, and involves a virtuous circle of growth featuring rising productivity and household incomes. Under Fordism, management recognizes unions for collective bargaining, and indexes wages to productivity growth and prices, while unions concede management's right to organize the labour process and define corporate strategy. The Fordist state promotes full employment, provides indexed welfare benefits for workers and the economically inactive through progressive taxation, and spreads the gains of workers in Fordist sectors to those in non-Fordist sectors through legislation.[30]

[24] Marangos 2003. [25] Lu 2007, 702. [26] World Bank 2020a.
[27] World Bank 2020b. [28] Kapelyushnikov, Kuznetsov, and Kuznetsova 2012.
[29] Cerami 2009. [30] Jessop 1992.

In the 1970s, these economies experienced simultaneous inflation and stagnation of economic output, to which they responded with a neoliberal turn. Neoliberalism promotes an institutional framework characterized by strong private property rights, free markets, and free trade, and relies on the state to create such a framework.[31] Under the neoliberal turn, flexible accumulation characterized by organizing production 'through dispersal, geographical mobility, and flexible responses in labour markets, labour processes, and consumer markets'[32] has replaced 'rigid' Fordism as the new mode of growth. Trade unions have been under attack, real wages have been under downward pressure, and the state has abandoned the target of full employment and deregulated the labour market. The state has also retreated from providing welfare benefits, often resulting in mass privatization of SOEs providing related services.[33]

As a result, workers under advanced capitalism between the late 1940s and the late 1970s saw constrained exploitation and decommodification, with the inclusion of some in non-agricultural employment and the exclusion of some from prime jobs. Thereafter, they have witnessed a comeback of relentless exploitation, recommodification, and recalibration of exclusion. In the United States, for example, the annual growth rate of the nominal average hourly wage of workers was 2.2 per cent between 1947 and 1979, but dropped to 0.7 per cent between 1979 and 2017.[34] While productivity increased steadily between 1960 and 2000, real wages increased between 1960 and 1973, and trended downward between 1974 and 1995.[35] Union membership as a percentage of employment rose from 7.4 per cent in 1930 to 28.3 per cent in 1954, and remained around 25 per cent until the early 1970s, but dropped steadily thereafter.[36] Wages and union density have experienced similar trends in many other advanced capitalist economies.[37]

Moreover, in advanced capitalist countries, the three decades in the aftermath of the Second World War were characterized by expansion of the coverage and levels of support for the unemployed, indexation of pensions to cost-of-living changes, and the introduction of family allowances and earnings-related benefits and pension schemes. In Europe, transfer payments and subsidies to households as a proportion of GDP increased from around 8 per cent in 1955–1957, to around 12 per cent in the late 1960s, and further to around 16 per cent in the mid 1970s.[38] In the UK, strategic sectors of the economy, such as coal, steel, and

[31] Harvey 2007. [32] Harvey 1989, 159 [33] Harvey 2007.
[34] Schmitt, Gould, and Bivens 2018. [35] Harvey 2007, 25. [36] Mayer 2004.
[37] Bengtsson 2014. [38] Esping-Andersen 1990; Marglin and Schor 2000, 60.

automobiles, were nationalized, and a substantial proportion of the housing stock was also in the public sector.[39]

In contrast, the neoliberal era has been characterized by austerity measures to reduce government deficits, which have adversely affected the social security system. Public expenditure on disability and sickness cash benefits as a proportion of GDP in countries within the Organization for Economic Co-operation and Development (OECD, an organization comprising mostly developed economies) dropped from 2 per cent in 1980 to 1.6 per cent in 2017. In these countries, public expenditure on families in cash as a proportion of GDP was 1.2 per cent in both 1980 and 2017, but payments in kind rose from 0.3 per cent in 1980 to 1 per cent in 2017. Against a backdrop of rapid ageing, the proportion of public expenditure on old-age and survivors' cash benefits rose from 5.7 per cent in 1980 to 7.7 per cent in 2017.[40] In addition, many SOEs providing essential public services were privatized. In the UK in the 1980s and 1990s, British Aerospace, British Telecom, British Airways, steel, electricity and gas, oil, coal, water, bus services, railways, and a host of smaller SOEs were sold off by the government, and public housing was also sold off to tenants on a large scale.[41]

Last but not least, in advanced capitalist economies under Fordism, regular, full-time, long-term employment prevailed, and working conditions in large corporations were generally superior to those in small firms.[42] Women and non-white people were largely excluded from job security. In addition, retail, hospitality, agriculture, sex work, and construction were constantly characterized by precarious work.[43] At the same time, in Japan, where the mode of growth was somewhat different from Western Europe and North America, workforce dualism was more pronounced: while workers in large firms enjoyed relatively high wages, employment security, and social benefits, their counterparts in small firms received low wages, with few or no social benefits and little employment security.[44] This period also saw a massive transfer of workers from self-employment and domestic work to wage employment.[45]

However, in these economies since the late 1970s, precarious employment has expanded.[46] For example, temporary employment as a proportion of wage employment among male employees in France increased from 3.3 per cent in 1983 to 16.7 per cent in 2018, before dropping to 15.4 per cent in 2020. This proportion in Spain increased from 14.5 per

39 Harvey 2007, 55. 40 OECD 2020. 41 Harvey 2007, 60–61.
42 Gordon, Edwards, and Reich 1982.
43 Mitropoulos 2005; Van der Linden 2014; Millar 2017.
44 Dohse, Jürgens, and Nialsch 1985. 45 Meng 2012. 46 Kalleberg 2009.

cent in 1987 to a peak of 32 per cent in 2006, before dropping to 24.1 per cent in 2020.[47]

## Limitations, Speculations, and Suggestions

Chronicling the post-1949 history of precarious labour in China in a single book is a formidable task, so some limitations must be noted. The world is in a tumultuous era. In China, efforts to overhaul the traditional growth mode have gained momentum, marketized reforms are ongoing, and tremendous uncertainties lie ahead for Chinese workers.

### *Limitations*

This book focuses on wage labour, and largely ignores non-wage labour. However, in reality, there are large numbers of such workers, including not only peasants and the self-employed but also workers in the putting-out system, in which the platform economy is the latest form.[48] Most workers providing services in the platform economy have no labour contracts with platform companies, and are excluded from labour rights enjoyed by employees. Studies have found that workers in the platform economy are subject to control from the platform through algorithms, and suffer from overwork and irregular hours, low pay, social isolation, and exhaustion.[49] In China in 2019, there were approximately seventy-eight million workers who received income by providing services in the platform economy.[50]

This book also fails to give sufficient attention to the diverse experiences of precarious workers in different regions of China. China is a large country with great diversity. Different places may implement national policies differently, and develop localized labour practices pertaining to precarious workers. This book uses the all-of-China-field-site research strategy to provide an overview of precarious workers in China since 1949, and the one-case multi-field-site strategy and the one-site-case-study strategy to give depth to the picture. While it does not claim to represent the whole country, readers should be aware that China is, in fact, more diverse than depicted in this book.

### *Speculations*

Looking ahead, both labour protection and further flexibilization in China are possible. The United States–China rivalry has been the basic

[47] OECD 2024. [48] Stanford 2017. [49] Wood et al. 2019; Qi and Li 2020.
[50] National Data Centre 2020.

geopolitical circumstance faced by China since the 2010s. Its implications for Chinese workers are twofold. On the one hand, it has harmed, and will continue to harm, the Chinese economy, and thereby Chinese workers, by disrupting GCCs, diverting export-oriented companies away from China, creating barriers to Chinese products' entry into international markets, and translating geopolitical tensions into even tighter control by the Chinese government over society, amongst other impacts. On the other hand, the United States–China rivalry exposes technological bottlenecks in the Chinese economy, and may serve as a catalyst for China's technological catch-up, which has the potential to benefit Chinese workers.

The labour implications of recalibration of China's economic relationship with the outside world are unclear. Doubt about globalization has been rising around the world, and anecdotal evidence suggests disinvestment by cost-chasing companies from China. In 2020, the world witnessed a pandemic caused by a novel coronavirus. On the one hand, it disrupted GCCs and reminded every country of the importance of onshore production of essential goods; on the other hand, it provided an opportunity for China to prove its reliability as a key node in GCCs, even under extreme shocks.

It is unclear how long China will remain a magnet for foreign capital. As foreign investors are major contributors to China's foreign trade and employment, outflows of foreign investment will adversely affect employment in China. It is too early to speculate how the strategic emphasis on internal circulation proposed by President Xi in 2020 will unfold to offset pressure on external circulation. In 2013, China launched the Belt and Road Initiative, which has dramatically boosted the country's outbound investment. Fieldwork investigations indicate that the impression that overseas Chinese firms employ mainly Chinese in positions that could be filled by locals is a myth.[51] However this initiative fares under China's inward-looking strategy, its direct impact on Chinese workers will be limited.

Ongoing technological upgrading to both processes and products in China is also a double-edged sword. Theoretically, it may both displace and create jobs, both deskill and upskill workers, and both reduce laborious and repetitive work and make the workplace safer, as well as strengthening management's control over the labour process. However, unlike workers in traditional developed capitalist economies, who first experienced mass automation in the 1960s and 1970s when labour

[51] Oya and Schaefer 2019.

unions were strong and wages were indexed to productivity, workers in present-day China have no genuine unions that are able to bargain with employers to share the productivity gains enabled by technological upgrading.[52]

The state will continue to play a key role in modulating labour precarity. On the one hand, the government's tight control over society has led to under-development of workers' organizations that can counter labour precarity. The Xi administration has been more coercive than its predecessors.[53] Moreover, in March 2018, the National People's Congress passed a constitutional amendment that withdrew the two-term limit on the presidency, allowing Xi to remain in power for life.[54] Whether refined coercion is Xi's personal administration style or the CCP's response to increasing domestic and overseas turbulence, the years to come are unlikely to see any reversal of the oppression of collective labour action. China's economic slowdown is likely to continue. Therefore, the government's promotion of flexible employment and lax implementation of labour protection regulations may also continue.

On the other hand, the government also has incentives to improve labour share in GDP. Its proposed new mode of growth involves boosting domestic demand to reduce reliance on exports. Only sustained wage growth can power sustained domestic demand growth.

Marketized reforms are ongoing. There is no sign that SOE reforms will shift away from the current direction of diluting state ownership, retreating from non-strategic industries, and adopting modern management institutions. This implies that the role of SOEs in providing decent employment will continue to be eclipsed. There is also no sign that the *hukou* system will be abolished in the near future, which will maintain the precarity of peasant workers. In addition, since the experience of developed economies shows that it is very hard to boost the fertility rate once the demographic transition has taken place, China's alarmingly low fertility rate is likely to continue, contributing to labour shortages in the years to come.

### *Suggestions*

Labour precarity is a phenomenon of global and historical relevance. Based on the contributions and limitations of this book and major dynamics in China in this regard, some directions for future researchers to consider can be suggested.

[52] Huang and Sharif 2017. [53] Fuchs, Tse, and Feng 2019.
[54] British Broadcasting Company 2018.

First, it is worth considering comparative studies of labour precarity between different places over the same period, between different periods in the same place, and between different workers in the same period and place. The dynamics and unevenness of the global economy give rise to fluctuations and diversity in working conditions across time, space, and labour, which calls for comparative studies between different regions, periods, and workers. As this book has shown, such comparative studies will enable a better understanding of working conditions and political-economic systems in individual countries and general convergences and divergences in working conditions on a global scale. Such studies might be facilitated by the analytical framework developed in this book. By incorporating the three mechanisms that generate labour precarity and have varying relevance for different economies, periods, and workers, this framework provides a powerful tool for comparative dynamic studies of labour precarity.

Second, the labour implications of China's new growth mode are worth examining. Technological upgrading and the rebalancing of internal and external economic circulation are key elements of this new mode. Both have profound implications for Chinese workers.

Third, non-wage workers in China deserve attention, particularly those in the platform economy. Technological advances have dramatically decentralized production, distribution, exchange, and consumption. In this regard, digital platforms have played a key role. The rise of the platform economy and the expansion of platform workers challenge the mainstream labour studies and the mainstream labour regulation framework, both centring on wage employment. While labour studies have devoted extensive attention to platform workers, most analyses have essentially treated them as wage workers. How their status differs from that of traditional wage workers and how such status generates unique vulnerabilities remain questions for future scholarship.

# Appendix List of Interviews

| No. | Interviewee(s) |
|---|---|
| O1 | Thirteen staff (individual interviews), Talent Pool, Beijing, July, August 2016. |
| O2 | An official of the provincial labour division and HR managers of three SOEs, Guangzhou, September 2016. |
| O3 | Local labour officials, Guangzhou, September 2016. |
| O4 | Managers of several labour agencies, Guangzhou, September 2016. |
| O5 | Officials of the provincial labour division and managers of two labour agencies, Shandong, October 2016. |
| O6 | HR managers of three SOEs, Shandong, October 2016. |
| O7 | Head of a large local HR company, Shandong, October 2016. |
| O8 | Labour officials of the municipal labour bureau, Shanghai, October 2016. |
| O9 | HR managers of several companies, Shanghai, October 2016. |
| O10 | Managers of several labour agencies, Shanghai, October 2016. |
| O11 | Managers of a logistics SOE, Shanghai, October 2016. |
| O12 | HR managers of several companies, Suzhou, October 2016. |
| O13 | Labour officials of a local district and managers of several labour agencies, Suzhou, October 2016. |
| O14 | Labour officials of a local industrial park, Suzhou, October 2016. |
| O15 | Managers of a petroleum SOE, Suzhou, October 2016. |
| O16 | Managers of three labour agencies and a staff member of the Dongguan HR Association, Dongguan, November 2016. |
| O17 | Official of the municipal labour bureau, Dongguan, November 2016. |
| O18 | MOHRSS researcher, Beijing, August, December 2016. |
| O19 | MOHRSS researcher, Beijing, September 2017. |
| O20 | Labour scholar, Beijing, July 2017. |
| O21 | Social security scholar, Wuhan, July 2017. |

W1 Agency worker, courier, male, from Anhui, Capital Express, Beijing, August 2016.

W2 Agency worker, courier, male, from Anhui, Capital Express, Beijing, August 2016.

W3 'Outsourced' worker, courier, male, from Hebei, Capital Express, Beijing, September 2016.

W4 First as an agency worker, then as a formal worker, manager, male, from Jiangsu, Capital Express, Beijing, September 2016.

W5 First as an agency worker, then as a formal worker, customer service worker, female, from Beijing, Capital Express, Beijing, September 2016.

W6 First as an agency worker, then as a formal worker, driver, male, from Beijing, Capital Express, Beijing, September 2016.

W7 Agency worker, manager, male, from Guizhou, Capital Express, Beijing, September 2016.

W8 Agency worker, courier, male, from Hebei, Capital Express, Beijing, September 2016.

W9 Agency worker, warehouse keeper, male, from Beijing, Capital Express, Beijing, September 2016.

W10 Agency worker, inward mail recorder, female, from Hebei, Capital Express, Beijing, September 2016.

W11 Agency worker, courier, male, from Hebei, Capital Express, Beijing, September, October 2016.

W12 Agency worker, manager, male, from Henan, Capital Express, Beijing, September 2016.

W13 Agency worker, courier, male, from Henan, Capital Express, Beijing, September 2016.

W14 'Outsourced' worker, courier, male, from Shaanxi, Capital Express, Beijing, September 2016.

W15 First as an agency worker, then as a formal worker, driver, male, from Beijing, Capital Express, Beijing, September 2016.

W16 Agency worker, courier, male, from Beijing, Capital Express, Beijing, October 2016.

W17 Agency worker, courier, male, from Henan, Capital Express, Beijing, October 2016.

W18 Agency worker, courier, male, from Shaanxi, Capital Express, Beijing, October 2016.

W19 'Outsourced' worker, courier, male, from Hebei, Capital Express, Beijing, October 2016.

W20 Agency worker, courier, male, from Heilongjiang, Capital Express, Beijing, October 2016.

W21 Agency worker, courier, male, from Henan, Capital Express, Beijing, October 2016.

W22 Agency worker, courier, male, from Shaanxi, Capital Express, Beijing, October 2016.

W23 Agency worker, courier, male, from Henan, Capital Express, Beijing, October 2016.

W24 Agency worker, inward mail recorder, female, from Hebei, Capital Express, Beijing, October 2016.

W25 Agency worker, courier, male, from Hebei, Capital Express, Beijing, October 2016.

W26 Agency worker, courier, male, from Beijing, Capital Express, Beijing, October 2016.

W27 First as an agency worker, then as a formal worker, manager, male, from Jilin, Capital Express, Beijing, November 2016.

W28 Agency worker, courier, male, Capital Express, Beijing, November 2016.

W29 Agency worker, manager, male, from Shandong, Capital Express, Beijing, November 2016.

W30 First as an agency worker, then as a formal worker, manager, male, from Beijing, Capital Express, Beijing, November 2016.

W31 Agency worker, postcard designer, male, from Shanghai, a logistics SOE, Shanghai, October 2016.

W32 Agency worker, sorter, male, from Hubei, a logistics SOE, Shanghai, October 2016.

W33 Agency worker, assembler, female, from Jilin, an auto parts SOE, Tianjin, December 2016.

W34 Agency worker, input preparer, female, from Hebei, an auto parts joint venture, Tianjin, December 2016.

W35 Agency worker, assembler, male, from Hebei, an auto parts joint venture, Tianjin, December 2016.

W36 Agency worker, assembler, male, from Hebei, an electronics joint venture, Tianjin, December 2016.

W37 Agency worker, warehouse keeper, female, from Hebei, a foreign electronics company, Tianjin, December 2016.

W38 Agency worker, assembler, female, from Shanxi, a foreign auto parts company, Tianjin, December 2016.

W39 Agency worker, packager, female, from Hebei, a foreign auto parts company, Tianjin, December 2016.

W40 Agency worker, quality controller, female, from Liaoning, an electronics joint venture, Tianjin, December 2016.

W41 Agency worker, assembler, male, from Shanxi, an electronics joint venture, Tianjin, December 2016.

W42 Agency worker, logistics worker, male, from Jilin, a foreign auto parts company, Tianjin, December 2016.

W43 Agency worker, logistics worker, male, from Hebei, a foreign auto parts company, Tianjin, December 2016.

W44 Agency worker, logistics worker, female, from Shanxi, a foreign electronics company, Tianjin, December 2016.

W45 Agency worker, quality controller, female, from Shanxi, a foreign electronics company, Tianjin, December 2016.

W46 Agency worker, assembler, female, from Shanxi, an auto parts joint venture, Tianjin, December 2016.

W47 Agency worker, assembler, male, from Hubei, a foreign auto parts company, Tianjin, December 2016.

W48 Agency worker, quality controller, female, from Hunan, an electricity SOE, Changsha, December 2016.

W49 First as a formal worker, then as an agency worker, warehouse keeper, female, from Hunan, an electricity SOE, Changsha, December 2016.

W50 Agency worker, security guard, male, from Hunan, a private property management company, Changsha, December 2016.

W51 First as an agency worker, then as a formal worker, group leader, female, from Hunan, an auto parts joint venture, Changsha, December 2016.

W52 First as a formal worker, then as an agency worker, and then as a formal worker, assistant engineer, male, from Hunan, an auto parts joint venture, Changsha, December 2016.

W53 First as an agency worker, then as a formal worker, quality controller, female, from Hunan, a foreign auto parts company, Changsha, December 2016.

W54 First as a formal worker, then as an agency worker, and then as a formal worker, warehouse keeper, female, from Hunan, a steel SOE, Changsha, December 2016.

W55 Agency worker, warehouse keeper, male, from Sichuan, a private logistics company, Guangzhou, December 2016.

W56 Agency worker, assembler, male, from Guizhou, a foreign electronics company, Guangzhou, December 2016.

W57 Agency worker, security guard, male, from Hunan, a private property management company, Guangzhou, December 2016.

W58 Agency worker, warehouse keeper, male, from Guangxi, a foreign cosmetics company, Guangzhou, December 2016.
W59 Agency worker, assembler, male, from Shaanxi, a foreign auto parts company, Guangzhou, December 2016.
W60 Agency worker, assembler, male, from Gansu, an auto parts joint venture, Guangzhou, December 2016.
W61 Agency worker, manager, male, from Liaoning, a logistics SOE, Guangzhou, September 2016.
W62 Agency worker, manager, male, from Guangdong, a logistics SOE, Guangzhou, September 2016.
W63 Agency worker, teller, male, from Guangdong, a state-owned bank, Guangzhou, September 2016.
W64 Agency worker, support worker, female, from Guangdong, a logistics SOE, Guangzhou, September 2016.
W65 Agency worker, telephonist, female, from Guangdong, a logistics SOE, Guangzhou, September 2016.
W66 Agency worker, manager, male, a logistics SOE, Guangzhou, September 2016.
W67 Agency worker, teller, female, a state-owned bank, Guangzhou, September 2016.
W68 Agency worker, manager, male, from Guangdong, a state-owned bank, Guangzhou, September 2016.
W69 Agency worker, assembler, male, from Henan, Foxconn, Shenzhen, December 2016.
W70 Agency worker, quality controller, female, from Guizhou, Foxconn, Shenzhen, December 2016.
W71 Agency worker, assembler, from Shanxi, Foxconn, Shenzhen, December 2016.
W72 Agency worker, assembler, Foxconn, Shenzhen, December 2016.
W73 Agency worker, quality controller, female, from Henan, Foxconn, Shenzhen, December 2016.
W74 Agency worker, assembler, female, from Yunnan, Foxconn, Shenzhen, December 2016.
W75 Agency worker, male, from Guangxi, Foxconn, Shenzhen, December 2016.
W76 Agency worker, assembler, male, from Hubei, Foxconn, Shenzhen, December 2016.
W77 Agency worker, assembler, male, from Hunan, Foxconn, Shenzhen, December 2016.
W78 Agency worker and student intern, assembler, male, from Guangxi, a private electronics company, Dongguan, November 2016.

W79 Agency worker and student intern, quality controller, male, from Guangxi, a private electronics company, Dongguan, November 2016.

W80 Agency worker, assembler, male, from Shanxi, a foreign electronics company, Dongguan, December 2016.

W81 Agency worker, assembler, male, from Hunan, a foreign electronics company, Dongguan, December 2016.

W82 Agency worker, assembler, female, from Guangxi, a foreign electronics company, Dongguan, December 2016.

M1 Male, born in 1930. In a wood processing factory affiliated with the central government (SOE) in Beijing, he was a formal worker between 1951 and 1982, a vice factory director between 1969 and 1978, and the party secretary between 1978 and 1982. February 2023.

M2 Male, born in 1940, junior college graduate. In a primary school in a county in Henan, he was a formal teacher between 1961 and 1962 and temporary teacher between 1962 and 1988. February and March 2023.

M3 Female, born in 1941, junior middle school graduate. She was a temporary teacher in a primary school in a county in Henan in 1958, and formal teacher in another primary school in the county between 1959 and 1962. After being transformed into a temporary teacher in a remote school in 1962, she quit the job because of family obligations and low pay and became a peasant. March 2023.

M4 Male, born in 1950, junior middle school graduate. In an equipment installation company affiliated with the municipal government of Wuhan (SOE), Hubei, he was a formal worker between 1970 and 1981 and union cadre between 1973 and 1976. March 2023.

M5 Female, born in the 1950s. She was a formal worker in an SOE in Wuhan in the Mao era and the daughter of a female temporary worker in street factories in Wuhan who passed away in late 2022. March 2023.

M6 Male, born in 1945, junior middle school graduate. He was a temporary worker at the bureau of electricity services in a county in Henan between 1969 and 1971 and was formalized in 1971. March 2023.

M7 Female, born in 1942, primary school graduate. She worked as a temporary worker in a grain station (state-owned unit) and a construction company (SOE) in a county in

Heilongjiang in the 1960s and 1970s. She married a formal SOE worker. March 2023.

M8 Male, born in 1941, a few years in primary school. He was a formal worker in a construction company affiliated with a county government in Heilongjiang (SOE) between 1960 and 1978 and temporary worker in a grain station (state-owned unit) and a power plant (SOE) in winter when construction projects suspended. March 2023.

M9 Female, born in 1945. She was a peasant and member of a work team organized by her production team to take on construction work contracted out by an aircraft manufacturing factory (SOE) in Xi'an, Shaanxi, in the early 1970s. April 2023.

M10 Male, born in 1947, junior middle school graduate. He was a temporary worker in a county-level supply and marketing co-operative in Xingtai, Hebei in 1965 before joining the army. April 2023.

M11 Male, born in 1940, primary school graduate and demobilized serviceman. He was a temporary worker in the tractor station of a commune administration (state-owned unit) between 1969 and 1974 in Weifang, Shandong, and was formalized in 1974. April 2023.

M12 Male, born in 1944, junior middle school graduate and demobilized serviceman. In a fertilizer factory affiliated with a county government in Shanxi (SOE), he was a temporary worker between 1970 and 1973, was formalized in 1973, and became the factory director in 1976. April 2023.

M13 Female, born in 1948, senior middle school graduate. She was a temporary broadcaster in the radio station of a commune administration (state-owned unit) in Shanxi between 1970 and 1972 and was then recommended to go to college by the commune. April 2023.

M14 Male, born in 1960, junior middle school graduate. He joined a coal mine affiliated with the municipal government of Jincheng (SOE), Shanxi, as a formal worker in 1976. April 2023.

M15 Female, born in 1960, a few years in primary school. She was a temporary worker at the bureau of roads in a county in Shanxi between 1979 and 1981 and was formalized in 1981. April 2023.

M16 Female, born in 1927, illiterate. She was a formal worker in a rubber factory affiliated with the municipal government of Jiaxing, Zhejiang, between 1958 and 1962, was dismissed in 1962, worked as a temporary worker in a candy factory, a textile mill, a coal mine construction company, and then a dyeing mill in the 1960s and early 1970s, and was formalized after three years of work in the dyeing mill. May 2023.

M17 Male, born in 1943, college graduate. He was a formal worker at the bureau of public security in a county in Shanxi between 1970 and 1984. June 2023.

M18 Male, born in 1947, junior middle school graduate and demobilized serviceman. In an agricultural machinery maintenance and manufacturing factory (SOE) of a county in Shanxi, he was a formal worker between 1970 and 2002, the director of the maintenance workshop between 1977 and 1981, the deputy party secretary of the factory between 1981 and 1984, and the party secretary of the factory between 1984 and 2002. June 2023.

M19 Male, born in 1949, senior middle school graduate. He was a temporary teacher in a primary school and a junior middle school in a county in Shanxi between 1968 and 1973, and was a barefoot doctor there between 1973 and 1978. June 2023.

# Bibliography


21st Century Economic Report. 2017. Beijing shi zhengfu gongzuo baogao: yao jiada zhongdi jiawei putong shangpin zhufang gongying bili (According to a working report of the municipal government of Beijing: the share of commodity houses at low to moderate prices in all offering should be increased). *21 shiji jingji baodao*, 4 January.

ACFTU. 1988. Chengshi funv zai jiuye deng fangmian mianlin de xin wenti (New problems faced by urban women in employment and other respects). *Zhongguo laodong kexue* (5), 12–15.

1999. *1997 nian zhongguo zhigong zhuangkuang diaocha* (*An Investigation of the Conditions of Chinese Workers in 1997*). Beijing: Xiyuan chubanshe.

2006. *Diwuci zhongguo zhigong zhuangkuang diaocha* (*The Fifth Investigation of the Conditions of Chinese Workers*). Beijing: Zhongguo gongren chubanshe.

2010. *Diliuci zhongguo zhigong zhuangkuang diaocha* (*The Sixth Investigation of the Conditions of Chinese Workers*). Beijing: Zhongguo gongren chubanshe.

2012. Dangqian woguo laowu paiqian yonggong xianzhuang diaocha (An investigation into labour dispatch in present-day China). *Zhongguo laodong* (5), 23–25.

2014. *Diqici zhongguo zhigong zhuangkuang diaocha* (*The Seventh Investigation of the Conditions of Chinese Workers*). Beijing: Zhongguo gongren chubanshe.

Adam, Jan (ed.). 1987. *Employment Policies in the Soviet Union and Eastern Europe*. London: Macmillan Press.

All-China Confederation of Industry and Commerce. 2007. *1993–2006 Zhongguo siying qiye daxing diaocha* (*A Large-Scale Survey of Private Enterprises in China, 1993–2006*). Beijing: Zhonghua gongshang lianhe chubanshe.

All-China Federation of Women. 2013. Woguo nongcun liushou ertong, chengxiang liudong ertong zhuangkuang yanjiu baogao (Research report on rural left-behind children and migrant children in China). *Zhongguo fuyun* (6), 30–34.

Anderson, Bridget. 2010. Migration, immigration controls and the fashioning of precarious workers. *Work, Employment and Society* 24(2), 300–317.

Andreas, Joel. 2009. *Rise of the Red Engineers: The Cultural Revolution and the Origins of China's New Class*. Redwood City: Stanford University Press.

2019. *Disenfranchised: The Rise and Fall of Industrial Citizenship in China*. Oxford: Oxford University Press.

Andreas, Joel, and Yige Dong. 2017. 'Mass supervision' and the bureaucratization of governance in China. In Vivienne Shue and Patricia M. Thornton (eds). *To Govern China: Evolving Practices of Power*. Cambridge: Cambridge University Press.

Arts Bureau of *Keji wencui*. 1994. Maixiang ershiyi shiji de beijing – beijing chengshi zongti guihua (1991–2010) jieshao (Beijing towards the twenty-first century – an introduction to the Beijing City General Plan (1991–2010)). *Keji wencui* (5), 73–77.

Athukorala, Prema-chandra. 2017. China's evolving role in global production networks: implications for Trump's trade war. In Ligang Song, et al. (eds) *China's New Sources of Economic Growth: Human Capital, Innovation and Technological Change, Vol. 2*. Canberra: Australian National University Press.

Bai, Huitian, and Lian Zhou. 2018. M xing jiegou de xingcheng: 1955–1978 nian difang fenquan yu difang gongye de xingqi (The formation of the M-shape structure: decentralization between 1955 and 1978 and the rise of local industry). *Jingji xuebao* 5(2), 1–42.

Barboza, David. 2010. China passes Japan as second-largest economy. *The New York Times*, 15 August.

Bengtsson, Erik. 2014. Do unions redistribute income from capital to labour? Union density and wage shares since 1960. *Industrial Relations Journal* 45(5), 389–408.

Bernstein, Henry. 2010. *Class Dynamics of Agrarian Change*. West Hartford: Kumarian Press.

Betti, Eloisa. 2018. Historicizing precarious work: forty years of research in the social sciences and humanities. *International Review of Social History* 63(2), 273–319.

Bian, Morris L. 2005. *The Making of the State Enterprise System in Modern China: The Dynamics of Institutional Change*. Cambridge, MA: Harvard University Press.

Blecher, Marc. 1983. Peasant labour for urban industry: temporary contract labour, urban–rural balance and class relations in a Chinese county. *World Development* 11(8), 731–745.

Bo, Yibo. 1957. Guanyu 1956 naindu guomin jingji jihua de zhixing jieguo he 1957 niandu guomin jingji jihua caoan de baogao (Report on the implementation results of the national economic plan for 1956 and the draft of the national economic plan for 1957). *Renmin ribao*, 2 July.

1991. *Ruogan zhongda juece yu shijian de huigu, shang juan* (*Review of Major Decisions and Events, Part I*). Beijing: Zhonggong zhongyang dangxiao chubanshe.

1997. *Ruogan zhongda juece yu shijian de huigu, xia juan* (*Review of Major Decisions and Events, Part II*). Beijing: Zhonggong zhongyang dangxiao chubanshe.

Bourdieu, Pierre. 1998. *Acts of Resistance: Against the Tyranny of the Market*. New York: The New Press.

British Broadcasting Company. 2018. China's Xi allowed to remain 'president for life' as term limits removed. https://www.bbc.co.uk/news/world-asia-china-43361276. Accessed 10 August 2018.

Buckley, Chris. 2020. Xi's post-virus economic strategy for China looks inward. *The New York Times*, 7 September.

Burgess, John, and Iain Campbell. 1998. The nature and dimensions of precarious employment in Australia. *Labour & Industry: A Journal of the Social and Economic Relations of Work* 8(3), 5–21.

Buttrick, John. 1952. The inside contract system. *The Journal of Economic History* 12(03), 205–221.

Cai, He. 2010. Cong 'dixian xing' liyi dao 'zengzhang xing' liyi – nongmingong suqiu de zhuanbian yu laozi guanxi zhixu (From 'bottom-line' to 'aggressive' interests: peasant workers' demand changes and industrial relations). *Kaifang shidai* (9), 37–45.

Cairns, Daniel S. S. 2015. New formalities for casual labor: addressing unintended consequences of China's Labor Contract Law. *Washington International Law Journal* 24(1), 219–252.

Cao, Ronggui. 2008. Zhongguo yiyuan gaige 30 nian (Thirty years of hospital reforms in China). *Zhongguo yiyuan* (9), 1–8.

Cary, Eve. 2013. China's people problem. *The Diplomat*, 5 February.

CASS and CAC. 1994. *1949–1952 nian zhonghua renmin gongheguo jingji dangan ziliao xuanbian, laodong gongzi he zhigong fuli juan (Selected Collections of the Economic Archives of the People's Republic of China, 1949–1952, on Labour, Wage, and Welfare)*. Beijing: Zhongguo shehui kexue chubanshe.

1998a. *1953–1957 nian zhonghua renmin gongheguo jingji dangan ziliao xuanbian, laodong gongzi he zhigong baoxian fuli juan (Selected Collections of the Economic Archives of the People's Republic of China, 1953–1957, on Labour, Wage, Insurance, and Welfare)*. Beijing: Zhongguo wujia chubanshe.

1998b. *1953–1957 nian zhonghua renmin gongheguo jingji dangan ziliao xuanbian, gongye juan (Selected Collections of the Economic Archives of the People's Republic of China, 1953–1957, on Industry)*. Beijing: Zhongguo wujia chubanshe.

2011a. *1958–1965 nian zhonghua renmin gongheguo jingji dangan ziliao xuanbian, laodong jiuye he shouru fenpei juan (Selected Collections of the Economic Archives of the People's Republic of China, 1958–1965, on Employment and Income Distribution)*. Beijing: Zhongguo caizheng jingji chubanshe.

2011b. *1958–1965 nian zhonghua renmin gongheguo jingji dangan ziliao xuanbian, gongye juan (Selected Collections of the Economic Archives of the People's Republic of China, 1958–1965, on Industry)*. Beijing: Zhongguo caizheng jingji chubanshe.

CCP. 2011. Zhongguo gongchandang dierci quanguo daibiao dahui xuanyan (Declaration of the Second National Congress of the CCP). In Literature Research Centre of the Central Committee of the CCP (ed.), *Jianguo yilai zhongyao wenxian xuanbian, di yi ce (A Selection of Important Official Documents since 1949, Vol. 1)*. Beijing: Zhongyang wenxian chubanshe.

Central Administrative Bureau of Industry and Commerce. 1960. *Ziben zhuyi gongye de shehui zhuyi gaizao (The Socialist Transformation of Capitalist Industry)*. Beijing: Sanlian chubanshe.

Central Committee of the CCP. 1966a. Zhongguo gongchandang zhongyang weiyuanhui tongzhi (A circular from the Central Committee of the CCP). *Renmin ribao*, 17 May.

1966b. Zhongguo gongchandang zhongyang weiyuanhui guanyu wuchan jieji wenhua dageming de jueding (Decision on the Proletarian Cultural Revolution by the Central Committee of the CCP). *People's Daily*, 8 August.

1995. Zhonggong zhongyang guanyu fazhan difang gongye wenti de yijian (Opinions on developing local industry by the Central Committee of the CCP). In Literature Research Centre of the Central Committee of the CCP (ed.), *Jianguo yilai zhongyao wenxian xuanbian, di shiyi ce* (*A Selection of Important Official Documents since 1949, Vol. 11*). Beijing: Zhongyang wenxian chubanshe.

1996a. Zhonggong zhongyang guanyu liji tingzhi zhaoshou xin zhigong he guding linshigong de tongzhi (Circular on immediately suspending the recruitment of new formal workers and long-term temporary workers by the Central Committee of the CCP). In Literature Research Centre of the Central Committee of the CCP (ed.), *Jianguo yilai zhongyao wenxian xuanbian, di shier ce* (*A Selection of Important Official Documents since 1949, Vol. 12*). Beijing: Zhongyang wenxian chubanshe.

1996b. Zhonggong zhongyang guanyu dali jinsuo shehui goumaili he zai qunzhong zhong jieshi dangqian jingji qingkuang de jinji zhishi (Emergent instruction on greatly tightening social purchase power and explaining the economic condition to the masses by the Central Committee of the CCP). In Literature Research Centre of the Central Committee of the CCP (ed.), *Jianguo yilai zhongyao wenxian xuanbian, di shier ce* (*A Selection of Important Official Documents since 1949, Vol. 12*). Beijing: Zhongyang wenxian chubanshe.

1997. Zhonggong zhongyang pifa zhongyang caijing xiaozu *guanyu taolun 1962 nian tiaozheng de baogao* de pishi (Comments on report on discussions about the adjustment plan in 1962 by the Central Finance Group authorized and issued by the Central Committee of the CCP). In Literature Research Centre of the Central Committee of the CCP (ed.), *Jianguo yilai zhongyao wenxian xuanbian, di shiwu ce* (*A Selection of Important Official Documents since 1949, Vol. 15*). Beijing: Zhongyang wenxian chubanshe.

Central Committee of the CCP, and State Council. 1995. Zhonggong zhongyang guowuyuan guanyu gongye qiye xiafang de jixiang guiding (Several provisions on the devolution of industrial enterprises by the Central Committee of the CCP and the State Council). In Literature Research Centre of the Central Committee of the CCP (ed.), *Jianguo yilai zhongyao wenxian xuanbian, di shiyi ce* (*A Selection of Important Official Documents since 1949, Vol. 11*). Beijing: Zhongyang wenxian chubanshe.

2003. Zhonggong zhongyang, guowuyuan guanyu jinyibu zuohao xiagang shiye renyuan zaijiuye gongzuo de tongzhi (Circular on further improving the service for the re-employment of laid-off workers by the Central Committee of the CCP and the State Council). In Literature Research Centre of the Central Committee of the CCP (ed.), *Shiwuda yilai zhongyao wenxian xuanbian, xia* (*A Selection of Important Official Documents since the Fifteenth National Congress of the CCP, Part II*). Beijing: Renmin chubanshe.

Central government. 1967. Guanyu jinyibu shixing jieyue naogeming, kongzhi 'shehui jituan goumaili', jiaqiang zijin, wuzi he wujia guanli de ruogan guiding (Several provisions on further economizing when carrying out revolution, controlling the purchase power of social groups, enhancing the management of finance, materials, and price). https://banned-historical-archives.github.io/articles/799609364f. Accessed 9 December 2024.

Central Intelligence Agency. 2024. China. https://www.cia.gov/the-world-factbook/countries/china/. Accessed 6 July 2024.

Central Office of Financial Leading Group. 1999. *Zhongguo jingji fazhan wushinian dashi ji* (*Major Events of Economic Development in China between 1949 and 1999*). Beijing: Renmin chubanshe.

Cerami, Alfio. 2009. Welfare state developments in the Russian Federation: oil-led social policy and 'The Russian Miracle'. *Social Policy & Administration* 43(2), 105–120.

Chan, Jenny, Ngai Pun, and Mark Selden. 2013. The politics of global production: Apple, Foxconn and China's new working class. *New Technology, Work and Employment* 28(2), 100–115.

Chan, Jenny, Mark Selden, and Ngai Pun. 2020. *Dying for an iPhone: Apple, Foxconn, and the Lives of China's Workers*. Chicago: Haymarket Books.

Chan, Kam Wing, and Li Zhang. 1999. The *hukou* system and the rural–urban migration in China: processes and changes. *The China Quarterly* 160, 818–855.

Chang, Jiang. 1999. *FESCO 20 nian* (*20 Years of FESCO*). Beijing: Beijing chubanshe.

Chao, Kang. 1977. *The Development of Cotton Textile Production in China*. Cambridge, MA: Harvard University Press.

Chapman, Janet G. 1963. *Real Wages in Soviet Russia since 1928*. Cambridge, MA: Harvard University Press.

Chen, Da. 1929. *Zhongguo laogong wenti (Labour Issues in China)*. Shanghai: Shangwu yinshuguan.

Chen, Gang, et al. 1990. *Zhongguo laodong fuwu gongsi* (*Labour Service Companies in China*). Beijing: Nongye chubanshe.

Chen, Hansheng, Muqiao Xue, and Hefa Feng. 1987. *Jiefang qian de zhongguo nongcun, di er ji (Rural China before 1949, Vol. 2)*. Beijing: Zhongguo zhanwang chubanshe.

Chen, Liping. 2015. Renshebu: shishi tichu xiugai laodong hetongfa jianyi (MOHRSS: putting forward suggestions to revise the Labour Contract Law when appropriate). *Fazhi ribao*, 18 November.

Chen, Meei-shia. 2001. The great reversal: transformation of health care in the People's Republic of China. In William C. Cockerham (ed.), *The Blackwell Companion to Medical Sociology*. Hoboken: Wiley-Blackwell.

Chen, Shaohui. 2003. *Cong jihua jiuye dao shichang jiuye: Guoyou qiye laodong jiuye zhidu de bianqian yu chongjian* (*From Planned to Marketized Employment: The Transformation and Reconstruction of Employment Institutions in State-Owned Enterprises*). Beijing: Zhongguo caizheng jingji chubanshe.

Chen, Xuewen. 1980. Mingdai zhongye zhejiang hangjiahu diqu nongye zhong shangpin shengchan he guyong laodong de tansuo (An exploration into commodity production and wage labour in agriculture in Hangzhou, Jiaxing, and Huzhou of Zhejiang in the mid-Ming Dynasty). *Zhejiang xuekan* (1), 51–56.

Chen, Yongjie. 2022. Guoyou, minying, waizi jingji fazhan shinian bianju (A decade of changes in the development of state-owned, private, and foreign economies in China). https://news.qq.com/rain/a/20220415A0627V00. Accessed 9 December 2024.

Chen, Yun. 2005. *Chen Yun wenji, di san juan* (*Selected Works of Chen Yun, Vol. 3*). Beijing: Zhongyang wenxian chubanshe.

Cheng, Tiejun, and Mark Selden. 1994. The origins and social consequences of China's *hukou* system. *The China Quarterly* 139, 644–668.

Cheng, Zhiming, Russell Smyth, and Fei Guo. 2015. The impact of China's new Labour Contract Law on socioeconomic outcomes for migrant and urban workers. *Human Relations* 68(3), 329–352.

Chesneaux, Jean. 1968. *The Chinese Labor Movement, 1919–1927*. Redwood City: Stanford University Press.

China Institute for Education Finance Research. 2018. 2017 nian zhongguo jiaoyu caizheng jiating diaocha: zhongguo jiating jiaoyu zhichu xianzhuang (A survey of household educational finances in 2017: the current condition of educational expenditure of Chinese households). https://opendata.pku.edu.cn/dataset.xhtml?persistentId=doi:10.18170/DVN/KE1JYM. Accessed 9 December 2024.

China Labour Data Centre. 1993. Quanguo zhiye jieshao fuwu jigou gongzuo qingkuang tongji (Statistics on labour agencies in China). *Zhongguo laodong kexue* (2), 47.

Chinese Labour Academic Association, and Beijing Municipal Labour Academic Association. 1999. *Zaijiuye fuwu zhongxin de jianli yu yunzuo* (*The Establishment and Operation of Re-employment Service Centres*). Beijing: Zhongguo laodong chubanshe.

Clarke, Simon. 2007. *The Development of Capitalism in Russia*. London: Routledge.

Cliver, Robert. 2020. *Red Silk: Class, Gender, and Revolution in China's Yangzi Delta Silk Industry*. Cambridge, MA: Harvard University Asia Center.

Cobble, Dorothy Sue. 2005. *The Other Women's Movement: Workplace Justice and Social Rights in Modern America*. Princeton: Princeton University Press.

Committee of Reforming the System of the National Economy. 1983. *Woguo jingji tizhi gaige de lishi jingyan* (*Lessons from Our History of Reforming the Economic System*). Beijing: Renmin chubanshe.

Condliffe, Jamie. 2018. Foxconn is under scrutiny for worker conditions. It's not the first time. *The New York Times*, 11 June.

Conquest, Robert (ed.). 1967. *Industrial Workers in the USSR*. London: The Bodley Head.

Cui, Fan, Ying Ge, and Fengchun Jing. 2013. The effects of the Labor Contract Law on the Chinese labor market. *Journal of Empirical Legal Studies* 10(3), 462–483.

De Backer, Koen, et al. 2016. Reshoring: myth or reality? https://www.oecd-ilibrary.org/docserver/5jm56frbm38sen.pdf?expires=1733717232&id=id&accname=guest&checksum=C23D3B684D6DE3BFDEC3A0268912C659. Accessed 9 December 2024.

Deng, Liqun, et al. 2009. *Dangdai zhongguo de laodongli guanli* (*The Management of Labour Power in Contemporary China*). Beijing: Dangdai zhongguo chubanshe.

Deng, Zhongxia. 1949. *Zhongguo zhigong yundong jianshi (1919–1926) (A Brief History of Labour Movements in China, 1919–1926)*. Beijing: Renmin chubanshe.

Department of Sociology, Tsinghua University. 2013. Duangonghua: nongmingong jiuye qushi yanjiu (The shortening of job duration: research on employment trends of migrant workers). *Qinghua shehuixue pinglun* 6, 5–8.

Ding, Xianjue, and Weiguo Yang. 1992. Guoying qiye gongxiao guagou qianyi (A preliminary discussion on linking the gross wage to financial performance of state-owned enterprises). *Zhongguo laodong kexue* (7), 7–11.

Doeringer, Peter B., and Michael J. Piore. 1985. *Internal Labor Markets and Manpower Analysis*. Armonk: ME Sharpe.

Dohse, Knuth, Ulrich Jürgens, and Thomas Nialsch. 1985. From 'Fordism' to 'Toyotism'? The social organization of the labor process in the Japanese automobile industry. *Politics & Society* 14(2), 115–146.

Dong, Baohua. 2011. *Laodong hetongfa lifa de zhengming yu sikao* (*Debates and Reflections on the Legislative Process of the Labour Contract Law*). Shanghai: Shanghai renmin chubanshe.

Dong, Yige. 2019. From Mill Town to iPhone City: Gender, Labor, and the Politics of Care in an Industrializing China (1949–2017). PhD Dissertation, Johns Hopkins University.

Editorial Board. 1988. *Youdian laodong gongzi zhuanyeshi* (*A Specialized History of Employment Relations and Wages at China Post and Telecommunications*). Beijing: Renmin youdian chubanshe.

Editorial Board of Chorography of Jiangsu. 1999. *Jiangsu sheng zhi, zonghe jingji zhi, shang (Provincial Chorography of Jiangsu, Chorography of the Comprehensive Economy, Part I)*. Nanjing: Jiangsu guji chubanshe.

Editorial Board of *Labour*. 1958a. Wuqiong de laodong qianli (Endless potential of labour power). *Laodong* (15), 6–8.

1958b. Laodong gongzuo dayuejin de yinian (A year of great leap forward in labour-related administrative work). *Laodong* (19), 2–3.

1958c. Yigong yinong, nengjin nengchu, biandi kaihua (Both-workers-and-peasants, both let-in and let-out, blossom everywhere). *Laodong* (13), 15–16.

Editorial Board of *People's Daily*. 1955. Jiaqiang laodongli diaopei gongzuo, kefu laodongli de langfei (Improving the allocation of labour power to avoid waste). *Renmin ribao*, 17 July.

1966. Quanguo dou yinggai chengwei Mao Zedong sixiang de daxuexiao (The whole country should be a grand school of the Mao Zedong Thought). *Renmin ribao*, 1 August.

Elfstrom, Manfred. 2021. *Workers and Change in China: Resistance, Repression, Responsiveness*. Cambridge: Cambridge University Press.

Elfstrom, Manfred, and Sarosh Kuruvilla. 2014. The changing nature of labor unrest in China. *ILR Review* 67 (2), 453–480.

Engels, Friedrich. 1987. Anti-Duhring. In Karl Marx and Friedrich Engels (eds), *Marx-Engels Collected Works, Vol. 25*. New York: International Publishers.

Esping-Andersen, Gosta. 1990. *The Three Worlds of Welfare Capitalism.* Princeton: Princeton University Press.

Fang, Hsien-t'ing. 1978. *The Triumph of the Factory System in England.* Philadelphia: Porcupine Press.

Fang, Yuan. 2006. Cong 'Quan Hong Zong' tan 'renmin wenge' (People's Cultural Revolution in the view of Quan Hong Zong). http://redchinacn.net/portal.php?mod=view&aid=28985. Accessed 8 January 2021.

Feng, Rui. 2002. Beijing chutai xin guiding, liudong renkou zinv jiaoyu jiangyou baozhang (Beijing issued a new regulation and the education of migrant children will be guaranteed). *Beijing wanbao,* 19 April.

Feng, Xiaojun. 2015. Zhizao jinzhang: Fushikang shengchan guocheng de jibenmaodun (Manufacturing Tensions: The Basic Contradiction in the Labour Process of Foxconn). Master's thesis, Peking University.

2017. Manufacturing conflict: the experience of a world factory in a changing China. *Modern China* 43(6), 590–619.

2020. *The Labour Implications of Technological Upgrading in China.* Geneva: ILO.

FESCO. 2013. Qicheng qiye paiqian yonggong bili diyu 10%, renli ziyuan waibao xuqiuliang jiang zengjia (Agency workers accounted for ten per cent or lower in 70% of investigated enterprises and the need for human resource outsourcing will increase). *Zhongguo xinshidai* (12), 76–78.

Frazier, Mark W. 2002. *The Making of the Chinese Industrial Workplace: State, Revolution, and Labor Management.* Cambridge: Cambridge University Press.

2010. *Socialist Insecurity: Pensions and the Politics of Uneven Development in China.* Ithaca: Cornell University Press.

Friedman, Andrew L. 1977. *Industry and Labour.* London: Macmillan.

Friedman, Eli. 2014. *Insurgency Trap: Labor Politics in Postsocialist China.* Ithaca: Cornell University Press.

Fuchs, Daniel, Patricia Fuk-Ying Tse, and Xiaojun Feng. 2019. Labour research under coercive authoritarianism: comparative reflections on fieldwork challenges in China. *Economic and Industrial Democracy* 40 (1), 132–155.

Gallagher, Mary E. 2011. *Contagious Capitalism: Globalization and the Politics of Labor in China.* Princeton: Princeton University Press.

Gallagher, Mary E., et al. 2015. China's 2008 Labor Contract Law: implementation and implications for China's workers. *Human Relations* 68(2), 197–235.

Gao, Hua, and Jun Huang. 2002. 1960 nian 'chixu yuejin' zhong de jiangsusheng chengshi renmin gongshe yundong. (The movement of urban communes in Jiangsu in the 'Continual Leap Forward' in 1960). *Zhejiang xuekan* (5), 51–56.

Gao, Mobo. 1999. *Gao Village: A Portrait of Rural Life in Modern China.* Honolulu: University of Hawaii Press.

Global Economic Database. 2024. China total exports growth. https://www.ceicdata.com/en/indicator/china/total-exports-growth. Accessed 17 December 2024.

Gong, Shuji. 1989. *Youhua laodong zuhe* (*Optimizing Labour Combination*). Beijing: Kexue chubanshe.

Gordon, David M., Richard Edwards, and Michael Reich. 1982. *Segmented Work, Divided Workers: The Historical Transformation of Labor in the United States*. Cambridge: Cambridge University Press.

Granick, David. 1991. Multiple labour markets in the industrial state enterprise sector. *The China Quarterly* 126 (June), 269–289.

Gregory, Paul R., and Irwin L. Collier Jr. 1988. Unemployment in the Soviet Union: evidence from the Soviet Interview Project. *The American Economic Review* 78(4), 613–632.

Gregory, Paul R., and Robert C. Stuart. 1974. *Soviet Economic Structure and Performance*. New York: Harper & Row.

Han, Jun. 2005. Shidi nongmin de jiuye he shehui baozhang (Employment and social security of peasants who lost land). *Kexue zixun* (07S), 28–31.

Harris, Nigel. 2015. *The Mandate of Heaven: Marx and Mao in Modern China*. Chicago: Haymarket Books.

Harvey, David. 1989. *The Condition of Postmodernity: An Enquiry into the Origins of Social Change*. Oxford: Wiley-Blackwell.

2003. *The New Imperialism*. Oxford: Oxford University Press.

2007. *A Brief History of Neoliberalism*. Oxford: Oxford University Press.

He, Guang, et al. 1990. *Dangdai zhongguo de laodongli guanli* (*The Management of Labour Power in Contemporary China*). Beijing: Zhongguo shehui kexue chubanshe.

He, Luli. 2005. Quanguo renda changweihui zhifa jianchazu guanyu jiancha zhonghua renmin gongheguo laodongfa shishi qingkuang de baogao (Report on the inspection of the implementation of China's Labour Law by the legal inspection group of the Standing Committee of the National People's Congress). *Zhonghua renmin gongheguo quanguo renmin daibiao dahui changwu weiyuanhui gongbao* (1), 82–87.

He, Zilin. 1989. Shilun shehui zhuyi tiaojian xiade shiye (An experimental discussion about unemployment under socialism). *Zhongguo laodong kexue* (2), 16–17.

Heimer, Maria. 2006. Field sites, research design and type of findings. In Maria Heimer and Stig Thøgersen (eds), *Doing Fieldwork in China*. Honolulu: University of Hawaii Press.

Hershatter, Gail. 1986. *The Workers of Tianjin, 1900–1949*. Redwood City: Stanford University Press.

Hinton, William. 1983. *Shenfan: The Continuing Revolution in a Chinese Village*. New York: Random House.

Hong, Huanchun. 1958. Guanyu mingdai ziben zhuyi shengchan de mengya wenti (On the sprouts of capitalistic production in the Ming Dynasty). *Lishi jiaoxue wenti* (4), 11–15.

Honig, Emily. 1992. *Sisters and Strangers: Women in the Shanghai Cotton Mills, 1919–1949*. Redwood City: Stanford University Press.

Hou, Chi-Ming. 1963. Economic dualism: the case of China 1840–1937. *The Journal of Economic History* 23(3), 277–297.

Howard, Pat. 1991. Rice bowls and job security: the urban contract labour system. *The Australian Journal of Chinese Affairs* (25), 93–114.

Howell, Jude, and Tim Pringle. 2019. Shades of authoritarianism and state–labour relations in China. *British Journal of Industrial Relations* 57(2), 223–246.
Hu, Angang, et al. 2014. *Zhongguo guojia zhili xiandaihua (The Modernization of the Governance of China)*. Beijing: Zhongguo renmin daxue chubanshe.
Hu, Zhongyuan, et al. 2004. *Beijing zhi: Youzheng zhi* (*Beijing Chorography: Postal Chorography*). Beijing: Beijing Press.
Huang, Philip CC. 1985. *The Peasant Economy and Social Change in North China*. Redwood City: Stanford University Press.
1990. *The Peasant Family and Rural Development in the Yangzi Delta, 1350–1988*. Redwood City: Stanford University Press.
2009. China's neglected informal economy: reality and theory. *Modern China* 35(4), 405–438.
2011. The theoretical and practical implications of China's development experience: the role of informal economic practices. *Modern China* 37(1), 3–43.
2017a. Dispatch work in China: a study from case records, part I. *Modern China* 43(3), 1–41.
2017b. Dispatch work in China: a study from case records, part II. *Modern China* 43(4), 355–396.
Huang, Philip CC, Yuan Gao, and Yusheng Peng. 2012. Capitalization without proletarianization in China's agricultural development. *Modern China* 38(2), 139–173.
Huang, Yu, and Naubahar Sharif. 2017. From 'labour dividend' to 'robot dividend': technological change and workers' power in South China. *Agrarian South: Journal of Political Economy* 6(1), 53–78.
Huang, Zongzhi. 2008. Zhongguo de xiao zichan jieji he zhongjian jieceng: beilun de shehui xingtai (The petty bourgeoisie and the middle class in China: a paradoxical social formation). *Zhongguo xiangcun yanjiu*, 1–14.
Hurst, William. J. 2009. *The Chinese Worker after Socialism*. Cambridge: Cambridge University Press.
ILO. 2015. Transition from the informal to the formal economy recommendation. https://normlex.ilo.org/dyn/nrmlx_en/f?p=NORMLEXPUB:12100:0::NO::P12100_ILO_CODE:R204. Accessed 14 October 2025.
Industrial Relations Arbitration Committee of Shanghai. 1948. *Shanghai wushiyi ye gongchang laogong tongji, 1948 nian ban (Statistics on Factory Workers in Fifty-One Industries in Shanghai, 1948 edition)*. Shanghai: Shanghaishi laozi pingduan weiyuanhui.
Inkeles, Alex. 1950. Social stratification and mobility in the Soviet Union: 1940–1950. *American Sociological Review* 15(4), 465–479.
International Federation of Robotics. 2014. *World Robotics, Industrial Robots 2014*. Frankfurt: International Federation of Robotics.
2024. Global robotics race: Korea, Singapore and Germany in the lead. https://ifr.org/ifr-press-releases/news/global-robotics-race-korea-singapore-and-germany-in-the-lead. Accessed 6 July 2024.
Investigation Team from the Institute of Economic Studies, Xiamen University. 1976. 'Wuqi' daolu kuan you guang, chengzhen jiumao bian xinyan (The

Wuqi road is wide and long, and the urban area takes on new looks). *Zhongguo jingji wenti* (Z1), 52–57.

Jessop, Bob. 1992. Fordism and Post-Fordism: a critical reformulation. In Allen J. Scott and Michael Storper (eds), *Pathways to Regionalism and Industrial Development*. London: Routledge.

Ji, Long, et al. 1991. *Dangdai zhongguo de jiti gongye, shang* (*Collective Industry in Contemporary China, Part I*). Beijing: Dangdai zhongguo chubanshe.

2000. *Xin zhongguo jiti gongye de wushinian* (*Fifty Years of Collective Industry in New China*). Beijing: Guojia qinggongye ju, Zhonghua quanguo shougongye hezuo zongshe, guoshi yanjiu lingdao xiaozu.

Jiang, Junlu, and Shaogang Wang. 2016. Lianghui guancha: laodong hetongfa xiugai qi bolan (An observation of the Two Big Meetings: whether or not to revise the Labour Contract Law sparks debate), https://www.chinalawinsight.com/2016/04/articles/labor-employment/%E4%B8%A4%E4%BC%9A%E8%A7%82%E5%AF%9F%EF%BC%9A%E3%80%8A%E5%8A%B3%E5%8A%A8%E5%90%88%E5%90%8C%E6%B3%95%E3%80%8B%E4%BF%AE%E6%94%B9%E8%B5%B7%E6%B3%A2%E6%BE%9C/. Accessed 9 December 2024.

Jiang, Zemin. 1997. Gaoju Deng Xiaoping lilun weida qizhi, ba jianshe you zhongguo tese shehui zhuyi shiye quanmian tuixiang ershiyi shiji – zai zhongguo gongchandang di shiwu ci quanguo daibiao dahui shang de baogao (Holding high the great banner of Deng Xiaoping Theory, and advancing socialism with Chinese characteristics fully into the twenty-first century – a report at the 15th National Congress of the CCP). *Lilun jianshe* (5), 1–22.

Jin, Baoyu. 2005. Zhongguo de nongye fazhan yu wenti (Agricultural development and problems in China). https://critiqueandtransformation.wordpress.com/2005/06/02/中國的農業發展與問題金寶瑜/. Accessed 4 September 2023.

Jin, Yihong. 2006. 'Tie guniang' zaisikao – zhongguo wenhua dageming qijian de shehui xingbie yu laodong (Rethinking 'iron girls' – gender and labour during the Cultural Revolution of China). *Shehuixue yanjiu* (1), 169–193.

Jones, Stephen Richard Henry. 1982. The organization of work: a historical dimension. *Journal of Economic Behavior & Organization* 3(2–3), 117–137.

Jonna, R. Jamil, and John B. Foster. 2016. Marx's theory of working-class precariousness – and its relevance today. *Monthly Review* 67(11), 21–45.

Kalleberg, Arne L. 2009. Precarious work, insecure workers: employment relations in transition. *American Sociological Review* 74(1), 1–22.

Kapelyushnikov, Rostislav, Andrei Kuznetsov, and Olga Kuznetsova. 2012. The role of the informal sector, flexible working time and pay in the Russian labour market model. *Post-Communist Economics* 24(2), 177–190.

Kohlmann, Thomas. 2017. VW's workers in China demand equal pay, https://www.dw.com/en/vws-casual-workers-in-china-fight-for-equal-pay/a-37821854. Accessed 17 June 2025.

Koo, Anita. 2016. Expansion of vocational education in neoliberal China: hope and despair among rural youth. *Journal of Education Policy* 31(1), 46–59.

Kornai, Janos. 1992. *The Socialist System: The Political Economy of Communism*. Oxford: Oxford University Press.

Kraemer, Kenneth L., Greg Linden, and Jason Dedrick. 2011. Capturing value in global networks: Apple's iPad and iPhone. Working paper, University of California, Irvine. https://economiadeservicos.com/wp-content/uploads/2017/04/value_ipad_iphone.pdf. Accessed 17 June 2025.

Kuruvilla, Sarosh, Ching Kwan Lee, and Mary E. Gallagher (eds). 2011. *From Iron Rice Bowl to Informalization: Markets, Workers, and the State in a Changing China*. Ithaca: Cornell University Press.

Labour Bureau of Shanghai. 1950. Guangyu shiye gongren fugong jiuye de baodao (Report on the re-employment of the unemployed). *Laodong gongbao* (4), 27.

Labour Bureau of Suzhou. 1985. Qianding laowu hetong, nongmin jincheng zuogong (Peasants became urban workers under labour service contracts). *Zhongguo laodong* (5), 15–16.

Labour Bureau of Wenzhou. 1993. Duoqudao kaizhan zhiye jieshao (Multiple ways for job introduction). *Zhongguo laodong kexue* (8), 11–14.

Lapavitsas, Costas. 2009. Financialised capitalism: crisis and financial expropriation. *Historical Materialism* 17(2), 114–148.

Lau, Lawrence J., Yingyi Qian, and Gerard Roland. 2000. Reform without losers: an interpretation of China's dual-track approach to transition. *Journal of Political Economy* 108(1), 120–143.

Lee, Ching Kwan. 1998. *Gender and the South China Miracle: Two Worlds of Factory Women*. Oakland: University of California Press.

2007. *Against the Law: Labor Protests in China's Rustbelt and Sunbelt*. Oakland: University of California Press.

2016. Precarization or empowerment? Reflections on recent labor unrest in China. *The Journal of Asian Studies* 75(2), 317–333.

2017. After the miracle: labour politics under China's New Normal. *Catalyst* 1(3), 92–115.

2019. China's precariats. *Globalizations* 16(2), 137–154.

Lee, Ching Kwan, and Yelizavetta Kofman. 2012. The politics of precarity: views beyond the United States. *Work and Occupations* 39(4), 388–408.

Lee, Hong Yung. 1980. *The Politics of the Chinese Cultural Revolution: A Case Study*. Oakland: University of California Press.

Lee, Joohee. 2017b. More protection, still gendered: the effects of non-standard employment protection acts on South Korean women workers. *Journal of Contemporary Asia* 47(1), 46–65.

Leung, Pak Nang, and Ngai Pun. 2009. The radicalization of the new working class: a case study of collective action in the gemstone industry. *Third World Quarterly* 30(3), 551–565.

Lewis, W. Arthur. 1954. Economic development with unlimited supplies of labour. *The Manchester School* 22(2), 139–191.

Li, Bote. 2003a. Quan Hong Zong shimo (The whole story of Quan Hong Zong). *Huaxia wenzhai zengkan* 334.

Li, Huazhong, et al. 1994. *Angang Zhi, xia (A Chorography of Anshan Steel Company, Part II)*. Beijing: Renmin chubanshe.

Li, Jiaqi, et al. 1997. *Shanghai gongyun zhi* (*A Chorography of Labour Movements in Shanghai*). Shanghai: Shanghai shehui kexueyuan chubanshe.

Li, Jinlei. 2023. Huji xinzheng laile! Guanxi ni de hukou (New *hukou* policy comes out! It is related to your *hukou*). https://www.chinanews.com.cn/cj/2023/08-03/10054825.shtml. Accessed 17 July 2024.

Li, Lin, and He, Tian. 2014. *Zhongguo fazhi fazhan baogao No. 12 (The No. 12 Report on the Development of Legal Governance in China)*. Beijing: Shehui kexue wenxian chubanshe.

Li, Longqian. 1959. Shilun mingdai kuangye zhong ziben zhuyi yinsu de mengya ji tedian (A preliminary study on the sprouts of capitalist elements and their characteristics in mining in the Ming Dynasty). *Xueshu yanjiu* (6), 32–37.

Li, Peilin, Yi Zhang, and Yandong Zhao. 2000. *Jiuye yu zhidu bianqian – Liangge teshu qunti de qiuzhi guocheng (Employment and Institutional Transformation – The Job-Seeking Process of Two Special Groups)*. Hangzhou: Zhejiang renmin chubanshe.

Li, Qi. 2003b. *Gaige yu xiufu: Dangdai zhongguo guoyou qiye de laogong guanxi yanjiu* (*Reform and Remedy: A Study on the Industrial Relations in State-Owned Enterprises in Contemporary China*). Beijing: Zhongguo laodong baozhang chubanshe.

Li, Shi. 2016. Recent changes in income inequality in China. In ISSC, IDS, and UNESCO (eds), *World Social Science Report 2016*. Paris: UNESCO Publishing.

Li, Xiaoying, and Richard B. Freeman. 2015. How does China's new Labour Contract Law affect floating workers? *British Journal of Industrial Relations* 53(4), 711–735.

Li, Xiaoying, and Zhong Zhao. 2012. Chengzhen laodongli shichang guyong guanxi de yanhua ji yingxiang yinsu (The evolution of employment relationships in the urban labour market and its influencing factors). *Jingji yanjiu* (9), 85–98.

Li, Xun. 2015. *Geming zaofan niandai (The Era of Revolution and Rebellion)*. Hong Kong: Oxford University Press.

Li, Yile, and Jie Meng. 2014. Zhongguo laodongli shangpinhua chengdu de biandong jiqi dui laodongzhe baochou de yingxiang (Changes in the degree of the commodification of labour power and its impacts on labour income in China). *Jingji xuejia* 12(12), 21–32.

Lin, Chaochao. 2012. Hefa hua ziyuan yu zhongguo gongren de xingdong zhuyi: 1957 nian shanghai 'gongchao' zai yanjiu (Resources of legitimacy and Chinese workers' activism: re-studying Shanghai Workers' Strikes in 1957). *Shehui* (1), 197–219.

2014. 'Da yuejin' hou de channeng guosheng yu chengshi gongye de zengxiao gaige (Industrial overcapacity and efficiency-improving reforms in urban industries after the Great Leap Forward). *Zhonggong dangshi yanjiu* (3), 133–145.

Lin, Chun. 2006. *The Transformation of Chinese Socialism*. Durham: Duke University Press.

Lin, Justin Yifu, Fang Cai, and Zhou Li. 1998. Competition, policy burdens, and state-owned enterprise reform. *The American Economic Review* 88(2), 422–427.

Literature Research Centre of the Central Committee of the CCP. 1983. *Guanyu jianguo yilai dang de ruogan lishi wenti de jueyi zhushiben (Notes on the*

*Resolutions for Several Historical Issues of the CCP since the Establishment of the People's Republic of China)*. Beijing: Renmin chubanshe.

2013. *Mao Zedong nianpu, 1949–1976, disanjuan (A Chronology of Mao Zedong, 1949–1976, Vol. 3)*. Beijing: Zhongyang wenxian chubanshe.

Liu, Guoguang, et al. 2006. *Zhongguo shige wunian jihua yanjiu baogao (Research Report on Ten Five-Year Plans of China)*. Beijing: Renmin chubanshe.

Liu, Mingkui, and Yuliang Tang. 1998. *Zhongguo gongren yundong shi, diyice. (A History of Labour Movements in China, Vol. 1)*. Guangzhou: Guangdong renmin chubanshe.

Liu, Shaoqi. 1985. *Liu Shaoqi xuanji, xiajuan (Selected Works of Liu Shaoqi, Part II)*. Beijing: Renmin chubanshe.

1993. *Liu Shaoqi lun xinzhongguo jingji jianshe (Works of Liu Shaoqi on the Economic Development of New China)*. Beijing: Zhongyang wenxian chubanshe.

Liu, Yongcheng. 1962. Lun qingdai guyong laodong – jianyu Ouyang fanxiu tongzhi shangque (On wage labour in the Qing Dynasty and a discussion with Comrade Ouyang Fanxiu). *Lishi yanjiu* (4), 104–128.

Lou, Jiwei, et al. 2000. *Xinzhongguo 50 nian caizheng tongji* (*Fifty years of Financial Statistics of New China*). Beijing: Jingji kexue chubanshe.

Lu, Feng. 1993. Zhongguo danweizhi de qiyuan yu xingcheng (The origins and formation of the unit system in China). *Zhongguo shehuixue* (2), 91–134.

2016. *Guangbian: Yige qiye jiqi gongyeshi (Changes of Light: The History of Beijing Oriental Enterprise)*. Beijing: Dangdai zhongguo chubanshe.

2012. Zhongguo nongmingong gongzi zoushi: 1979–2010 (The trend of wages of peasant workers in China: 1979–2010). *Zhongguo shehui kexue* (7), 47–67.

Lu, Nanquan. 2007. *Sulian jingji tizhi gaige shilun: Cong liening dao pujing (A History of the Reform of the Soviet Economic System: From Lenin to Putin)*. Beijing: Renmin chubanshe.

Lü, Xiaobo. 1997. Minor public economy: the revolutionary origins of the danwei. In Xiaobo Lü, and Elizabeth Perry (eds), *Danwei: The Changing Chinese Workplace in Historical and Comparative Perspective*. Armonk, NY: ME Sharpe.

Luo, Pinghan. 2003. *Da qianxi: 1961~1963 nian de chengzhen renkou jingjian* (*The Great Relocation: Population Downsizing in Urban China between 1961 and 1963*). Nanning: Guangxi renmin chubanshe.

Lüthje, Boy, Siqi Luo, and Hao Zhang. 2013. *Beyond the Iron Rice Bowl: Regimes of Production and Industrial Relations in China, Vol. 4*. Frankfurt: Campus Verlag.

Ma, Xuejun. 2016. Batou baogong zhi: jindai zhongguo gongyehua zhong de guyong he shengchan fangshi (Gangmaster contract system: employment and production in the industrialization of modern China). *Shehuixue yanjiu* (2), 102–122.

Ma, Zengrong. 2012. Qinhan shiqi de guyong huodong yu renkou liudong (Hiring activities and population movements in Qin and Han Dynasties). *Zhongguo wenhua yanjiusuo xuebao* 54, 1–28.

Maddison, Angus. 2007. *Chinese Economic Performance in the Long Run*. Paris: OECD Development Centre Studies.

Mao, Tse-Tung. 1971. *Selected Readings from the Works of Mao Tse-tung*. Beijing: Foreign Language Press.

Mao, Zedong. 1977. Kang mei yuan chao de weida shengli he jinhou de renwu (The great triumph of the Korean War and tasks thereafter). In Mao Zedong's Works Editing and Publishing Committee of the Central Committee of the CCP (ed.), *Mao Zedong xuanji, diwujuan* (*Selected Works of Mao Zedong, Vol. 5*). Beijing: Renmin chubanshe.

1982. *Mao Zedong nongcun diaocha wenji (Collections of Mao Zedong's Rural Investigations)*. Beijing: Renmin chubanshe.

1986. Lun shi da guanxi (On the ten major relationships). In Literature Editing Committee of the Central Committee of the CCP (ed.), *Mao Zedong zhuzuo xuandu, xiace (Selected Readings of Mao Zedong, Part II)*. Beijing: Renmin chubanshe.

Marangos, John. 2003. Was shock therapy really a shock? *Journal of Economic Issues* 37(4), 943–966.

Marglin, Stephen A., and Juliet B. Schor (eds). 2000. *The Golden Age of Capitalism: Reinterpreting the Postwar Experience*. Oxford: Oxford University Press.

Marshall, Thomas Humphrey. 1950. *Citizenship and Social Class and Other Essays*. New York: Cambridge University Press.

Marx, Karl. 1973. *Grundrisse*. London: Penguin Books.

1996. *Capital Volume I. Marx-Engels Collected Works. Vol. 35*. London: Lawrence & Wishart Ltd.

Marx, Karl, and Friedrich Engels. 1988. *The Economic and Philosophic Manuscripts of 1844 and the Communist Manifesto*. Amherst: Prometheus Books.

Maschmeyer, Richard A., and Ji-Liang Yang. 1993. Results of the contract responsibility system in the People's Republic of China: an analysis of two state enterprises. *Thunderbird International Business Review* 35(3), 253–272.

Mayer, Gerald. 2004. *Union Membership Trends in the United States*. Washington: Congressional Research Service.

Mazat, Numa, and Franklin Serrano. 1995. An analysis of the Soviet economic growth from the 1950's to the collapse of USSR. http://www.centrosraffa.org/public/bb6ba675-6bef-4182-bb89-339ae1f7e792.pdf. Accessed 7 January 2021.

Meisner, Maurice. 1999. *Mao's China and After: A History of the People's Republic*. New York: The Free Press.

Meng, Jie. 2012. Zhanhou huangjin niandai shi zenyang xingcheng de – dui liangzhong makesi zhuyi jieshi de pipanxing fenxi (How did the golden age after the Second World War came into being – a critical analysis of two Marxist explanations). *Makesi zhuyi yanjiu* (5), 35–46.

Meng, Jie, and Yile Li. 2013. Gaige yilai laodongli shangpinhua he guyong guanxi de fazhan – bolanni he makesi de shijiao (The development of the commodification of labour and wage employment since the Reform – perspectives from Polanyi and Marx). *Kaifang shidai* (5), 85–117.

Mi, Hong, and Zhenghua Jiang. 1996. Minguo renkou tongji diaocha he ziliao de yanjiu yu pingjia (Study and evaluation of statistical surveys and other references about population in the Republican era). *Renkou yanjiu* (3), 44–52.

Mikhalev, Vladimir. 1996. Social security in Russia under economic transformation. *Europe–Asia Studies* 48(1), 5–25.

Millar, Kathleen M. 2017. Toward a critical politics of precarity. *Sociology Compass* 11(6), 1–11.

Ministry of Commerce. 2022a. Zhongguo waizi tongji gongbao 2022 (Statistical bulletin of FDI in China 2022). http://images.mofcom.gov.cn/wzs/202211/20221102151438905.pdf. Accessed 21 October 2023.

2022b. 'Sanjia mache' zhiyi de waimao daidong jiuye 1.8 yi ren (Export, one of the three driving forces of China's economic growth, creates 180 million jobs). http://www.ce.cn/xwzx/gnsz/gdxw/202205/20/t20220520_37601152.shtml.Accessed 6 July 2024.

Ministry of Education. 2012. *Zhongguo jiaoyu tongji nianjian 2011 (Educational Statistical Yearbook of China 2011)*. Beijing: Renmin jiaoyu chubanshe.

2024. Quanguo jiaoyu shiye fazhan tongji gongbao (Statistical bulletin of educational development in China). http://www.moe.gov.cn/jyb_sjzl/sjzl_fztjgb/. Accessed 17 July 2024.

Ministry of Labour. 1950. Zhongyang renmin zhengfu laodongbu gongzuo baogao (Report on the work of the Ministry of Labour of the central government). *Yunnan zhengbao* (5), 96–98.

1991. *Zhongguo laodong nianjian 1988–1989 (China Labour Yearbook 1988–1989)*. Beijing: Zhongguo laodong chubanshe.

1992. Laodongbu bangongting guanyu guanche quanmin suoyouzhi qiye zhaoyong nongmin hetongzhi gongren de guiding zhong youguan wenti de fuhan (Reply from the administrative office of the Ministry of Labour pertaining to problems in the implementation of the provisions on the recruitment of peasant contract workers in state-owned enterprises), https://www.shui5.cn/article/0f/176902.html. Accessed 9 December 2024.

1993. *Zhongguo laodong nianjian 1990–1991* (*China Labour Yearbook 1990–1991*). Beijing: Zhongguo laodong chubanshe.

Ministry of Labour, and the Ministry of Personnel. 1991. *Zhongguo laodong renshi nianjian 1949–1987* (*The Yearbook of Chinese Labour and Personnel 1949–1987*). Beijing: Zhongguo laodong chubanshe.

Ministry of Labour and Personnel. 1982. *Laodong jiuye he laodong fuwu gongsi wenti yanjiu* (*A Study on Employment and Employment Service Companies*). Beijing: Laodong chubanshe.

Mitropoulos, Angela. 2005. Precari-us? *Mute* 1(29), 88–96.

MOHRSS. 2014. Laowu paiqian tonggong tongchou bu baokuo fuli he shebao (Equal pay for equal work excludes welfare benefits and social insurance). *Xiandai rencai* (5), 8.

2024. 2023 niandu renli ziyuan he shehui baozhang shiye fazhan tongji gongbao (Statistics on the development of the course of human resources and social security in 2023). https://www.mohrss.gov.cn/SYrlzyhshbzb/zwgk/szrs/tjgb/202406/W020240617617024381518.pdf. Accessed 17 July 2024.

Mou, Yongan, and Hongzhang Jie. 1955. Yange kongzhi zhaoyong linshigong (Stringent control on recruiting temporary workers). *Laodong* (7), 13.

Municipal government of Beijing. 2005. Beijing chengshi zongti guihua (2004–2020) (General Plan (2004–2020) of Urban Beijing). *Beijing guihua jianshe* (2), 5–51.

2016. Beijing shi guomin jingji he shehui fazhan di shisange wunian guihua gangyao (Summary of the Thirteenth Five-Year Plan for the Economic and

Social Development of Beijing). *Beijing shi renda changwei hui gongbao* (1), 20–81.
Muravyev, Alexander. 2014. Evolution of employment protection legislation in the USSR, CIS and Baltic States, 1985–2009. *Europe–Asia Studies* 66(8), 1270–1294.
National Bureau of Labour. 1980. *Zhongguo laodong lifa ziliao huibian* (*A Collection of Labour Legislative Documents in China*). Beijing: Gongren chubanshe.
National Committee of Hygiene and Birth Control. 2014. *Zhongguo weisheng he jihua shengyu tongji nianjian 2014 (China Hygiene and Birth Control Statistical Yearbook 2014)*. Beijing: Zhongguo xiehe yike daxue chubanshe.
National Committee of Hygiene and Health. 2023. *Zhongguo weisheng jiankang tongji nianjian 2022* (*China Hygiene and Health Statistical Yearbook 2022*). Beijing: Zhongguo xiehe yike daxue chubanshe.
National Committee of Reforming the Economic System. 1998. *Zaijiuye gongcheng zhinan* (*A Guideline for the Re-employment Project*). Kunming: Yunnan chubanshe.
National Data Centre. 2020. Zhongguo gongxiang jingji fazhan baogao 2020 (Report on the development of the sharing economy in China, 2020). https://www.huiqiyidiantong.com/Upload/2020/08/26/2020_08_26_1598426737_569116.pdf. Accessed 6 January 2022.
National Healthcare Security Administration. 2024. 2023 nian yiliao baozhang shiye fazhan tongji kuaibao (Statistics on the development of the course of health security in 2023). https://www.nhsa.gov.cn/art/2024/4/11/art_7_12348.html. Accessed 17 July 2024.
National People's Congress. 1999. Zhonghua renmin gongheguo xianfa xiuzhengan, 1988 (An amendment to the Constitution of the People's Republic of China, 1988). In National People's Congress, *Zhonghua renmin gongheguo xianfa (Constitutions of the People's Republic of China)*. Beijing: Renmin chubanshe.
National Post Bureau. 2016. 2015 nian youzheng hangye fazhan tongji gongbao (Statistical bulletin of the development of the postal industry in 2015). http://www.chinawuliu.com.cn/xsyj/201605/11/312023.shtml. Accessed 8 January 2021.
National Post Bureau, and Deloitte. 2014. Zhongguo kuaidi hangye fazhan baogao 2014 (China express industry development report 2014). https://www2.deloitte.com/content/dam/Deloitte/global/Documents/Consumer-Business/gx-cb-chinas-express-sector-chinese.pdf. Accessed 8 January 2021.
Naughton, Barry J. 1988. The Third Front: defence industrialization in the Chinese interior. *The China Quarterly* 115, 351–386.
1997. Danwei: the economic foundations of a unique institution. In Xiaobo Lü and Elizabeth Perry (eds), *Danwei: The Changing Chinese Workplace in Historical and Comparative Perspective*. Armonk, NY: Me Sharpe.
2006. *The Chinese Economy: Transitions and Growth*. Cambridge, MA: Massachusetts Institute of Technology Press.
NBS. 1984. *Guanghui de sanshiwu nian, 1949–1984* (*The Glorious Thirty-Five Years, 1949–1984*). Beijing: Zhongguo tongji chubanshe.
1985. *Zhongguo gongye jingji tongji ziliao, 1949–1984 (Statistics on the Industrial Economy of China, 1949–1984)*. Beijing: Zhongguo tongji chubanshe.

1987. *Zhongguo laodong gongzi tongji ziliao 1949–1985 (China Labour and Wage Statistics, 1949–1985)*. Beijing: Zhongguo tongji chubanshe.

1989. *Zhongguo laodong gongzi tongji ziliao 1978–1987 (China Labour and Wage Statistics, 1978–1987)*. Beijing: Zhongguo tongji chubanshe.

1999. *Xin zhongguo wushinian tongji ziliao huibian* (*Collected Statistics on Fifty Years of New China*). Beijing: Zhongguo tongji chubanshe.

2000a–2023a. *Zhongguo tongji nianjian 2000–2023 (China Statistical Yearbook 2000–2023)*. Beijing: Zhongguo tongji chubanshe.

2010b. *Xin zhongguo liushinian tongji ziliao huibian* (*Collected Statistics on Sixty Years of New China*). Beijing: Zhongguo tongji chubanshe.

2010c. *Zhongguo nongcun zhuhu diaocha nianjian 2010* (*China Rural Household Survey Yearbook 2010*). Beijing: Zhongguo tongji chubanshe.

2014b–2024b. 2013–2023 nian quanguo nongmingong diaocha jiance baogao (Oversight investigative report on peasant-workers, 2013–2023).

https://www.gov.cn/xinwen/2014-05/12/content_2677889.htm

https://www.gov.cn/xinwen/2015-04/29/content_2854930.htm

https://www.gov.cn/xinwen/2016-04/28/content_5068727.htm

https://www.gov.cn/xinwen/2017-04/28/content_5189509.htm#1

https://www.stats.gov.cn/sj/zxfb/202302/t20230203_1899920.html

https://www.stats.gov.cn/sj/zxfb/202302/t20230203_1900299.html

https://www.stats.gov.cn/sj/zxfb/202302/t20230203_1900710.html

https://www.stats.gov.cn/sj/zxfb/202302/t20230203_1901074.html

https://www.gov.cn/xinwen/2022-04/29/content_5688043.htm

https://www.stats.gov.cn/sj/zxfb/202304/t20230427_1939124.html

https://www.gov.cn/lianbo/bumen/202405/content_6948813.htm. Accessed 9 December 2024.

NBS. 2021. *Zhongguo maoyi waijing tongji nianjian 2021 (Statistical Yearook of Trade and Foreign-Related Economic Activities in China in 2021)*. Beijing: Zhongguo tongji chubanshe.

2024a. Guojia shuju (National data). https://data.stats.gov.cn/easyquery.htm?cn=C01. Accessed 17 July 2024.

NBS, and the Ministry of Labour. 1989. *Zhongguo laodong gongzi tongji nianjian 1989* (*China Labour and Wage Statistical Yearbook 1989*). Beijing: Laodong renshi chubanshe.

1990. *Zhongguo laodong gongzi tongji nianjian 1990* (*China Labour and Wage Statistical Yearbook 1990*). Beijing: Zhongguo tongji chubanshe.

1993, 1994, 1996a, 1996b, 1997, 1998. *Zhongguo laodong tongji nianjian 1993–1998* (*China Labour Statistical Yearbook 1993, 1994, 1995, 1996, 1997, 1998*). Beijing: Zhongguo tongji chubanshe.

NBS, and MOHRSS. 2020. *Zhongguo laodong tongji nianjian 2020 (China Labour Statistical Yearbook 2020)*. Beijing: Zhongguo tongji chubanshe.

2023. *Zhongguo laodong tongji nianjian 2023 (China Labour Statistical Yearbook 2023)*. Beijing: Zhongguo tongji chubanshe.

Ning, Kang, et al. 2010. *Dongguan laodong zhi* (*Labour Chorography of Dongguan*). Guangzhou: Lingnan meishu chubanshe.

OECD. 2020. Social expenditure – aggregated data. https://stats.oecd.org/Index.aspx?datasetcode=SOCX_REF. Accessed 6 January 2021.

2024. Temporary employment. https://www.oecd.org/en/data/indicators/temporary-employment.html?oecdcontrol-00b22b2429-var3=2020. Accessed 18 July 2024.

Ouyang, Fanxiu. 1961. Ming qing liangdai nongye gugong falü shang renshen lishu guanxi de jiefang (The emancipation of agricultural wage labour from legal subordination in the Ming and Qing Dynasties). *Jingji yanjiu* (6), 49–73.

Oya, Carlos, and Florian Schaefer. 2019. *Chinese Firms and Employment Dynamics in Africa: A Comparative Analysis*. London: SOAS, University of London.

People's Bank of China. 2020. 2019 nian zhongguo chengzhen jumin jiating zichan fuzhai qingkuang diaocha (A survey of the assets and liabilities of urban households in China in 2019). https://finance.sina.com.cn/money/lczx/2020-04-24/doc-iirczymi8099086.shtml. Accessed 7 January 2021.

Perry, Elizabeth J. 1993. *Shanghai on Strike: The Politics of Chinese Labor*. Redwood City: Stanford University Press.

1996. Labor's love lost: worker militancy in Communist China. *International Labor and Working-Class History* 50(fall), 64–76.

Perry, Elizabeth J., and Xun Li. 1997. *Proletarian Power: Shanghai in the Cultural Revolution*. Boulder: Westview Press.

Personnel Bureau of Fenyi, Jiangxi. 1985. Banhao xiangzhen laodong fuwu gongsi anzhi nongcun fuyu laodongli (Well operating township-level labour service companies to place rural surplus labour). *Zhongguo laodong* (9), 27–28.

Picot, Georg, and Arianna Tassinari. 2014. Liberalization, dualization, or recalibration? Labor market reforms under austerity, Italy and Spain 2010–2012. Lisbon: The Welfare State in Portugal in the Age of Austerity Conference, 9–10 May 2014.

Piore, Michael J. 1972. Notes for a theory of labor market stratification. Working papers 95, Department of Economics, Massachusetts Institute of Technology.

Polanyi, Karl. 2001. *The Great Transformation: The Political and Economic Origins of Our Time*. Boston: Beacon Press.

Porket, Josef L. 1989. *Work, Employment and Unemployment in the Soviet Union*. New York: Palgrave Macmillan.

Prosser, Thomas. 2016. Dualization or liberalization? Investigating precarious work in eight European countries. *Work, Employment and Society* 30(6), 949–965.

Pun, Ngai. 2005. *Made in China: Women Factory Workers in a Global Workplace*. Durham: Duke University Press.

Pun, Ngai, and Huilin Lu. 2010. Unfinished proletarianization: self, anger, and class action among the second generation of peasant-workers in present-day China. *Modern China* 36(5), 493–519.

Pun, Ngai, and Jenny Chan. 2012. Global capital, the state, and Chinese workers: the Foxconn experience. *Modern China* 38(4), 383–410.

Pun, Ngai, Huilin Lu, and Huipeng Zhang. 2012. *Dagongdi: Jianzhuye nongmingong de shengcun tujing (The Great Construction Site: Life of Peasant Workers in the Construction Sector)*. Beijing: Beijing daxue chubanshe.

Qi, Benyu. 2016. *Qi Benyu huiyilu* (*The Memoir of Qi Benyu*). Hong Kong: Zhongguo wenge lishi chubanshe.

Qi, Hao, and Zhongjin Li. 2020. Putting precarity back to production: a case study of Didi Kuaiche drivers in the City of Nanjing, China. *Review of Radical Political Economics* 52(3), 506–522.

Qingdao Branch of the ACFTU, and the All-China Federation of Women. 1994. Dangqian nü zhigong xiagang cunzai de zhuyao wenti (Main problems pertaining to the layoffs of female workers at present). *Laodong neican* (11), 31.

Qiu, Huihui. 2007. Huawei yingdui xin laodong hetongfa, wanming yuangong zixuan quliu (Huawei responds to the Labour Contract Law. Nearly 10,000 employees face the choice of leaving vs. remaining), *21 shiji jingji baodao*, 27 October.

Que, Mingkun, Hua Wang, and Huiying Wang. 2019. Gaige kaifang 40 nian woguo minban jiaoyu fazhan licheng yu zhanwang (Looking backward, looking forward: forty years of privately invested education in China since the Reform and Opening-up). *Zhongguo jiaoyu xuekan* (1), 29–36.

Raeburn, Nicole Christine. 2004. *Changing Corporate America from Inside Out: Lesbian and Gay Workplace Rights*. Minneapolis: University of Minnesota Press.

RedChinaCn. Net. 2014. Beijing nuojiya gongchang zaici bagong (Nokia workers in Beijing are on strike again). http://redchinacn.net/portal.php?mod=view&aid=22630. Accessed 11 August 2018.

Ren, Zemin. 1988. Guanyu jiejue qiye fuyu renyuan wenti de sikao (Thoughts on solving the redundancy problem in enterprises). *Zhongguo laodong kexue* (11), 21–23.

Representatives of No. 302 Construction Team. 1967. Xuelei banban de hetong baogong waibaogong zhidu (The bloody and tearful institution of contract labour and outsourced labour). *Hongse fengbao*, 27 February.

Research Office for Economic Laws of the Legislative Affairs Commission of the People's Congress. 1982. Tianjin shi chengzhen jiti suoyouzhi qingkuang diaocha (A survey of urban collective units in Tianjin). In Ministry of Labour and Personnel (ed.), *Laodong jiuye he laodong fuwu gongsi wenti yanjiu (Studies on Employment and Employment Services Companies)*. Beijing: Laodong chubanshe.

Research Team of the Institute of the Economic System and Management, the National Development and Reform Commission. 2015. Guoqi gaige licheng huigu yu dangqian gaige zhongdian (Review of the history of the reform of state-owned enterprises and key points in current reforms). *Zhongguo jingmao daokan* (7), 27–29.

Ricketts, Erol R., and Isabel V. Sawhill. 1988. Defining and measuring the underclass. *Journal of Policy Analysis and Management* 7(2), 316–325.

Rostow, Walt Whitman. 1960. *The Stages of Economic Growth: A Non-Communist Manifesto*. Cambridge: Cambridge University Press.

Schmitt, John, Elise Gould, and Josh Bivens. 2018. America's slow-motion wage crisis: four decades of slow and unequal growth. Economic Policy Institute. https://www.epi.org/publication/americas-slow-motion-wage-crisis-four-decades-of-slow-and-unequal-growth-2/. Accessed 6 January 2021.

Schwarz, Solomon. 1960. Unemployment in Soviet Union? *Current History* 39(231), 280–283.

Sheehan, Jackie. 2002. *Chinese Workers: A New History*. London: Routledge.

Shen, Fuxiang. 2010. *Zhengrong suiyue – Shoubu gongren zaofanpai huiyilu (The Radiant Period – The First Memoir of a Worker Rebel)*. Shanghai: Shidai guoji chuban youxian gongsi.

Shen, Yuan, and Yuhua Guo. 2012. Xinshengdai nongmingong chulu hezai (What is the remedy for the plight of migrant workers). *Shehui kexue bao*, 1 November.

Shen, Zhi, et al. 1998. *Shanghai laodong zhi (A Chorography of Labour Issues in Shanghai)*. Shanghai: Shanghai shehui kexueyuan chubanshe.

Shi, Guoheng. 1946. *Kunchang laogong (Workers in a Factory in Kunming)*. Shanghai: Shangwu yinshuguan.

Shi, Jianyun. 1996. Lun jindai zhongguo nongcun shougongye de xingshuai wenti (On the ebbs and flows of the rural handicraft industry in modern China). *Jindai shi yanjiu* 93(3), 25–43.

Silver, Beverly J. 2003. *Forces of Labor: Workers' Movements and Globalization since 1870*. Cambridge: Cambridge University Press.

Silver, Beverly J., and Eric Slater. 1999. The social origins of world hegemonies. In Giovanni Arrighi and Beverly Silver (eds), *Chaos and Governance in the Modern World System*. Minneapolis: University of Minnesota Press.

Silver, Laura, and Christine Huang. 2022. Key facts about China's declining population. https://www.pewresearch.org/short-reads/2022/12/05/key-facts-about-chinas-declining-population/. Accessed 29 September 2023.

Sina Caijing. 2013. Deerfu Beijing shubai gongren bagong, buman laowu paiqiangong shenfen (Disgruntled about being agency workers, hundreds of Delphi workers in Beijing are on strike). https://finance.sina.cn/sa/2013-02-06/detail-ikftpnnx6963295.d.html?from=wap. Accessed 11 August 2018.

Sirkin, Harold L., Michael Zinser, and Justin Rose. 2014. The shifting economics of global manufacturing. https://www.bcg.com/publications/2014/lean-manufacturing-globalization-shifting-economics-global-manufacturing.aspx. Accessed 11 August 2018.

Smith, Chris, and Jenny Chan. 2015. Working for two bosses: student interns as constrained labour in China. *Human Relations* 68(2), 305–326.

Smith, Chris, and Ngai Pun. 2018. Class and precarity: an unhappy coupling in China's working class formation. *Work, Employment and Society* 32(3), 599–615.

Social Bureau of Shanghai. 1947. *Shanghai gongchang laogong tongji, 1946 nian shi (Statistics on Workers in Shanghai Factories, 1946 Edition)*. Shanghai: Shanghai shi shehuiju.

SOE News. 2017. 2017 zhongguo 500 qiang qiye bangdan laile (Fortune 500 list of China in 2017). http://industry.people.com.cn/n1/2017/0911/c413883-29528018.html. Accessed 11 August 2018.

Sohu Net. 2012. Nanzi zhaogongzuo bei heizhongjie pianqian, suohui wuguo tongsi gongzuo renyuan (A male jobseeker cheated by an unregistered labour agency, stabbed its staff to death after failing to get money back). http://news.sohu.com/20120215/n334747713.shtml. Accessed 11 August 2018.

Solinger, Dorothy. 1999. *Contesting Citizenship in Urban China: Peasant Migrants, the State, and the Logic of the Market*. Oakland: University of California Press.

Song, Ping. 1957. Laodong jiuye wenti (On employment problems). *Laodong* (21), 2–3.

Song, Ruilai. 1989. Guoying qiye yinru shiye jizhi de biyaoxing he kenengxing (The necessity and feasibility of introducing the unemployment mechanism in SOEs). *Zhongguo laodong kexue* (2), 13–14.

Song, Shiyun. 2009. Xin zhongguo chengzhen zhufang baozhang zhidu gaige de lishi kaocha (A historical examination of reforms of housing security institutions in urban New China). *Zhonggong dangshi yanjiu* (10), 102–110.

Standing, Guy. 2011. *The Precariat: The New Dangerous Class*. London: Bloomsbury Publishing.

Stanford, Jim. 2017. The resurgence of gig work: historical and theoretical perspectives. *The Economic and Labour Relations Review* 28(3), 382–401.

State Council. 1953. Zhongyang renmin zhengfu zhengwuyuan guanyu quanzhi nongmin mangmu liuru chengshi de zhishi (Directive on persuading peasants not to flow into cities blindly by the State Council of the Central Government). *Laodong* (4), 1.

1957. Guowuyuan guanyu fangzhi nongcun renkou mangmu wailiu de zhishi (Directive on preventing blind outflows of rural population by the State Council). *Zhonghua renmin gongheguo guowuyuan gongbao* (1), 8–9.

1958. Guowuyuan guanyu gedanwei cong nongcun zhong zhaoyong linshigong de zanxing guiding (Interim provisions on recruiting temporary workers from rural areas by the State Council). *Laodong* (1), 4–5.

1981. Guanyu yange kongzhi nongcun laodongli jincheng zuogong he nongye renkou zhuanwei fei nongye renkou de tongzhi (Circular on tightening control over peasants' flows into cities for work and the conversion of agricultural population into non-agricultural population). *Shanxi zhengbao* (2), 9–11.

1983. Guowuyuan guanyu chengzhen laodongzhe hezuo jingying de ruogan guiding (Several provisions on co-operative operations by urban workers by the State Council). *Zhonghua renmin gongheguo guowuyuan gongbao* (10), 420–423.

1994. Guowuyuan guanyu gaijin gongye guanli tizhi de guiding (Provisions on reforming the management system of industry by the State Council). In Literature Research Centre of the Central Committee of the CCP (ed.), *Jianguo yilai zhongyao wenxian xuanbian, di shi ce* (*A Selection of Important Official Documents since 1949, Vol. 10*). Beijing: Zhongyang wenxian chubanshe.

2002. *Kaituo zaijiuye zhilu – Guoneiwai cujin jiuye de zuofa* (*Widening the Opportunities of Re-employment – Practices of Employment Promotion at Home and Abroad*). Beijing: Yanshi chubanshe.

2005. Guowuyuan guanyu guli zhichi he yindao geti siying deng fei gongyouzhi jingji fazhan de ruogan yijian (Several opinions on encouraging, supporting, and guiding the development of non-public economies such as self-employment and private businesses by the State Council). *Shanxi zhengbao* (8), 3–7.

Statistics Bureau of Beijing. 2005. Beijing shi tongjiju 2004 nian guomin jingji he shehui fazhan tongji gongbao (Statistical bulletin on the economic and social development of Beijing in 2004 by the Statistics Bureau of Beijing). *Beijing shi renda changwei hui gongbao* (4), 25–40.

Statistics Bureau of Beijing, and the Beijing branch of NBS. 2016. Beijing shi 2015 nian ji 'shierwu' shiqi guomin jingji he shehui fazhan tongji gongbao (Statistical bulletin on the economic and social development of Beijing in 2015 and during the Twelfth Five-Year Plan). *Beijing shi renda changwei hui gongbao* (19), 53–80.

Su, Xing. 2007. *Xin zhongguo jingji shi* (*An Economic History of New China*). Beijing: Zhonggong zhongyang dangxiao chubanshe.

Swider, Sarah. 2016. *Building China: Informal Work and the New Precariat*. Ithaca: Cornell University Press.

Tao, Chunfang, and Xiaoxian Gao. 1991. *Zhongguo funv tongji ziliao, 1949–1989* (*Statistics on Women in China, 1949–1989*). Beijing: Zhongguo tongji chubanshe.

Teiwes, Frederick C., and Warren Sun. 2011. China's new economic policy under Hua Guofeng: party consensus and party myths. *The China Journal* 66, 1–23.

Tian, Yipeng, and Si Qi. 2005. *Danwei shehui de zhongjie (The End of the Danwei Society)*. Beijing: Shehui kexue wenxian chubanshe.

Tilly, Charles. 1999. *Durable Inequality*. Berkley: University of California Press.

Tu, Guoming. 2007. Shanghai shi qiye laowu yonggong de xianzhuang wenti yu duice (The status quo, problems, and solutions of labour dispatch in Shanghai enterprises). In Changzheng Zhou (ed.), *Laowu paiqian de fazhan yu falü guizhi* (*The Development and Legal Regulation of Labour Dispatch*). Beijing: Zhongguo laodong baozhang chubanshe.

United Nations Children's Fund, et al. 2023. 2020 nian zhongguo ertong renkou zhuangkuang: shishi yu shuju (Conditions of children in China in 2020: facts and data). https://www.stats.gov.cn/zs/tjwh/tjkw/tjzl/202304/P020230419425666818737.pdf. Accessed 17 July 2023.

Van der Linden, Marcel. 2014. San Precario: a new inspiration for labor historians. *Labor Studies in Working Class History of the Americas* 11(1), 9–21.

Vosko, Leach. 2000. *Temporary Work: The Gendered Rise of a Precarious Employment Relationship*. Toronto: University of Toronto Press.

Walder, Andrew G. 1986. *Communist Neo-Traditionalism: Work and Authority in Chinese Industry*. Oakland: University of California Press.

Wallerstein, Immanuel. 1983. *Historical Capitalism*. London: Verso.

Wang, Aiyun. 2011. Shilun xinzhongguo chengli hou woguo shenfen shehui de xingcheng jiqi yingxiang (A preliminary discussion about the formation and influence of status society in China after 1949). *Zhonggong dangshi yanjiu* (12), 48–60.

Wang, Feng. 2016. Qiyejie huyu xiuding laodong hetongfa, tansuo yonggong shichang linghuoxing (Employers appeal to revise the Labour Contract Law and explore the flexibility of the labour market). *21 shiji jingji baodao*, 16 November.

Wang, Fenglu, et al. 1999. *Beijing zhi, zonghe jingji guanli juan, laodong zhi (Chorography of Labour Issues, Comprehensive Volume on Economy and Management, Chorography of Beijing)*. Beijing: Beijing chubanshe.

Wang, Haiyan, et al. 2009. China's new Labour Contract Law: is China moving towards increased power for workers? *Third World Quarterly* 30(3), 485–501.

Wang, Jiaoping. 2007. Laodong hetongfa lifa de beihou (Behind the making of the Labour Contract Law). *Gongren ribao*, 10 July.

Wang, Jiye, and Jian Wang. 1996. *Woguo eryuan jiegou maodun yu gongyehua zhanlue xuanze* (The *Rural–Urban Dualistic Contradiction and the Choice of Industrialization Strategy in China*). Beijing: Zhongguo jihua chubanshe.

Wang, Jun. 2001. *Mao Zedong yu zhongguo gongyehua* (*Mao Zedong and China's Industrialization*). Fuzhou: Fujian jiaoyu chubanshe.

Wang, Shaoguang. 1995. *Failure of Charisma: The Cultural Revolution in Wuhan*. Oxford: Oxford University Press.

1997. *Fenquan de dixian (The Limits to Decentralization)*. Beijing: Zhongguo jihua chubanshe.

Wang, Xiaozhang. 2009. Cong 'shengcun' dao 'chengren': gongmin quan shiye xia de nongmingong wenti. (From survival to recognition: migrant workers from the perspective of citizenship). *Shehuixue yanjiu* (1), 121–138.

Wang, Xuexi. 1985. Zigui shashi jianli laowu guanxi (Labour service relations were established in Shashi, Zigui). *Zhongguo laodong* (4), 29.

Wang, Zhenxia. 2018. Zhongguo zhufang zhidu gaige 40 nian: huigu yu fansi (Forty years of reforming the housing system in China: review and reflection). *Caijing zhiku* (2), 128–136.

Weber, Max. 1978. *Economy and Society: An Outline of Interpretive Sociology, Vol. 1*. Oakland: University of California Press.

Wen, Tiejun. 2013. *Baci weiji: Zhongguo de zhenshi jingyan 1949–2009 (Eight Crises: Lessons from China, 1949–2009)*. Beijing: Dongfang chubanshe.

White, Gordon. 1987a. The changing role of the Chinese state in labour allocation: towards the market? *Journal of Communist Studies* 3(2), 129–153.

1987b. The politics of economic reform in Chinese industry: the introduction of the labour contract system. *The China Quarterly* 111, 365–389.

White III, Lynn T. 2014. *Policies of Chaos: The Organizational Causes of Violence in China's Cultural Revolution*. Princeton: Princeton University Press.

Wildau, Gabriel, and Emily Feng. 2017. China broadens campaign against overcapacity. *Financial Times*, 23 November.

Wood, Alex J., et al. 2019. Good gig, bad gig: autonomy and algorithmic control in the global gig economy. *Work, Employment and Society* 33(1), 56–75.

World Bank. 2020a. GDP (current US$) – Russian Federation. https://data.worldbank.org/indicator/NY.GDP.MKTP.CD?locations=RU. Accessed 6 January 2021.

2020b. Russia: unemployment rate. https://www.theglobaleconomy.com/Russia/unemployment_rate/. Accessed 6 January 2021.

2022. New World Bank country classifications by income level: 2022–2023. https://blogs.worldbank.org/en/opendata/new-world-bank-country-classifications-income-level-2022-2023. Accessed 5 July 2024.

2024a. GNI per capita, Atlas method (current US$) – China. https://data.worldbank.org/indicator/NY.GNP.PCAP.CD?locations=CN. Accessed 5 July 2024.

2024b. GDP growth (annual %) – China. https://data.worldbank.org/indicator/NY.GDP.MKTP.KD.ZG?locations=CN. Accessed 6 July 2024.

2024c. Research and development expenditure (% of GDP) – China, United States. https://data.worldbank.org/indicator/GB.XPD.RSDV.GD.ZS?locations=CN-US. Accessed 6 July 2024.

Woronov, Terry. 2015. *Class Work: Vocational Schools and China's Urban Youth*. Redwood City: Stanford University Press.

Wright, E. Olin. 2000. Working-class power, capitalist-class interests, and class compromise. *American Journal of Sociology* 105(4), 957–1002.

2016. Is the precariat a class? *Global Labour Journal* 7(2), 123–135.

Wu, Jie (ed.). 1995. *Zhongguo jingji wenku: Laodong jingji juan* (*A Collection of Works on China's Economy: The Volume of Labour Economy*). Beijing: Zhongyang bianyi chubanshe.

Wu, Qingjun. 2010. *Guoqi gaizhi yu chuantong chanye gongren zhuanxing* (*The Reform of State-Owned Enterprises and the Transformation of Traditional Industrial Workers*). Beijing: Shehui kexue wenxian chubanshe.

Wu, Yiching. 2014. *The Cultural Revolution at the Margins*. Cambridge, MA: Harvard University Press.

Wu, Zhi. 1936. *Xiangcun zhibu gongye de yige yanjiu* (*A Study on the Cloth Industry in Rural China*). Shanghai: Shangwu yinshuguan.

Xie, Guihua. 2008. *Zhuanxingqi de chengshi laodongli shichang – Guanyu xiagang yu zaijiuye de shizheng yanjiu* (*The Urban Labour Market in the Transitional Era – An Empirical Study on Layoffs and Re-employment*). Beijing: Zhongguo renmin daxue chubanshe.

Xie, Zengyi. 2017. Yonggong chengben shijiao xia de laodong hetongfa xiugai (The revision of the Labour Contract Law from the perspective of labour costs). *Faxue* (11), 66–76.

Xing, Can. 2024. Lexiang chengshi shenghuo, woguo chengzhenhua lü dadao 66.16% (Enjoying the city life, the urbanization rate in China hits 66.16%). http://paper.people.com.cn/zgcsb/html/2024-01/22/content_26038567.htm. Accessed 5 July 2024.

Xiong, Yihan. 2012. Xinshengdai nongmingong yu gongminquan zhengzhi de xingqi (New-generation migrant workers and the rise of citizenship politics). *Kaifang shidai* (11), 90–104.

Xu, Feng. 2013. Temporary work in China: precarity in an emerging labor market. In Judy Fudge and Kendra Strauss (eds), *Temporary Work, Agencies, and Unfree Labor: Insecurity in the New World of Work*. London: Routledge.

Yan, Ruizhen, et al. 1990. Zhongguo gongnongye chanpin jiandaocha de xianzhuang, fazhan qushi ji duice (The status quo, trend, and counter-measures of price scissors between agricultural and industrial products in China). *Jingji yanjiu* (2), 64–70.

Yan, Zhongping. 1955. *Zhongguo mianfangzhi shigao (A History of the Cotton Textile Industry in China)*. Beijing: Kexue chubanshe.

1989. *Zhongguo jindai jingji shi (1840–1894), xiace (Economic History of Modern China, 1840–1894, Part II)*. Beijing: Renmin chubanshe.

Yan, Zhongqin, et al. 1987. *Dangdai zhongguo de zhigong gongzi fuli he shehui baoxian* (*Wages, Welfare, and Social Insurance of Employee-Workers in Contemporary China*). Beijing: Zhongguo shehui kexue chubanshe.

Yang, Jisheng. 2016. *Tiandi fanfu: Zhongguo wenhua dageming lishi* (*Turn Upside Down: The History of the Chinese Cultural Revolution*). Hong Kong: Tiandi tushu.

Yang, Renshu, et al. 1990. *Dangdai beijing quxian gongye* (*County-Level Industry in Contemporary Beijing*). Beijing: Beijing ribao chubanshe.

Yang, Wenjian, Fengxian Qiu, and Xiao Li. 2013. Eryuan kunjing xia de shidi nongmin tudi huan baozhang wenti fenxi (An analysis of exchanging land for social security of landless peasants under the plight of rural–urban dualism). *Gonggong guanli xuebao* (1), 71–78.

Yu, Faming. 2000. *Xiagang zhigong laodong guanxi wenti toushi* (*An Exploration into the Employment Relationships of Laid-Off Workers*). Beijing: Jingji kexue chubanshe.

Yu, Mingchao. 1998. Zhongguo shengzhi wenti yanjiu (A study on the regionalization of China). *Zhanlue yu guanli* (4), 18–30.

Yuan, Lunqu. 1990. *Zhongguo laodong jingji shi* (*An Economic History of Labour in China*). Beijing: Beijing jingji xueyuan chubanshe.

Zeng, Xiangquan, et al. 2008. *Laodongli shichang zhongjie yu jiuye cujin* (*Labour Agencies and Employment Promotion*). Beijing: Zhongguo renmin daxue chubanshe.

Zhai, Huanjun. 1990. Jianguo qian laodong jingji shi, disanjiang (The history of the labour economy before 1949, the third lecture). *Zhongguo renli ziyuan kaifa* (4), 39–41+47.

Zhang, Letian. 2005. *Gaobie lixiang: Renmin gongshe zhidu yanjiu (Farewell to the Ideal: A Study of the Rural Commune System in China)*. Shanghai: Shanghai renmin chubanshe.

Zhang, Lu. 2014a. *Inside China's Automobile Factories: The Politics of Labor and Worker Resistance*. Cambridge: Cambridge University Press.

Zhang, Shaochun. 2018. *Wuqi ganxiao yanjiu (A Study on Wuqi Cadre Schools)*. Beijing: Renmin chubanshe.

Zhang, Xinmin. 2012. *Laowu paiqian lilun yu shijian* (*Theory and Practice of Labour Dispatch*). Beijing: Zhongguo laodong shehui baozhang chubanshe.

Zhang, Xuebing. 2014b. Jihuawai yonggong: dangdai zhongguo shi shang de yizhong ziyuan peizhi xingshi (Out-of-the-plan employment: a form of resource allocation in the history of contemporary China). *Zhonggong dangshi yanjiu* (1), 57–68.

Zhang, Zhuoyuan. 2008. 30 nian guoyou qiye gaige de huigu yu zhanwang (Retrospect and prospect of the reform of state-owned enterprises in the past thirty years). *Qiye wenming* (1), 15–18.

Zhao, Minghua. 2012. *Guoyou qiye gaige zhong de gongren – Zhongguo fangzhi chanye de gean yanjiu* (*Workers in the Reform of State-owned Enterprises – A Case Study in the Textile Industry in China*). Beijing: Shehui kexue wenxian chubanshe.

Zhao, Xuewei. 2017. Gaige kaifang qian qingnian qunti de fei wending jiuye yanjiu (A study on precarious employment of young people before the Reform and Opening-up). *Qingnian tansuo* (3), 83–89.

Zhao, Zhongheng. 1985. Gaohuo gudinggong zhidu de youyi changshi (Beneficial attempts to flexibilize the fixed worker system). *Laodong* (6), 8–10.

Zhao, Ziyang. 1983. Guanyu diliuge wunian jihua de baogao (Report on the Sixth Five-Year Plan). In Office of the Standing Committee of the National

People's Congress (ed.), *Zhonghua renmin gongheguo diwujie quanguo renmin daibiao dahui diwuci huiyi wenjian (Collections of the Documents from the Fifth Session of the Fifth National People's Congress of the People's Republic of China)*. Beijing: Renmin chubanshe.

Zheng, Dongliang. 2010. *Laowu paiqian de fazhan yu guizhi – Laizi guoji jingyan he guonei shijian de diaocha yanjiu* (*The Development and Regulation of Labour Dispatch – An Investigative Research Based on International Experience and Domestic Practice*). Beijing: Zhongguo shehui baozhangbu chubanshe.

Zhou, Guoliang. 2016. Cong rengong chengben bianhua kan laodong hetongfa shishi yu xiugai – Jiyu Shanghai rengong chengben diaocha shuju de shizheng fenxi, shang (The implementation and revision of the Labour Contract Law from the perspective of labour cost changes – an empirical study based on labour costs survey data in Shanghai, Part I). *Zhongguo laodong* (13), 4–11.

Zhou, Kaichang. 2007. 'Laowu paiqian' zai cujin jiuye shehui zeren tixi zhong de dingwei (The location of 'labour dispatch' in the system of promoting employment-related social responsibility). In Changzheng Zhou (ed.), *Laowu paiqian de fazhan yu falü guizhi* (*The Development and Legal Regulation of Labour Dispatch*). Beijing: Zhongguo laodong baozhang chubanshe.

Zhou, Yonghao, et al. 2005. *Beijing zhi, renmin tuanti juan, gongren zuzhi zhi (Chorography of Labour Organizations, Volume on People's Organizations, Chorography of Beijing)*. Beijing: Beijing chubanshe.

Zhu, Bangxing, Linge Hu, and Sheng Xu. 1984. *Shanghai chanye yu shanghai zhigong (Industries and Workers in Shanghai)*. Shanghai: Shanghai renmin chubanshe.

Zhu, Chuan. 1980. Chengzhen jiti jingji de suoyouzhi wenti he jige zhengce wenti (Several problems about ownership and policy of urban collective economies). *Jingji yanjiu* (2), 3–11.

Zhu, Cishou. 1999. *Zhongguo gongye laodong shi* (*A History of Industrial Labour in China*). Shanghai: Shanghai caijing daxue chubanshe.

Zhu, Tinglin. 1985. Jiahexian nongcun chuxian laowu shuchu 're' (A fever of providing labour services in rural Jiahe County). *Zhongguo laodong* (11), 27.

Zhuang, Qidong, Lunqu Yuan, and Jianli Li. 1986. *Xinzhongguo gongzi shigao* (*A History of Wages in New China*). Beijing: Zhongguo caizheng jingji chubanshe.

# Index

www.ingramcontent.com/pod-product-compliance
Lightning Source LLC
Chambersburg PA
CBHW071248180926
51613CB00002B/170
*9781009640534*